I0754434

THE PRISON OF WELTEVREDEN;

AND A GLANCE

AT THE

EAST INDIAN ARCHIPELAGO.

BY

WALTER M. GIBSON.

ILLUSTRATED FROM ORIGINAL SKETCHES

NEW YORK:
J. C. RIKER, 129 FULTON STREET.
1855.

Prison of Weltevreden.

ONSECRATED to the elevation of the native races of the East Indian Archipelago, in religious truth, in morals and social virtues; and to the mitigation of the selfishness and asperity of European dominion in the East; through the development of a closer sympathy between Western Intelligence and Eastern Imagination; under the fostering influence of the faith and enthusiasm of woman,—of the WOMEN OF CHRISTENDOM, to whom this work is earnestly inscribed by the

AUTHOR.

GENERAL VIEW

OF THE SCOPE, TREATMENT, AND AIM OF THIS WORK.

In its Scope

It embraces some mention of early influences, which led the author to adventure in the East; his voyage thither in his own vessel, visiting many small islands but little known, in the South Atlantic, and Indian Oceans; his arrival in the Malayan Archipelago, and sojourn in the interior of Sumatra; where he saw apparent evidences of semi-human beings, and became acquainted with princes and nobles of the island, and their families; visiting them at their homes, partaking of their hospitality, studying their literature, and observing their religion, laws, customs and social habits;—as peculiar to the Malay race, and as affected by European influences; and forming intimate friendly relations, which were interrupted by the jealousy of Dutch officials; causing his arrest, the seizure of his vessel, and his confinement for fifteen months in the prison of Weltevreden, in the Island of Java; where he underwent a most extraordinary and oppressive prosecution at the hands of the government of Netherland India; and at the same time, meeting within his prison cell, a most novel and interesting experience of Malay and Javanese character; finding teachers of all that he wished to learn of these isles, and docile pupils to listen to all that he wished to impart; finding many evidences of a refined and tasteful civilization, of a happy disposition to receive the truths of a more convincing creed than their own, and a simplicity of character, and a heroism of devotion,—in many instances bordering upon the regions of romance; which brightened many prison hours, and finally enabled him, when his life was in danger, to effect his escape.

In the Treatment

truth has been adhered to, but not in the naked form of daily occurrence. Events of like character are grouped together; and only those are introduced, which illustrate some point of view in the Glance that is presented. The romantic beauty and poetic life of Indian isles is arrayed in the vesture of Eastern story; whilst the graver facts of the country's resources, and of European influence and dominion, are set forth in more sober garb. Some names have been changed, of persons who still live in the presence of a power, that might look with disfavor on the parts they enacted, as set forth in these pages; and many things of deep interest have been suppressed, to screen those who are thus exposed:—and thus some other licenses taken; but otherwise, facts alone are presented, and all are but a small portion of what might be said about isles and races so little known to this western world;—about weak and worthless princes, and simple, heroic women; about climes of perpetual spring, lands of unfading verdure, rocks seamed with gold, groves filled with spices, and an unsurpassed beauty and bounty of nature; every where surrounded by miasma, by cruel things in the water, on the earth, in the forest, in the air; and in the shape of European civilization, enlightenment, religion and dominion.

The Aim

is to open up new regions of thought and feeling, and in presenting real pictures of oriental character, to point out new avenues to the oriental mind; to show forth childlike races claiming by their simplicity, docility, obedience and truthfulness, the highest paternal care of a superior civilization; to show how this has been wielded to gratify selfish ends alone,—producing a harvest of vice and hate; and to show the effects of another policy,—studying the simple character, meeting it with congenial sympathy, wishing to serve rather than to be served, teaching with patience and some fraternal regard; and receiving in exchange, a childlike love and devotion: to show that this result might be universal throughout the beautiful islands of the Indian Ocean, among their simple and numerous races; who by their numbers, by the defences that the Creator has set up around them, by the deadly barriers that save them from any permanent Caucasian intermixture, must ever be the sole producers of the chief Eastern treasures for which the selfish world has contended ; and demand that attention from self-interest, which ought to spring from an enlightened, Christian philanthropy.

CONTENTS.

THE Prison of Weltevreden, in 1853, was an irregular group of thick-walled barracks, one story high. There was a gloomy Hall of Justice in front, where the examination of prisoners provisionally detained took place. The visitor who did not wish to enter the chambers of the Hall, would pass along beneath an archway; and then came in view of the house of the head jailer. Further on, he would enter an open court, with a row of commodious, cleanly, prison chambers on either side, devoted to prisoners of state and to unconvicted persons: beyond this, passing through a gateway in a lofty wall, he would enter another open court, between rows of smaller, and more closely guarded cells, whose iron studded doors, and close barred gratings, showed that they were the abodes of convicted men; another and smaller court was beyond this, with inclosures and rows of cells on either side; these were smaller, filthier, more closely guarded than the preceding ones, and the abodes of still greater unfortunates; but farthest of all, at the bottom of the quadrangle, there was to be seen a range of low, gloomy walls, of heavy, black-stained, iron-embossed doors, with crevices for light and air. There the deadly silence of a church vault reigned behind; except now and then, might be heard the footfall of a Dutch sentry; or the hoarse, heavy rustle of the chains of some wretch doomed to death or to lifelong woe.

On the afternoon of the 26th January, 1853, in the first cell, on the right hand of the first court, a prisoner was pacing his chamber floor, with a look of deep thought, and some excitement. He is a man in early manhood, but his bleached and marked face, show a greater number of years than he has yet passed. He has been in prison a long time, and his soul has been sorely tried; but now he has heard news, that give him hopes of speedy liberty; and he feels a thronging rush of emotions at the thought of beholding the bright world again. He had heard of a favorable decision by his judges; and each time he hears the outer gate of the prison swing open, he expects to behold an officer with the order for his release.

He has packed up the few effects of his scanty wardrobe, and some trifles, the work of his brain and hands during his prison hours, each of which he would preserve as mementoes of a painful, yet strangely interesting portion of life. He paces to and fro, to calm the tumult of his heart,—throbbing with longings to work out in deed, some visions that had broken in upon him like prophecies in his lonely prison room.

As he walks, his face droops, and there is a shade passing over it; he thinks how little less cheerless will be the wide world to the prison he leaves behind. He thinks of some ties and duties, that would demand his devotion when free; and he recalls many, so many strange and happy memories; but all are mingled with pain, much more than seems to be the common lot of men.

His hopes of freedom bring melancholy; the sadness of intense feeling. He is touched with it deeply; but not love, nor the memory of it, has place in his thoughts; and yet they are busy with pictures of woman, some one of his own race; some wise and sympathetic soul with whom he fain would talk. He needs the faith which the jealousy of man never gives to that fellow-man, who steps out upon a new and untrodden course.

As he muses, the prisoner pauses at the bars of his room window. The sun has set, and the stars are fast spangling a lovely Javan sky: softly, deeply blue, and of a dreamy, mysterious loveliness like the daughters of the Javan land. The sky and daughters of the sacred isle, had often soothed the prisoner in his solitude, and lulled him to a forgetfulness of the past,—awakening hopes of a new and happier life among these coral isles.

But with the thoughts of freedom return the memories of the sky of his own land, and the daughters of his own race. He looks northward and westward, where the clear blue sky, the fresh invigorating air, and noble, fair faces, thoughtful not dreamy, nerve the soul to its highest and best essays.

As he muses on, his head and heart are busy with many plans and warm hopes. The prison gate swings open; an officer appears; the well-known face of thee, good Brower, who had often brought such change of joy and woe to the tenants of this sad house of care. The prisoner steps forward to meet him; he sees a paper in his hand, and his heart beats strongly; but there is a cloud on the face of Brower; for the good sheriff was joyful when he brought joy, and sad when he brought sadness. The paper is seized,—is read; 'tis a decree from superior judges, ordering another trial, and casting the prisoner back upon the doubt, and pain, and gloom of his prison life.

On a fair evening, in the Java sea, on board of one of America's largest and fleetest clippers, homeward bound from China, a lady was seated on the quarter deck, leaning upon the t'gallant rail, and gazing earnestly upwards at the starry splendors of a lovely Indian sky.

She gazed with a quiet joy upon the stars, and some faint, waning tints of a rich tropic sunset; and a gentle murmur of the waters rippling by the ship's sides, made soothing melody to her soul; yet was she sad in her revery.

Though each breath of air wafted that ship on its way to her native land and home,—to the loved ones around the old home's hearth; yet there was a painful gap of space, a weary lapse of time to pass away, ere the joys of home would be her's.

She was feeble in health; and there were causes more besides to make the voyage dull and unpleasing; and to make the long time that was yet to pass away look still longer. She longed as only a prisoner, and a lonely passenger at sea can long, for some companionship, to help chase away the dreary solitude of that quarter deck.

The lady sighs and thinks of home, feeling that there alone, and not till seated there, can she hope for any answer to her soul's want; and she sighs, not that it should be thus, but that home is so far off, that there are three or more weary months to pass away, before reaching it; and there is no hope of pleasant voice and look to brighten with some cheer the long, long days, that must be lived through on board that cheerless ship.

She sees no hand of Providence, leading that ship; as it silently wings its way on that unruffled sea, beneath that calm, starry sky of the Indian Archipelago. She sees only those twin isles, the "Two Brothers;" and a little way off, the "Watcher," which seem in some way typical of herself and her heart's longings; and though she sees it not, those longings arise from some sympathy, with the near approach of the workings of that hand, which was leading that ship on a pathway on which ship had never gone before.

The great clipper glides onward, through the phosphorescent waters, amid the deepening shades of night. Her officers pace her decks in confident security, and the word is passed that all is well. They have looked at the charts, and think their pathway clear; they see no hidden rocks, nor reefs, nor shoals in the course they would pursue for the night. There were some coral ledges marked down, which their observations placed about three miles off on their starboard bow; but their place on the chart was wrong.

The lady sighs again, and says: What ray of hope, of cheer to this solitude, is there on the long track of waters before me? What hope,——there is a rebound, and quivering shock felt throughout that ship: there is a dull, grating sound rising up from the waters beneath her bows; and see the confused hurry of officers and men, as they cry, Aground! aground! we're aground!

The ship had struck on Brower's shoals.

On the morning of the 25th April, 1853, the Palmer, a large American ship, was to be seen leaving the roadstead of Batavia, with all her canvas spread, to catch the soft land breeze, that came in aromatic wafts from off the Java shore.

Her commander, crew, and passengers were all on deck, looking towards the port they were leaving, with a gaze of intense anxiety. Two long twelve-pounder cannon were run out for a stern chase, and stout, rugged-looking seamen, were standing by with hands already blackened with powder: and there were other signs, which would seem to show a state of war, or the attack of some hostile sea rover. But it is neither war nor piracy, that is the cause of this ship's warlike trim.

There is a man on board, for whom this anxiety is shown; for whom these guns are pointed. He has just come up from out of the ship's hold, where he has been lying hid for some time. He looks very pale, bleached by long, unchanging stay, within confining walls; and this pallor contrasts strangely with thick, black hair on his head, and long, unsightly black hair on his lips; but this is not his own; his own lighter hair peers from beneath, and his strange-looking, ill-fitting garments do not seem to have been made for his person.

It would be easy to judge from this man's disguised costume

and countenance, and his anxious, hunted look, that he was a fugitive; and it would be no less easy to judge from the stir on board around him, and the lookout towards Java, that he had just escaped from that island; and the people on board were expecting a pursuit, and stood ready to beat off all attempt to retake him.

The land breeze now freshens up, and the clipper surges ahead, at a rate that would defy the pursuit of any craft, with sail or steam, in those seas. The city of Batavia has sunk from view; but a Dutch war steamer's long, black wreath of smoke is yet to be seen above the horizon.

Edam, with its wild ruins, and the Thousand Isles, are passed; then Onrust, that grave of sailors; next Cramat, with the Tchandys of the old Brahmins; and then the Kambuys, Great and Little, the fruity Babi, the lofty Gunung Laoo, near by the Pulo Merak with its curious cove, rise upon the view, and are lost astern of the swift-winged ship. There are clustering here, and lining the Sunda Straits, that great gateway of the trade of the East, some of earth's fairest spots of island verdure and shade, and filled with the brightest of winged life, and tropic beauty.

The lovely Sunda Isles glide quickly past in review. The shoaly channelled Zutphen group, the pirate prahu's safe retreat; then little Thwart the Way, with its noisy, foaming shore, the lofty Rajah Bassa of the great Malay land, Sebookoo, by the Lampong's Bay and Pulo Bessi; but chief of all, is the sublime and lovely Crockatoa, with its marvellous marine gardens by its shores, its deep verdure and boiling fountains, where the angler can cook the fish caught within his rod's reach, from the ocean tide, laving the island's coral border; and lastly appears Pulo Intan. The Batoo Hadjy, or Pilgrim's rock of the Diamond Island, is waning to the view; 'tis gone, and now that ship is alone between unbroken sky and water, on the great Indian sea.

The sun has set; and the weary crew and passengers are retiring to an early rest. The officer of the watch is pacing to and fro, and the man at the wheel is watching his compass, and the shaking skysail.

There are three persons, who are lingering on that quarter-deck: they are gazing wistfully out upon the sparkling sea, and then at the splendor of the Indian night sky; and two of these are ladies, and the other is the fugitive.

He draws near, and they speak of the beauty of the sea and the stars. The ladies were talking of the cheatery of star-raised hopes; of the treachery lying beneath these gentle Indian waters; and of the frailty of the great ship, that now bore them on so swiftly and so safely.

And why did the ladies think thus? And then they tell of the revery of one, some three months before, on this same quarter-deck, at a point within two degrees of where their ship now is; and they tell how the starry and ocean depths they were then looking at had been questioned, seeking to find a solace in their shadowy looks and great mysterious voices; and how the heart had gathered hope from them, and the soul was soothed with the melody of whispering wavelets; soothed to a sense of peace and quiet trust. But just then the coral rocks were beneath the ship's bows, and she struck upon Brower's hidden shoals. How the vessel had been got off, and barely kept afloat to run into a port near by; and how, after three months refitting, she had sailed; and at the moment of departure, he had himself escaped on board; of all this, the fugitive himself best knew.

It was curious,—a fact outvying in strange coincidence many

a rare device of fancy. He, too, had had a revery, on the evening of a day, just three months ago: and he had been looking from close-barred gratings up to the same blue and glittering space, seeking hope in the skyey depths; he thought he read there what he sought, and he was about to go forth, to enjoy the sweets of wandering free once more; but the cold hand of ruthless power, under a cloak of justice, was then near by; and Brower, the sheriff of Weltevreden, came with an order of re-arrest, that cast the prisoner back upon his despair.

All this is true—on the same day, almost the same hour, these two reveries were broken by the wreck and the re-arrest; by Brower the sheriff, and by Brower's shoals.

They begin to tell to each other something of the past. The ladies had heard some rumors, from a prison in Batavia; but all was vague about him, who came on deck that morning. He had come amid hurry, excitement, and the roar of cannon. Where had he been? why imprisoned? and above all, how had he escaped?

The questions of the ladies conjure up an eventful and exciting past. A host of strange people, of wild and lovely scenes, and stirring deeds, that would require much time to unfold. But there is a long voyage before them; and they all shall have pleasure on many a fair day, and many a soft evening, in telling and listening.

The Palmer is a beautiful ship; of frigate size in length of keel, from deck to kelson, and in the width of her beam. Her sides, bows, and stern, sweep around in continuous curves. She has long polished masts, of bright-grained heart of pine, tapering from the thick columnar base in the hold, up so gracefully to the slender royal shafts on which the gilded trucks are poised. The Palmer's yards are of man-of-war's weight and width, on which are bent a full suit of sails, from spanker to jib, from main to sky-sail, springing so trimly from the clews, and spanning each spar with a graceful arch. The whitest of pine glistens on her quarter-deck, one third of the ship's length; and at the break of it, steps lead down to the main deck, on each side of a covered companion-way, leading into

THE CABIN OF THE PALMER.

In it there is a range of state-rooms, starboard and larboard, four of each, ample as chambers, with beds, not berths, of four feet width, with springy mattress, like beds ashore. The polish of bird's-eye maple, by the side of deep-hued mahogany, glistens from panel and stanchion. A partition of rich panelling and stained glass, cuts off ten feet of the after part of the saloon, superbly cushioned and carpeted, from the main portion forward, which is filled with the dining table, and the cushioned seats on either side.

At this table, eleven persons are seated, on the second morning of the homeward voyage of the ship from Java. Her commander sits at the forward end: he is yet young, not past his thirtieth year. He is backward and faint of speech in the cabin, though forward and firm enough on deck: he does not speak much or well, except in a gale of wind, to men on the yards, reefing refractory sails.

His fair young wife sits on his left; who had preferred life at sea with her bronze-faced sailor, to a quiet home with father and mother. Their baby, a crowing urchin, the pet of the cabin, little Charley boy, is just now nestled in the lap of the lady who sits next to his mother; and this is the lady of the revery on the quarter-deck.

The baby's nurse sits next to the lady; a spare-looking, talkative, cheery old dame; she has spent her life singly, has seen much of the world—nursing and voyaging; yet prouder of nothing more than to be a famous child manager and pleaser; and somewhat vain of her knowledge of making crullers and doughnuts, and all manner of domestic pastry.

The old nurse finds sometimes a willing, sometimes a gruff, impatient listener to her exploits with babies and short crust, in her neighbor on her left. We shall follow that course round the table. The nurse's left hand neighbor is a man about forty-five years of age; he is a huge, broad-chested, dark-looking man of war. He is terrible to look at, and terrible in his strength and courage. The ancient god of force seems incarnate in that man.

He was a boatswain on board an American ship of war, stationed in the Chinese waters. He became chafed at times, and disturbed the ship's people with his Titanic play. At one time, he was ordered under arrest, and several marines were sent to seize him; but as they came within reach of the nervy palms of the boatswain, they fell around him like rotten reeds blown down by a strong wind; and had these been the days of Samson, without powder and bullet, he might have withstood the whole ship's company with a handspike; or even Samson's weapon against the Philistines.

But our boatswain must yield to the overwhelming power of the enginery of war. He was discharged and disrated; and he shipped on board the Palmer, at Canton, to return home, to seek some redress at the hands of the Chief of Marine at Washington.

Whilst the Palmer was repairing at Onrust, the navy yard of the Dutch, near to Batavia, the boatswain, like the rest of the passengers, spent his time ashore in this city. The fame of his strength was common talk among the natives and the foreigners of the port. Mynheer took his pipe from his mouth, and stared at the shaggy, lion-headed American, as he passed by; and the Malay and Javanese said that the rakshashas, the giants of old, Laksamana or Panji, had come back to earth again.

But there was one who took umbrage at the boatswain's renown—a merchant, and a man of wealth; but an athlete, and a prize-fighter at heart—who handled the boxing glove more readily than the pen, and preferred the bowling alley to the counting-room. He too was hugely built; but plump, florid, and round limbed; a marked contrast to the square built, bull-necked boatswain; though they were alike in age, stature, and girth.

They met at the hotel, where the merchant had rooms. The two gladiators frankly gave and took words of good feeling and good fellowship. An admiring crowd stood off, looking on, and whisperingly discussed the strong men's animal points. These two drank to each other's health, and toasted the sages and the heroes of their countries.

The merchant warmed fast with wine; his voice grew louder; he bantered the boatswain about his strength; he challenged him to exchange a few buffets with the gloves; but our man of war kept cool; he was a guest, and he would not take up the gauntlet of his host. The latter taunted and pressed on the boatswain, and seized him by a lappel of his coat as he was about to depart: he pulled till the lappel and part of the back was left in his hand; still the boatswain would retreat, and would meet the boxing merchant some other day. But no, the latter would have a trial of strength then: he seized his retreating guest by the remaining lappel, taunted him with cowardice, and tore lappel and almost the whole of a new uniform coat from the boatswain's back.

Now, our man-of-war's-man's blood was up. He bared his brawny arms. He closed with his challenger, and the garments of the merchant were torn from him like wetted paper. They grappled, they swayed to and fro, they heaved, they lunged, and the merchant was hurled to the ground.

The lookers on, were the mate of the Palmer, another American, some merchants of the city, and a lawyer. These rushed forward to help the fallen man; but the sailor scattered them right and left, and kept his foot upon his prostrate foe. One, more forward than the rest, came within the boatswain's grasp, who seized him by both legs, like a helpless child, and hurled the rash man out of a window near by, who was only saved from a desperate fall, and probable death, by a balcony rail against which he struck.

The boatswain's foot was loosened, and the merchant sprang

up. He rushed upon his enemy with infuriated rage. They struck and tore each other with terrible power; and in a moment their broad, massive faces were bruised and gashed, and their garments were hanging in tatters and clotted with blood.

The merchant staggered, and again he went down. Three lookers-on rushed forward to stop the maddened American from leaping upon him. The boatswain seized them one by one, and felled them sprawling upon the prostrate gladiator; laid hold upon a huge, heavy, round Dutch table, overturned and slammed it down upon the struggling four, jumped on top, leaped and kicked forth upon it for a few seconds, an infuriated war-dance; and then stalked forth, conqueror, bloody, ungarmented, and awful.

The boatswain, and the stout mate of the Palmer, who is on his left, at the after end of the cabin table, now listen with quiet deference to the garrulous nurse; or to the passenger, who has a place, at the after end of the starboard side. He is the late fugitive, and is speaking of Sumatra, a chosen land with him, of which he hopes to tell much, to many in his own and other lands. He will tell his story in another way, in these pages, as he told it to those who sailed with him in the Palmer.

Next to him is a pale, slender, slow-spoken man, about thirty years of age, eight of which he had passed as a missionary in China, and he is a great amateur in Chinese literature. He had married early; but Chinese diet or climate, or missionary life in China seems fatal to American women; for his wife soon died, like many other missionary wives who had gone out. The young missionary needed another companion; and the men at home, who sent him forth, the American Board of Foreign Missions, had made large provision to meet the wife-wants of the gospel laborers it sent forth. At one time, they provided for the return of the widowed missionary to seek another partner; but finally it was decreed, that those who wished to supply the place of a lost partner, should stay in the field of their labors, and have one sent to them.

Our worthy minister sent for one, and he often spoke of the novel feeling, in awaiting an unknown spouse. In due time, the matrimonial order was filled from a female school for missionary wives; was shipped, and duly received in China by the eagerly expectant consignee, who accepted the shipment, pronounced it good, and put his own name upon it: and now, this matrimonial consignment, a slender, quiet young lady, with a mild, pale and kindly face, sits beside her missionary spouse. She is an invalid, and they are returning home, to save her from the speedy grave of the missionary wife.

Another missionary sits next to the invalid wife. A stooping, pale-faced, elderly-looking man; though older with infirmity than with years. His thin hair is almost white; but it is a flaxen whiteness, and its natural hue; and the pallor and wrinkles of his face, are the bleachings and markings of failing health, the speedy product of "Celestial" air and food.

But the face of the elder missionary, as we shall call him, has a good, earnest, and benevolent expression; and his eyes beam forth occasionally from out of the surrounding drapery of disease, with a sparkle of true missionary enthusiasm. His head swims, his sight is dim, and his hand wanders at times, in quest of food upon the table. Then there is put forth a woman's hand to obtain what the sick man wants; and there is a woman's voice by his side, that rouses the sluggish invalid from his torpor. That voice has a foreign sound, a Scandinavian accent, and belongs to a Swedish face, with a look of middle age, round, florid, and fair, that left Sweden some ten years ago for England, and there entered the British missionary service to go to China, as a teacher; where some twelve months before this time she married our elder missionary, who had not long lost a wife.

The Swedish lady sits on the right hand of the commander, and completes the table circle. She leads the way in conversation among the cabin's company; and has been addressing the fugitive passenger a multitude of questions about his wanderings in the Indian Archipelago, about the Malays, his imprisonment, his trials and his escape.

He feels, as one often feels who has seen much of life, and met a strange fate, like many a one of earnest thought, and of some fine-fibred feelings, easily jarred: he shrinks from the direct challenge of curiosity, to tell, like a hireling story-teller, of that which has been most eventful in life.

He is feeble now, not yet recovered from late pain and excitement: he looks very thin, and ghastly. After a time, he will be glad to tell his brave rescuers, and kind-hearted providers, something of what he has lately seen and undergone. It will be the only return he now can offer for the mate and boatswain's timely rescue with the boat; for the comfortable berth he now finds on board; for the change of garments from the elder and younger missionary; and for the abundant gift of toilet luxuries from the ladies.

The commander wishes to know something of the yellow-skinned people on the pepper coasts of Sumatra; the boatswain is more curious about the bloody pirates, who cut off heads and skin stout sailors alive; the mate damns the Dutch, and would know, why the big-breeched smokers had dared to lay rude hands on the flag of his country; the elder missionary asks about the gospel among the Malays; the younger about the books of the Javans; and the ladies ask if there be any truth in a story, that some heroic daughter of a Sumatran chief or Javan noble, had brightened the cell of their fellow passenger, while in the Prison of Weltevreden.

This curiosity was not immediately gratified, but his story was gradually drawn out, day after day; and as the interest in narrating and listening increased, he would make a preparation of notes during the day, for the afternoon's story on the quarter-deck; and the book is mainly made up from those notes; many of the first chapters being only slightly changed from the words then prepared. But the exact order of telling has not been preserved; little attention has been paid to the circumstances attending each narration on board the Palmer; and only such comments of the listeners as had a bearing upon the object of the work, have been retained. He first told of the early influences that led him to adventure in the East; then of his voyage to Sumatra; and afterwards of his imprisonment, and all that occurred to him in the island of Java.

THIRD DAY.

THE dark clouds of the night before have rolled mutteringly away to the land of storms, leaving a bright tropic day; and now, the slanting rays of the declining sun shed a golden light, and a softened warmth along the polished quarter-deck of the Palmer.

All of the cabin's company are seated there, on the light rattan settees of China. They are grouped around the passenger from Java, who begins now the story he had promised

ABOUT HIS UNCLE.

I had an uncle, who, when a youth, ran away from home, a good home; from a kind father, and an affectionate mother, to go to sea, to become a sailor, to live a life of adventure, and to see strange people and far-off lands. He went through all the bitter trial of a friendless apprenticeship on board ship; the tyranny of a brutal captain; the cruel, harmful jokes, and snubbings of more brutal men; all this with hard labor, and bitter weather on deck, and with coarse food, and a foul berth in the forecastle, he struggled through sufferingly, until he became a man, and could hold an even hand with a harsh life and the tyranny of his fellow-men.

His thoughts, like those of all sea-roving young souls, wandered among the isles of the Southern seas. He had daily strolled in boyhood upon the wharves of his native seaport town, to gaze upon the mighty ships that sailed to the Indies. He had read with eager relish, all stories of Eastern lands; and he beheld in dreams, Arabs, Hindoos and Malays, with brown skins, bright turbans, and jewelled robes, moving in pomp and dazzling array.

He found the captain of an East Indiaman, who needed an apprentice, and would take him. He thought of the glory and fortune he would win on the ocean, and in the Indies; but how leave his mother. He prepared a glowing story to tell her; but he felt that she could never view the adventure as he did; and his heart failed him.

The time approached for the ship to sail. He had daily watched the reeving of ropes, the bending on of sails, and all the preparations for a long sea voyage. The day of sailing had arrived; the ship is in the stream, ready to up anchor, the moment the captain shall come on board. Still my uncle has not dared to break unto his mother, his desire to go with this ship. He feels that she would never consent for him to go: he persuades himself also, that she cannot understand all the advantages of the voyage, and all the motives that lead him to wish to go. He beholds, with boyish hope, a glorious voyage accomplished in a very short time, when he shall return in triumph, with fame and fortune, wherewith to gratify his mother, and others whom his young soul does love. He meets a young sailor whom he knew, about to put off for the ship. The signal flag of the gallant craft is floating from the main; and waves him on to glory and the glittering East. The judgment of the boy and his sense of duty, are lost for the time, in the strange visions of the young roving heart. He resolves to go. He writes a few hurried words of love and assurance to his mother; and, in a few hours, he is on board the ship, at sea.

I shall not tell you of the various fortunes of this uncle in the East. He had passed from the bitter life of the friendless apprentice, to that of the sailor man; and yet neither the fame nor the fortune of his boyish dreams had been found. He felt the sting of disobedience, along with his other hardships; and yet he would not return to his country, till he could show those at home something for his hopings, and his wanderings. But there came a time, when his pride was broken; when his heart yearned to go back to his mother, and try to wipe away the error of the past, by soothing her failing age; and then there came the news of his mother's death.

After this there was little in his country, for which the desolate, disappointed man, now cared. He made his home in the East. He entered the service of an Arab merchant of Muscat; and after a time, fell into the favor of the Imaum. He made many voyages to the Malay Islands, chiefly to Acheen, in the island of Sumatra.

Whilst on a return voyage, and touching at Bombay, he found letters from a sister, whom he remembered as a little child, but was now married to a man of wealth. The sister longed to see her much thought-of, and long lost brother. His heart was touched with home memories. He arranged his affairs on his return to Muscat, and after many affectionate adieus from Eastern friends, he departed for the home of his sister.

The sun-bronzed man was embraced by a fair and dignified lady; they who had once romped together, a ruddy, round-faced boy, and a curly-haired, rosy-cheeked girl. Time's changes at home were sad for him to dwell upon. He prepared to return to the scene of his interests; and where he had spent eighteen years of his life, those years when faith is strongest, and hopes are brightest. In speaking to his sister of his future in the

East, he said that he wanted one of her children to share his fortunes with him there. He singled out her third son, a child rocked upon his own much-loved sea. His love for this nephew grew strong from the first moment of his seeing him, though the child could barely lisp his name. There was a strange bond of sympathy between them. And when the uncle was gone, he regularly sent from Muscat, or Ceylon, or Acheen, some word or gift for his nephew Walter, who now tells it to you.

As I grew up, in boyhood's inquiring age, I heard them often speak at home of my adventurous uncle; who had caressed me in my childhood, and had chosen me to be his heir, and his partner in foreign lands. The spirit of adventure, to see strange people and far-off countries, sprang up in me, as soon as I had learned to read about them; and that was at a very early age. I felt a longing to go to sea, and to join my uncle, even in my seventh year.

It was about this time my uncle made a strange, abrupt return. I was much with him during this visit,—rambling together often on the sea beach, to listen to the melody of the tossing waters, which we both loved so much. And then he talked of Arabia, and of the islands of the far East: and more than all of Sumatra: of the perfumes that wafted from her shores; of the many dainty fruits, and myriad bright-feathered birds of her flowery groves: of the Malay princes, and of the mighty wars with Portuguese, Spanish, Dutch and English.

And then he spoke of a great city in the centre of the island, a city once of mighty extent and population, whose Sultans had given laws to all the rest of the Malay nations. But this great city had decayed; and its empire had been divided into many small, and feeble portions. Now the Malays looked for the restoration of the sacred city; and their traditions had pointed to fair-skinned men from the West; who should come with wisdom and great power; and who should destroy the robbers of Islam, the evil genii of the woods, and a great plunderer called Jan Company. All these scenes, all these events and legends, stirred up a spirit which, from that time forth, grew upon my soul.

My uncle returned to the East. The bronze-faced man was gone. The stories of the sea and of the islands had ceased; but the wonders of Sumatra, the glittering pomp of Eastern princes, shone in every bright scene that met my eyes; and then as I rambled on the beach, I often beheld with revery's eye, far out at sea, where water and sky did meet, where the sun's glistening rays were dancing amid the mirage of its own making; there I beheld the sacred city of the Malay isle, with its shining walls and temple roofs; and then I wondered who should help, who should teach, and who should do good to the people of the Indian seas.

When the story of the uncle was ended, the captain expressed his wonder how that any man, who had ever traded on the coast of Sumatra, could weave such fine fancies, as did the uncle around the thieving, cut-throat Malays; and the boatswain muttered something about too nice a yarn, and bending on too much fancy tac'le, and too long in getting to sea among the Dutch and the pirates. But the ladies and the missionaries smiled approval, and hoped on the following day to hear more of the early influences that led the narrator to the East.

FOURTH DAY.

When the sun's declining rays, caught by the spanker, left one half of the Palmer's quarter deck in shade, the ladies and the missionaries were grouped around the fugitive on the weather quarter, when he began to relate

ABOUT AN OLD TEACHER.

I received my limited share of bookish lore under the direction and tuition of a good and remarkable old man. He was famous for his stories. The ordinary routine of the tasks and the teaching of his class, was often stayed to tell some stirring tale of heroic life or travel.

The old worthy had been a missionary among the red men, and bois brulés, of the remote North West, and on the Pacific borders: and the boy-hearted old enthusiast, often led away his pupils from their books, to lead them on in story by the beaver dams on the streamlets of the Winnipeg and the Wimpigoos, among the wigwams and the deer haunts, and the browsing buffaloes on the prairies of the Saskatchawan, and then across the rocky bound of Oregon, and down the Okanagan to the shores of the Pacific.

There, our good teacher loved to pause, and point out to us, far away, upon the grand ocean, beautiful islands, the chosen scenes of the lavish bounty and beauty of nature, where flowers for ever bloomed, and spring-time had no end. Such was the picture the good old man's enthusiasm presented to the eye of all his young hearers; and with me, the stories of my uncle, and my own dreamings of Sumatra were revived; and thus another step was my heart led on towards the East.

Were I telling the story of my life, I would have much to say about many haps in early boyhood: even a childhood of adventure. I was a wanderer from home, and left to my own guidance at the age of fourteen. I entered a youthhood rich in a wild young heart's revelry, amid all that adventure sought, and romance could wish for; and wretched too in all that unthinking, lonely, unadvised youth could bring upon itself, of unseasonable trials, trouble and care.

I fled from my studies with the old missionary, to seek a home among the red men he had so much spoken of. I wandered off with a hunting party, and marched many a day with my boy's feet, over wide tracts of wild forest; or with light-footed dogs, and the flat, metal-sheeted traineau, glided over the fragile ice crust of deep, boundless, bleak snow wastes. I followed in adventure's steps, in the great Empire city; and above all in my own adopted State. How glowing and bright was the life of those early days; and how rich then, the revelries of the wild young heart!

And then came the trials and cares of the unadvised youth. When I was yet a boy, I met in my wanderings in the backwoods of South Carolina with a fair gentle girl of my own age, who had never been more than half a day's ride from the plantation of her father. We often sauntered together in the still woods of Milwee on summer days; we would wade, barefooted, the shallow pebbly streams; cross the deep and rapid creeks, with mutual help of hands to our tottering steps, as we walked the unsteady swinging trunk that bridged them over. We rambled hand in hand to gather wild grapes and the muscadine, then we would rest beneath the dense shade, and at the foot of some great tree, and talk of our boyish and girlish fancies; and then without any thought as to mutual tastes, character, or fitness, or any thing that had to do with the future; but listening only to the music of our young voices; to the alluring notes of surrounding nature; and having only our young faces to admire, we loved; and long ere I was a man, we were married.

It was about this time, that I made the next step towards the Islands of the Indian Ocean, through the influence of a wealthy and intelligent planter. He was a man of expanded mind, and enthusiastic temperament; and had a great relish for travel, and bold enterprise in unknown countries. He often spoke of the hidden wealth of the Eastern world; and said how it had been a dream of his youth to go into the heart of Asia, and then among the marvellous islands of the Indian Ocean. He oftentimes traced out a route on the Eastern Hemisphere, which I followed with eager eyes. I recalled again the first impulse given to my boyish imagination; and now, aroused by this man's fervor, the Sumatran land began to gleam in revery before my eyes again; and the Indian Ocean lay outstretched, a shining path before me, even in those early days, leading to fortune and to honorable renown.

The region of country in which I dwelt, the upland border of the state, is a chosen spot of nature to foster the ardor of young thoughts of novel and lofty enterprise. There are no groupings of earth, and woods, and streams, that offer wilder and richer pictures, than can be seen along the windings of the Keowee, so deeply fringed with borders of laurel and muscadine; on the Wild Wolf Creek, from the mighty beetling crags of Table Rock, in the sweet valley of Jocassee, on "Horse Shoe" Chauga, famed in Kennedy's romance, and then beyond Tugaloo in the Currahee, in the rich beauty of the "leaping liquid silver" of Talula and Tecoa; and thus a host of wild and lovely vales, and frowning peaks, and shining streams, in this Switzerland of America, were the scenes of my early oriental dreamings.

I was indeed but a dreamer then; in those days before I became a man; or I had not found my calling. I felt myself fit for little, in a planting country, sparsely peopled, where few or none were wanted but those, who could handle the plough, the hammer or the axe; who were shrewd in the exchange of peddlers' wares; or could drub some knowledge of books into rude backwoods, barefooted boys, in an "old-field-school," for which pursuits I had but small skill, and less of taste.

I longed to look at the sea again. It was a strong, yearning wish I felt. I gazed with pleasure on the swift waters of the Savannah; and as I thought of them flowing on towards the ocean, my heart almost tempted me, at times, to launch forth in a well-stored canoe, descend to the river's mouth, and there join any great ship going to any distant land. It was a boy's thought; whilst I had a man's cares to fix me in my backwoods home. But now, in the midst of my boyish longings, death came to chill all dreams, and cloud my life; yet after a time my young widowed heart felt free to range again; and I wanted to fly on the wings of the wind towards the rising of the sun.

FIFTH DAY

The Palmer was still in the trade-winds: she rolled gently yet swiftly on, under a full spread of canvass: the sky was bright overhead, with a skirt of white fleecy masses just above the horizon: the watch off duty lay outstretched on the t'gallant forecastle, basking in the softened rays of a declining tropic sun; and the passengers were lounging on the settees of the quarter-deck, or leaning over the t'gallant rail, watching the yellow sea-weed floating past amid the deep blue waters, when he of the Southern backwoods sat down to relate his departure from his early home, some travels, and what led to

THE PURCHASE OF THE FLIRT.

I left a curious little cabin home, on the banks of the Savannah. It had been the work of my own hands, and of that neighborly help, ever so readily lent by the Southern planter and backwoodsman. It was a rude little wooden hut; but the pine log walls, and the oak-board roof, and the mud and stick chimney had been a pleasant home; and the corn cake baked on my own hearth stone eat sweetly in those days, when coarse fare and a draught from the water brooks was luxury.

The best of my early years were spent on the waters of the Savannah: on both of its banks,—on the Carolina, and on the

Georgia side. I have travelled those waters, from the Tybee mouth to the utmost limit where a steamer's keel can run; then with shoulder to a boat pole have urged, with slow and straining step, the flat-bottomed cotton barge up to the shoals on the Seneca. I have canoed on Keowee and Twelve Mile, and have waded, or crossed on some simple log, every branch and spring stream running down from the Saluda Hills on the one side, and the Currahee on the other

I love the land by the Savannah's waters. I have wandered over, and explored, every wood and hollow, every steep and ravine, from Chatooga and Chauga, from Conneros and Generostee, from Twelve Mile and Eighteen to Six and Twenty on the Carolina side; and then from Tugaloo and Tecoa, from Big Cedar and Little Lightwood Log, to the Great Broad in Georgia.

I love the people that live by these waters; the clear-headed, generous, independent men; and the fair, trusty, warm-hearted women of the southern backwoods.

I lived the philosopher's coveted life, in my early unambitious years, among these people, in these woods, and by these streams. A light labor got me all I wanted then, of simple dress, and simple food: the homespun garb, both inner and outer one, from the coat to the stocking feet, was carded, spun, dyed, woven, and made up, by the same hands that cooked the backwoods fare. And I cared not for more than this supply of simple wants, and my pine log home.

When this light labor was laid aside, which was often done, then I turned to other toil, with my rifle and hatchet and hunting knife, in the woods; and I roused the red deer abounding in the glens and valleys, and on the hill sides around Oconee, and the Valhalla of later days.

In one of my chases among the wilds of Pickens, I was

wooed by a deep, silent, and shaded hollow to shelter from the noonday heat, and take my hunting meal; and as I lay on a cool, green bank, watching the leaping and eddying play of a limpid mountain stream, that purled and brawled over its pebbly bed, I saw amid the bubbles of a little shoaly point, a glistening speck of bright metallic lustre.

I found among slaty and crystalline stones, a dark pebble, bearing upon its face a gout of pure, white, silvery metal, from which the dim coating of native ore had been burnished, when swollen waters had hurried it onward in the streamlet's bed, rubbing against its fellows.

The glistening of that metal had greater charm than the chase of deer. I sought along the stream for more of the material of coin, of which so little was seen in those mountain wilds ; and as I sought I came to a curious dent in the streamlet's bank, covered with the growth of the surrounding ground, but which showed that the hand of man had been burrowing in that wild glen many years ago.

I then recalled some backwoods stories of the Cherokees, when masters of these forests, how in some frontier warfare they had dealt out death with silver bullets, found in some mountain haunts, never seen by the white man's eye.

Many a search had been made, and I dare say is making to this day, to find out the silver mines known to the Indians; and when I found the pebble with the silvery gout, and looked upon the cut in the little creek's bank, I doubted not but that I had fallen upon one of the Indian mines.

I returned home with the piece of shining ore, and showed it to one who knew much about gold, and silver and lead mining; and he at once pronounced what I had found to be a piece of native silver, often found in ductile gouts and threads on the surface of some lump of the dark quartose stony ore, in which it is mostly hid, and from which by grinding, and by heat or metallic flux only can it be brought forth.

The miner made me a tempting offer to lead him to the spot, where I had found the silver ore; but I cared not to share my secret, and sought it again alone. I went this time with pick and spade, to dig into the cut in the creek bank. I saw plainly, that the bed of earth into which I dug had been before disturbed, and was like the filling in of some old pit. I pierced through this mingled soil, and came to a bed of dark and crystalline rock and earth, and still deeper I found the same dark stone and quartz; and of this I brought away a load not knowing whether I had found silver or not.

The miner's mortar and crucible showed that I had found a silver mine. Now there were visions of great treasure, and of a pomp and pride of wealth, which those backwoods had never known; and now the rude forest home, and the simple dress and fare had lost the quiet charm which once they had worn for me.

The desire arose to buy the lands in which the silver was found; but they were part of a great, encumbered, law-entangled domain; and so utterly rugged and barren, that no one could seek their purchase, with the plea of wishing to till the soil.

Still it became my great wish to own this land, so that I could work out the imagined silver masses unmolested; but towards the carrying out of this wish, my chief means were a rifle, a mule, some old books, and the little furnishings of my rough log shelter.

But I had youth,—the youth of nineteen; and a large share of that age's ardor and over sanguine hopefulness: and then from my point of view, in those backwoods, when my young mind, had been so long growing up untrammelled and luxuriant, I felt not those checks in looking forward to any achievement of fortune or of fame, which spring from the discipline of arts and letters, and the training of society.

In speaking of this,—my state of mind, and the finding of the fancied great silver mine,—I merely wish to tell of one, the most pleasing one to the curious ear, of the many causes, along with the death I have spoken of, that led me to leave peace, and quiet joys, and a simple life in a fair sylvan home, to go and enter into the common strife for gain with the rest of the money-groping world.

There were some calls to common practical pursuits, which led me into the business world; but beneath this outside of every-day toil, there glowed the hope in that hopeful time to get the means to draw forth a silver wand from the hills of Oconee, that would open up a road to the charmed East; and with that in view, I left the pine-log home, the homely fare, the homespun garb, and the unfettered life of the backwoods.

I soon learned that an adventurous spirit, and ambitious hopes, and all lack of training to any labor of the head or hands, were but poor stock in trade among the busy marts of men; and I soon felt that what had made me feel so rich among the forests, would in the city keep me very poor.

The drudge and the routine of the daily life of trade, soon drove away all dreams of the past. But wealth was eked out of this dull toil; even as the bright gold is dug out of the dull earth: and so I gained some fortune, and then I travelled.

Of my ramblings then, it is not my object to speak; except to glance at so much as led to the once longed-for journeyings in the East.

Among other countries, I travelled throughout the republic

of Mexico. I followed the track of Scott's conquering army: by the battlements of Ulua; through the woody pass of Cerro Gordo: at Plan del Rio, Jalapa, Perote, Puebla; and then among the smiling huertas, overtopped by the snowy peak of Orizava.

I saw something of the havoc at Molino del Rey, and upon the cypress steeps of Chapultepec. Then I wandered by Chalco; and mounted to the snows of the Muger Blanca: visited the silver lands of Guanajuato, and ranged through miles of hot galleries, down a thousand feet and more in the earth's bowels, in those old emptied metal veins of Rayas, La Luz, and Valenciniana; from whence dollars are still poured out, by millions every year. And here I thought of the Peruvian, whose mountain chase led him to the silver-loaded caverns of Potosi; and then I thought of the silver gout and the creek bank by Oconee.

I was in the hot plains, in the Tierra Caliente, and sojourned at Cuernavaca, at the old hacienda of Cortez of Atlacamulco; then explored the hand wrought halls and corridors within the womb of Montezuma's mount of Xochycalco,—abode at Miacatlan, Temisco, and Cocoyotlan,—visited the Aztec republics in the hills,—went a day's journey within the wondrous caverns of Cacahuamilpa; and then on the road to Acapulco, looked forth towards the Pacific, and thought of early plans of fortune and renown as I looked on the pathway to the East.

I became known to many of the leading men of Spanish America abroad; and soon formed a large circle of South American friends on my return home. There was one,—a diplomat from a Central American State, who offered me a gratifying position, and prospect of great moneyed gain, if I would fit out and equip a small, swift and stout-built vessel, for the service of his government, which I resolved to do.

I found the craft that was needed,—a man-of-war built schooner, long and low in the hull, broad in the beam, sharp at the bows, with raking masts, and large yards. Some six and ninety feet in the length of her keel,—four and twenty, the width of her beam; and her burthen less than one hundred tons, though admeasured to be three and fifty more.

I had the schooner fitted up with great care in her equipment, and taste in her adornment. She was to be the nucleus of a little fleet of a small republic, whose banner had never yet floated over a keel of its own; but now the pennant of a Centralian flag ship was to float from the masthead of the Flirt.

Her hull was repaired, her copper cleaned, her decks calked, her shrouds set up, her running gear all rove, her crew aboard, and about to bend on her new suit of sails, when trouble and loss ensued, and the pleasant and harmless scheme of the Centralian navy failed; yet still, I held the Flirt, and I longed to have a sail in her. I had lost the chances of winning great profit and naval glory; but my beauteous ship was ready for sea; the sea, on which I had longed so much to range, in a vessel of my own.

You will not care to know all the causes that should have stayed me, or that sent me forth. A vessel was on my hands, bought for a purpose which could not be achieved. She was not fit for the common carrying of trade. Her sale would have been a great sacrifice at home, which was so promiseful of profit abroad; and so I thought I had some cause to make a venture in the little ship, and felt; being most willing to believe, that Providence bid me go.

Let me glance back to a soft sunny afternoon on the 19th of

May, 1851. I am reclining on Beacon Hill, on Block Island, with telescope in hand, ranging the horizon, and scanning every sail that breaks the ocean line, or looms up from behind Montauk Point. Each mackerelman coming out of Buzzard's Bay, with a square foretopsail, has been the object of my eager gaze, —and for three weary days the mackerelmen have mocked my straining eyes.

Once more a square foretopsail heaves in sight, with low hull and raking spars; but she stands off from the island, and bears up channel towards Point Judith. I wave a little flag from the Beacon heights, and now she heads up for the island shore, and signals are in her shrouds: I run down to the beach,—a fisherman is about to push off in his boat. I want to jump in with him; but rumor has filled the island with wild stories of a strange craft hovering on the coasts, and he refuses to pull me to the dark, dashing little craft, now backing her foresail, within a mile, off shore. I offer five, ten, all the dollars I have,—and at last am afloat in the fisherman's skiff, and soon alongside of, and on board the Flirt.

We ran up to Newport, came to anchor, and spent there the night, the next day, and got under way again on the morning of the following day. As we stood out of the harbor, a well manned cutter loosed her sails, and bore up in our wake, seemingly wishful to dare the Flirt to her best, and so we crowded on all sail, running swiftly down past the sandy flat of Conanicut, and threading our way with ease, among and ahead of the fleet of mackerelmen that whitened the Narraganset Bay. Block Island again is passed; the last dim line of land is lost to view, and of all that we left behind that morning, the last speck that breaks the receding horizon's verge, is the pursuing cutter, which soon is gone, and the Flirt is fairly out at sea.

* * * * * * *

The Boatswain had drawn near, on hearing the name of the schooner. He had known her well, when she was with the Gulf Squadron, and at Vera Cruz. It was to him like the hearing about an old friend; and he told how that she was the stiffest little sea-boat that ever sailed out of Chesapeake Bay, on the eastern coast of which she was built. She had run down many a degree with exploring Wilkes, and the gallant Nicholson; and with many a story of the old cruisings of the Flirt, the ex-man-of-war boatswain amused the passengers of the Palmer, on the evening of the fifth day of her homeward voyage from Java.

SIXTH DAY.

There were eleven persons in all, who sailed in the Flirt for Brazil. There was a young man in the cabin, who had done much in the fitting of her out, and was now passenger for Bahia. He had introduced a friend to the owner, once a naval captain's clerk, afterwards a trader's mate, and now was chosen master of the schooner.

The mate was a stout, gaunt man-o'war's-man, who dropped from the stern of the St. Lawrence frigate one night into a fishing boat, and joined the schooner. He shipped as seaman, but took the place of a former mate, who ran away from the Flirt on her leaving port.

There were five men before the mast; three Americans, one Italian, and one Chilian; besides these, an old Spanish cook; then the owner and his servant, and these were all who sailed in the Flirt for Brazil.

She had a small cargo, as ballast, some eighty tons of ice—had no armament,—not one cannon, not a keg of powder, nor any small arms, not a musket or rifle; and there was nothing except a small, breach-loading carbine, two small brass pistols, which the master carried in his breeches pockets, two old rusty war-pikes, and a harpoon; nothing else but these for offence or defence were on board of the Flirt, when she sailed from America in 1851.

She was soon in the fogs and squalls of the tepid Gulf Stream, and the little craft being in bad trim, labored heavily.

The owner became very sick, and lay for many days in his berth. His cabin companions were better seamen, and fed well and drank well, whilst he was a prey to nausea.

He remained full a month below, with only a chance venture on deck, and knew little of the ship's progress, or of the state of affairs on board, except as reported to him. He began to hear stories from his servant of dislike shown by the men for the master; the stories increased,—the trouble grew greater; and he felt that he must arouse, if he would save his ship.

There was a man on board, who was the type of the traditional mutineer: short, thickset, with a thick upturned nose, on a mottled, gnarled face, hedged around with coarse, black, bushy hair. He was the first to slight orders, and then with malicious and wanton bravado, stood on the t'gallant forecastle, with a mock quadrant in his hand, mimicking, in an insulting way, the action of the master in taking an observation of the sun.

This was unheeded for a while, till the master spoke in half jeering half threatening words about the man's mimicry; to which he replied; and then the master unwisely bandied words with the man for a time. The latter was ordered to be silent and go forward, but he answered with effrontery, setting the master's authority at defiance.

The spirit of mutiny was on board, and if not quelled the vessel would be in danger. It was necessary to put the rebel sailor in irons; but he refused to yield to the master's order, and the crew stood back, with an air that showed they were ready to join whichever party should be conqueror.

By the help of the owner and his Italian servant, the mutineer was secured in the forecastle, whither he had sullenly retreated with the harpoon in his hand,—he was brought up on deck, manacled both hand and foot, and then put down into the run of the cabin, over which a grating was placed.

After a few days stay in this close, dark hole, and being fed on biscuit and water alone, the bull-dog pluck gave way, and the sturdy rebel begged to be released, promising to ask the master's pardon, and to do his duty better and quieter than before.

He was let loose, and there was quiet on board again; but the peace was short. There arose complaints about the food, about the mode and filth of the cookery. The Spanish cook was removed, and the Italian was installed in the caboose in his stead: but the new cook pleased no better than the former. The spirit of complaint was abroad in the ship. The master was mocked more than before. His orders were disobeyed, and insubordination reigned on board the Flirt.

On the morning of the 5th of July, whilst the master and the owner were standing by the cabin companion-way hatch, all of the crew came aft in a quiet manner, with the late mutineer at their head.

He began to speak about the old grievance of the cookery, and then of the need of water, and some fresh provisions. But the chief complaint was that he and his shipmates did not know where they were, and they did not believe that the master knew. He then said that they had been six weeks at sea, with a sharp-built, fast-sailing, stout and steady craft, lightly loaded; and yet, by reason of sailing by the wind nearly all the time, and taking in sail at the sight of every cat's paw, they had not crossed the Line, a run of some twenty odd days from home; but seemed to be a long way off, baffling about in the "variables" on the skirt of the North Atlantic trade-winds.

He went on to say, that he and the crew had lost all confidence in the seamanship of the master; and as they were about to run short of many stores, they demanded that the schooner should make for the nearest place, where a supply could be obtained.

During this harangue the master had gone down into the cabin, and as he remained there when the man had ceased speaking, the owner addressed the crew, saying, that the master could have no object, either in going slowly, or in running off his course; and as he was the only one on board who could make any pretensions to navigation, it was absolutely necessary that they should still trust to his direction. The leader of the crew then replied, that there was bad feeling and plotting on board, and it was the interest of the owner and all concerned to steer for the nearest port, so that ill-sorted people might part company, as well as to get needed supplies.

It was resolved to do so; and that evening, in concert with the master, the vessel was headed for Porto Praya, the nearest place to get supplies; although the distance was but a little less than to the nearest port on the coast of South America; but they counted upon a favoring wind all the way, and hoped to make the run to Porto Praya in one third of the time that they would be in reaching the nearest point of the coast of Brazil. The vessel was now very much lightened: her ballast was apparently all melted away: the schooner having risen considerably out of the water, and fresh water had been pumped out of the hold for about two weeks.

Baffling winds followed the Flirt on her course to Porto Praya. What had been supposed would be a run of about one week or less, was lengthened to eighteen days. On her way thither, she met the Sumter, commanded by Captain Reid, from Cork, with 300 troops on board, bound for the Cape of Good Hope.

The owner and master went on board the transport ship, and obtained several things of which they were in greatest need.

They entered the harbor of Porto Praya on the afternoon of the 22d of July. The owner immediately went ashore with the master, and called at the American consulate: the consul was absent from the island, and they found a young Americanized Portuguese, having been educated in the United States, acting in his stead, and with him made arrangements to obtain some water, and various ship stores.

On the third day after their arrival, when the owner thought he had adjusted the various disagreements on board, and had requested the master to go ashore to make some final purchases prior to their departure, whilst he remained on board to make ready for a start, the Captain of the Port came alongside the Flirt to inform him, that, in compliance with the request of the acting American consul, the commandant of the Fort of Porto Praya desired the owner and the mate of the Flirt to appear before him.

They were led into the presence of Major Morraes, the commandant of the troops, and acting Governor of the Island of St. Jago, where they found the American consular representative, the Captain of the Port, the master of the Flirt and his friend in the cabin; and then they learned that the master felt aggrieved about his loss of authority at sea, and was anxious for an official investigation of the matter.

The Governor had an authority from a U. S. naval commander to examine the papers of American ships touching at Porto Praya, and all evidences of the legality of their voyage. He instituted a close and judicious inquiry, and in a short time he underwent a very decided change of opinion in regard to the affair, to what had been previously created in his mind.

The master's mind seemed also to have undergone a change for before the audience closed, he fully concurred with Major Morraes, in the view that he had taken of the difficulties at sea, but he wished to return home, and so the owner was constrained to part with his navigator,—whose friend left the schooner at the same time.

What else ensued, the owner of the Flirt related thus to his fellow-passengers on board the Palmer:

After this I stayed three more days at Porto Praya. Commandant Morraes pointed out to me what there was curious in the island of St. Jago, of which Praya is the capital. This is a crumbling ruin of old Portuguese power; once a flourishing rendezvous for the ships of King John and Emmanuel, and the great Prince Henry of Portugal, when Vasco de Gama doubled Africa's farthest southern point; and when bold Sequeira, the conquering Albuquerque and heroic Galvan followed after him to the conquest of the Indies, and of the islands of South-eastern Asia.

A few old guns,—many useless and dismounted,—line the edge of the rocky bluff upon which the ruin of Praya stands, defended by some two or three hundred ragged negroes and convict Portuguese, who subsist on theft, and some scanty rations of coarse food; for the worthy Governor informed me, that he had not received any pay, or any attention from the Home Government, for about eighteen months; but as he had spent some twenty-two years of his life there, and elsewhere on the coast of Africa, he felt some pride to keep up a show of power as he best could.

Commandant Morraes seemed to be a disappointed man, infirm and soul-weary. He had commanded at Mozambique, and had dreamed of advancing the pillars of Portuguese dominion on

Madagascar, and to all the old landmarks in the East; but the spirit that founded empire in the Brazils, that girded Africa with forts, and that built up Goa and conquered Malacca, was dead in his country. A vicious and distracted court, and a corrupt aristocracy at home, needed every milrea of a lean exchequer for Braganza's dynastic struggles, and to revel in Lisbon's hideous vice.

The Commandant seemed to wake up to some of his old adventurous fire, as we talked together, and as he listened to some of my reveries and purposes. He glanced at the remnant of Portuguese possessions, and hinted at what might be done with them. The Cape de Verdes were an abandoned group of once fair islands, in ruinous state, every now and then devoted to famine. St. Jago lived on the visits of strangers, Mayo was a mere salt-pan, and St. Vincent a foreign steamship station. At Mozambique, a feeble, neglected garrison was cooped up by the barbarian queen of Madagascar, and Portuguese power struggled for an existence upon that island. The glory of Goa was gone; the trade of Macao had been drained by the thrifty Hong-Kong; and the turreted white flag waved no longer in the great Eastern Archipelago, except at the penal ruin of Dhelli on Timor.

Portugal wanted some young and unvitiated energies to raise up her scattered ruins, and turn them to profit. America had ample means, abundant small capitals, controlled by young and energetic heads, ready to embark in any hazard promiseful of profit, and some national fame; and why not buy the Cape de Verdes, or Mozambique, or Timor? for the Commandant spoke, as though he thought the Anglo-American people were in the market, for the purchase of every misgoverned, half-ruined spot of earth, where any planting, or trading, or mining could be carried on.

The worthy major dwelt especially upon the advantage of the purchase of the Cape de Verde islands, to make good plantations out of their generous soil, with the plentiful black labor which vagabonded over it in ragged uselessness, as bad as when in the jungles of Africa; and these might be obtained for the price of one good estate in America.

But I felt no interest in the Cape de Verdes, with all the profit and power that might be created out of their wastes, and ruins, and their motley population of vagabonds. I would not have been tempted by an offer of change of place with the worthy Governor,—to give up my taut, trim, well-appointed little Flirt, to lord it over the ruin-crowned bluffs of Porto Praya, and its breechless black garrison.

I was soon eager to be at sea once more. The Commandant wished me to change my course from Bahia to Lisbon. My cargo for the former part was almost gone; and in a few days there would not be left on board the Flirt a diamond of the Rockland Lake, of the size of one of the smallest brilliants of Brazil. By going to Lisbon, I would most likely obtain a cargo for South America, and I would see some interesting portion of the old world.

Major Morraes had an only, a motherless child—an invalid daughter just entering into womanhood—whom he wished to send away from her dreary home at Porto Praya, where she drooped daily, to live with some relatives in the gay metropolis of the home land; and he proposed to charter my cabin for the passage of his daughter and her domestics.

I could not have refused the surrender of my comforts to the sick lady, had there been no other conveyance; but there were Portuguese vessels in port, homeward bound. I did not wish to go then to the old world; I did not wish to see Lisbon, and I found a plea not to go, though much I desired to escort home the fair child of Major Morraes.

On the sixth day after casting anchor at Porto Praya, I was ready again for sea. The water casks were filled, and the schooner's stern was garnished with plantains, and yams, and two lean pigs. For these I was indebted to the poor Commandant, and in return, I presented him with a piece of curtain tapestry, two small silver cups, and some other trifles.

I appointed the mate to take the place of the sailing-master who had left; and found at Porto Praya a Swede, who filled the berth of the promoted first officer. Both had no other knowledge of seamanship but the commonest duty of a man before the mast; and I, notwithstanding my many voyages at sea, was no sailor, and I was not qualified then to take charge of the navigation of a vessel.

The Commandant came down to the beach, to wave me an adieu, as I dashed through the heavy surf that rolls into Porto Praya. He had just parted with his daughter, and was heavy-hearted. The Flirt had her anchor apeak, her sails were unfurled, and I soon gladly welcomed the ocean heave and the ocean air once more. As the crumbling ramparts, and the rocky crest of Porto Praya faded to the view, we passed a brigantine, that had left the roadstead some hours before us; and this was the Rosa de Lima, bearing to Lisbon the invalid daughter.

The chronometer had been ruined by some hand that had left us at Porto Praya; and all time tables and other guides for reckoning at sea, were found gone, when the need of them arose,—and it seemed a wild risk to run a small ship across the ocean without any guide of art, or a skilful hand on board; but I thought not of the risk, because I did not know, and could not feel its full extent; and so, with faith in a Hand that had led me safe o'er many a strange path before, I struck out with compass alone to guide my little ship, across the ocean, for the coast of Brazil.

SEVENTH DAY.

SABBATH ON BOARD THE PALMER.

A FLOOD of golden rays, gilding and shining through a pyramid of soft fleecy clouds, reaching from the. ocean line to the sky vault's top, led in a Sabbath of calm and softened sunniness.

The crew had worked on the Lord's day before; and the commander of the Flirt, and his fellow-passengers, had then passed a day of painful turmoil and unrest; and all seemed glad to give this one to still repose, and musing thoughts alone.

When the sun's rays no longer shot down from overhead between the sails, but came slanting, and were caught by the canvas fore and aft, leaving the polished deck in shade, the men of the Palmer came with clean shirts and shining faces, and, ranged in order, sat down against the bulwarks; whilst the people of the cabin sat by, on the break of the quarter deck; then the young Missionary standing up in the midst, read from the word of God, and spoke of the Redemption; and this was the story on board the Palmer on the seventh evening of her homeward voyage from Java.

EIGHTH DAY.

A VISIT AT SEA.

The tenth day after leaving Porto Praya we were some few degrees south of the Line, and it was one of the blandest of those gently breezy trade-wind latitudes. The light wafts of air over a tranquil sea, barely filled the schooner's mainsail, and she glided on an even keel; yet swiftly on, through the yielding flood of placid blue;—for this was her play,—a light wind and a smooth sea;—and in it she could count sea knots, far faster, than the great leviathan clippers of the ocean.

The wavelets rippling against her sides,—the faint creaking of the spars aloft,—the mainsail's lazy flap from time to time, and the low murmur of the tropic breeze, wafting us so gently on;—these sounds, and the balmy air,—the clear rose-tinted sky, the ocean's blue and heaving breast, strewn with golden threads and bulbs, the yellow weed from ocean's fields; all this—these sights and sounds, and breezy kissings, filled my soul with a gush of grateful feeling.

A sense of relief from cares and fears, just gone by,—a spirit of pride in treading the deck of my own swift and graceful craft, and a feeling of glorious freedom, of unchecked power to range the world at will, stole over my soul; and I felt heedless, which way my clipper headed on this bland, breezy, trade-wind sea.

There was a cry of, Sail ho!—a stirring sound at all times,

and in all places; but more so, amid the great wastes of the less frequented parts of the ocean. I examined with my glass the speck just visible to the sailor's eye, and made out a large brig, some three points off our lee bow, and heading north-east.

I had been wishing to speak a vessel, on account of some little wants and information which we needed; and now ordered the schooner to be headed so as to run athwart the path of the stranger; but, as with a slightly freshening breeze, we began to near him, he bore away, going right before the wind, clapping on stu'n-sails, and every inch of canvas that his spars could bear.

The retreating brig played shy in vain, for the taut and saucy schooner, with mainsail filled, bore swiftly down upon the clumsy merchantman. We ran up the stars and stripes, which were answered by the tri-color of France; but this time the Frenchman was shy of the old ally of his country, and wishful to give him a wide berth; for here was a suspected portion of ocean highway, between the two coasts of Brazil and Africa, where lawless adventure had been so often met with under the starry bunting of freedom, and on board of such craft as mine.

The long, dark hull, and sharpened bow, the range of ports, the raking masts, the heavy spars, and great spread of canvas; all this coupled with the present course,—a seeming chase, might give indeed a suspicious look, and fill the trader's mind with some fear of having met a lawless rover.

The Flirt sped on; she was soon close upon the brig; she ran under his quarter; then, to show the ease with which she could walk around him, shot ahead, luffed in the wind's eye, backed foresail, and came to, easy, graceful, and still, as a sea-bird resting on the crest of a wave.

The Frenchman answered our manœuvre, by coming to also. Ere the Flirt had stayed her headway, my light and graceful gig was loosened from the davits; and ere the ripple was stilled by the schooner's sides, I was afloat with my mate and four oarsmen, pulling towards the stranger.

A lot of red caps and excited faces lined the bulwarks of the brig. I mounted the sides, by help of a tasteful man-rope. As I stepped over the gangway, I was met with bows and smiles, mingled with an anxious, inquiring shade of look, from a short, stout little man, who stood cap in hand, in the midst of an evidently intensely excited and curious crew.

After giving a cheerful response to the little man's salute, he led me, without premising with one word of parley, into a tasteful marquee or cabin on the main deck. I was saluted, on entering, with a shrill, harsh clamor, from macaws, parrots, monkeys and marmozets, hung around in cages, or chained in the saloon. The polite commander hastened to inform me, that he had lately obtained them on the coast of Brazil, and had sailed from Parahiba, ten days ago, with a load of cotton and sugar; and then went on to give me more details about his vessel, cargo, and voyage; but I interrupted him and said, smiling, that I thought he mistook me and the object of my visit; as I had not boarded him either in the exercise of the right of search of a man-of-war; or in the spirit of plunder of a rover of the sea; but to ask a few things much needed by myself and men, which I hoped would be an excuse for the liberty I had taken, to cause him to stay his course.

At my words the face of the worthy Frenchman widened with a look of relief, and shone with smiles; and he expressed himself as being only too happy, if in his power to meet my small request. I told my wants, how my chronometer had been ruined at Porto Praya,—that I had there lost my nautical almanac, and had nothing but the unaided quadrant to help me find my way across the ocean; and then there were some medicines much needed by a sick man on board the Flirt.

My longitude was corrected, a spare almanac given me, and the other small wants provided for, and more than I had asked, with sailor-like alacrity and liberality; and I was glad to have a good Ohio cheese, half a dozen of Philadelphia ale, and a lump of Rockland ice in my boat, which were gratefully received as a most welcome treat. After this mutually pleasant interchange of favors, as the sea was still calm, the commander would have me taste of refreshment with him, and talk over the news we brought from our different points of the world.

The ocean inspires a free range of thought; and sunny placid waters, with light breezes, lull and soothe the heart to a forgetfulness of the matter-of-fact cares of the busy, wearying turmoil on shore. Whenever harsh duty on board gives some small respite, and when the sun and soft tropic wafts of air play upon the gently swelling sea, then will sometimes the most soddened sin-seared sailor-man, out of whom every vestige of faith and bright hopes, and the young heart's adventurous romance, has seemingly been storm-washed and toil-worn away a long time ago, often let his thoughts wander from his filthy, comfortless forecastle, to the shining seas and sunny isles of early dreams, where brave men should win treasures and glory, and the smiles of gentle women in a flowery land.

Much as steam, and the careful search of almost every nook of the earth has taken away from the romance of the sea, yet still there are few seamen, whose thoughts do not wander wild at times: few who are not rovers at heart; but rovers in quest of bold and honest adventure, among strange people for trade or travel in unknown isles; and not rovers of the black flag, with the death's head and the raw bones.

3

Such was our theme, the pleasant sea-wander far off, where ports, and tariffs, and tonnage were not known. We had talked of my taut and stanch little ship, which we could see as we talked, now rising with and heading to the ocean swell. I had spoken of her strength and fleetness, and comfort on board; of my tastes, and untrammelled power to range; and as I spoke on, the fervid Frenchman followed me with glowing looks, and then broke forth into glowing words, in being borne along with my gallant skiff among the islands of the Indian ocean.

He had ever longed for some such wide-world wander, on sea and shore; yet not ever idly strolling, but working while wandering. A hearty tilling of the soil for a time, and then with the fruit of his health-braced limbs, to launch forth with his own keel on the broad, free seas, to visit his brethren of all hues and habits, scattered throughout the fair earth.

All his life at sea, as yet,—before the mast and aft,—had been one unchanging course of soul-wearying drudge; at the behest of dainty men on shore, who sickened at the smell of the sea. He was now going for them this round of drudge in his clumsy craft, with a freightage of the lash-wrought sugar, and ardent spirit of Brazil, which life his soul abhorred.

The beautiful Flirt now wooed his roving heart; and I, the poor and cargoless sea-wanderer, loomed up a viking in his imagination. And thus he viewed me, and my little ship; his roving fancies, warming him at last to such a pitch that he hinted at, then urged outright, that I should head for France with him, and there join means on board my clipper for a partnership of congenial trade and travel all over the globe.

In the fast flow of words in a tongue to which my ear was but little, and my lips still less practised, I had no chance to interpose a word of my own thinking;—of wish for, or dissuasion from his scheme. But I had felt some little borne away by the candid, hearty warmth of the man; though not so far as to dream one moment of going 'bout-ship, to head for France, to join interests with the captain of the brig in a partnership of free sea life, such as the polity of the chief governing powers of the world do frown upon, however harmless it may be.

Yet as he spoke on, fanned as we were by the soft winds, and rocking gently on the breast of the boundless sea, the wild scheme did not seem so wild then, as to think of it ashore. And so I listened, and let the roving skipper go his bent.

On we went, steering for that land, late rioting in the frolic of tumbling down thrones. We were soon at anchor, and treading the vine fields of republican France. Ere many days, we were afloat again, on board the beauteous Flirt, with forecastle, hold, and cabin, well filled with choice wares, and arms, and brave men. We were wafted by gentle tropic gales, and gliding o'er the heaving bosom of the Indian sea: we were in the midst of coral isles, of cocoa groves, and jewelled princes, and warriors with brown skins, with whom we were about to enter into magnificent relations of friendship and trade—when suddenly, we were recalled to the old brig by an uproar of mingled volleys of French and English oaths, and a clattering of feet and handspikes on the main deck.

The active Gaul leaped foremost out of his cabin; and when I had joined him by the main hatch, I saw one of my sailors, a little bullet of a man, one from the land of steady habits, standing over a prostrate Frenchman: he was holding a Porto Praya monkey in one hand, and shaking defiance with the other at the soup eaters, whom he bid come on: the rest of my men were squaring away with their tar-blackened fists, at the crew of the Cesar; who though outnumbering mine five-fold, were kept at bay by the little band of Flirts.

The monkey, a great pet of the forecastle, who followed the men daily to the crosstrees, and came down by the run on the stays, had been smuggled into the boat, and was now the cause of war. During the time of the entente cordiale, the tricks of Blister had been shown off: a Frenchman had seized him with careless grasp, had been bitten, and being maddened with the pain, had dashed poor Blister on deck with murderous force, and stamped upon him, but had scarcely done so, when down he lay, his own full length.

The struck man rose, furious to spring upon the one who had dealt the blow; and the little dark, knotty, gnarled Connecticuter stood ready for him. The French captain ordered his men to stand back; but they, with handspikes in hand, were advancing with wicked looks. The wind had now freshened, and my master was making signals to return. The brig was getting stern way upon her, and not an instant was to be lost in regaining the Flirt.

I said a word to the mate, who sprang into our boat, and made all ready for shoving off. I pulled my chief fighting man back, and said a few words of peace to the threatening Frenchmen; but they were not to be soothed by mild words; one of their shipmates had been struck down by one of my piratical crew; and sacré and tonnerre, they felt insulted until he was avenged.

My men had backed at my order towards the gangway; they were passing over,—the Frenchmen crowding on, gesticulating and cursing, and giving and receiving blows. My men were all over the ship's side, the sea was rising,—the mate cries out, the boat will swamp; let go, I cry, and over I leap.

And now with hands to their oars, my crew give way, amid

a yell of oaths and cries, of "pirates," "beasts," and of threats to sink us; but the wind is up, and there is a shout,—to square away the yards, silencing the motley din; and they were the last words I heard of my late partner, in imagined glory and adventure.

The sea had risen fast indeed: the long, deep roll of mid-ocean, was breaking in foaming surges; and my little shell, awhile o'ertopped the schooner, and then it was lost to view. A few hearty pulls from strong and willing hands;—and we were astern of the buoyant Flirt, now lifting with, and heading to, defiant of the ocean's roll. We could not run alongside,—lines were hove, and foot-ropes let down astern; and quickening fear, and some practice in rope-climbing, soon landed us safe on deck.

It was time; for the sea was up, and the wind was straining back the foremast to its utmost bend;—but soon the yards swing round; the clipper pays off; and on she bowls before the whistling squall.

And where was the Cesar?—far astern, and dimly seen through the mist of the rising storm; and there was the tri-color of France, waving defiance or adieu. Up went the flag of America, answering to either; and thus we dipped and waved, till the storm mist shrouded us from view.

* * * * * *

NINTH DAY.

The owner of the Flirt resumed the story of the voyage, in his vessel from the Cape de Verde Islands, towards the port of Bahia, telling of many mishaps and trials owing to the errors of dead reckoning, and his own and officers' unskilled hands, in working a way to the

COAST OF BRAZIL.

We had been groping our way by compass and helm, aided from time to time, by speaking a passing ship, until we had, by the showing of the log, run down latitude and longitude enough to have reached the South American coast; when, on the afternoon of the eighteenth day of our run from Porto Praya, a gleam of fire was dimly seen to the westward.

On nearer approach, I descried a ship on fire, and glimpses of land beyond. On approaching nearer still, I could see, by the light of the column of flame that was licking the topmost spars of the burning craft, a crowd of boats hauled up on the beach of a deep, bluff-crowned cove, and from which there seemed to have just landed a troop of sailors, and a host of naked and manacled black men; and then I doubted not that I beheld a burning slaver, abandoned after the safe landing of its live African cargo.

We stood off and on till morning came, and then we beheld the thick-wooded coast of Brazil; but not knowing off what part we were, though judging from the reckoning to be north of the point to which we steered, we ran down the coast, till we came to a bold reef, with an inlet leading into a roadstead, in which were many ships riding at anchor; and beyond this, a fort, crowning commanding heights.

The port seemed too small for the one we sought; but we needed some refreshments and repairs, and entered the roadstead, which proved to be that of Maceio; here I resolved to make some small purchases, and then go on my way again on the same day of our arrival; but there was a strange fate following the Flirt. The Brazilian Custom-House required that I must enter my vessel in what was called franquia, and afterwards must submit to a routine of clearance, that required several days.

On the afternoon of the third day of our forced stay, all hands—officers, crew, and my servant—all, except a lad in the forecastle, had been made drunk by some of the poisonous aguardiente of the country, brought on board the vessel whilst I was ashore. The master and mate, though steady and sober men, drank freely: both mere sailors before the mast; but the mate, who had been obtained at Porto Praya, proving to have more skill than the master, had necessarily taken charge of the chief duty of sailing the vessel; hence there was a grudge between them, and they sought the first chance to warm themselves into a fighting mood, in order to settle their ill blood.

The master was tall, muscular and bony; the mate short, round-limbed, and the heavier of the two. Both were bold and hardy alike. As they drank, they began their taunts, and quickly came to blows. The crew took sides, and a general melée ensued on the quarter deck of the Flirt.

The battle between the two principals was long and obstinate. In their struggles, they rolled down the companion-way into the cabin, the mate uppermost, and striving to choke his foe, with all his might; but the master, drawing a spring-knife from his pocket, stabbed furiously at the mate, gashing his hands, face, throat, and breast in the most horrible manner.

After the butchery of his antagonist, the master was seized with a sudden revulsion of soberness and remorse; accompanied the wounded mate ashore, and surrendered himself to the police of Maceio. The crew of the Flirt being in a wild and riotous state, were made prisoners by some men brought from a neighboring ship; and they were sent ashore for confinement, till they should become sober; and to afford an opportunity to remove some dangerous characters among them. The magistracy of Maceio chose to see in this sailorly row, a design to disturb the peace of Brazil, and issued orders fcr the arrest of the commander and crew of the Flirt.

There was no American consul nor resident in the place. I retreated to the house of the British Vice-Consul, where, after some parley, I was allowed to remain on parole. The men were called up severally before a Court of Instruction, and underwent long and trivial interrogations. The Brazilian Government was in want of a light, swift craft, to send down to Buenos Ayres, which they were then blockading; and merchants of Maceio said, that there was a disposition to trump up some charge in order to confiscate the trim and beautiful Flirt.

Many days had been passed in sham investigation. I had been summoned to appear before the Fiscal and Judges of Instruction, but had refused. Nothing had been elicited from the crew, to substantiate a shadow of a charge, and yet the Brazilians seemed determined to retain my vessel, and would have done so, by sending her to Rio de Janeiro, there to await the destructive delay of Brazilian law, or of my own Government's interference; but there was a prompt deliverer close at hand.

On the seventh day of my stay at Maceio, the lad, the lonely keeper on board the Flirt, descried a war steamer passing down the coast. He immediately hoisted the ensign, with the stars union down. The steamer observed the signal of distress, ran into the roadstead, proved to be the British steam sloop-of-war "Conflict;" and her commander, Captain Drake, on learning the cause of the signal, came ashore, saw me, looked at my papers, made some inquiries of other parties, satisfied himself, and then, without remark, desired me to accompany him to where they were holding the Court of Instruction.

We found a Presiding Judge, a Fiscal, or Solicitor, the Chief of Police, and Captain of the Port, composing a tribunal of justice, before whom one of my men was undergoing an interrogation. At the sight of the British officer, the Court showed much emotion, and seemed disposed to disperse.

The commander of the Conflict hastened to say to the Court, that he appeared before them in behalf of a citizen of a power friendly with his own, and without representative or protection at this place. He did not assume any right to interfere in the behalf of the American captain; but he would say to the Court before him, judiciary, police, and prosecution, that he doubted their sincerity in seeking any end of justice, since they, the same men, had so lately connived at the landing of a large cargo of slaves from the African coast, in sight of their port, the flames of the abandoned slaver having illumined the buildings around where he stood. He doubted not, they regretted the destruction of that American clipper, which must otherwise have fallen into his hands; and now sought to replace it with the one then lying in their port, which, according to their own rigid search, and all evidence before them, carried not a cannon, or more than a single small arm on board; was manned by a feeble crew of seven men, including officers; her commander being evidently no seaman, but a quiet gentleman, with some novel taste for travel. There was not a shadow of evidence to imagine treason, or any other such absurdity, under such circumstances; and therefore he would advise the authorities to let the Flirt and her people go in peace.

The result showed that he was wont to utter, and they to listen, to such dictation. They showed the craven spirit every where seen in Spanish and Portuguese America, among the vicious stock of mingled race, now holding sway over the old masters from the Peninsula. This court of mestizoes rose with much trepidation, and said they were glad to learn from the Senhor Capitão that the American and his vessel were clear of all suspicion, which would save them the trouble of further investigation; and they were ready to permit the schooner and her people to depart.

The English captain not deigning to await the conclusion of the Court's reply, turned on his heel, and left the Hall of Justice along with me. We had not proceeded far, when the Captain of the Port overtook us, with the papers of my vessel in his hands, which my brave protector bid me refuse, until I had received ample compensation for my forced stay and expenditúre.

I replenished my stores, I shipped a new officer, and a small crew of coast hands, and then set sail for Pernambuco, the nearest port where I would find an American Consul, and could ship a good crew, and make a fresh and better start.

TENTH DAY.

THE commander of the Flirt began to give some account of Pernambuco, the city of the Reef, built upon the islands of Recife, Boa Vista and San Antonia, which rest in tranquil waters, protected from the surges of the Atlantic by the most wonderful breakwater in the world,—a perfect dam of coral, sloping seaward, and presenting a high wall face on the shore side. He went on to speak of the observations that he had made during a month's stay, in regard to the trade and growth of the city, the manners and customs of its people, the fertility and forest splendor of the surrounding country, its varied animal kingdom, of the Government, and social life, of the clergy, women, and slaves, and much, besides, about Pernambuco and the Empire of Brazil; but he was interrupted by the young lady passenger, who observed that she doubted not, that Brazil was a very wonderful country for sugar, logwood and diamonds, and that it would be interesting at another time to hear about its growth and progress, including the fortunes of the Braganzas, the imperial Pedros; but at present she would prefer, that the narrator would put to sea again with his Flirt, and reach the Malays, the Dutch, and the Prison from whence he had escaped, by the nearest route he could take.

This being the desire of the rest of his hearers, he turned from Brazilian politics and statistics, to glance at some circumstances which preceded his departure from Pernambuco; his shipment of a new crew; the offers made to him to charter his vessel for Buenos Ayres, prevented by the blockade; for the river Amazon, stopped by a Government prohibition; then, finding no opportunity for such employment as he had hoped, his endeavor to sell his vessel, but trade being dull, could find no purchaser; but, in the midst of his strivings and lookings around for something to do, his falling in with a Hamburgh captain, an old cruiser in the East Indies, who told him news about the long lost uncle, and revived the memories of Sumatra; but at this time, the American Consul at Pernambuco, getting word of an American ship being ashore on the Brazilian coast, off Cape St. Roque, and needing help; and the Flirt being the fleetest vessel and of lightest draught in port, his engaging her to go to the rescue, with instructions to take any cargo saved to Rio de Janeiro.

He went and found the stranded vessel abandoned and stripped; nothing to save, what should he then do, the wide ocean being before him; there being nothing for him to do in Brazil; the returning home, a fruitless sacrifice; then thoughts of the Eastern islands, of the uncle and his strange fate, rose up to view; and there, while at sea, while beating down the Brazilian coast, he resolved to steer for the East, and, with a bounding heart, he headed for the Cape of Good Hope; and then, on his way thither, he stopped to visit a curious island: and thus he told of what he saw and heard of

TRISTAN D'ACUNHA.

We had passed the parallel of Africa's most southern lands, and were midway in the South Atlantic, between those stormy points of the Horn and Good Hope. The unwearying pigeon of the Cape, and the heavy-winged albatros, were chasing us with varied evolution; now sweeping over, now darting under the stern, or clustered together and fluttering on the water in our wake, greedily picking up some garbage from the schooner. Then came the long-tailed marline bird, screaming and flying to and fro, high overhead; these signs of birds, with thick masses of white clouds in the south, bid us look out for land that must be near.

We were, by our reckoning and observation, full sixteen hundred miles from the nearest point of continental coast; but our chart showed some pin-point dots,—the spots of land that we were nearing, and which I had wished to see.

The vessel, urged on by a fresh south-western wind, fast ran down the heavy cloud masses that embanked the horizon ahead; the birds came thicker, with more of the screaming marlines; we had got out of the ocean's roll, and the sea came chopping as under the lee of a protecting shore; but the man in the chains still hove his lead, and felt no check to his line.

The day had been harsh, blustry, and lowering. We strained our eyes at the piled-up hills of clouds that seemed to wall up some shore from our view, which we feared we would not sight before nightfall. Later on, the clouds began to break overhead, though still enshrouding the horizon. In the break above, we gazed with pleasure at the skyey blue, that had been veiled from us for some time; and then at a white, sun-gilded cloud, peering above the dark mass that walled up half the sky. But the glistening of this cloud was strange; and while the dark mass moved on, and broke, and lowered, there this dazzling cone remained, piercing like a mighty pyramid's peak the blue above; and as nearer we came, it larger grew; and then the dark mass broke away below, and we found ourselves at the base of a lofty, snow-capped mount, within a few hundred yards of the shore of Tristan d'Acunha.

Though near enough to fire a musket-ball on shore, yet our lead found no bottom; and the steep, bold mount, that shot up in sheer unbroken ascent, eleven thousand feet overhead, seemed but a summit above the sea, of some mighty mountain, whose base lay many a hundred fathom down below, on the ocean's bed

This mountain island, some seven miles around, presented a bald wall of rock sheer down to the water's edge, in all its circumference, except a small patch, a cable's length of shingly beach, backed by a ledge of green and level land, walled in by the beetling black rock of the mountain's side, from which there gleamed a shining silvery streak, and which a nearer view showed to be a great gushing spout of water, springing boldly from a cleft in the rock's dark face, and thundering down upon the beach, a flood of melted snow, convenient for, and most grateful to thirsty crews.

The ledge of green was tilled, in terraced plats, around a range of neat, snug mud huts; and there were cattle browsing, and further signs of man were seen, and then he soon appeared himself. A whale-boat, like a large canoe, was launched from the shingly beach; it came bounding bravely through the surf and the chopping sea, and when within hail of the Flirt, then lying to, the words, "Schooner ahoy," came ringing across the water in right good, pleasant-sounding Saxon.

Four men came over the gangway of the schooner; a white-haired patriarch, short, and bent with years; a youth of twenty, showing a mingling of the blood of some dark straight-haired race with Saxon; another youth, tall and ruddy; and the fourth was a short, thick, coarse-limbed, and a sailorly-looking man in the face, though not in his garb; for he, like all the rest, had goat-skin cap, and shoes, and coverings for the legs, with some other things of savage dress; and these men were, the old Governor of the island, two grandsons, and a son-in-law, who came to welcome us to the wild isle we saw.

I learned then, and partly since, that the old man was once a sergeant in the British East India Army, and had left his service in 1810, to cast his lot on the then deserted Tristan d'Acunha. After some years of a rude and desolate life, with an old negro and a boy, he went with a frail craft on an adventurous cruise to the Cape of Good Hope, and brought back a partner, a woman willing to leave all the world beside, to share with him the green clefts and ledges of that lonely ocean peak.

Their solitude was blessed with daughters, who grew up lithe and strong-limbed, like the wild goats, which these damsels chased with equal speed of foot; and they were seen by hunters of other game, adventurous men in search of whale, who were willing to leave their huge prey, to join the Dianas of the mountain isle.

And then, from a wreck,—that of the Blendenhall,—a man and woman were strangely saved, and cast upon this shore. All of these, the founder of this lonely state, his wife, and old retainers, the children and those they married, with their increase, along with that of the couple saved, numbered, at the time of my visit there, eighty-four souls in all.

Old Governor Glass ruled by right of age, and a founder's claims to chief suzerainty of the soil, and as yet there had been no contending rival. He alone sat in judgment, to uphold the laws of his own making; and with his simple code and prompt administration, all legal lore and the delays of law were there unheeded and unknown.

No custom-house, nor bank; no factory, nor doctor's store of drugs; no traffickers, tax-gathers, nor deep-mouthed, purchased politicians; no strutting soldier, and no wranglers about unloving dogmas, were there; whilst the use of money was a myth of other lands.

The islanders had some cattle and sheep, and grew barley and potatoes on their narrow ledge of level land, which held not more than two hundred acres of farming soil. What they had to spare of their meat and esculent food, along with fresh milk and eggs, they exchanged with whaling ships that chanced that way, for a few ship's stores, but chiefly powder and shot, with which to chase the goats and conies, that swarmed in the clefts and up the steeps of their island mountain.

On the summit of this mountain, a crater's mouth showed where the earth's inner molten mass had been belched forth; but now, where the liquid lava once had boiled and raged, down some hundred feet from the crater's brim, there flowed a cool, pellucid lake, filled with strange fish, unlike to any of the many kinds that swarm around the island.

We found no safe anchorage during our stay off the island,—part of two days and a night; but there is a point about one mile and a half southeast of the small patch of landing beach, where there is a detached bank in twenty-five fathoms of water, exposed to the ocean's roll from north to south by east; and as two ships have been lost there, from the wind veering round to the northeast, while they were at anchor, no vessel should trust to a hawser on that bank.

This absence of good anchorage has saved the islanders from hurtful contact with ships' crews, and thus has favored the growth of simple tastes, of industrious habits and kindly intercourse; and the culture of some knowledge of books, of which they have a small stock, and prize most highly, and they were eager for newspapers of any ancient date that we could spare.

Fain would I have stayed some time ashore, could I have moored my vessel in safety; but the south winds blew; the Flirt was tossed in a fretful sea, and seemed straining to start on her eastern way. I returned some gifts, pleasing to the islanders, for the fresh food they brought; and after exchanging kind words, gave the schooner the helm, and off she flew; and when the shingly beach, the green ledge, the rude hamlet, the leaping stream, and the dark rocks of Tristan d'Acunha had faded from our view, still the glistening snow-peak was seen, when far on our way to the Cape of Good Hope.

All the listeners to the story of Tristan d'Acunha were eager to learn more about these islanders, and their dot of dominion, so far away, alone in the great ocean; more about their social habits; their personal looks, especially of the women; their amusements, notions of property, and, above all, their ideas of religious worship.

These queries could not well be answered; for the visit had been too short, and foul weather cut off that intercourse, which otherwise would have taken place; and furthermore, the commander of the Flirt had left the islanders with the promise and firm intention of paying a lengthened visit on his return from the East, and still hoped to do so, and learn all that was interesting concerning the little insular state.

The boatswain had a word to say about Tristan d'Acunha; he had sighted it in many an East India voyage. A fight took place off the island, some time during the last war, when Commodore Biddle in the Hornet, sunk the British brig of war Penguin. Seven years before that time, in 1808, an American seaman, Jonathan Lambert, of Salem, left his ship, along with a boy and an old African, and settled on the island. He went there to establish a station, to supply fresh provision and water to whalers, and to ships going round the Cape. In one of his cruisings with his boat, on a visit to the little islands near by, called Nightingale and Inaccessible islands, he was drowned; but as Sergeant Glass appeared at Tristan d'Acunha shortly afterwards, with the companions of Lambert, it has been suspected that the American settler met with foul play. At any rate, the boatswain thought the Government at Washington ought to look into the matter, as the island was American by priority of settlement, was a good station for India-bound ships, and would be of great use in time of war.

ELEVENTH DAY.

The Flirt was upon the Agulhas banks, on the tenth day after her departure from Tristan d'Acunha, the dim outline of the African sands, on the coast of the Cape, being just visible from her decks; and after three-and-twenty days' sail in the Indian Ocean, was in sight of the island of St. Paul. This island shows a strong likeness at a distance to a spermaceti whale, when approached from the southwest, there being near the extremity, resembling the head, a lofty, natural column of rock, which might well be mistaken for the spout of the whale. This natural minaret is honey-combed with innumerable holes, which are filled with the nests, the eggs, and the young of sea birds, who fly in screaming clouds round their grand columnar aviary. This shaft stands in front of a deep cove, which forms almost a circle; the incomplete segment being partially filled up by the base of the natural column, leaving between this and the horns of the crescent a mere boat channel, for entrance into the cove. This natural basin has steep, stony banks, like the walls of a dock, and affords no convenient place for landing. Its waters, and those surrounding the island, swarm with small fish of various kinds, having fine, firm, white meat,—sweet-tasted, and free from small bones.

An adventurer from the Isle of France took possession of St. Paul's many years ago, and resided on it for some time. He was not at home when the Flirt paid a visit to the island, there was no evidence of any human being then residing there. It is about one mile and a half long, and half a mile wide on the average; covered with a coarse, stunted, fern-like growth, and is of volcanic origin, as there are several hot springs upon it, which send forth steaming and scalding streams into the sea.

The next land that lay in the course of the Flirt, was the small group of islands called Cocos, which are strung continuously together, by connecting shoals and coral banks, and lie on the ocean like a Titanic necklace of emerald beads and coral links, the land-locked sea within being inaccessible except to small craft of the lightest draught. An enterprising trader by the name of Ross, took possession of this group; and as his own Government had made a treaty with the Government of Holland, in which it had conceded a political and commercial monopoly to the latter, of all islands in the Indian Archipelago, south of the equator, he courted the protection of the authorities of the Netherlands at Batavia; obtained the privilege to hoist the Dutch flag, and took with him a large company of poor natives of Java, to cultivate his insular dominions, the chief production of which is the cocoa nut, whence cocoa nut oil is obtained in great abundance; and with which Governor Ross freights his schooner twice a year for Batavia.

It was not the object of the commander of the Flirt to turn aside or stop on his way across the Indian Ocean. Madagascar, Mauritius, St. Paul's, and the Cocos had courted his curious eye to take a passing glance, but he hastened on to the great Malay Isle, whose mountain summits soon broke upon his view, and thus he spoke to his friends on board the Palmer of his

FIRST SIGHT OF SUMATRA.

On Christmas eve, we were sailing with a gentle wind over a smooth sea. We were nearing thick masses of land-clouds, when there came a faint aroma of sweet woody scents, wafted on the breeze; as we sped through the yielding vapory banks, the fragrant air came strong and pleasurable, like distant strains of song; then the retreating clouds presented to our gaze a dark blue peak, piercing the skyey blue above; the wood, and blossom, and gum-scented breeze came stronger and more thrilling, rivalling in pleasure sweet melody on the waters; and the peak, and the odor-laden winds, were the first sight and first welcome breath of the land of long dreams, the Island of Sumatra.

I shall not stop to speak of what I saw of the Straits, and of the Islands of Sunda, through which we have just passed; of Crockatoa and Anjier, of Thwart the Way, and Bessie, and of all those pleasant spots which first greet the ocean traveller, at this entrance of the Indian seas.

I felt a deep heart's thrill on entering the threshold of the East Indian Archipelago:—those islands of so much fabled wealth and wonder, of so much real value and interest, and so much less known than any other portion of the peopled earth.

To my right was the olden Jabadiv, the "land of barley," of the Alexandrian geographer, the sacred Isle of the Hindoos, and the Java of English and Dutch dominion; an island rivalling Cuba in size and fertility, and sixfold its number of souls; once a land of great empires and oriental pomp, sending forth its embattled fleets and hosts to the nations around them, then warring with European power and skill, and falling by the hands of the buccaneering men of Portugal, of England and of Holland, and now yielding a coffee harvest, the chief support of the almost bankrupt sovereignty of the last and the meanest of its masters.

To my left was a greater island still, though less fruitful and less peopled, and not so rich in historic lore and dynastic fame; but the chief seat of a great race, who without war, or proselyting zeal, had scattered their language, and customs, and traditions among numberless nations around;—from Madagascar to Polynesia, from Malacca to Papua, the teeming millions of the many thousand isles within the Indian Ocean, all bear some marks of the intellectual sway of the Malays of Sumatra.

Before me was the greatest of all, an island continent; full of hidden wonders, and unexplored rivers, and plains, and mountain ranges; where the human form with hairy skin lodged in the trees; where man sought the head of his fellow man, as the best of gifts to lay at the feet of his bride; and where an adventurous gentleman had become the prince and civilizer of a barbaric race, and filled the world with the fame of Brooke and Borneo.

And around these were the countless smaller isles of the Indian seas; and many of them large, rich, and greatly peopled states. There were the fragrant isles of spices, so rich in soil, yet so poor in product, making Molucca another name for sordid monopoly. There was Celebes, with its trading Bughis, and their maritime laws; then Magindinao, the Lanuns' land,—the great pirate isle; Papua, with its ferocious tribes, and birds of paradise; Banca, the great tin mine; Bali, the little Bali with its heroic race, twice conquerors of the Dutch; Sumbawa, the sandalwood island; Timor, the last remnant of Portugese dominion in the Indian seas; and still thousands more of fair island spots, rich in a gorgeous animal and vegetable life, had wooed many a fancy from the hard path of a toiling life in a cold land, and might well produce a deep heart's thrill with their full charm of verdure and fragrance, bursting upon weary and storm-tossed senses.

It was my plan to steer direct for Singapore, the great central point, and chief trading port for all nations in the Indian seas: there I hoped to hear some tidings of my uncle; and there I designed to refit for a short cruise to the northern part of Sumatra, the north-eastern portion of Borneo, and to other points in the Archipelago, where the native races of these islands are independent, and where I thought there was no risk of coming in contact with European jealousy and power.

Calms and currents kept us lingering for many days in the Java Sea, and creeping slowly through the Straits of Banca. While the schooner was at anchor, waiting for a wind to stem the adverse current that prevailed, I cruised in my boat among the fairy dots of land, upon the Lampong coast; roused up some of the strange marine monsters that sport in the green slimy ooze along those shores, which seems to be a deposit of decomposed animalculæ,—took a good look at Lucepara,—visited the Nanka group, great and little, which my sailing-master explored in quest of water, finding none;—and then when off Parmesang Hill, I went with my boat to the opposite coast, pulled up a rapid creek, explored the jungle, and it was there, on a New-Year's Day, I first trod the soil of Sumatra.

We had reached, on a pleasant afternoon, the north-western end of the Straits of Banca—the Sumatra and Banca shore just to be seen from either bow: one half hour more, and the Flirt would have been out of sight of Manopin Hill, and beating up against the northwest monsoon in the China Sea; but a black-arched battlement of cloud rose up to bar the way; up sprang the dark disc, and on it came with tropic speed and wrath, rolling with foam over the waters. The Flirt was all snug in storm trim, as she careened to a furious and blinding squall; and drove on heedless of the helm, among dangerous shoals, and upon an unknown coast, with no other guide in the thick darkness that surrounded us, but the lead line. The water rapidly shoaled, and when the lead found bottom at three fathoms, though not knowing whether on a bank or the coast, we let go our anchors, and rode out the storm in safety.

When daylight came, we beheld the Banca shore, and the fort of Minto, about two miles distant. Whilst I was scanning with my glass the small craft and native boats at anchor, and entering the roadstead of Minto, I observed a small Dutch cutter standing in; she had been hovering near the schooner in the straits the day before: she now ran close alongside the Flirt, and ladies were to be seen on board, whose deep brunette skins and fine youthful forms, draped in novel and tasteful costume, could readily be distinguished. One hailed us in merry voice, and at the same time a clear, shrill, pleasant feminine laughter from many voices, came ringing over the waters: and then the ladies mocked with their parasols my use of the telescope, levelled at them whilst the cutter passed by, and came to anchor near the Fort. I resolved to go ashore and take a glance at this noted Dutch depot for tin; leaving orders to be all ready to make sail in the afternoon, when I should come on board.

TWELFTH DAY.

When the commander of the Flirt first stepped on shore at Minto, he was surrounded by a crowd of half naked natives, who made a great clamor, repeating very distinctly the word *shabandar*, and pointing to a low building near the beach, above which the Dutch flag was flying. At the doorway of this building he was met by a stout, portly man, in the early prime of life—the type of the old Dutch burgomaster in form, but not in complexion; his skin being almost as deeply shaded as the turbaned natives around him. This was the Shabandar or Havermeester of Minto. After an exchange of salutations, he invited the commander very cordially to partake of some refreshments, then before them. The novelty of the visit was commented upon;—the first American vessel that had ever anchored in the roadstead of Minto, within the knowledge of the Havermeester. He was gratified at the visit; it was so rare to meet with a traveller of any information upon the island of Banca. If he wanted wood or water, or any thing to be done on board of his vessel, it should be attended to, and he pressed him to delay his departure, saying, it might be no loss of time, to stay even several weeks.

The north-west monsoon was then blowing in the teeth of all vessels proceeding to Singapore; and no sailing craft, even one as sharp built as the Flirt, could then reach this port in less than twenty or twenty-five days; whereas a few weeks later, on the setting in of the south-east monsoon, she might make the run in less than three days. As the commander had no urgent business at Singapore, had no cargo, and the vessel was his own, why would he not rest awhile at Minto? It was true, the Havermeester said, that the place had slight attractions to offer, there being no other society except a few families of the officers of the small garrison; yet he was sure they would be highly gratified by the visit, and offer a hearty welcome. With these, and other pressing words, the commander felt tempted to stay, and await the change of the monsoon, which would take place in about three weeks; and he sent his boat back to the schooner, with orders to countermand the preparation for departure that afternoon.

The Havermeester conducted the commander to the residence of the Governor, or Resident, as the chief magistrate of all islands or provinces is named in Netherland India: he afterwards led him to the quarters of the several officers of the garrison; and then to his own house to spend the evening. The incidents and conversations during these visits, were thus related by the commander of the Flirt, on board the Palmer, when he spoke of

THE VISIT TO MINTO.

I found the Resident in company with the commandant of the fort, seated beneath a large tree, in the small park near the esplanade of the fort; some of the noted beverage of Schiedam and of the gaseous fluid of Seltzer was before them, of which I was invited to partake, immediately after my introduction by the Havermeester.

The Resident seemed about thirty-five years of age, well

made, and of a handsome presence; but he had a cold eye, and a skeptic's smile played upon his lips, as I spoke of my voyage in my little ship, and visits to out-of-the way islands, without cargo or freight, or any fixed haven in view. It will seem strange, said the Resident, to our plain matter-of-fact, trading Hollanders, to hear of a man sailing with a good vessel, fit for valuable use, over the dull, wearisome sea, to visit the bleak rock of Tristan d'Acunha, a poor potato patch for whalers,—the bleaker one of St. Paul's—a roosting and nesting-place for gulls and boobies; or to visit the pestilential, morass coast of Sumatra.

I observed that my cruise would not have seemed strange to the plain, and trading Hollanders, of the sixteenth and seventeenth century, when the roving Houtmans, and Heemskerks, followed in the footsteps of Antonio de Abreu, and other rovers of Portugal, over the same dull sea I had crossed, to seek out what there was rich or rare, in desert or peopled islands; but the monopoly which some of those Hollanders founded, did think strange of independent rovers who came after them; and seized the vessel of one—the brave Roggeween—who chose to stop in these seas without leave.

But the roving Houtmans, and Hemskerks, as you term them, came with sanctions from home, to seek in an open field of adventure, for new outlets and markets for the trade of the fatherland; and they founded, and those who followed after them reared up a power, which won the right to bid Roggeween, or any one who should come now without leave, to depart from the shores of any island in the Indian seas.

They went forth, I said, with that sanction only, which every commander of a ship carries with him, who has submitted to the marine police regulations of his country, and proceeds in general quest of a market. They went, indeed, into an open field of adventure, for the rich lands of the Malays and the Javanese had been a common plundering ground for Arabs, Portuguese, and English, long before the coming of the present power. The former had menaced the shores of the great islands of the Archipelago with a shadowy and unsubstantial dominion, and it did not seem that more than that was done now.

It will not seem so to you Americans, said the Resident with some warmth, who have deemed the Spanish territory of Cuba an open field for adventure, which you have lately failed to annex, and fifty of your countrymen, with the son of one of your statesmen at their head, have expiated at the garotte the penalty of the failure (and as the Resident said this, he held up a newspaper, containing the news of the ill-fated expedition of Lopez).

My heart sickened as I heard for the first time—and being the first news from home—the details, accompanied with bitter, insulting comment in the Dutch official paper of Batavia, of the scourging and strangulation of the misguided men, who were slain at the Moro; and therefore it was, perhaps, with some little rising emotion, that I said to the Resident:

The community of the American people has not sought to make an adventuring ground of any well-settled dominion. It has placed those of its citizens who have done so, beyond the pale of its protection. Some of these were led to believe, that the great body of the natives of Cuba did not desire the presence of twenty thousand alien soldiery for the protection of their industry, and therefore they went, at their own hazard, to aid in driving the oppressors away. They failed, and suffered the pain of their own individual failure, and not that of the American people to annex the island of Cuba.

And then other matters in relation to the East Indian Archipelago were discussed from our different points of view. After a time, the subject was changed, the spirit of polite taunt was laid aside, and the ill-suppressed scowl that had darkened the face of the Resident, gave way to an official smile, as he led the way to the Residency, and introduced me to his family.

Thus at the threshold of Netherland India, was I met with a strong anti-American feeling, cloaked under a guise of diplomatic politeness; and this I believe to be the feeling of Dutch officers generally in the East. England has been the former cause of fear and jealousy; but now America, since the movement towards Japan, takes her place as rival with Holland, for a share of the monopoly of the East Indian Archipelago.

A warmer reception awaited me at the house of my Creole friend, the Havermeester. I found there, with his fair wife, two youthful ladies of fine features, and graceful forms, in whose veins a shade of the finest Javanese tint was mingled. Their eyes showed a glowing curiosity, and that my visit had been looked for.

We knew no language in common; they no English, French, or Spanish, and I no Dutch or Malay, with which to make an interchange of thought. But the younger of the Creole ladies, closing her fan, and holding it at both ends with a forefinger and thumb of each hand, brought it to her right eye like a telescope; and as this was followed by a burst of rich, loud-ringing laughter from the other lady, I knew that I was in the presence of the fair mockers on board the cruiser, in the morning.

The same graceful pantomimist talked on with her hands. She pointed to me, and pointed to the west, and making a large circling sweep with her hands, and dilating her eyes, said, "America;" then her hands made a wave-like motion through the air, as she said, den zee, den zee; and saying, with a questioning look and tone, Flirt? Minto? tin? I shook my head, to say that I did not come to Minto with my vessel for a cargo of tin. Java? Koffy? said the lady. Another shake of my head. Then she held up her right hand to her mouth, with the thumb and forefinger almost touching at their tips, seeming to bite at something small and pungent, which caused her to put out the tip of her tongue, draw up her face, and half close her eyes, saying, Sumatra? as she did this. But I showed by another shake, that I came not to seek pepper in Sumatra; and to all the attempts of my questioner to know what had brought me to the East, I smiled, and looked a negative.

What had taken me to the East?—a question wonderingly asked by so many since, by curious friends, and by those who had the power to question. What had, indeed, caused a man to go with a small ship into regions of spices, flowers, and placid tropic seas?—where none came but with great ships, to be quickly laden with bitter berries, a nauseous weed, and foul drugs, rejected of all beasts of the forest and fowls of the air, to pamper the vicious stomachs of the temperate zone.

What had brought me to Java, Sumatra, or Borneo, if I came not for coffee, pepper, arrack, and tobacco? What was in their woods and groves—even the many-trunked banyan or waringin, pillared, aisled, and vaulted, like fitting temples for Jehovah on earth; or the graceful tamarind, with arrowy leaf; or the tough, dark teak, noblest timber for ships; and mysterious, deadly upas: or what was there of fruits—the fragrant mango, the mild, pulpy dookoo, and delicately luscious mangosteen: or what of flowers—the many parasitic pendants of evergreen boughs—the odorous champaka, and pigeon flower, and the kumbang melati, the richly fragrant flower of love; or of beasts—the great elephant, the fierce tiger, the rhinoceros, tapir, and exquisite little musk deer: or winged creatures—the huge vampire bats of Java, stupefying the senses with their musky wings; the swallows, casting out from their throats the glutinous nests, the so much prized stimulant of sensual Chinese: and then those bright bodies of mingled glistening hues of gold, ruby, silver, and turquoise, floating in the balmy air, and justly called the birds of paradise;—what was there in all these, unfit for freight or traffic, that a man should risk so much, and come so far to see?

And what could I come to learn about the eleven millions of docile, and industrious people, of the famed land of Madjapahit, and Matarem, once faithful subjects of Rajahs, and Susunans, and now of Governors General, ever laboring for all their cruel and unrighteous masters with childlike zeal; or the four millions of Sumatra—the wandering, fighting, romantic Malays—the Scandinavians of the East, and vikings of modern times: or the three millions of Borneo, the frank and loyal Dyaks, yet bloody hunters of human heads; or the two millions of Celebes, famous for adventurous trade and female rule: or the one million of Bali, brave little Bali—that dot on the eastern seas, that had twice victoriously withstood the power of Holland: what was there in all the twenty-five millions of human beings of the East Indian Archipelago, in all the wonders of its islands and seas, that I should come for, if I came not with calico and cutlery, for coffee and tobacco?

What could I come for? said the dull Dutch guardian of tin at Minto; and, as he said, plain, trading Hollanders would, like himself, wonder to learn. What did I see, to make such a cruise to pay? many an American friend wanted to know; and what, said the fingers and eyes of the graceful young Dutch Creole, could bring you here, if coffee and pepper did not?

I reached out my hand over the rail of the verandah where we sat, and drew towards me the limb of a jessamine bush, which becomes a tree of twenty and thirty feet high in these islands. I inhaled the sweet fragrance of its blossoms. I then pointed to some banana and cocoa-nut trees, loaded with their fruit; to a tame musk deer, running about in the yard; to a bird of bright plumage, the pet of the lady of the Havermeester—to many other objects that were new to me, and then imitating her waving and rocking motion with the hands, repeating her words of den zee, and pointing alternately to the fruit, flowers and animals, and to my eyes, nose and lips, gave her thus a pantomimic answer to her wish to know what brought me to the East Indian Archipelago.

The Havermeester, who had left us after introducing me, now returned. The ladies asked to know more about what our fingers and eyes had not fully explained. And then he said to them, as he afterwards translated to me, that I came, more wishful to fill my head with knowledge, than my vessel with merchandise; that I saw more in these islands than cargoes for ships; was more desirous to know and be known to my fellow-men in the East, than to trade with them: and something he added, causing the ladies of the cruiser to smile, and look a little confused. And I judged that he spoke of some especial curiosity which led me to come ashore at Minto.

At a late hour, a Malay servant of the Havermeester, with a cocoa-nut bark torch, led me through the grounds of the fort, and along by the sentries in the pathway leading to it, and then through the native town or kampong, to the boat landing. This servant, or oppas, as he was called, then left me, whilst he went to rouse up the boatmen of the Havermeester, to take me on board my vessel.

Whilst standing alone near a small embankment, where four thirty-two pounder cannon are planted, and fixed at point-blank range, a man started up from an embrasure in the embankment, and spoke to me in French. He said that he was a soldier of the garrison, and a Belgian; and he wanted to desert and serve me on board my vessel. He had been vilely beaten for a trifling fault, with a loaded cane, on the soles of his feet and elsewhere, most degrading to man; he loathed the brutal Dutch service, and would gladly serve me for nothing, until I should return to America; and then he went on to say, that my visit, and my conversation with the Resident, had been that evening the gossip of the garrison. He thought that Providence had sent me and my ship to save him. He had crept out of the barracks after dark, and had followed me from the house of the Havermeester. If I would say the word, not only himself, but eleven other soldiers, countrymen of his, were ready to come on board my vessel, this night, or any other that I would be pleased to take them off and receive them.

Whilst these words were rapidly uttered, I could just discern, by a clear starlight, the stout frame, yet thin, haggard face of a young man, about twenty-five years of age. I had begun to speak, when the glimmer of the torch of the returning oppas caused the soldier to dart out of sight, within the embrasure of the embankment, saying as he fled, he should watch for me when I went ashore again.

Two lascars bore me on their shoulders over the slimy ooze of a beach left bare by an ebbing tide, and eight lascars pulled me alongside of the Flirt; then, on board in my snug cabin, I was soon forgetful of the polite Havermeester, the suspicious Resident, the merry Creoles, the bastinadoed Belgian, and all that happened to me on the day of my first visit at Minto.

THIRTEENTH DAY.

During the second and third day after the arrival of the Flirt in Minto Roads, there was a steady fall of rain, with gusty weather, which deterred communication between the vessel and shore. On the afternoon of the third day, a naval officer came on board the schooner, to pay, as he said, a friendly visit to the American captain; but, as was afterwards shown, he came as a spy, by order of the Resident at Minto.

On the morning of the fourth day, two officers and the physician of the garrison, came on board the Flirt, and invited the commander to dinner on shore. He found a very agreeable and instructive acquaintance in the doctor, who spoke very good English, and had spent many years in India. His term of service had just expired, and he was preparing to return to his native country. He expressed a desire to visit America, and took much pains to gratify the wish of the American commander for information, who thus spoke of him on board the Palmer, and of his visit to

THE HOSPITAL AT MINTO.

After dinner, the doctor accompanied me to the sick ward, where he had about forty patients, one half Chinese, one third Malays, and other people of the Archipelago; and the remaining portion were soldiers, all in a comfortable and cleanly state. I was very much struck with the quiet and patience of the native invalids as contrasted with the groaning and restlessness of the sick Dutchmen; and this greater passivity under suffering, of all colored races more than white, seems to prevail throughout the world; but this is most strikingly seen among the islanders of the Eastern seas; and they possess another physical property, the ready healing of their bodies from wounds or disease, which appears in strong contrast with the fevers, festers and gangrenes, which attend any severe fleshly hurt received by their European masters. The doctor pointed out the case of a Malay woman, who had been fearfully mutilated with a hatchet; she had received a furious blow in the face, striking the cheek bone, glancing down the jaw and slicing off the face, a large flake of flesh which hung down upon her shoulder; and whilst attempting to ward off other blows, was struck between the fingers of the right hand, which was split in two down to the wrist; and yet about a week's care, with simple bandages of linen and applications of pure water alone, had restored the wounded flesh to a healthy state, with every promise of recovery; and the doctor spoke of other native cases, who had been readily cured of wounds, which would have been inevitably fatal to a European. He ascribed this ready curability of the Malay and Javanese to the simple diet of rice, birds and fish upon which they feed.

The doctor pointed out what was curious to observe in the fort, barracks, and native town, and surrounding country, and this was the substance of his discourse to me about

THE ISLAND OF BANCA.

This island is one hundred and twenty miles in length, and will average forty in width, and there are between fifty and sixty thousand people upon it; one half of these are the aborigines, living in the forest and hilly fastnesses of the interior; they are like the Sundese of Java, the Dyaks of Borneo, and the Alfuras of the more southern islands;—the rudest of savages, and living in as wild a state as when the first European visited these shores. They have no political organization of their own, and offer nothing in their savage life that deserves particular mention.

One third of the population are the all-conquering Malays living upon the coasts, who have invaded this, as they have every other island in the East Indian Archipelago, with their language, customs, and trade. The remaining portion are Chinese, the workers of the tin mines, who vary in number between eight and ten thousand. Junks full of these people arrive from China with every change of the monsoon—and the same junks return well filled with thrifty Chinamen, carrying home the savings of their labor in the mines: and thus there is a continual ebb and flow of the Chinese population; but the Government will not allow their number to exceed ten thousand, on account of the turbulence of their character;—for they are engaged in constant feuds; and are riotous, like the various factions of foreign laborers upon your railroads and canals in America.

Tin, for which the island is famous, is found in pellets and nuggets, of native ore, in surface deposits of alluvial soil; and is extracted by a rude process of washing. The yearly quantity obtained is about 70,000 piculs, or 4,500 tons of your weight. Double or triple the quantity might be obtained, but the Government does not wish to glut the tin market, with the bounty of metal which Banca is capable of yielding.

Is not this policy, I said, a remnant of that old unwise spirit of monopoly, which destroyed great quantities of spices and spice groves, to enhance the value of what remained? The greater abundance and cheaper price, would have caused a more general use; and such would be the case with tin: were it cheaper and more plentiful, it would be largely used as a substitute for lead, for water pipes and other purposes.

The Government thinks otherwise, said the doctor;—it owns all the land of the island; and no person, Dutchman or stranger, can work the mines without its permission, and must deliver all tin obtained to Government, at the fixed price of 13½ florins per picul, or five dollars and fifty cents of your money for 125 pounds; and as that weight of tin in your markets would be worth about twenty three dollars, you will perceive that the Government of Holland must derive a royal revenue from the tin mines of Banca.

There is a neighboring island, a little more than one third the size of Banca, called Billiton, upon which tin of a fine quality has recently been discovered; and this island has been granted to Prince Henry of the Netherlands, to enable him to recruit his diminished revenues. He has appointed two agents, who are now about to commence the working of the mines.

Whilst walking upon the esplanade, the doctor observed; You will perceive that the means of defence of Minto, these simple earthworks, with half a dozen cannon mounted upon them, hardly deserve the name of fort, and the little garrison is but little more than the force of a guard-house. One hundred and twenty soldiers are all the military force upon the island, to keep in order the ten thousand turbulent foreign laborers; and moreover there is an element of weakness in this garrison, as in all others throughout Netherland India;—more than one half being Belgians, who have been averse to the Dutch service, and ever ready to desert from it, since the separation of their kingdom from that of Holland.

But this Government, by its conciliatory management of the native princes and chiefs throughout the Archipelago; and by its admirable system of police surveillance, is enabled to control sixteen millions of subjects, with less than ten thousand European troops. The princes whilst they retain the veneration of their people, are willing to resign their substantial power, and the direction of their domains to the superior intelligence of their European masters, from whom they receive a stipendiary revenue. The want of energy of the unambitious princes, has long ceased to threaten the disturbance of Netherland sovereignty; and that is further maintained by the fidelity of natives, who constitute the entire police force. The oppas,—chief Malay or Javanese attendant, whom you have seen accompany the Resident, Havermeester and other officers, is directly paid by the Government, and reports instantly the slightest irregularity in the conduct of his master.

You may call the subsidiary relation of the native princes with the Government, a wicked conspiracy of sordid intelligence with imbecile rank to fleece the simple masses; and the police surveillance, a base system of espionage; but there has been nothing in the history of other European dominations in the East, or of Christian and civilized domination over weak and ignorant aboriginal races upon your own continent, which would furnish to Holland a more disinterested example.

When I returned on board the Flirt, after my visit to the doctor, I found in my cabin a stranger, a man about thirty-five years of age, with the complexion and features of mixed European and native race. He informed me that he was master of a barque, then lying in the roads, belonging to the island of Bali, which had been chartered by the Dutch Government to convey some troops from Batavia to Palembang in Sumatra, where the Government was at that time engaged in a war with some native tribes.

He went on to say that he had called partly from curiosity and partly to make an offer of services. He had met with American commanders at Singapore, and other points in the East Indies, from whom he had received many obliging favors, and so felt anxious to avail himself of every chance to make a return to their countrymen. He seemed to have much knowledge of the trade, manners, and customs throughout the Archipelago, and possessed of that general information most needed by a stranger desiring to cruise in the Indian seas. It was his design, after transporting the troops on board his vessel to Palembang, to sail for Singapore, expecting to stop on the way at the island of Linga, the Sultan of which he knew. He then spoke of the remarkable floating town of Palembang; and of the easy navigation of the river upon which it was situated. My curiosity was greatly excited, and I had a desire to accompany the Balinese barque on its route to Singapore.

I told the Havermeester my wish to go to Palembang. He said the risk was great, there was little to see, and nothing to be gained. The water way thither was deep and swift in its flow: at the mouth was a bar, not easily passed; and pirates, ever ready to cut off a small, unarmed ship, lurked with their prahus in many coves and islet channels near by; the banks swarmed with caymans, tigers, and serpents; over the water hovered clouds of fierce insects; one dozen of which could drain the life-blood of a man, and war raged not far from the town; and the law of war was there, among the people under the control of the Dutch Governor, who was a cold, harsh man: and thus the Havermeester warned, and said he wished me to spend the rest of the northwest monsoon at Minto.

I saw the Resident again. He was more cheerful and polite than before. He had heard of my desire to follow the troops on board the barque from Bali. He said I would behold the Venice of the East, a city amid waters, whose people were famed for their skill in rare filigree work in gold, and in curious lacquered ware, richer than that of Japan. My light vessel would easily pass the bar of the river; and with the wind that then prevailed, could stem the stream with ease, whilst her row of ports and warlike rig would keep far off all prowling Malays; and so the Resident seemed to wish me to go.

My friend, the doctor, knew much about Palembang. It was the largest town in Sumatra, and was well worth a visit to see; but he did not think, with the Resident or Havermeester, that there was such peril or ease in going there. Knowing, said the doctor, the Creole's frank and friendly nature, and knowing that you have pleased him, you may look upon his opposition to your going, as given with the best intent; but knowing otherwise of the other man, I would warn you to consider well what he suggests.

The opposing and encouraging counsel, and all that was said, served but to strengthen my desire to go to Palembang. I was not then prepared to visit Sumatra, as I had planned before; but I had found a good companion and a good escort. I had my vessel in good repair, and my men were willing to go. The great island of early dreams would now be seen; and so I resolved to follow the transport ship from Bali.

I had made known my wish to have a Malay servant to wait in my cabin, and to help me learn his language. I said that I wanted a simple man of the country,—one who knew nothing of European service. On the day I had made ready to leave Minto, a man was brought to me, being furnished with a pass by the secretary of the Resident. He was a Malay, about thirty-five years of age, of short size, with a broad, yellow face, which had a look I did not like at first; but Bahdoo Rachman, as he was called, thrusting his fingers like two combs together, placing them with palm down upon his head, then crouching low at my feet, and making other signs to show his submissive will to serve me; he thus chased away my first dislike, and I hired him for fifteen Dutch East India rupees, or five dollars a month, out of which he had to buy his own rice, fish, and curry—his chief food; and this was deemed good wages for a servant man in Netherland India.

I had obtained some small stores from the chief ship-chandler at Minto, a shrewd, jocular, little old man, who had gotten many a dollar of cumshaw from American and British captains at Hongkong, and his native Whampoa. He spoke glibly the few words of the mongrel Anglo-Portuguese lingua-franca of the open ports of China; and had learned, with the Chinese trader's aptitude, the many little courtesies which were most grateful to the American and English customer. And Lim Boo Seng was a good sample of his trading countrymen, every where thrifty and successful in the East. I went to see him before leaving.

Whilst I ate of kimlo, a Chinese chowder of chicken, tripang, bamboo pith, and various herbs most tastefully seasoned, along with a dish of shrimps and shredded cocoa-nut, the little ship-chandler entertained me, in his jargon, with much gossip about Minto, and the condition of his countrymen on the island of Banca.

The Government was bad to Chinamen; they had to hide their dollars, and look very poor. When a Chinaman came to Minto, and when he went away, he had to pay money. When he bought a wife, he had to pay for marrying her; and when he died, every day that his body lay in his own house, he had to pay for the privilege of staying above ground. The Chinaman works all the gold and the tin, and does all the trading; the Javanese works the fields; the Malay spies; and all, said Lim Boo Seng, are robbed by the Kumpany Wolanda.

Before leaving my host, he gave me a letter,—several columns of tea-chest marks upon a broad sheet of yellow rice paper; and this I was to deliver to his friend Oey Soch Tchay, at Palembang, who would give me good pork, yams, chickens, milk, and fruits for my ship, and entertain me with kimlo and tchoo as he had done. He gave me some curious miniature blocks of best Banca tin; and with many pleasant words of good will, I and Lim Boo Seng parted.

I then went, Bahdoo following me, to pay a last visit at the house of the kindly Havermeester. In speaking of home, I mentioned a name that caught the ear of his lady. She questioned me, and then it seemed that I and her husband descended from a common ancestry of not very ancient date,—from a scion of European nobility, awhile an exile in Holland, afterwards embarked for the East, there found a faithful companion in a simple, loving Javanese girl; and the husband of my hostess was the fruit of that love.

This was an exciting discovery to my Creole friend, and to his fair European wife, who was eager to bring out all the strong points of her husband's claim to European lineage,—a strong wish felt by every Creole, of white and colored race, throughout the world. I had the miniature of one who bore the name, and was a lineal descendant of him from whom we traced our descent: the lady was curious to see the portrait, which I was glad to offer in return for pleasant attentions; and her husband accompanied me on board my vessel to obtain it, and there to bid me a final adieu.

Whilst the Havermeester had stepped aside to order his boat, and whilst I stood near the embankment where the guns at point-blank range were planted, I saw a soldier lying face downwards, and seeming to sleep, on the grass within the covert from whence the Belgian had come, some nights before. He raised his head, and I saw that it was the same man. He made a slight beckoning motion. I went near, and heard him say, I will be on board your vessel to-night, with eleven of my countrymen well armed, who want to desert with me, and to serve you.

When we were ready to push off, my servant suddenly recalled to mind something he had left, and needed very much. He piteously entreated the Havermeester to ask of me to let him go to his house, promising to be on board before I had got up my anchor. I left Bahdoo behind, and went with the Havermeester to obtain the miniature, who returned with it on shore. When I wished to get under way, I found that two of my men were unfit for duty, and having only four able men and a boy, we could not get up the anchor, and so I went ashore again to get some help, and to bring off Badhoo, who delayed his return.

Near where I landed, I saw a young native woman, dressed like one of those poor unmarried followers called *nyaees*, who are seen at all times at the heels of every Dutch trooper and officer in the East. She was seated near where I had seen the soldier lying two hours before, and was wringing her hands,—sobbing, and uttering accents of despair. I asked a Dutch sailor the cause of her grief; and he said that her man, a Belgian soldier, had just been marched off to the guard house.

I saw the Havermeester again. He shook my hand with as much warmth as before; but he met me with a constrained look. He could not explain, but expressed a hope to see me again at Minto, when he could receive me as a relative, though so remote a one, but whom it was his delight to have met. He would send me a boat's crew to help me get under way; and as he bid me God speed, there were marks of anxiety in his face.

I had sent one of my men to the store of Lim Boo Seng to get some forgotten article of ship-chandlery. The man came back, saying there was trouble at the Chinaman's shop; women and children were making an uproar; and all the words that my sailor could get out of the son of the old man, one who helped his father in the store, was "Resident," and "papa."

I was struck with some vague fear: a blow seemed to have been dealt out to every man with whom I had spoken, or who had spoken to me freely. And yet I thought, how can that be? Who could have told what the Havermeester, or Chinaman, or Belgian said to me? You may see, as I group these facts together, who was the spy; but I, during the excitement and occupation of the time, did not then suspect the simple Bahdoo, but took him gladly with me on board.

As soon as the longshoremen who had helped to get up the anchor, had left the Flirt, the Dutch war cruiser in the roadstead loosed her sails, and followed in the wake of the schooner. The Balinese barque, which had left some hours before, expecting me to follow, was still to be seen bearing towards the mouth of the Palembang river. I had lost my desire to follow. The late events, and the watching cruiser, led me to expect trouble, for which I was not prepared. I felt a strong presentiment of coming danger. A light squall came up, and the sun having just set, the cruiser was soon lost to view; and then I gave orders to my sailing master to head the schooner for Singapore.

* * * * * * * *

FOURTEENTH DAY.

SABBATH ON BOARD THE PALMER.

FIFTEENTH DAY.

Some spirit of storm, some genii of the Indian isles, seemed to bar the way of the Flirt into the China sea. The same black-arched wall of thunder cloud, that had before shut off the way from out the straits of Banca, again rose up. The schooner beat up against it for a time amid thick darkness, strong wind, and rain; and when at last the storm wall was rent, and broke away; the transport barque was seen by a clear starlight, a cable's length ahead, and riding at anchor within gunshot of the bar of the Palembang river.

The wind and the current setting in from the sea of China against the Sumatra shore, had driven the Flirt far to the west, when her commander had hoped that he was north of Manopin Hill, which overlooks Minto. He had not wished for this encounter on leaving port, and fain would pass the barque; but as he began to stand off, he was hailed from the water, and then beheld a boat right under the schooner's bows, and one minute later, the master of the transport ship was on the quarter deck of the Flirt.

The Balinese had some hint of the misgivings of his consort, and he sought to remove his doubts; spoke of his hopes of the pleasant sail in company, and then reminded him that they had agreed to bear an equal share of the expense of a skilful pilot, familiar with the rivers and coast of Sumatra, with Linga and the neighboring islets. An officer going to join the garrison at Palembang, had come with the master of the barque. He spoke of much that was rare and worthy to be seen; and the commander of the Flirt was induced to follow his friends in the barque.

Whilst the commander and master, and the Dutch officer were yet talking, they descried a large Malay prahu that had shot out from behind a thick-wooded islet near the bar,—bearing down towards the schooner. The manœuvre and direct approach seemed hostile. There was an anxious look-out on board the schooner, for with her handful of men, and utterly defenceless state, she might be overpowered and plundered by the nimble pirates, before succor from the barque could reach her.

As the crowded prahu neared with threatening aspect, and the people on board the schooner made ready their small means of defence, to beat off any piratical assault, the sailing master of the Flirt, an experienced officer in the Indian seas, ordered the ports to be thrown open, ends of blackened spars to be run out, and lighted lanterns carried along the deck. The prahu checked her course, and bore away, leaving the people on board the Flirt much relieved.

The incident inspired a spirit of wakefulness, and led to a discussion in the cabin of the Flirt, about piracy in the East Indian seas. The master of the barque related many curious incidents, and the substance of his discourse was told by the commander of the Flirt, to his friends on board the Palmer, on the afternoon of the fifteenth day of her homeward voyage from Java, when he spoke of

PIRACY IN THE MALAYAN ARCHIPELAGO.

I have often had to deal with pirates, said the Balinese captain, and there are plenty of them—though many people think not—still to be met with, cruising about in these seas. Eight years ago, I went with a small fore and aft schooner to Selwatti and the coast of Papua, to collect a cargo of tripang to carry to Banyarmassing in Borneo.

I had got my load and was making for home. I had run through Morti Straits, between Pulo Morti and Gilolo, and was coming in sight of Pulo Tagulanda, when I saw a large war prahu, bearing down upon my little craft. This was my first command, and I had not kept a sharp look-out, so that the pirate was within gunshot, before I or any of my men had seen him.

It was about sunset. The land breeze was going back, and the sea had fallen almost a dead calm; and it was the sound of the pirate oars that first made us look out. The prahu was one of the biggest; was crowded with coolies at the oars, and with tall fighting men on the split bamboo deck above. I could now make out the scarlet jackets, always worn by the Lanun pirates; they twirled their limbs in battle postures, brandishing their long spears and golok swords; then a clang of gongs broke forth mingled with shouts and yells, and all the fuss and fury they put on, whether to cut off a boat or a big ship.

My whole force being twelve Dyak sailors and their wives, and two Chinamen, cook and carpenter, the best policy was to keep still and bide our fate, knowing that Lanuns do not kill when no fight is made; and so it was with us, when the pirates had sprung over the schooner's sides, as they always do, all at once, by laying hold with a long, hooked bamboo upon the bulwarks of any craft, whether of schooner or frigate size; and then with the muscles of arms and feet, jerking themselves upward, turn somerset in air, and with a flying leap alight on deck, and go to work with poisoned kriss, rushing first at the cabin to slay the master; but they did not do so this time, for I knew their talk, hailed them as they cleared the bulwarks; and they, seeing me and my folks all quiet, and crouched down on the quarter-deck, put up their krisses, ordered us to get down into the prahu, plundered the schooner of what they wanted to carry away; the panglima, or chief captain and his officers, taking the money, arms, and fine garments; the men, the coarser booty; and then they set fire to the schooner.

I and all my men except the two Chinese, were stowed away under the bamboo deck. We were made to squat down, with knees raised up, our wrists were lashed down to our ancles; and then, putting us back to back, we were made fast in couples, with thongs of cocoa-nut bark cord. In this hampered and tortured state, we lay all the time of our stay on board the pirate craft. But my poor cook and carpenter fared worse. They were kicked and beaten as dog-eating beasts, the moment they reached the Lanun deck; they were forced down on their backs, with their hands lashed behind them; their pig-tails were run through a hole in the deck, and being hauled on with all the strength of a man, so as to raise up the scalp from the skulls of the tortured men, was made fast below; and in this way the wretched Chinamen passed the time on board.

The prahu was worked by forty coolies at the oar—poor naked slaves, mostly kidnapped from the small islands around Timor. The fighting deck was manned by fifty men, tall Lanuns, and some of the Rayat Laut, or sea people, regular pirates of these seas; and their craft was commanded by a half-breed Malay Dyak, an old fierce villain, called Panglima Besar, the Great Admiral, as his name signifies.

The fighting men never put a hand to an oar. They would feel themselves disgraced by having any thing to do with work; and utterly degraded, if, in some desperate encounter, they should owe their safety to any interference of the coolies, who are allowed no part in the business of fighting and robbing.

We had a steady breeze after leaving Pulo Tagulanda. The long, deep, sharp-built prahu made good time with its heavy mat sail; and after a run of five days, we came in sight of Tanjong Oonsang, on the north-eastern coast of Borneo; ran along shore about one degree, put into Kinibatangan river, ascended one of its branches a short distance, and came to anchor at a small place called Kota Baroo, where we were put ashore, and sold the same day,—the women to some small chiefs living up the country, and myself and men to several panglimas, or pirate captains, then holding rendezvous at Kota Baroo.

My purchaser was called Panglima Djamaloodin, a young chief from the Brunai country. In a few days after he bought me, he put to sea with a complement of thirty coolies, myself among the number, and thirty-five fighting men, chiefly Malays and Dyaks. We steered south-east down the coast, doubling cape Oonsang, and then struck out a course due south, until we came to, off the island of Menimboora, which is near the most eastern point of Borneo. The pirate had passed several trading prahus without noticing them, and it was plain that there was some especial expedition on foot.

We came into a small bay after sunset. Our sampan, or canoe tender, was launched. The Panglima, with six men well armed got down into it, each one having his kriss, a two-handed pedang sword, and a long senapang, or musket of Dyak make; and I and three coolies were ordered to paddle them ashore. We went about a mile up a small creek, and pulled into a thick rotan jungle, where Djamaloodin and four of the armed men got out, leaving two in the sampan, with their senapangs pointed at myself and companions, ready to fire at the first one who made a suspicious move.

In about half an hour after the Panglima had left, we heard the firing of several shots; then we heard faint sounds of screams of women. Again we heard them nearer and louder, and in a little while the commander appeared, bearing up the body of a woman, whom he held around the neck and waist in a way to confine her arms, whilst one of his men held up her feet. Two other women were following, driven along with the muzzles of the senapangs, by the three men behind them. All the time whilst in the sampan, and when we got on board the prahu, the woman in the arms of the Panglima, whom I now saw by a clear moonlight to be quite young and exceedingly pretty, continued to scream, and to make violent efforts to get loose.

When on board the prahu, the Panglima tried very hard to soothe his prize. She seemed to be quieted by his caresses, and her struggles and sobbings had ceased altogether. I was just thinking how foolish to make such a fuss at first, and then give up so easily, when suddenly I heard a quick rush of feet over head, a sharp cry of pain from a man, a plunge into the water, then another and another, and by and by two good Dyak swimmers came up on my side of the prahu with the Panglima's captive in their arms.

When the resolute young woman was brought on deck, I heard the Panglima, who, it seems, must have been wounded by her, call out binatang, or wild beast,—a common expression of spite and anger; then I heard the sound of a heavy blow, and the fall of a body just above me, and a scream from the same voice that had shrieked in the jungle. A horrible order was then given to all the pirates. Two crevices between the bamboo splits just above my head were pried open with spears. I saw some delicate little fingers passed through; and the prises being taken away, the bamboo splits tightened up, squeezing blood from those fingers, and screams of agony from the poor girl, who, it seems, was laid on her back, her hands stretched out and made fast in the atrocious way I have told you.

The scene on the bamboo deck, had drawn off all attention for a time from the coolies below. The bamboo vice had hardly griped the girl's fingers, when I seized a pointed stick, pried open the splits, and shoved out the fingers. The victim, on feeling herself loosened, sprang up, and I saw her plunge into the water again, followed by a dozen of yelling pirates. She dove right down. For a minute I looked on the water, whilst the baffled pirates struck out in various directions; but no girl was to be seen, and I am sure the poor creature went resolutely down, and perished beneath the waters.

I began to think of myself. I knew that some cowardly cooly would tell of what I had done; and then it would be folly to hope for mercy. With the chance of a cruel death before me on board the prahu, I thought I had better now make an effort for my life, whilst confusion still prevailed. I was quickly in the water, and being as good a swimmer as any of the race of my mother, I felt that I might bid defiance to the pursuing pirates, of whom I got several yards start before I was descried. My limbs were almost free, whilst they had on their tight fighting clothes. As soon as I had got under shelter of a piece of rotan jungle, I sank down, being a tolerably good diver, and remained under water about half a minute, then rose up gradually. As my head got above the surface, I could feel the lunge in the water, from the heel of the last pirate who passed over me.

I remained in the jungle a short while, till the pirates gave up the search, and they returned on board the prahu. I then got on to firm ground, and walked up the creek bank, to the point where we had pulled in with the sampan; there I struck into the path taken by the Panglima and his men; for with all my suffering and state of apprehension, I felt a strong curiosity to go to the place where the women had been captured, thinking I had something to tell that might be of satisfaction to their friends. I had not gone far, when I saw a gleam of light; by and by, a red, smoking mass, at the edge of a small sawah, or rice field: and going nearer, I beheld the burnt ruins of several large cabins. Among the red embers, I saw the roasted bodies of two human beings; and three more lay near by—two men, a boy and a girl, and an old woman; the men with bullet-holes in them, and all terribly gashed with ragged kriss wounds.

I turned sick at the sight of what I knew must have been the pirates' work. I felt afraid to stay any longer on the island, expecting to be massacred by any of its people who should find me near the scene of the bloody violence. I returned to the creek bank, and remained there till daylight, hoping to find some fisherman's sampan, with which I could put to sea. I found one as I expected, and on the same day was picked up in a half-dead state in the Straits of Macassar by a Chinese junk bound for Samarang.

At the conclusion of the story of the Balinese captain, the young Dutch officer who had accompanied him, an assistant surgeon going to join the garrison at Palembang, said to me in French: You will hear a great many strong stories about pirates in these seas, and especially in the yarns, as you say in English, of your brother sailors; but from my experience on board of several of the cruisers of my Government in these seas, I can vouch for the entire correctness of the captain's story, as regards the actuality of piracy of such a character in the Archipelago. The kind of vessels, weapons, habits, costume, mode of attack, and all the particulars set forth in the narrative, I know to be strictly correct.

Piracy continues to infest these seas, almost as much as before the first European keel entered them. Great pirate communities still exist in the islands of the sea of Mindoro, of Sulu, and Molucca, issuing forth sometimes in fleets of prahus, carrying many hundreds and even thousands of warriors. They cut off large ships that lie becalmed, make descents upon small islands, and several times have dared to attack Government ships of war, and not always without success. Holland has striven to establish and maintain an efficient maritime police within the Archipelago; and with that intent, stipulated with Great Britain in the treaty of 1824, for a joint action in the suppression of piracy in the Eastern seas. But England has been negligent in doing her part in compliance with that article of the treaty, and Holland alone is insufficient to accomplish the task.

I said to the Dutch officer that I thought the insignificance of British interests, situated on the outskirts of the Archipelago, at Pulo Pinang, Malacca, Singapore, and Labuan, bore such a slight proportion to the great treasure-fields of the Netherlands, in Java, Sumatra, the Moluccas, and all throughout the Archipelago, that the more negligent patrol of the less interested party ought not to be wondered at; but the world had heard of the labors and wise policy of Sir James Brooke, who with some aid from the British Government, seemed to have done more towards breaking up great nests of piracy, and restoring a vitiated and dissolute people to the amenities of civilized life, than all the power of Holland had accomplished during its empire in India.

You derive your information, said the Dutch officer, from British writers, who furnish you in America, with plentiful abuse of every European nation that has braved the power or competed with the trade of England. Brooke was an adventurer, who took advantage of the weakness and cupidity of a miserable Malay Rajah, and secured a possession in Borneo. England being prevented by treaty from gaining any possessions in any part of the Archipelago, south of Singapore—was eager to sustain one of her subjects in a territorial foothold upon this great island; and thus, under the cloak of his sovereignty, secure what would be too gross a breach of national faith to attempt otherwise. Hence the support of Brooke in the so-called suppression of piracy, which resulted in the cession to his government of the island of Labuan.

The Balinese captain, who had not been a party to the conversation that was carried on in the French language, roused up at the mention of Sir James Brooke; and learning the statements of the Dutch officer, said with some warmth;—Rajah Brooke has done more to break up the pirates in these seas, than the Company (the Netherland India Trading Company) ever did or will do; and the British have spent ten times the value of Labuan in breaking up the bloody Serebas and Sakarran pirates. I remember well the different times, when old Cochrane, and Keppel, Mundy and Belcher, with the Dido, the Nemesis, the Agincourt, the Spiteful, and Brooke's own little Royalist, punished the rascally Tunku Ali Omar at Brune; and broke up the murdering, head-hunting Dyaks, all along the west coast of Borneo. Six months charter of any one of those ships, was worth all the trashy coal that can ever be got out of Labuan; and as for Brooke being an adventurer, I can say, that there is not another government in all India, on the continent, or among these islands, where so much has been done to raise up the people of the country, as in Brooke's Rajahate of Serawak.

The Dutch officer replied by some allusion to Malacca, the birth-place of the Balinese captain; hence his British predilections. The latter made a reply offensive to the Dutchman, who muttered something in which the word liplap was heard,—a contemptuous designation of half-breeds in the Archipelago, as the word cheechee is in continental India. The bronze-green skin of the Dano-Malay turned of an ashy hue, with a dark mottled shade, his dark eyes dilated with bitter ferocity, and with arms thrown back, and fingers claw-like, curving and spread out, he seemed about to make a wild-beast spring, when I stepped forward and interposed between the European and the infuriated half-breed. A semblance of peace was restored; and with ill-suppressed flashings of hate and vengeance, the Balinese captain returned with his passenger, at a late hour, on board the barque.

* * * * * * *

I know something about those bloody pirates, said the Boatswain. When a lad I was on board one of our Beverly whalers, homeward bound, running through Gasper Straits. We were hard up for grub, nothing but beans, which some Beverly skippers think is enough for men any time, but not so with ours. He wanted to send a boat ashore, to get some yams, and other small truck from the yellow scamps on Banca; and running in too close, we got becalmed under the lee of the land, and there lay all night. A small prahu came alongside and wanted to exchange some trade for powder, but we had none. Our old man had been in these seas afore, and told us to keep a sharp look out. It had just struck seven bells in the first watch after the dog watches. I was lying on the booby hatch, thinking of the folks in old Maine, and looking out landward; all at once, I see three dark looking things, low in the water, shoot out of a small bight of a bay, and make towards our ship. The old man told us to make ready for pirates, who were coming down upon us in big, long prahus. We had some small arms, and two nine pounders; but our powder was run out. The chances were small for us to beat off ten times our force, with handspikes, harpoons and whale spears. Five minutes more, and all our throats would be cut; but quick as thought, the old man had all the bottles brought out, smashed and strewn on deck, fore and aft, starboard and larboard, and bid me and the cook to stand by the coppers, that luck had full of boiling slush at the time. I had just got a ladle in my hand, when over they came, the yellow varmint, just as the Balinese skipper said, flying over the bulwarks; but wasn't there a screech from a hundred yellow devils, as they lit with naked feet on the broken glass, that lay pretty thick; then the old man let them have the few shots we had left, and charged with the harpoon and whale spears. The villains were checked; they yelled with pain, and over they went, back to their prahus. Now was our time, myself and the cook, and we let them have it hot and fast, the scalding anointment; and they struck out for land with another kind of chorus to what they came down upon us with. We had five bodies to throw overboard.

SIXTEENTH DAY.

When morning came, the American schooner got under way, and bore up close in the wake of the Balinese barque that stood in towards the mouth of the Soonsang branch of the Palembang River. They crossed the bar at about three-quarters flood tide when there was three fathoms water upon it, and five fathoms immediately within the bar. At some points there is no less than four fathoms water on the bar at flood tide. In coming in towards the bar, there are several beacons, which were all passed to the south-east of them, except the two outside, which were passed between bearings got:—Tacked first with Eastern apparent point of river bank, (but in reality, an islet in mid-channel,) S. W. by S. ½ S.; the W. point of entrance, N. W. by N. close to outermost S. E. stake in two and a half fathoms: northern point of land in sight after passing all the beacons north by west. Steered up near the eastern bank of the stream, having a slack current of not more than one and a half knots an hour; yet the wind falling to a dead calm, the barque was obliged to launch all her boats, and haul on her head with oars, at a creeping rate; whilst the schooner having sweeps—long oars to be handled by four men, and being fitted with rowlocks in her ports, she glided with good speed up stream, with only two sweeps out, her weak force preventing her from using her full complement of six. The Flirt was making three knots against

5*

the stream, and might have made a run of thirty and some odd miles before nightfall; but as her consort was dragged along slowly, and her men in the boats becoming exhausted, the barque and schooner came to anchor in eight fathoms water, in mid-channel, about fifteen miles from the bar, where the river was about half a mile wide. At this point, after coming to anchor, they were visited by a Malay chieftain, and the commander of the Flirt thus described to his friends on board the Palmer, the visit, and his first observations upon

THE SOONSANG RIVER.

As with measured tread on deck, and sailor's song, the long blades of the sweeps rose and dipped, the schooner glided on up stream with rippling sound. On either bank, a thick cane jungle, overtopped here and there with the atap palm, came down to the water's edge. Dark and shapeless caymans lay upon, and mingled with muddy rafts of logs, lodged on bars, and by the jungle border; and from the dark green, leafy, wooded shore, there came thrilling wafts of flowery, woody aroma.

Towards nightfall, a gentle breeze from the eastern bank brought sweeter quaffings of scented air, rich as the music swell that first stole over me from off the island's ocean shore; and then, as the shade grew deeper, mingled sounds rose up, blending with the bird-notes of the day; but harsher,—some hoarse and ruttling; then distant, hollow boomings, and long-drawn notes, cracklings in the brake, the monkey's chattering cry; and the quick, strong tiger caterwaul.

On the western bank, some dwellings could be dimly seen through openings in the jungle;—low huts, on high posts of small bamboo frames, with broad leaf roofs; and when off these signs of human habitation, we came to anchor, midway between them and the wild conservatory and concert on the eastern side.

A skiff was seen to put off from the point where dwellings were seen. It was urged quickly along by four paddle blades; and as it neared the schooner, a long bright skiff was made out, some thirty feet in length, with both ends raking and tapering off to points, like sharp gondola beaks; the sides and whole body of the buoyant skiff were glistening with the hue and polish of fine-dressed maple-wood; and this was a tambangan—the Sumatran canoe.

A young and rather handsome man stepped from the tambangan on board the schooner. His face of mingled gold and olive tint, wore the look of a tasteful and inquiring mind. He was all robed in silk; a long and flowing coat made of deep green, hand-spun thread, flecked with gold; a scarlet vest, buttoned from the throat down to the waist, around which the ample girth of a fantastic figured skirt, was lapped and folded, then under-tucked to hold it on the hips; and from out these laps and folds, a diamond crusted hilt and part of a golden sheath were seen.

The movement of the young man was staid and easy; and he bowed and held forth his hand with a strongly impressive grace. I should have listened in vain to the softly modulated words that came from his mouth, had not an interpreter been near. The Balinese captain had left his vessel simultaneously with the approach of the young chieftain, and now stood beside him on my quarter-deck.

When seated in my cabin, my Sumatran visitor said in very soft-sounding words, that he was a Demang, or chief in authority over the campong or village of which we beheld glimpses through the jungle. It was called Moora Soonsang, whose people were fishermen—spending all the time in the using or in the making of nets; and in the gathering and curing of atap (a species of palm leaves) for the trade of Palembang.

His eyes, to use his own words as translated to me, had wondered at a strange banner coming up the river, not like that of Arab, English, or Company, or any other that he had seen; and he had looked with much heart-liking upon the little black ship, like the ulang bird, with golden beak and proud swelling breast, walking with dipping feet against the running waters; and he, the slave, had presumed to come and see the pretty ship, and him who ruled her ways.

After my reply to his complimentary words, we spoke of my country, voyage, condition of my vessel and object in visiting Palembang. When I came to speak of having no arms, no means at all for defence or offence, the Demang shook his head with a good-humored expression of disbelief. Many evil men prowled about these waters, which the American captain must know, said the Demang; and he is too wise to float on a sea-bird that has no beak or talons.

The *orang badjak*—pirates—said he, lie in wait with prahus

near every *quallah* (a river mouth); all the length of Pulo Percha (a native name of Sumatra). No towns are near the quallahs, and the coast of Pulo Percha has no people except alone the Moora Soonsang; which only is not burnt and harried, because fish soon spoil; atap is of great bulk and little worth; and poor fishers make poor slaves; but this pretty ship, this cabin filled with rich things, would make good plunder, and the pirate kriss would not spare the gentleman before me, if his ship's open mouths, pointing to the ports, have no biting teeth.

The Demang said that no man had ever entered the Malay country before, without kriss or senapang, powder, and ball. The Portuguese, the English, the Hollander, had all come with great guns and much power. The people from the land of the starry flag he saw must be *betuah* (meaning sacred, not to be hurt, as some men are believed to be by Malays), if they went abroad without arms, fearless of Dutchmen and pirates.

The Demang had brought in his tambangan, to present to me, some fine large trout shaped fish, called *ikan guramee*, a large bunch of bananas, some mangoes and a lot of fat snipes, with which I was told the jungle abounded, and were caught by scores in nets. For these I gave him a small can of French preserved butter, and some fine cut Turkish tobacco, with which he went his way well pleased.

You were much too polite to that Malay rascal, said my Balinese friend, as soon as the silken robe of the Demang had passed over the gangway. He is a spy of the Dutch—very likely a friend of the pirates; and would sell you to either for the price of the smallest of one of those sparklers on the handle of his kriss. You must keep a sharper look out for the beastly Dutch and the oily Malays.

I was unwilling to believe that the half-breed's caution was called for on this occasion, and I could not think that the gentlemanly Oriental whom I had just seen, was no more than a mean, petty, pensioned spy.

I think, said the commander of the Palmer, that the Balinese captain was about right in his advice. I never met with a Malay in all my cruisings, whether cooley, lascar, trader or rajah, who was not a treacherous scamp; and I always made short talk with them, and made them toe the mark pretty straight, whenever any of the run-a-muck scoundrels came about me.

Alas! said the lady of the younger missionary, is not that the echo of that harsh expression of mistrust uttered everywhere by white civilization against its colored inferior? The Indian of our frontier, the Hindoo of the Ganges, the black man of Africa, and the children of these isles are all esteemed inbornly evil alike; and ungrateful, for the good they receive!—at the hands of their stronger and wiser white brethren.

SEVENTEENTH DAY.

On the second day, the progress of the barque and schooner was slow and labored as on the day before. After a toilsome pull with boats and sweeps for about twenty miles up a stream, averaging thus far six fathoms in depth, and 700 yards in width, we came to anchor near the entrance into the Oopang,—a broad, deep channel, diverging from the Soonsang, and running southwesterly into the straits of Banca.

On the morning of the third day, we began early our toil with boats and sweeps. After passing the Oopang, I learned from Bahdoo, that the name of Soonsang ceased, and the main stream received the name of Moosee, or Ayer Moosee,—so called from the Ulu Moosee,—a wild hill country, near Bencoolen on the west coast, in which it takes its rise. The current now became stronger: the oarsmen pulling at the head of the barque, gave up with exhausted arms, and my small force, barely enough to man two sweeps, could urge no longer the sharp-prowed clipper onward;—and so ere noon, the barque and schooner let go their anchors in the stream.

Here I resolved to take a peep at the jungle, that had so wooed my curious gaze; and started on a cruise with my long-boat,—taking with me, Bahdoo, a sailor, the carbine, our only fire-arm, a hatchet, a pike, some boiled rice, and a small keg of water.

To avoid the hot rays pouring down upon the water at noon, we ran under the thick overhanging shade that lined the banks, and roused up the caymans, or *buaya*, as Bahdoo called them, which he seemed to dread very much; and gave me to understand, that they have oftentimes seized people and dragged them out of their tambangans, a story which I heard vouched for afterwards by Europeans. The monkeys sprang from limb to limb,—some with young ones in their arms, and stopping at times to give us a stare and chatter; whilst birds of great beauty were roused, and rose up with varied cry, from the thick brake and heavy-leafed forest.

Some five miles from where we had started, we came to another large divergent branch on the right bank, like the Oopang on the left; and this would lead us, said Bahdoo, to the Banyoo-Assin, or Sour-River, a great stream like the Moosee, by which large ships could ascend to Palembang. The splendor of the leafy and flowery border of this branch, which seemed about 400 yards wide, and the gentleness of its current, tempted me to a sail upon its waters.

On the left bank of the stream, a short way from the entrance, I espied what seemed the dark entrance of a cavern; and on coming nearer, I found it was the mouth of a small creek about forty feet wide, over which the limbs of lofty trees were closely interlapped; forming a thick tunnel roof above the unsunned waters of the creek, that issued forth, cool as from out of some Alpine cave.

I was wishful to explore this tree-roofed stream, but Bahdoo implored me not to go; he spoke of *binatang*,—wild creatures on the ground, in the trees, and in the air;—he made wild cries like beasts; and then his face changing to a deeper fear-stricken look, he spoke of *orang utan*, fierce and hairy wild men, who lived in the thick tree-tops, overhanging this creek, and would drop into our boat, or pelt us with cocoanuts from overhead. Whilst Bahdoo was on the point of crouching down in his usual way of entreaty, the sailor, who was as curious as myself, and seeing my wish to go on, seized both oars, and with a vigorous pull shot the boat within the leafy tunnel.

Farther up this curious vaulted aisle, the air was chill,—an awful silence reigned, and things around were dimly seen, although the hour was but little past noon-time. As we went on, we came to where the arch widened, the green roof rose up, and the air came warmer, and a few rays shot down from above; —then further on again the arch narrowed, and the roof lowered, —so low in one place did the matted limbs come down, that we were forced to stoop our heads, and pull the boat along by the branches that brushed her gunwale.

After pulling about fifty yards, the woody vault of the cavern enlarged again; and we saw before us, a smooth glassy avenue, lined with a close array of massive columns, whose tops were lost to view within the enshrouding canopy of green; the end of the vista was lost in gloom, till, as we sped along, light began to dawn, and a little further on, it came pouring in from a break in the cavern wall.

We had come to an opening in the bank, leading into an open plain of marshy grouud, thickly strewn with bodies of mighty trees, thrown down by the fierce simoon a long time ago; for they lay covered with a coating of soily loam, and thickly matted, creeping vegetation; so that the sod-enwrapped corses of these old giants of the forest, seemed like a net-work of raised pathways, on which to thread a way through the yellow ooze of a deadly looking swamp.

Wishing to take a nearer view of some gorgeous flowering

trees, that skirted the farthest side of this open ground, I stepped out to try my feet upon the raised green paths, and ordered Bahdoo to follow; but again the Malay uttered cries of entreaty, pointing to the swamp and then to his legs, making hideous grimaces of disgust and pain: but as his clamorous fear on entering the creek seemed thus far to have no foundation, I thought his alarm was feigned—some trick of laziness—and so paid no heed for myself, yet let him stay with the boat,—and took the sailor with me.

The pathways rose and sloped, and were barred with crossing paths in all directions, making most tedious and unsteady walking; so that we found great need of the pike and boat-hook we had taken in our hands. As we went on, we felt a stinging sensation about the legs, but our uneasily balanced foothold prevented us from stooping to find out and remove the cause of the annoyance. We saw around us, snipe in great abundance, a species of blue stork, and other birds.

There was a portion of raised ground near the centre of the swamp, which was a mound of the sod-covered logs. Down we thrust our pike and boat-hook to their utmost length into some open spaces, and still there seemed more crevice way down through this piled up raft of huge timbers. I further saw, as I removed the soddy coating, that the wood seemed of a brittle, stony consistence, and I was eager to make more thorough research; when I was aroused by a cry from the sailor, who pointed to blood that stained his stocking—I was at the same time recalled to a sense of pain about the ankles; and I then thought of the pantomime and reluctance to come of Bahdoo.

The stinging sensation increased, and as I continued to strike and rub my pantaloons, I saw blood staining my own stockings. We beat a retreat for the boat in order to find out and remove this hidden enemy. The pain increased, the blood came faster; the sailor stamped and cursed, as he stumbled unsteadily along; and as we both approached the boat, walking as though on hot plates, and striking our legs with our hands, I could see a broad, chuckling grin on the face of the Malay.

Achih,—achih,—said Bahdoo, as he stooped down to roll up my pantaloons, and held up to me a small red leech, about two thirds of an inch long, which he had taken from my bleeding limbs. When we had got rid of the enemy, and washed ourselves, my oppas showed me that this little leech could jump; and thus got upon pedestrians like the troublesome, flesh-burrowing seed-ticks, I often suffered from in the forests of South Carolina; but tenfold more hurtful and bloodthirsty.

Bahdoo now hoped that I was content to return; but I wanted to see how much farther on this canopied creek extended; and so, after a lunch in the boat, we plied the oar along the deep shaded waters, till again the light broke in and we came to another open space, which was high and dry, and covered with clumps of very lofty, and some beautiful, long-leafed flowering trees. One tree with a large, thick varnished leaf arrested my attention, and Bahdoo said, *pooh'n gatah percha;* and of this I broke off a small branch.

My breaking of the twig seemed to rouse again some hostile genii of these woods, for a moment after doing so I heard cries from Bahdoo and curses from my sailor, who had followed me into this inviting grove of beauty; and then I saw them with one hand buffeting the air, and with the other rubbing their faces, whilst a swarm of large black insects buzzed around, and darted violently at them,—and then some of the vicious creatures flew at me and I felt most keenly stung. The sailor and Malay waved and fought with their hands;—they ran, and off went the swarm, leaving me, who had stood still, without moving a hand,—for I had had some experience with mad bee swarms in our western forests.

Bahdoo plunged into the creek, and the sailor followed; and when I reached the boat, they had set up such a splashing as to disperse the winged enemy. I felt the stings I had received, two on the hands and one in the face, most keenly—more acute than those of bees. I resorted to the simple remedy of pressing the end of a key barrel over the pustule raised by the sting, and soon obtained relief; and the Malay and sailor seemed to get relief from the mud with which they had besmeared themselves.

In half an hour, we were all right again;—but now, my sturdy Jack as well as Bahdoo, began to think we had better bout ship: still I was loth to leave this caverned creek, and wanted to see the end of it, for the sun was yet high; and I agreed after another half hour's pull, taking an oar myself, to turn back.

For a time, nothing but the sounds of the oars, the dip and splash, and ruttle on the rowlocks, broke upon the still cool air within the wood-caverned water-way. By and by Bahdoo, who was steering, stooped his head, and held the back of his hand to his ear: the oars were held in rest, and then we heard a crackle in the leafy mass above, and a little ahead of us;—a few strokes more, and another rest; and then a loud rustle and shake of limbs broke upon us, right overhead, and Bahdoo cried wildly, moonyet besar,—orang utan,—orang utan,—a great monkey! a wild man! a wild man!

I heard gruff animal sounds mingled with rustles, jumps and shakes amid the tree-top limbs; but as yet had seen nothing of what caused them. I sprang out of the boat, and Bahdoo, without bidding, quickly followed,—the sailor after him, with the carbine in his hand: the heavy leaps and shakes continued, and after some time gazing upward, I got a glimpse amid a thick bower of foliage, at a height of about eighty feet, of a dark brown form seeming to me as large as a human being; and when Bahdoo saw it, he cried out, Orang Kubu! Orang Kubu!

I raised a shout, and we all cried out at the top of our voices. I struck at some low drooping limbs with the pike in my hand; and then we heard rustles and leaping sounds at other points in the great treetops near the form we had seen;—this one shifted, slid down a limb, came nearer to view, and then we could partly see a very human-like form, holding a little creature with a very human-like face, peering down upon us.

The sailor had raised the carbine, and was about to fire, when I bid him stop; it seemed like murder to shoot at that human face, for I had heard something of wild and hairy races, roaming in the forests not far from the waters of Palembang. I again raised a shout,—Bahdoo made a peculiar piercing cry, and again the creature moved; it leaped, others leaped, and the huge tree shook. Downward came the sounds, leaping, rustling, crashing, then dark bodies shot before us, down, plunge into the creek.

We had stood with weapons grasped, expecting an attack; but after hearing a quick flounder and splash in the water, up sprang five or six large creatures, for a moment but dimly seen, then up the bank and away into the thick forest on the other side.

Three fourths of the day was now gone, and I had seen enough for one day's excursion. The boat was put about, and rowed quickly down the canopied stream,—pulled with hands again through the narrow neck, where the leafy top brushed our backs. Our fatigue felt lightened, when we shot out of the leafy cavern into the warm daylight on the main stream we had left; and our increasing fatigue was all forgotten when, upon turning the bend of the stream into the Moosee, we beheld the graceful, golden tipped spars of the Flirt walking up among the towering tree-tops.

A light breeze had risen, filling the clipper's main and foretop sail, with which she walked away from the lumbering barque, that crept slowly behind, with all sails set. It was sweet after the day's fatigue and adventure, to sit upon my quarter-deck, and feel the cool wafts of air, that blew perfume from the woods, and played with the folds of the flag of America, which I felt proud to think I was the first to bear up this noble Sumatran stream.

When we had come to anchor, while I sat eating my curry, real, mild, savory East Indian curry, prepared by Bahdoo; and while sipping the fragrant tea of my friend Lim Boo Seng, the costliest leaf, brought from the centre of China, and gathered, as he said, by monkeys on certain inaccessible rocky ledges on mountain sides, and while proving the merits of the mangoes brought by the Demang,—a visitor was announced, and the young surgeon from the Bali barque entered my cabin.

He was curious to know what I had seen and met with, and expressed a regret, that I had not signified a desire to have company in my excursion. And then I spoke of the diverging river branch, the covered creek, the brittle stony woods, the gutta percha limb, the leeches, the insects, and the orang utan.

I had entered, said my visitor, the Djarang, a strait or channel, connecting the Moosee with the Rantoo Stenno, a branch of the Palembang waters, which joins the Soonsang not far from the Campong Soonsang. There are several of these channels, diverging from the main branch of the Moosee; the Padang, Kamoodee, Kombang, Oopang, Djarang, Troosang, Punchian, Chetar and Rantoo Stenno, forming numerous deltas, which are much subject to inundation during the north-western monsoon;

and that was why nearly all the cabins we had seen were deserted at that time; but, said he, they will be peopled again on the return of the south-eastern monsoon, and a rice crop will be planted and gathered, before the season of freshets has returned.

In other parts of Sumatra, said the intelligent officer, where vegetation is even more exuberant than you behold it here, and forest trees are grander and loftier, you will meet with many deliciously embowered lakelets, and canopied creeks like the one you ascended; and in the interior there are large tracts of country, thickly strewn with huge timbers of ancient date, some half, and some wholly carbonized, according to the heat and pressure of superincumbent soil, to which they have been subjected.

He had often suffered from the little swamp leech, called *achih*, which deterred me from further mineralogical researches. Europeans wore nether garments that could be drawn tight around the ankles, whenever obliged to traverse swampy tracts of country in Sumatra, and in Borneo. The natives pass marshes with bare legs, so that they can quickly remove the leeches, as they leap upon them; which they can the more readily do, as they look straight forward and downward as they go along, and not staring right and left, and round about them, like Europeans.

He said that the gutta percha tree was found in great abundance on the western coast, especially in the territory of Bencoolen, where tracts of ten and twelve miles square were almost entirely covered with this valuable gum tree. The native name, *gatah percha*, signifies *band* or *ribbon* gum; probably because it is commonly formed into strips for various purposes; but one of the native names of this island being Percha, it may have been the design to call it the gum of Sumatra. Traders, who care little about names, have changed the *gatah* to *gutta;* as they have *cayu putee* to *cajeput*, and orang *utan* to orang *utang*, which latter signifies a debtor, instead of a wild man, to the ears of a Malay. And then he commented upon the human-like creatures that I had seen. He had heard much about a wild race of human shaped beings, covered with hair, called *orang kubu*, or *brown men*, who were to be found in the country north of Palembang, between it and the territory of Jambee,—living on the streams that flow into the Banyoo Assin; but he had never heard of them upon the Moosee, or any of its own branches; yet it need not be surprising that the Kubus should be found upon the Moosee and its branches, as there was a direct communication by cross channels, between it and the Banyoo Assin.

A great many extraordinary and improbable stories are told about the Kubus and other wild aboriginal races, by the Malays, who call them all by the general name of orang utan. Some account of them was given by a lieutenant in the army of Netherland India, who spent many years in Sumatra.

This lieutenant said that the orang kubu are to be found in the large tracts of forest, watered by the Lakitan, Batang Lekoh, Rawas Ulu, and Lalan, tributaries of the Moosee and the Banyoo Assin, and forming boundaries between the territory of Palembang and the Sultanate of Jambee. He spoke of them as a race of beings, living in a state of nature, as simple as wild beasts. They were much stronger built than the civilized men of the island; symmetrically formed, of powerful frame, and capable of enduring any hardships incident to their brutish life.

Some of these creatures, he said, wore a small strip of bark about the loins, and both sexes daub themselves with mud and gum from trees, to avoid the bite of insects; but they seem to have no idea of the use of garments for a covering. The men have long, shaggy beards (an appendage almost denied to the civilized Sumatrans), and the bodies of males and females are covered with long, flowing hair.

Their food consists of wild berries and fruits, and of fish, and several species of reptiles which they eat raw. They do not cultivate the earth in any manner whatever. When traversing the forests, they are accompanied by a species of large, wild dog, who keep watch against the attack of tigers and bears, and also serve as sentinels, to prevent the surprise of their masters by the Malays, who hunt them for slaves. He said that the sagacity and fidelity of these dogs, almost indicate the possession of greater reasoning faculties than shown by the Kubus.

These creatures make rude shelters of tree bark, while many lodged in the tops and hollows of trees. Their only weapon and tool is a pointed bamboo, of which even the orang utan avail themselves. The bow and arrows, and sumpits, or bamboo tubes for blowing out small darts, in use among the Dyaks, the Alfuras, and other wild tribes of the East Indian Archipelago, are unknown to these hairy men of Sumatra.

They have sometimes been known to approach the abodes of civilized people, when pressed with hunger, or as, in some cases, when pursued by wild beasts. The lieutenant gives an instance of a Kubu female, who was induced to live with a Malay. At first she rejected cooked meat; and when she began to partake of it, she seemed to suffer much pain in her stomach. For some time, she could not be prevailed upon to wash her body with water, instead of smearing it with liquid gum from trees.

The greatest number of these beings are to be found in the country of the Batang Lekoh; and these appear to have some slight traits of civilization, some of them being engaged in gathering benzoin or frankincense; and in fact are the chief collectors of that article of commerce, which they exchange for some trinkets and pieces of colored cloth. They are extremely cautious of approaching the Malays, for the purpose of trading, for fear of being caught and retained as slaves, which very often happens; and it, said he, is doubtless the treachery of the civilized man which keeps those poor wild creatures more isolated than they otherwise would be.

This mistrust of civilized man, has led to a very curious custom of trading, somewhat resembling that described by Herodotus, between the Carthaginians and certain wild tribes in Africa; but more singular still, in the case of the Kubus, as described by the Dutch lieutenant, and afterwards to me by many Arab and Chinese traders I have met with. The Kubus deposit the gum they collect, and other articles to exchange, in a certain place, when traders are in the neighborhood; then they strike with a club upon a suspended hollow log, called taboh by the Malays, making a loud, drum-sound—and run off back into the recesses of the forest. The traders come to the spot, take away the gum, and leave what they think proper. After they have gone the Kubus cautiously venture out of the thicket, and carry off what has been left for them. Sometimes this mode of barter is reversed—the traders depositing trinkets and cloths—then beat a gong, and retire; whilst the wild men come and take away what has been offered, and honestly and generously leave all that they have got of gum or other articles. Thus, the chief material for the purifying incense used in the ceremonial of the church of Rome is gathered by these rude hands.

Marsden, who resided many years on the western coast of Sumatra, in his account of the aborigines of the island, says that he had heard of two species of people, dispersed in the woods, and avoiding all communication with the other inhabitants:

these were the orang Kubu, and the orang Gugur: the former being, as he understood, very numerous on the south-east coast between the Palembang and Jambee territories. He speaks of having heard of several that had been caught and put to work as slaves; and of a young Kubu female that was captured by a man in the Laboon country. He says that the Gugurs are much scarcer than the Kubus, differing in little, but the use of some uncouth kind of speech, from the orang utan of Borneo,—they being entirely covered with hair. But Marsden is rather skeptical about the existence of these beings of doubtful humanity.

You will have an opportunity when at Palembang, said the Dutch officer, to learn something more definite about these creatures; and may probably see some of them in the possession of the old pensioned Sultan, who resides there. I did learn much more about these wild people at Palembang and at Batavia, which I shall relate in the course of my narrative.

EIGHTEENTH DAY.

On the fourth day after entering the Soonsang, the barque and schooner were still toiling up stream towards Palembang. In the morning they passed the island of Kumbaroo on the right, and the Pladjoo River on the left. On the banks of this river's mouth, and on the island, are some vestiges of fortifications;—the scene of a severe engagement between a Dutch naval force, of five ships of war, and some troops of the late Sultan of Palembang.

The channel of the Moosee increased in depth, as the branches outflowing from the main stream were passed; and above the Pladjoo, it had deepened to ten fathoms in mid-channel, with a width of stream of about five hundred yards. A few miles from the mouth of the Pladjoo, the floating town burst upon the view; and the commander of the Flirt thus described, on board the Palmer, his

ARRIVAL AT PALEMBANG.

We began to see tambangans of many shapes and sizes, darting past, or shooting athwart our bows; some very plain—the rough, scooped log alone, half-filled by some lonely fisher, and he half covered by his broad, bowl-shaped tudong hat; others richer with varnish gloss outside, and carpet within, where turbaned men were seated; and little boys in tasteful dress, with amber skins, and sparkling eyes, paddled these gay skiffs along.

Large, laden prahus passed by, in which long ranks of rowers, shaded by the broad banana leaf, sang as they rowed along: one tuneful voice breaking on the ear awhile, with shrill and pleasing strain; and then a chorus rang out from those long ranks, keeping time with the dipping dayong blades; and thus, amid song and forest splendor on either side, with thronging oriental scenes upon the water, did we approach the Venice of Sumatra.

A breeze sprang up, and the graceful clipper, with her stars floating at the gaff, glided proudly up the thronged water broadway, amid the junks of China, the prahus of the Archipelago, and the heavy craft of Holland; and before thousands of curious gazers, looking out from houses resting on rafts, that rose and fell with the sink or swell of the tidal stream, which they lined on either side.

After letting go my anchor in ten fathoms water, in the midst of junks and prahus, at the lower end of the town, I went ashore to call upon the Dutch authorities in the fort, about two miles higher up. The Havermeester, or Shahbandar, as more commonly called at Palembang, was a middle-aged Creole, with a mild and kindly look of face, the son of an English trader of Padang and a Malay mother; and he seemed heartily glad to welcome one who spoke his father's tongue.

The Shahbandar introduced me to the Dutch lieutenant commanding the Pylades, a small gun brig, then lying at Palembang. He was a man past the prime of life, with coarse features marked with strong drink. After some conversation about my voyage, and object in coming to the East, he led me to the fort, where he introduced me to a man about thirty-five years of age, of short stature, with plain unmilitary features, mild expression, and very slovenly dressed; and this was Col. de Brauw, the Resident and Commander-in-chief, in the territory of Palembang.

On returning to my vessel on the following day, from a visit on shore, I found a stranger in my cabin; a tall and venerable man, of most noble and commanding presence. His dark features were pure Arab, of the finest type; and were crowned with a muslin turban of snowy whiteness; from his shoulders hung, down to his ankles, a green silk robe; within this he wore a yellow silken vest, and a pure white skirt, gracefully tucked and folded; and rich embroidered sandals on his feet, made up the striking costume of him, who advanced to take my hand, and who introduced himself,—Seyd Scherriff Ali, Panyorang or Prince of the Arabs of Palembang.

He had stood near, amid a group of Arab and Chinese merchants, when I talked with the Shahbandar. He had heard that I came from America, a mighty country to him; of the greatness of whose people he had heard much; at Muscat, and even here in Sumatra. He had learned from my words with the Shahbandar, that I came with my beautiful vessel for no purpose of trade; but to see the beauty and wealth of the island, to tell of to my countrymen. He was glad to see such a man, and he had come to invite him to his house, to talk with him. And all this I understood with the help of my list of Malay words and sentences already learned from Bahdoo—a few words of English, which he knew, and much pantomime between us.

I stepped into his ornamented tambangan. We sat down on a rich carpet in the centre, and were shaded by a payong, or huge parasol. Eight pretty little boys dressed in white and green, between the ages of six and ten, plied the bright paddle

blades,—one half forward and the others aft of us, whilst a stout Malay sat on the tambangan's stern-peak, and with a large, broad dayong, guided it along, swiftly down the stream; then gracefully rounding to, and shooting across an eddying current into a calm canal, brought us to the steps of the house of the Arab Panyorang.

We stepped on to a floor beneath a long verandah roof. A second floor, raised a step higher, lay beyond this, and here my stately companion stopped, and pointing to a graceful silk-covered lounge, a petarana, invited me to rest, whilst he reposed upon another. A small table richly japanned was placed between us, on which were a profusion of small, varnished, wooden plates, filled with sweetmeats, cakes and fruits of various kinds.

When we first sat down, several men and youths had assembled upon the verandah floor, and gazed at me with curious looks. After a few minutes, when I had ceased to taste of the dainties that were pressed upon me, a motion from the hand of the Panyorang dispersed the curious throng, all save one, a youth about seventeen, with fine features, the finest type of the comely race of Yahman;—mild and mind-beaming eyes, which he fixed with earnest look upon me, as he sat on a mat, and leaned on the petarana, near the feet of the Panyorang. "My grandson Abdallah bin Aboubaker bin Ali," said the old man, as he gazed on the youth with wistful eyes.

Our discourse in Malay was a labored work of broken sentences and signs. I had a small blank book cut and lettered, in which I had already a goodly vocabulary of words and sentences, gathered from Bahdoo, the Balinese captain, and every one I had met with, who knew any thing of Malay, whom I had always pressed into the service of teaching me. And now, with vocabulary and pencil in hand, I talked with the Panyorang, as

I had with all I had met with in the East; learning more as I talked on.

The Panyorang spoke of Raffles, the Tuan Besar Ingres,—the English Great man, as Sir Stamford Raffles, the famous British Governor in the Archipelago, and enlightened founder of Singapore, is called and remembered by the Malays of Palembang. He said, that the people did not believe that the great good man was dead, and looked for his coming again.

The Panyorang had taken part in the wars of Badroodin, the late Sultan of Palembang. He had gone to meet the English General Gillespie, near Pulo Burong, to capitulate for the surrender of this town, when the Sultan had fled into the interior. After that time the English had unwisely given up all that the Tuan Raffles had gained, to the Dutch Company, who grasped at all things for Holland, and wanted to make slaves of Arabs, Malays, and Chinamen, all alike. The Panyorang said, The Portuguese are gone; the Spaniards are very weak; the English have abandoned the Archipelago by treaty; and there is no power to stay the all-devouring Dutch, unless it comes from America. Was it coming? Had I come to see, when and where Americans should come?—he was anxious to hear.

I said, my ship is very small; many prahus and junks upon this river are larger. I have no arms. I have no merchandise, no gifts, nor any thing to give me power. I have but a feeble handful of poor sailors, and poor myself; then why should the Panyorang suppose that I was sent by a great power to prepare a way for conquest, or commerce?

The Dutchmen near the *benteng* (the fort) had said, that the American was a spying bird; he had come with small show of means, that none might suspect; his vessel was a war-built ship, and she might have a consort lurking near, or at Singapore, that could quickly fill her empty hold with men, and those gaping ports with guns; and he, the Panyorang, must say, that he should wonder to see a gentleman (*tuan betul*) come into these dangerous and troubled countries, with an empty and unarmed vessel, unless for some affairs of his Government, and with its strong protection near by him.

An ill-founded suspicion as to the object of my visit to the East, arising from ignorance and jealousy, had met me at the threshold of Netherland India. An absurd importance attached to my untrader-like appearance and movements by Dutch authorities, had already prompted overtures of desertion and rebellion on the part of disaffected soldiers and vassals; and this jealousy, ignorance, and suspicion, was soon to involve me in a most extravagant charge of crime, and the Government of the Netherlands in a vexatious and expensive prosecution.

I asked the Panyorang, had he not heard of curious and adventurous Arabs, who had in olden times come to Pulo Percha, to Java, and other lands in these seas; who had come without power, trusting alone in God; and without armies or ships of war, had grown great and rich in these Heaven-blessed lands. Then why should he be surprised at my coming?

The Panyorang said I spoke truly. The children of the prophet had indeed come without power; without the power of war; but with the power of Allah, and they had conquered the land. Every chieftain of Sumatra has some of the blood of the true sons of Islam in his veins. And the children of Yahman and their children's children, are many in the land of Pulo Percha; —fifteen thousand in all; of these, two thousand at Palembang, over whom your slave is chief; said the Panyorang, bowing.

My brethren, and myself, said he, have some substance: we have chiefly merchandise and ships; there are eleven square-rigged ones, belonging to the Arabs of this town. My own, the Djelanie, carries three hundred koyangs (about 900 tons), and the Maimoon, Lachmady, Faid Alim, and others belonging to my brethren, are fine ships. The Company is jealous of us; they wish to destroy the commerce of the Arabs, and make us slaves like the Chinese and Malays. We wish for a Company that would have more power to keep the country—that would have less jealousy and fear, and would give more freedom to trade; and I did think that you might give us the promise of such a one.

These ideas and statements of the Panyorang, which I have just uttered in plain English in the course of a couple of minutes, cost in its original utterance, at the least, ten times that amount of time, of mutual struggles with words and pantomime, between myself and the venerable Arab. I was strongly impressed with his extensive knowledge; though amusingly vague as regarded America; with his quickness of perception, and above all with his polished and dignified manner; and I thought the title of Panyorang, or Prince, well befitted the stately old man.

I had talked of America, of the America that was the child of England, as he spoke of it,—of the number and mighty size of her ships, of the greatness of her cities, of her marvels of steam and telegraph, of the wealth, of the happiness, of the numbers of her people; and as I spoke on with labored words, with moving hands and animated face, the grandson had fixed his eyes upon me with eager look; and when I rose to depart, he said some words to his grandfather; and Abdallah returned with me in the tambangan.

When on board and in my cabin, I showed the young Arab what I had of curious things; books, pictures, dresses; but he was most curious about maps: he pointed to the colored divisions upon a map of the globe with inquiring look; and when I mentioned America, he pointed to it with dilated eyes, then to me, and to himself, and taking hold of my hand, with many signs and words gave me to understand that he wished to sail away with me.

I had been at first sight much pleased with the fine, earnest, intelligent look of Abdallah; but now I felt touched with this spirit of adventure to see the world, or his liking for me, I did not know which the young Arab expressed. I spoke to try him. I might not go back to America in one, two, or three years. But would I not stay on the sea with my ship all that time? if so, he wished to serve me. His father, Aboubaker bin Ali, was the captain of the Djelanie, and sailed to Singapore and Batavia; but Abdallah wished to sail much further. I was pleased. I promised to speak with the Panyorang and the captain; and Abdallah left me with a joyful countenance.

Whilst the Arab was taking leave, the Balinese captain entered. Take care, said he, glancing at Abdallah, these Arabs are greater rogues than the Malays, though not in so small a way. They have an old Panyorang, called Scherriff Ali—a swamp snake,—who has grown fat on English, Dutch, Chinese and Malays; he has about a dozen wives, and several dozen grandchildren, who paddle him about in his rambahya, or big tambangan. He deserted old Sultan Badr Oodin, and gave up Palembang to the British; and when the Dutch got into possession of Palembang again, by treaty, he tried to sell the place to the British governor Raffles, who was then at Bencoolen. He is a cunning old fellow; and if the Dutch were not afraid, they would hang him up right off; but the Malays half worship the Arabs, as being the true orang Islam; and so the Arabs do as they please, and are the real masters of the native people.

The Balinese captain did not know the person of the Panyorang; but he could assure me that he had a general idea of the history of every body of any consequence in the Archipelago; and I had had some occasion to believe that his general knowledge was almost as extensive as he boasted. Yet I was inclined to think that he viewed every thing native, from an ordinary European false point of view;—the half native imitating his Caucasian progenitor, in the East the same as the West; yet I could not then refute the assertions about the Panyorang's motives in his dealings with British, Dutch, Raffles, and the Sultan Badr Oodin; but one thing I had observed, that the little boys in the tambangan were all Malays; and not one of the little fellows, whom I had examined very attentively, recalled to my mind the slightest resemblance to the Panyorang, or any thing Arab,—and so I received all the other assertions of the captain with an entire reserve of judgment.

It is too true, said the elder Missionary, that this captain only uttered the sentiments of all Europeans in the East; who from the beginning, deal with the natives in the spirit of dealing with rogues, and never seem to wish to believe that a Malay, Javanese or Chinaman, could possibly have a good or honorable sentiment. These, like our Indians in America, like Africans, like every other people not Caucasians, are looked upon as born bad—designed by Providence to remain so; and to be used or abused, according to the interest or whim of the superior race. When they shall be treated with a parental kindness and forbearance, with some love and patience, as though dealing with children; acting firmly and without suspicion; showing that you seek their interest as well as your own; giving them no poison; giving them good advice and faithful protection; then I am sure they would repay with the love and fidelity of children; for all these races seem glad to look up to the white man. He is indeed their superior, and should be their affectionate elder brother. But what has he been throughout all India and China? we will not look elsewhere. Has it not been his sole object to come to the East to seek wealth, wrung out of toiling simplicity and ignorance, with which he returns home to make a vulgar, barbaric display, whether in England, America or Holland? What a mission has been here for power and civilization! For two hundred years and more, the three millions of Christian Dutchmen have been the masters over seven generations of about fifteen millions of Mahometan and Pagan Malays, Javanese and other races of the Archipelago,—not less than one hundred millions in all; and for what purpose?—to fill the plethoric coffers of stolid men of Amsterdam and Rotterdam, the old Company of sordid monopolists; and now to support a poor royalty, a vicious younger branch of the once energetic family of Nassau.

What glory for Holland, if she had sent ten thousand of her men from home, solely to teach and elevate the people of Java and Sumatra; to teach them the hopes of immortality of her church, the security of her laws, the advantages of her literature, and the amenities of her civilization. The gratitude of this people would surely have given more, than has been wrung from them by ten thousand soldiers, and by systems of surveillance and order, for the sake of making easy the collection of revenue, the sole object of European Government in the East.

That all sounds very well, said the Commander of the Palmer, in his usual blunt way; but when I hear of missionaries going among Malays or Chinese, without scrip or purse, trusting to the gratitude of the people, they go to teach for their subsistence, and caring nothing for pay or honors,—then it may be time for reproaching governments for not carrying out missionary operations on a grand scale. You will do far more good to the Chinese and Malays by thrashing work out of them, and making them wide-awake to trade; making them feel that they must do it honestly, than by teaching them a lot of home stuff, which no more suits these down-Easters, than pigtails and black teeth would ours at home.

Both were extreme,—the kindly old missionary with his Utopian plans for bettering races of men—the product of ages of vitiation; and the worthy captain, in thinking that there is not enough humanity left in them, for philanthropy to go to work upon, with any plan whatever. The Chinese, Hindus, Malays, and other people of the East, may become wiser, stronger and happier, when missionaries of the gospel shall go forth among them, more zealous and unencumbered, and less as mere stipendiary agents of a company; and when merchants and ship captains who go East, shall get some other ideas of a race, than what they learn from lascars and coolies,—the vicious offspring of trade,—the helots of commerce in all parts of the world.

NINETEENTH DAY.

On the day following his visit to the Arab Panyorang, the commander of the Flirt took dinner with Governor de Brauw at the Residency. He met a large, and fine-looking company of ladies and officers at the Governor's table, where he was received with marked attention, as the chief honored guest.

After some remark about the peculiar dainties of Palembang, the Governor spoke of the warlike condition of the country. Hostile parties of natives came into the neighborhood of the fort, and with the pepper, cinnamon, dammar, and gold dust brought from the interior, purchased firearms and ammunition from Arab and Chinese traders, who affect a friendliness to the Europeans, but secretly aid the native princes in their insidious warfare.

This state of brigandage, as he termed it, had continued since the departure of the British forces from the Dutch possessions in the Archipelago, which had been seized by England at the time of the incorporation of Holland into the empire of Napoleon. The Government of Great Britain had reluctantly complied with an act of national justice, in restoring to the Netherlands their possessions in the East, whilst the agents of that Government sought by intrigue to render valueless the restoration, by inciting the native princes to a maintenance of their independence.

This was especially true of Sir Stamford Raffles, the founder of Singapore. He had kept up, whilst in power in Java and Sumatra, a correspondence with every prince of note in the Archipelago; with no one more than with the fierce and bloody Sultan Badr Oodin, who sat on the throne of Palembang at the time of the restoration.

This cruel and treacherous prince, had ordered the massacre of the people of the Dutch factory, established in his dominions. The British Government affected to chastise him for this; took his kraton, or palace at this place; but after obtaining from him the tin mines of Banca, they allowed his sanguinary character full license as before. When the Netherlands came into power again in the Archipelago, the Sultan Badr Oodin was deposed, and his younger brother, Nayem Oodin, a good prince of easy nature, was elevated in his stead.

The British resumed their machinations. The quiet prince was dethroned, and his elder brother recommenced a reign of terror over Palembang. He waged a fierce, and for a time, a successful warfare against the forces of the Netherlands. He drove every European out of his dominions; but the General de Kock returned the ensuing year with a fleet and army, with which he defeated the forces of the perfidious Sultan, and took him a prisoner of war to Batavia.

The younger brother was reinstated Sultan of Palembang; but again a secret British influence began to incite this weak prince to hostile acts; he was deposed, and the Government of the Netherlands assumed the protectorate of the Sultanate, which it has endeavored to maintain up to this time; but the infatuated natives, regardless of the advantages of regularly administered laws, increasing the security of life and property and all the advantages of a well regulated trade, still clamor for the return of the race of their tyrants, who made sport with the lives, property, and female honor of their subjects; they resist all our good intentions, and bite like their own tigers, at the hand that would feed and help them. We point in vain to the comfortable and contented Javanese, as an evidence of the beneficence of our rule.

Sumatra and Java, said Major Van Blommestein, an officer with a slightly creole complexion, and a good-humored intelligent countenance, are like the wolf and the house-dog in the fable. The Javanese mastiff will fatten with a chain around his neck; but this gaunt, fierce Malay wolf of Sumatra, will never be tamed or made profitable in any way. We must deal with Sumatrans, as the Americans have dealt with the Iroquois and the Mohawks, or let them alone altogether.

To this, the commander of the Flirt replied, that the American Government had paid many millions of dollars for the sovereignty of the Indian lands, and said that territory not greater in extent than Sumatra, which he understood to be upwards of eleven hundred miles long, and an average of one hundred miles broad, had cost not less than forty millions of dollars;—say ninety millions of guilders,—more probably than the net revenue of the whole Archipelago, since it had been in the possession of Holland. Was she willing to pay for sovereignty at that rate?

You Americans, said the naval commander, with a laugh of apparent good humor, can beat all the world in telling a good story, as well as in every thing else. How can you be so rich, when your chief city of Washington was mortgaged to some of our folks in Amsterdam,—Hope and Company I believe, and was at one time about to be sold under the hammer, to satisfy the claim of our poor Dutchmen: and would have been sold, had not your terrible President, the one who defeated the

British by lying quiet behind some cotton bales, laid an embargo upon the revenues of the country; and unlike Camillus, saved the capitol with hard money instead of the sword.

When the somewhat rude and prolonged laugh of the Dutch officers had subsided, the American commander said: that it was true, some portion of the small lot of ground, where the American Legislature assembled, had been mortgaged by a city corporation for money borrowed in Holland; and when the Dutch creditors had sought to foreclose the mortgage, the then President of the United States (General Jackson) had recommended to Congress to assist the municipality of Washington in releasing itself from its obligation, which no more concerned the credit and wealth of the country at large, or perhaps not as much, as the credit of Holland was concerned, when her late king sold her cabinets of rare paintings—the work of her sons of genius, never to be replaced—to meet the expenses of a vicious court life. It is true, that the same Hope & Co., who held the mortgage on the town lots of Washington, also had a claim upon William of Nassau: but there was no Congress, holding the untold millions of a free people to help him; and so, the capitol,—the Valhalla of Netherlands art, was sacked by an auctioneering Brennus, and carried off by the barbarian dilettanti of Europe. And as for the cotton bales of New Orleans, it might have been better for the Netherlands to have had a few of them in the Archipelago, with some of the same rifles that were planted behind them, when Lord Minto and Sir Stamford Raffles went to Batavia.

Several officers sprang up to reply, or to make some other kind of demonstration, when the Resident rose, with calm and impressive dignity, proposed that the company should drink to the health of the President of the United States, and of

William the Third, of Nassau;—which was done. The first one heartily, by the ladies present; and the latter received a boisterous vociferation from the loyal Dutchmen. Afterwards the Resident proposed, that the two gentlemen of the sea—his guest, and his naval friend of the guard ship—should pledge each other, which was done, and apparent cordiality was restored, and continued at the whist parties of the gentlemen and among the music of the ladies in the drawing-room; and when the guest took his leave, the Resident and his chief officers present, accepted an invitation to dine on board the American clipper.

After leaving the Residency, the commander not finding his Malay servant at the gate of the Fort in waiting with a torch, set off alone towards the boat landing. He took a contrary direction and wandered off among the native campongs, far beyond the precincts of the fort.

He was tempted by the soothing freshness of a tropic night, which are ever cool and breezy at Palembang, like the softest of Indian summer evenings in South Carolina. The deep, ruttling roar of some wild elephants broke harshly upon the stillness of the night: they were some just caught, chained to trees outside the fort,—their trunks drawn up and tethered to a pendent limb; and in this irksome plight, tortured with hunger and thirst by man, who wanted to get the benefit of their labor, by destroying their native sense of liberty, the poor huge brutes, with imbecile strength, broke the weary air with wailings at the tyranny of the ruthless little animal that had bound them.

These were not the only captives; other poor children of nature, were making softer lament against cruel jailors, the godlike masters of brute and bird. A plaintive sound—a soft, moaning human-like note, said ku-whoo—ku-kur—ku-kuruboo, —then a deep gurgling bar of sound came from the throat of the buruug kukur, (the Sumatran dove,) filling the night with its taught notes of a sad sounding melody.

But he soon had cause to think that it were well for man, that the brute and bird were all he made to mourn. As he followed a narrow way between lines of low bamboo huts, he heard a pleading cry of female voices, drowned at times by oaths and brutal words from coarse Dutch voices; and a minute later, saw by the torch light of an oppas, three Dutch officers, who were driving before them two weeping and sobbing young Malay women;—the officers striking and thrusting at the poor girls with their canes, as these stopped and turned round,—and uttered words of entreaty.

The officers looked amazed at the presence of the stranger. One of them, who had been on board the Balinese barque, recognized him, and asked in French what mad curiosity had brought him wandering among the Malay campongs beyond the protection of the fort, where a lonely European's life was not worth an hour's purchase. You see we have a picket of soldiers in our rear, as a necessary guard for a night frolic

The commander explained how he had lost his servant, and his way; and that he was on no such errand as theirs. He did not wonder that they needed guards, when the children of the country were driven thus like wretched cattle. The officers, who were urging the poor girls with such brutality forward, were coarse-looking men, half-drunk; they growled in Dutch about the stranger—who was he—what the blixem did he want—gave the girls a rude shove, and marched on.

The barque acquaintance, who was sober, walked a little in the rear with the commander, to whom he promised to furnish a tambangan, to put him on board his vessel. You may think very hard of what you see; a case of abduction, kidnapping—a terrible outrage upon helpless innocence—it is nothing of the sort. These two officers, a lieutenant and adjutant in the mess to which I belong, had bargained with an old Malay hadjy—a pilgrim as the rascal calls himself,—having been to Mecca; but you will meet with, in the Archipelago, more hadjys than ever got sight of the mausoleum of Mahomet. They had purchased of him two girls, said to be *prawan*, or virgins, just brought from the Ulu or hill country.

You must know that the government does not want the officers of the army in the East to be burdened with wives; whoever takes one, must give security to the amount of ten thousand florins,—a fabulous sum for any poor devil of an officer under the grade of colonel: but the benevolent government, though fearful of the disqualifying encumbrance of a family, affords facilities for a general concubinage; and so my friends here, wishing to obtain those allowable army followers, called nyahees, who are left behind at every station,—made a bargain with the hadjy as I have just told. He did not bring the girls to the rakit,—our floating barracks on the river,—at the appointed time. Some dodging was suspected; and so, whilst the captain of our mess was gone to the Residency to meet the American commodore (for some of our benighted Dutchmen, and they of the highest at Minto and Palembang, will have it that you are something of the sort in disguise), along with the jolly Havermeester and our drunken admiral; these friends started off in search of their purchases,—persuading me to accompany them. We found the hadjy, who made piteous protestation, that by no fault of his had he failed to come. He had told some lying story to the mother of the girls, who had come with her children to Palembang. When she found that they were to be sold to soldiers, she set up a howl, and the young ones along with her;—no doubt the hadjy wanted to keep too much of the price of their virginity to himself. He could not deliver his merchandise, but pointed it out. My friends had swallowed enough of schiedam, not to be baulked: they had some trouble with the old lady, and started up a wicked looking crowd with krisses, which fortunately our bayonets kept off from us. The girls make a rather unusual disturbance which I don't understand; for the buying and selling of them is as common as the traffic of snipes in the market; and nothing more common, than for a mother to sell her own children.

The party had now reached some large bamboo house frames lined with fine matting and close wicker work; they were afloat on raft foundations, and moored by enormous twisted bamboo cables to the river bank, which has no shoaling beach, but runs steep down at the water's edge, like a canal embankment,—there being sixty feet depth of water, within less than that distance from the shore.

The party stepped along a floating, mat covered causeway, into the rakit, as the floating houses of Palembang are called. The girls were thrust into a small verandah room, and left in charge of an oppas; whilst the officers and commander entered upon another part of the rakit, filled with clouds of tobacco smoke, and coarse sounds, in which the Dutch dom and blixem prevailed.

The commander was quickly pledged with schiedam, and with the haansche bier of Rotterdam, the chief Dutch guzzle in the Archipelago. Gentlemen, said a lieutenant in very bad French, with red hair and short nose, rising up unsteadily with tumbler in hand,—let us drink to the health of the Governor's guest at dinner, who has condescended to leave the parlor to come and take tea in the barracks. We can give him a heartier bumper, and a warmer look and shake of the hand, than our cold, smiling, fish-blooded chief.

Silence there, about the Resident; said a dark-complexioned, severe looking officer, in Dutch. I will not hear Col. de Brauw spoken of disrespectfully by any one here. Yes, you shall by me; said a pale, thin, slight-formed man, who had been addressed as captain. I say, that De Brauw is a false-hearted dog: he has played false with one half the officers in the garrison: he stole the credit of an action at the storming of Singa Rajah in Bali, from a sergeant in his company, which got him his promotion: he basely lied, as you all well know, to the chief, Ferdano Mantri,—promising to show him the beauties of a war ship just arrived; and then confining the brave, confiding native on board, to be sent to Batavia. You all know that Ferdano Mantri was a noble and enlightened chief, feared by us because loved by his people;—his bravery, and the fidelity of his adherents, made him dangerous; and so our government needed a De Brauw to decoy a brave man into a base trap. I know the Resident has power, more than common Residents; he has tried it on me; he has put me under arrest for the unnoticed peccadilloes of his own cringing clique. Go tell him that I said so; that he may ruin me sooner than he now intends; he has power indeed;—an adjutant of the King,—a royal bastard of the Hague.

The dark-complexioned officer made some retort in Dutch, which was answered by a bottle hurled at his head. All the revellers sprang to their feet,—making wild din, with oaths and drunken scuffle. The dark and the pale faced officer had thrown down the table that stood between them, and locked arms in hostile grapple;—and all the rest were engaged in separating them when their unexpected guest slipped away unseen from the midst of the mêlée.

He went out, the way he entered, to the causeway leading ashore; he saw the oppas asleep on his guard at the verandah room, and heard sobbing sounds coming from within. He had thought of no plan to help these seeming victims; but now these moans smote upon his heart. He approached the door, undid the fastenings,—the sound of their removal being unheard amid the din still going on within. The girls were seen by some faint rays of moonlight, cowering in a corner—Come out and run; quick, quick, I am your friend! said their liberator in Malay.

They rose up, they looked around them, then at the open door; they seemed to feel around with their hands; they approached the door with crouching movement; they looked out fearfully; their friend stood aloof; the roar of voices, crashing bottles, and breaking chairs, came from the mess-room; out sprang the girls, and with a few bounds, they crossed the causeway, and were lost amid the gloom on shore.

The commander got ashore, without being seen by the awakened oppas. He had now learned the way to the boat landing. He reached it, and there he found his truant Bahdoo, asleep in the tambangan, which brought him ashore, where the fellow had been dozing at the time his master left the Residency.

The commander was surprised to see in his cabin, the next morning, the Balinese skipper, in company with the pale-faced captain of the previous night's brawl. These two had met elsewhere, in the Archipelago, and were old friends. The Dutch officer had taken an interest in what he had heard about the American commander, who, with his vessel had become for the time being the sole topic of conversation in the garrison and among the native campongs. He had been sorry that the blackguardism of the night before had hindered his design to become better acquainted; that row, by the way, having ended with some bruised bones and cut faces; and he pointed to an ugly mark on his right cheek;—but with the soberness of the morning, peace has returned, and little damage has been done; except, the loss of two girls, who broke prison in a most unaccountable way; and our lieutenant is now busy trying to discover how they got out, and by what help, and where they have gone to.

The infantry captain went on to say that he had heard from his friend of the barque, of the great desire of the American gentleman to know something about the interior of Sumatra. He was happy to have it in his power to gratify his curiosity to a great extent. He had commanded a topographical corps and surveyed all the up-country of Palembang, and all the head-waters of the Moosie, fighting as he surveyed,—having lost in the mountains during the last expedition, more than two hundred of his men,—slain by the lances of the Malays.

He drew a compact roll from a side pocket and showed a finely executed map of the Palembang territory, including a portion of the territory of Bencoolen on the ocean side, or north-western coast; and of the Sultanate of Jambee and Kubu country on the east; and as he pointed to various localities on the map he made the following comments in answer to various questions upon

THE TOPOGRAPHY OF THE TERRITORY OF PALEMBANG.

It comprises about one fourth of the surface of the island of Sumatra; extending from 101° 40′ to 106° 0′ of longitude east of Greenwich; (the Captain reckoned from the Meridian of Paris); and from 6° 40′ to 3° 30′ South Latitude.

The boundaries are;—on the north-west, a lofty range of mountains called Bukit Barisan; portion of a chain which runs the whole length of the island near the ocean side on the west; precisely like the Cordilleras of South America. This Sumatran range has an average elevation of 4,000 feet; there are several volcanic peaks; the Gunung Planak; the Bukit Ulu-Moosie, and the Gunung Dempoh;—the latter attaining an elevation of 9,000 feet. On the north, and north-east, are the territories of the Sultan of Jambee, whom our Government chooses to call a vassal; although not one of our people dare set foot within the dominions of his Jambee Highness. On the east and south-east,—the China Sea, and Straits of Banca; on the south, —the Java Sea; and south-west,—the territory of the Lampongs, who occupy all the southern end of Sumatra.

The rivers are numerous, and many of them navigable to a great extent. You have seen, that the stream you have ascended could be navigated by a line of battle ship up to this place. It is of extraordinary depth, far deeper comparatively at Palembang, than your Mississippi at New Orleans; and you could ascend with your schooner, when not drawing more than ten feet of water, one hundred and fifty miles higher up, as far as Moora Klingie on the Moosie. For a hundred miles beyond that point, it is navigable for penchalangs,—long, freight tambangans, which will carry thirty and forty tons weight. I should say that there was at least 1,500 miles of good steamboat and ship navigation within the territory. All these streams, about a dozen principal ones, and numberless tributaries, run into a singular circle of water, like so many ribbons attached to a hoop; and this central position was most judiciously selected for a fort and palace by the old Sultans.

The rivers of Palembang are like a bundle of serpents, grasped by the middle; seven wildly-tossed necks stretch out towards the coast, and seven jaws pour the floods of the interior into the China Sea; behind the point where grasped, the coiling forms are spread in wild contortion over the whole breadth of the land; and at the grasped point,—the deep neck of waters, between the island of Kombaroo, and the mouth of the Pladjöo, the late Sultan, the terrible Badr Oodin, a fitting holder of the serpents, gave us a bloody reception in 1818, and 1821.

The roads are few; there are hardly any other means of communication between the different points in the territory except by water. A tambangan inland and a prahu at sea, is the chief home of a Sumatran; I mean of course the Malays. There are some pathways, through the great forests and swamps of the interior, which are utterly impassable to European troops. All our expeditions into the interior have been by water.

We have a bamboo fort, at a point on the head-waters of the Moosie, called Tebing Tinggi, a corruption of Benteng Tinggi, signifying, high fort; and we have some small military posts, at Lahat, Roopit, Klingi, and other places in the interior; but they cost an immense sacrifice of men and money to maintain them; and perhaps we will be forced to abandon them; as we did our posts in the Siak and Indraghiri territories, in the northern part of Sumatra. The rulers at the Hague, are like some of yours in America; ready to drop a thing, regardless of glory, when it ceases to pay. They would leave Sumatra to itself; for it is an expensive wild beast, that destroys a good deal of the substance produced by the tame animal of Java; but if we go away, the British, or you Yankees will come in, and set on the Sumatran tiger to worry the Javanese buffalo. We would grow rich with those nice plantations, Java and the Moluccas alone; but little Holland is a grasping old fool, in trying to hold the great wilderness of Sumatra, Borneo, Celebes, and all the Archipelago besides. It is like one of your people, who owns a snug paying plantation in the old States; after increasing a little he becomes ambitious to own big tracts of lands; buys up small states of Indian territory; the little plantation is worn out to meet the tax bill for hunting grounds; and by and by a lot of those nomadic gentlemen, you call squatters, set up a title with rifle in hand to the unsettled dominions of the ruined planter; which he never enjoyed except on paper; as Holland enjoys Sumatra, Borneo, and Papua on maps.

We have few reliable data, to determine the population of any portion of Sumatra; I should say, four millions of souls was the lowest estimate, of which I would allow one third of a million for this territory. The official report gives a much lower number: but the official population estimates are all below the mark. The government wishes to speak very moderately about the extent and populousness of these great islands. The population of this town is seventy thousand, of which two thousand are Arabs,—the oligarchs, that really rule the land, through the religion of the people: four thousand are Chinese; who here, as elsewhere in the Archipelago, are like the Parsees of Hindustan, and the Jews of Europe;—the ever thrifty and wealthy peddlers of the east, the true men of trade, with about as little soul, and as much cash, as the great and little peddlers of Amsterdam, London and New York. And all the rest of the people of Palembang are chiefly Malay; except some Javanese settlers induced to come here by our government, in order to check a little the fierce Malay element of the population.

Within the walls of this fort, and at other posts in the territory, we have two thousand troops, two thirds of which are Javanese and other natives. We have no foothold outside of the fort, beyond the range of the guns. The Malays would give us for food to the caymans, in one night, if our fortifications were gone. We dare not wander in the campongs single-handed. The Malay is quick with his kriss, and you would do well not to venture on shore alone. The people are hospitable to strangers,—would no doubt receive you kindly, but they might mistake you for a Dutchman, and give you a point of poisoned steel before they had discovered their mistake. You would do well to apply to the Resident for a couple of soldiers for an escort when going ashore; but be cautious in your intercourse with that man. He has shown you great attention; he has drawn in his claws, and held out the velvety paw; but mark that cold eye, and rigid face which accompany the languid smile, and you will read the coldest of treachery. He is now about to send me again into the interior, and I expect to receive orders for the march at any hour. Whilst I was making up my knapsack, this morning, our Balinese friend spoke to me about an admirable little breech-loading carbine which you possess, the very thing I want, and am willing to give any price within my means that you will name.

The carbine was produced, and examined, the officer was in raptures; he had never seen any thing more efficient than the clumsy muskets of the service. This small arm was loaded by raising the chambered breech with a spring, which closed again by the first pull of the trigger. The Dutchman handled it with delight. But the owner regretted to have to say, that it was the only firearm fit for use, that he had on board his vessel, and he did not wish to part with it. A couple of good muskets, as well as a liberal price, were offered; but no, the carbine must stay on board the Flirt; and the topographical captain, failing to secure the object of his visit, went ashore disappointed and in a bad humor.

After the departure of the Dutch officer, the Balinese proposed a visit to the Chinese quarters; he knew a wealthy Chinaman, who possessed one of the improvising verse singers of the country, a curiosity to hear and see; they went, and the circumstances of this visit were thus related on board the Palmer, on the nineteenth day of her homeward voyage from Java.

TWENTIETH DAY.

I WENT with the captain of the barque in a large tambangan manned by his own lascars, quick-handed Buginese boatmen, who threaded a way with nimble skill, among the thronging, bright-polished proas, upon the Moosie, and the many canals of the Chinese campong. We sped with well-plied dayong, past a Chinese josh with curving roof, beyond this beneath a high-springing bridge, like a crescent over the water; then darting under a curiously fashioned house, floating on two rafts, ran along between these, beneath the house floor, till we came to steps which led us at once within the chief room.

A fat, smiling, pleasant-looking little man, with close-shaved shining skull, and long plaited queue, in sack of purple silk, and white silk trowsers of Chinese cut and fulness, met us at the top of the steps; and I was introduced to Teo Chan Beng, one of the wealthy men of Palembang. When seated, on fantastic rattan chairs;—fruits, sweetmeats, and warm tchoo were placed before us. In a little dainty pot, of the measure of a cup of our own table, was tea, that filled the room with fragrance, when poured into the tiny bowls, which Chinamen poise on thumb and fore-finger, and tipping over to the lip, thus love to quaff in dainty drops the soothing drink of their country.

Our host spoke a few words of the trading jargon of Canton,

and a few Chinafied English words; I met none in the East who did not. I had my vocabulary in hand, and with blunders and pantomime, I talked with Chan Beng, as I had done with Arab and Malay,—laughing and learning, as I blundered along.

The Balinese spoke to his friend:—he smiled, and called Sedap,—Sedap; we heard a shrill, sweet voice, then a bound, and in sprang, into the room, with a panther-like leap, a pretty, lithe young creature, a Malay girl, with soft skin, bright eyes, and limbs, that moved and played, and lifted her up like wings, around which a bright scarlet silk sarong her only dress, was gracefully folded.

The master stilled the bounding of the nymph-like slave; for after staying a moment, she was about to leap out again; he drew her gently towards him like a father; he spoke of me; and then my companion said many things; she shook her head; they seemed to urge, and after a time, she stepped out into an open space, the Chinaman took up a *kechapi*,—a small guitar, and tuned forth a simple melody, which Sedap followed with swaying head, with twining arms, and twirling, fingers; and with her soft piping voice.

When the song had ceased, I spoke to her, asking her name, age; the simple things, we ask of a child. She was called Sedap Malam, or Pleasant Night; and she looked like the soft starry sky of her own clime; she had seen twice fourteen monsoons, or fourteen years; she came from the Ulu, far away, where her mother had sung pantuns,—the songs of her country, before her,—Tuan Beng was mother now, and father too; he was a good papa, and she sang for him all the day.

And what was my name? and much more the emboldened nymph now asked, urged on by the jovial host, who laughed with Sedap at the blunders I made. She repeated names, and many

English words, with a justness of accent most surprising, which I thought was owing to a musical ear; but I met with many a Malay afterwards, who uttered the words of our language, though not knowing it, with the utmost truthfulness of tone.

I had heard of Malay minstrels, pouring out pantuns, made as they sang. Sedap was of the inspired race, a Malay improvisatrice. I asked her to sing for me; something never sang before; and what about, said she; some story of Laksamana; ah, no, there was nothing new to be said of him; then of herself: what of the Fair Night? its stars were always the same; then choose yourself; yes, I will sing of something new, of a *juro mudi*, a captain, of *kappal hitam kecheel*, the little black ship. And then with a monotone, yet soft and pleasing, she sang these words as I then partly understood, and were afterwards more fully explained.

THE PANGLIMA OF THE LONG BLACK PRAHU.

1. A black cloud[2] comes up the Moosie;
White clouds[3] are floating above;
The bangu[4] in the swamp,
Flies away with swift wing.

2. Blue eyes[5] shine from the black cloud,
Like machang[6] fierce, like kukur[7] soft.
The moon fades away,
Behind bukit Iskander.[8]

3. A beard floats o'er the black cloud;
Brown like the kandidi's[9] wing.
The hills of the Ulu[10]
Roll down into the Moosie.

4. A voice thunders from the black cloud;
The white ones roll away.[11]
The coolies stay the dayung,[12]
By the Moora Klingie.[13]

5. Tuan besar[14] is eating nassee; [15]
Blue eyes and brown beard by his side.
The nyonya[16] is eating her heart; [17]
Kasih-an[18] the tuan besar.

6. The Wolanda[19] darkens his brow;
Merika,[20] is betuah.[21]
The claws of the Alang[22] are strong,
The rajah-walie[23] has stronger.

7. Who comes with tambangan of Bali;
Brown beard floating o'er the black cloud.
Soft, and breezy days,
Of musim tunggara[24]

8. Sedap Malam is eating her heart;
Blue eyes are shining.
The Panglima of the long black prahu
Must never go down the Moosie.[25]

The songstress sang the last verse with a mirthful look, and as she uttered the last word, sprang with a laugh out of the room. You will understand but little of the spirit of the song from the words I have just given; but I have endeavored to conform as much as possible to the original measure, in which I am aided by retaining many of the Malay words. I will now give you a few notes of explanation which will help you to a better idea of the meaning of the improvised song.

I need hardly tell you that the panglima and the prahu were myself and my schooner[1]; and the black, and white clouds, her hull[2] and sails.[3] The bangu is a large stork.[4] You will observe in this verse, as in the others, little or no apparent connection between the first and second couplet. The great art of the Malay pantun is to conceal a certain subtle connection between the first and second part, which, as in this case, is sometimes skilfully done; but I must say, I could never discover it in many of the Malay pantuns I have heard, which were often unmeaning and absurd.

It will not be necessary to say, whose eyes were complimented, as shining from the cloud; like a tiger[6] fierce, and a turtle dove,[7] soft. The Bukit Iskander, or Hill of Alexander,[8] is a hill about three miles north-east of the town of Palembang, upon which there is a stone shrine, surrounded by a thick grove, which is filled with apes and *tupei* or squirrels, who feed on offerings of fruits and nuts brought to the shrine by superstitious Malays.

This hill is but one among a great number of places in Sumatra which are named after the Grecian conqueror of India. Frequent mention is made in Malay history, traditions, and poetry, of Alexander the Great,—of *Zu'l karnain*, the two-horned, as he is called in the East. It is said that he crossed the Straits of Malacca, and performed many wonderful exploits in Sumatra. All noted places of doubtful origin, are associated with the name of Iskander; the same as in Mexico, where all remarkable places, whose true history is not known, are honored with the name of Montezuma. It is stated in the chronicles of the old empire of Menangkabau that a Malay princess, Sindang Beedok, married a descendant of Alexander, called Patee ; and all the early Sultans of Palembang prefixed Iskander to their other names. Of course, the presence of Alexander in Sumatra must be regarded as fabulous.

But is there not a possibility, said the elder missionary, interrupting the narrator, that Nearchus, the admiral of Alexander, who sailed into the Indian Ocean, and touched at Serendib or Ceylon, also touched upon Sumatra, and left those traditions of the conqueror; or that probably some of his galleys were blown by the Etesian winds, as the Greek admiral called the monsoons, upon the Golden Chersonesus, a name by which Sumatra was known to the ancients?

The commander did not suppose that any Greek galley ever got half the way from the mouth of the Indus to Sumatra. He supposed that the stories about Alexander in the Archipelago, were entirely Hindoo traditions. A large portion of the literature of the Malays, were translations from the Hindoo.

But, said he, I am wandering from the song. The improvisatrice speaks of a kandidi, a kind of snipe[9] which I found exceedingly fat and plentiful at Palembang, and then of the Ulu, or up-country,[10] which tarnishes the waters of the Moosie with its brown soil, during the wet monsoon. The white clouds roll away, the sails are furled;[11] and the schooner comes to anchor; as when the paddle blade,[12] broadside to the stream, checks the boats, at the trading head-quarters on the Klingie.

The "great man,"[14] as all residents are called, is eating rice.[15] By the way, rice claims three names among the Malays; *pahdee*, when rough; *berass*, when cleaned; and *nassee*, when cooked. And as rice is the chief food with them; so to take nassee, is equivalent to taking soup with us, that is to say, dinner. The lady of the great man, the nyonya, as a married woman[16] is called, is eating her heart,—*in love*,[17] and pity on[18] the husband. The allusion to such speedy conquests, are but the common compliments of the Malay language.

The Dutchman[19] of course is angry; but America[20] is not afraid, he is invulnerable;[21] and if the hawk[22] has strong claws, the eagle[23] has stronger. The presence of the stranger that arrived at the house of Chan Beng, was pleasant like the delightful days of the south east monsoon,[24] and Sedap Malam is in love too, like the nyonya, with the captain of the long black ship, who must stay for ever at Palembang.[25]

My interpreting companion informed me, that his friend Beng had bought the girl, when a child, a helpless orphan, from a mercenary relative into whose hands she had fallen. At the age of eight she showed a taste for song, and verse; and when twelve years of age, she had become so much noted, that several panyorangs, Arab, and Malay, had offered large sums for her; but Teo Chan Beng was rich, he loved Sedap Malam as his own child, was careful and watchful over her like a father, for she is not like the common pantun singers and dancers of the country, of doubtful character; he had a merry, honest, good heart entirely unlike nearly all his gross countrymen ; and would not listen to the offer of the sultanate of Palembang, in exchange for his rare singing bird.

I spoke of a letter I had for one Oey Soch Tchay, whom I had not yet been able to find. My host knew him; and in half an hour I was face to face, with a dark, pockmarked, very fat, and very merry Chinaman; and this was Soch Tchay. He was accompanied by a young friend called Pood Djang.

The letter of Lim Boo Seng, which I had carried about me, was now brought forth ; and three bare necks with glossy heads and oblique eyes were craned over the long columns of tea chest marks; whilst various sounds, short bell-like grunts,—chah—hey—wong,—mixed with smiles and nods at me, showed that friend Lim Boo Seng had spoken like a cordial, good reference in his letter of introduction.

My new Chinese friends were urgent that I should visit their own rakit, and after a cordial shake of the hand and assurance of welcome at all times from Teo Chan Beng, I was again threading a way along the canals and among the floating houses on the western side of the Moosie.

Oey Soch Tchay lived in a huge ark, sixty feet long and thirty wide, afloat in a rapid and eddying part of the stream; it was made fast with bamboo cables to bamboo piles, driven into the shoal water, a short way off from the main channel; whilst the end of the dwelling, that lay river-ward, rose and fell like a steamboat ferry bridge, when moved by the swelling or sinking waters.

The raft foundation on which it floated, was like an open logged pen. Around and within this pen, in the water beneath the house and outside, were to be seen a crowd of light yellow and dark brown bodies, plunging and splashing, thrusting arms between the open bamboos, clambering upon them ladder-like, and then leaping back into the stream that rushed beneath the rakit. This was the afternoon hour, when men and boys thus publicly bathed in Palembang's Broadway.

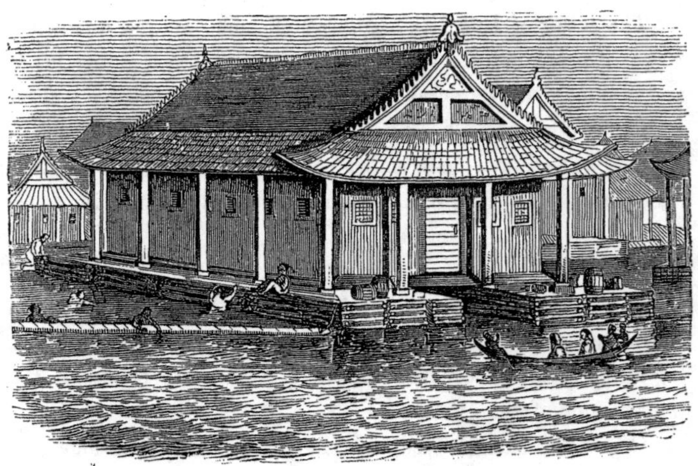

Oey Soch Tchay was wishful to show me his large junk, which made sea voyages; and I learned that his countrymen at Palembang owned eleven square-rigged, European-built ships, barques, and schooners, besides a great many junks and prahus. He sent cargoes of rattans, also tiles, which are well made near this town; also benzoin, damar, pepper, and other merchandise, to Singapore and Batavia.

He had plentiful stores to supply me, as Lim Boo Seng had said, and all needful things of provision, cheap and good. You will not care, at this time, to listen to lists of prices, and other minute particulars of trade; but it may not be dull matter to tell, that I could get a hundredweight of rice for sixty cents, fourteen fat fowls for a dollar, plump snipes and very plentiful, at five Dutch doits, or one cent and a half a-piece; large yams, one hundred for two reals; and fruits—mangosteens, mangos, dookoos, rambutans, and durians, for almost nothing,—a few coppers for the supply of my ship for a day.

Whilst I talked, with a group of curious and good-humored Chinamen around me, who are by no means the dull animals at home they seem abroad;—of a sudden, we heard a floundering in the water,—screams, shouts, and the cry of buaya! buaya! I saw affrighted yellow skins clinging to the bamboos, then I saw a movement and whirl in the water stained with blood, at a point at which the scared bathers were gazing; then a bubble and plunge, and up rose a yellow body with a torn and bleeding leg, and making weakly arm strokes to reach the rakit's side.

The wounded bather, a Chinese youth, about fifteen years of age, was brought into the verandah of Soch Tchay. He had been seized by a large buaya or Sumatran alligator, which are very dangerous to natives, on all rivers, creeks, and lakes of the island, and in among the canals of the town of Palembang; yet rarely, as in this case, venturing to disturb a party of bathers. They said he had tasted of man before; and, like the tiger who had once feasted on human flesh, ever afterwards made more desperate efforts than usual to taste again this new and delicate relish, so much superior to fishes, snakes, monkeys, and water-birds, their usual food.

The youth was fearfully torn from the hip to the knee. Being strong and active, he had struggled hard, and loosened the hold of the monster's jaw, which however had gripped again, at each loosening jerk, and at last had only let go, when a tambangan's prow was launched for the rescue of the struggling victim. The wounded limb was swathed in wetted cloths, as I had observed at the hospital of Minto; and I was told that the mangled flesh I had seen, torn to the bone, would be well and sound in two or three weeks

I took kimlo, tchoo, and tea, with Oey Soch Tchay, and his friend, Pood Djang, and passed a pleasant and entertaining evening with my Chinese friends.

DINNER ON BOARD THE FLIRT AT PALEMBANG.

According to invitation, the Resident of Palembang came to dine on board the Flirt. He was accompanied by the Assistant Resident, the Shahbandar, the commander of the brig of war, the Chief of Commissariat, Major Commandant, and other officers of the garrison.

The schooner was dressed very handsomely for the occasion. A profusion of flags, red, yellow, and tricolored, borrowed from Dutchmen, Arabs and Chinamen, were strung from jib-boom to maintop, whilst the stars and stripes floated from the flag-staff astern.

The white pine main and quarter deck, was holystoned, and made clean and shining like a housewife's cake board; the shrouds newly set up and tarred; the bulwarks fresh painted; the brass mountings of binnacle, and companion way hatch, and the fancy woods of tiller, rail, and skylights, all rubbed and scoured to their highest polish and lustre.

But the cabin was a work of art, an ocean boudoir, rarely seen. When on the coast of Brazil, that land of rare woods, the commander had shipped a lot of mahogany, amarilla, and other finely grained, and fine-colored timber for decoration; also a roll of rich scarlet brocatelle, received as a present for the remnant of ice:—and during the many days passed on the Atlantic, and the Indian Ocean, the taste and fancy of the commander and the skill of a Portuguese carpenter, a choice cabinet workman, were busy in beautifying that cabin.

The state-room, and ward-room of the old man-of-war, now made a saloon of elegant space. The bulkhead, berth stanchions, and sides, were elaborately wrought in woods of various hues, and with tasteful scroll-work and devices. The scarlet brocatelle hung in heavy valence folds around the saloon, and was drawn up at the berths by silken tassels and cords:—brocatelle covered cushions lay on the transom; and the flowered silken drapery hung in rich folds around mirrors and pictures, that completed the decoration of the cabin of the Flirt.

This ornament and beauty of the vessel has been dwelt upon, on account of its having been a cause of such a crowding of visitors to admire it, and had much to do with the after fate of the commander and crew.

The Resident and his officers examined the vessel with critical look. The naval commander pointed out her strength as a battery, and said that such a craft was never meant to sail without guns. The host then led his company into the hold; it was a great empty space, except a few tons of iron lying along the kelson. The naval commander pried about in the forecastle, and under the run of the cabin, but nothing of what he sought was to be seen; yet, still he searched with eager eyes, and struck about with his cane as though he hoped to find some pistols and bowie knives stowed away in the hollow timbers.

Whilst at dinner, the Resident was lavish in praise of the trim and decoration of the schooner. He had often heard how Americans loved to beautify their ocean homes, and make of them floating palaces; and now his conception was more than realized by the tasteful beauty of the Flirt. He wished that his countrymen would trim their broad bowed galliots into somewhat more elegant shape; and pay some attention to decorative naval architecture.

The commander of the guard ship said, that the broad-bowed

galliots were typical of the square and sturdy character of their makers; whilst the American clippers, and these words he said in English, with a coarse leer on his face, owed perhaps "their sharpness to sharpers."

The idea of Dutch grossness is commonly associated with their fleshly build; their breadth of beam, their heavy chops, and protuberance of paunch:—the people of Holland have been usually pictured, as gross built, smoking, sleeping burgomasters; but this is rarely true of the outward man, the grossness is within. These officers on board the Flirt, were all of short or slender make, and had all the outward seeming of gentlemanly propriety of person; but their first acts after greeting the host, were to feel the stuffing of the cushions, to examine the curtains, to scrutinize the table-cloth; and finally to examine the quality and ask the price of every article that he wore.

But none carried this display of vulgar and offensive curiosity so far as the naval commander: his prying and insulting search of a vessel, on board of which he came as a guest, was not noticed; nor some insulting allusions to his host;—but when he made the insulting remark about the countrymen of him who had invited him, he lost the privilege and forbearance due to a guest:—he was met as he had been met before, and thus was harmony once more broken up by this man; and his taunting demeanor was shown on other occasions, until at last, he had an opportunity of gratifying his malignant hatred of every thing American by trampling upon an American flag.

After the visit of the Resident, the commander moved his vessel higher up the river, near where the Ogan, a deep bold stream, pours into the Moosie. Great numbers of the men of note among the Malays of the interior, who had before feared to pass the fort, came to visit the schooner. She was surrounded at times with a fleet of tambangans, penchalangs, and small river craft of all kinds; whilst her decks were covered, and her cabin filled with curious natives.

Men of all ranks, and representatives from all parts of the territory of Palembang, and even of Sumatra, came to see the beautiful American ship; and her commander talked with Panyorangs, Demangs, Tumungungs and other chieftains of the country,—with men from Jambee, Siak, Indraghiri, and with some of the warlike Passumese. Every day of his stay at Palembang was crowded with novelty and incident, among a strange, curious and interesting oriental people. A narrative of the observations made, the conversations held, notes of which being most industriously taken, would embrace much, not only of the history, art, trade, manners, customs, and riches of the territory of Palembang, but of the island of Sumatra. But this book is to be confined chiefly to those incidents of personal adventure related on board the Palmer, which afford a glance at the East Indian Archipelago. One of these incidents, a visit to a Malay chieftain, some of whose friends had been entertained on board the Flirt, was thus related on board the Palmer.

TWENTY-FIRST DAY.

According to the word of a messenger, the day before, a rambayah, or long covered barge, came to bear me to the house of the chieftain, who had sent me some presents of varnished ware and a message of strong desire to see me.

Twelve young men plied the propellers, half paddle, half oar of the rambayah. The song of the steersman with long dayong in hand, followed by the chorus of the coolies, with their dipping blades, fell with a pleasant charm upon my ears, surrounded by Sumatran forests, and gliding over Sumatran waters. On the left bank of the Moosie, we entered a narrow creek, bordered by a dense wall of festooned and matted foliage that rose up from the water's brink some fifty feet on either side. The cocoanut, banana, and mango, spread their limbs in shade overhead and dropped their fruit in the stream. The thick, dropping bounty, the clustering bouquet of beauty; the lavish waste of thrilling aroma; and the babel concert of birds, mingled with the song of the rambayah men, pressed upon every sense, and prepared me with enthusiasm to meet the Malay lord of this jungle beauty and profusion.

On a little bamboo jetty, I beheld a group of many colored silken robes, and large sunshades; and when I could discern the forms and faces of those they robed and shaded, I singled out a chief-like form,—a stately old man,—with mild and venerable expression on his light bronze face. He bowed low, when I stood before him, took my right hand between both of his, called me his son, most welcome to his house, and thus was I received by Panyorang Osman Laksana.

A large company surrounded the Panyorang; young men of his family, some men wielding lances, and a number of coolies; one bearing a huge payung, walked with his broad shade, close behind the chieftain and myself, as we moved, side by side, towards his house.

We came in sight of a group of low buildings; some plaster and bamboo villas, surrounding a central court, and forming a Malayan serai. There were some novel sights to me of atap roofs, of verandahs strung thick with lamps, and other features of a rich Sumatran abode; but one thing chiefly fixed my gaze, —something that had been dimly seen from the water; a lofty pole, a clean cocoa tree trunk stripped of its broad leafed tuft; there on the top of this mast reared up by nature, floated the flag of America.

The Panyorang looked with mirthful pleasure at my surprise. I was curious to know where it came from, and ventured many surmises; but the Panyorang said, that cloth of silk and cotton, and of all colors, was plenty in his country; and skilful hands were not wanting to fashion it into curious flags, as well as handsome robes. Thus I beheld, and I doubt not, for the first time beheld by any one, an American ensign, made by Malay hands unfurled upon Sumatran soil.

As I entered the main dwelling, a salute was fired from some small brass pieces called *lelahs*, which have flaring mouths, like blunderbusses. The Panyorang said that Sumatra gave *selamat sampeh*, the welcome to America.

I found, as in the house of the Arab Panyorang, a succession of floors, ascending from the verandah floor in front. On the inner

and upper one, he seated me, and then himself upon a silk covered settee; the young men and lance bearing followers, sat upon mats, a step below us; whilst the coolies crouched down, with their heads between their knees, on the bare verandah floor.

The walls of the inner room were adorned with inlaid arabesque work, and showed a rich lacquered surface. The bountiful gums of the island, are skilfully applied to dwelling walls, to water skiffs, to wardrobes, and vessels for food of all kinds. They are covered with curious devices, and the lacquer applied with heat, has a fine porcelain surface, long resisting weather and water, and glistening with metallic lustre, as did the chamber walls of this Suma tran dwelling.

The Panyorang was curious to have me explain the use of the vocabulary in my hand. I showed him the alphabetic arrangement; the a, b, c, corresponding with the ailf, ba, ta, of Arabs and Malays. He pointed out various common objects, which I happened to have noted down; and referring to the letter, read out to him the Malay word; and other things he pointed out, the name of which I had not; and then he repeated it, and I wrote it down; the old chieftain looking on with curious eyes, as I inscribed the words he said.

An hour and more he spent, with eager relish, in teaching me. Then he repeated the names and ages of all his people present, and seemed wishful that I should have a record of them. He called, and a young man approached, crouching low, with a reed, ink, and some Chinese rice paper; and as the Panyorang repeated the names of persons, the young man wrote them in Arabic letters alongside of my own writing.

My name was written in various ways, with the peculiar titles of the country prefixed to various portions. Besides names of persons, the names of places were spoken of,—towns and territories in America. The Panyorang was wishful to know if it was as large as Holland.

I took a large piece of paper, and with a reed traced a rude outline of the globe in hemispheres; and as I marked out the continents and countries, the young man, the *juro-tulis*, or scribe, as he was called, wrote in Malay the names of the places I had traced. Beginning with Sumatra, and the other large islands of the Eastern seas, I went on, mapping the countries of Asia, and Africa; and then Europe, the land, I said, of the English, Portuguese, Spanish and Dutch; then after pointing out the Atlantic space of ocean, I drew the outline of the western continent; and showed the Panyorang how great was America.

After tracing the outlines of portions of the world, as far as the curiosity of the Panyorang extended, I presented to him, this rude draft of a map. He received it with a look of much pleasure: he called to some one in an inner room, and an aged woman appeared. This was Nemastiapa, his wife; she held a

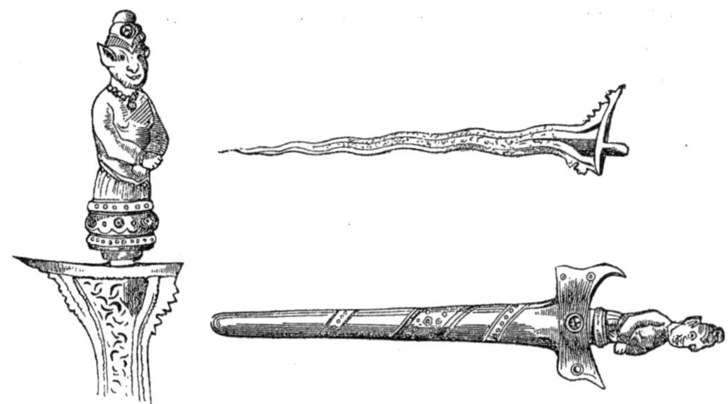

kriss in her hand, which the old chief took from her and presented to me. He said that no man could hurt me whilst I wore it; the point of a hostile kriss would be blunted against me; this one had been made of *besi malela*, of hardest steel, by a cunning hadjy in the sacred city of Menangkabaü. I heard afterwards that some krisses acquired such a reputation on account of some lucky escape from death of the owner, attributed to the influence of the kriss, that they were frequently valued at two and three thousand rupees.

A repast was served up, in dishes of finest wood richly lacquered. Rice and birds were the staple of the meal,—the flesh stewed in cocoanut milk, and the rasped nut mingled with rice, both sweet and salt seasoned. There were savory dishes of beans and bamboo pith; and fruits were served before me, the mangosteen, the nannas, and manga minyala, in their natural state as I thought; but when I took them by their stem, they came apart; and I found their substance finely jellied, and re-enclosed within the original rind.

As we eat, I heard a rude, though pleasantly plaintive music. A troop of matronly women appeared, with Nemastiapa at their head; they all sat down on mats behind the Panyorang; they were followed by three young girls, who placed themselves on the floor, a step below us. These wore a scarlet sarong or skirt, held in its fold and position by a silver girdle, curiously made of many joints, called a *tali pendeng*; the arms and bust were bare, except the partial covering of wreaths of white odorous flowers, the fragrant kumbang melati, or flower of love, which were twined in rich clusters, among plaits of their glossy, jewel-bedecked hair; and these were *menyanyee*, the singing girls of the country.

They stood forth in postures, their flexible arms doubling backward almost as far as forward; and their fingers, tipped with curved silver points, played with fantastic motion; and thus without any movement of feet, except, from time to time, a change of position, they swayed their bodies, they twined their arms, and twirled their fingers in all the mazes of the Sumatran ronggeng dance.

This posturing was accompanied by the kechapi, and the karonchong, a gingle of small bells; and after a while the voices of the girls, chanting songs of love and war, kept time with the mazy play of their limbs. The voices sounded shrill and sharp, the usual tone of these singing girls of the Malays; and not soft and tuneful like the notes of Seedap Malam, who gave forth a melody I heard nowhere else in the East.

Two men stepped forward, their heads covered with a yellow cloth, that hung down like a veil. They joined in song with the girls; they all took parts in some story of warriors, evil genii, or *djins*, and princesses; a *palawan*, or hero loved; and a *tuan putree*, a royal Malay lady was won; a magician scowled upon the happy state; by evil spells he seized and bore away, through air, the hapless lady; the hero finds a *widadiri* (or *bidiyadiri*), a Malay wood nymph; he obtains a charm, regains the beauteous putree, and thus the *wayang*, or Sumatran opera is performed.

When the play and song had ceased, I took some money to present to the girls, having heard from my Bali friend, that it was expected of guests to pay for all such entertainment, by gifts to these wandering minstrel performers; but the Panyorang, observing the movement of my hand, motioned with earnest and dignified expression of face, to put back my gift. He had invited his son as a friend. He was not an Arab, or Chinese trader.

Whilst we sipped tea, and eat of *manisan*, various sweetmeats, at the close of the repast, the young man, the juro tulis, took the place of the ronggengs, and sat down crosslegged upon a mat, with a manuscript in his hand, from which he read with a drawling monotone, yet a somewhat pleasing sound. He read of ancient wars, heroes and princesses; of which I understood but little then; but afterwards learned that it was concerning the Javanese conquest of Palembang.

Browijoyo, one of the most powerful Sultans of the great Empire of Madjapahit in Java, made war upon the people of Palembang and conquered them; and his son Aria Damar became Sultan of the country. One of his race married Patee, the descendant of Alexander and of an Indian princess, who had gone in quest of the conqueror to ask the honor of being the mother of a race of heroes; these were Patee and his descendants down to Badr Oodin, and many princes and princesses, who now wandered in the Ulu; but a day of deliverance was near, a Secunder Zulkaram; some tradition promised hero was coming, the Wolanda would be driven out, the royal race would return to the *astana malaghay*, the palace of their forefathers, and the blood of Iskander and Browijoyo would sit enthroned once more by the waters of the Moosie.

Then the juro tulis recited some verse in a quicker, more song like tone. His story was about rakshashas, or huge, hairy giants; of wicked djins; and of *dewi* and *widadiri*, the lovely forest and mountain nymphs of the beautiful olden Malay mythology, which, like the Greek, peopled the streams, and caves and tree-tops with young virgin forms, who faithfully watched over mankind to defend them from the foul spirits of the sea and air.

The juro tulis told of a rajah, Chindeh Balang, a prince of the Passumah, who had three daughters: Sareena, gracious; Chayah, light; and Seenee, delicate limbed; who were married to three Panyorangs of hideous form and evil mind, called Kandung, humpbacked; Berbulu, hairy; and Binchee, the hateful; whom the father dared not to refuse, by reason of their power and ferocity. The good rajah died, and his sons-in-law went to war, the one with the other, in dividing the lands and the people of Chindeh Balang; and after a time, these wicked princes called in the aid of some hideous djins of the sea to whom each one promised the gold, cinnamon and other precious things of the country, if they might have the strongest youths and fairest maidens of the Passumah.

These djins came and took the gold and cinnamon and other precious things; and made slaves of all the people themselves; and the evil Panyorangs too, who were shut up in iron cages and sent across the sea to Ternate. The sea djins drove far away all of the race of Chindeh Balang, and said; our rajah shall be rajah instead; but the people of the Passumah loved the memory of Chindeh Balang, they groaned under the rod of the sea devils, and they fled to the cave of the Bukit Dempoh for a refuge.

A widadiri, resplendent as *din'ari*, and softly lovely as *silam* (the morning and evening twilight), appeared before the people of the Passumah, upon a white elephant, bearing a beautiful child in her arms, which she said was the daughter of the princess Retna Komala, the Precious Gem of the Redjang Tinga (a district on the head waters of the Moosie), and of a long-lost son of Rajah Chindeh Balang. Its life had been sought by the three bad Panyorangs; but the princess had confided her daughter to an old woman, a *dukun*, who lived at the foot of Pemalang Kambing, where the widadiri had watched the growth of the child; and she now brought her to strengthen the hearts of the people of the Passumah Ulu Manna; and that they might now take charge of their rightful sovereign, Zaydee Komala, the Flawless Gem.

This grand-daughter of Chindeh Balang grew up more lovely than all the virgins of the Passumah; and the people watched over her in the Ulu that she might not fall into the hands of the dark-minded djins of the sea. Whilst she lived, the pirates would have no peace in the lands of the Passumese; for these loved their royal race, and would give tribute and service to no other, and thus the minstrel sang of this fair princess.

ZAYDEE KAMALA

Illustrious Princess; Flawless Gem;
Beautiful Night in the Ulu.:
Bright Rays of morning light,
Shining on Gunung[1] Dempoh.

Face of the moon, fourteen days old;
Hue of gold, ten times refined,[2]
Hearts of men of Passumah,
Fuller than coffers of Company.

The kancheel[3] gave its form;
The melati stem its bend;
Melati[4] blooms no fragrance,
By the Flower of Ulu.

Flawless Gem of Passumah;
Dazzling eyes of men,
Modest eyelash drooping,
Like the Waringin[5] shade.

Tender voice of the laweet[6]
Moaning the absent mate:
Proud voice of white-maned waves,
Lashing Karang[7] Nagosurie.

Light of eyes; Substance of heart[8];
Life of the fainting soul;
Allah blesses; men adore
Flawless Gem of Passumah.

The mountain[1] of Dempoh, where the princess resided, being so lofty, rugged and inaccessible, is a favorite asylum for mythic nymphs and persecuted ladies, whose highest standard of beauty in the estimation of Malay poets is the round face and the golden skin.[2] The little musk deer,[3] a perfect one, not larger than a rabbit, when full grown, bounds among the crags of Dempoh; whilst the smooth slopes are fragrant with the small cream white, festival flower[4] of the Malays; flourishing under the Sumatran banyan,[5] whose drooping limbs, touching earth or rock, put forth roots where leaves once grew, and other columns appear, supporting the great forest temple roof.

The sea swallow,[6] which collects a certain weedy gum, exuding from ocean rocks, to build those nests eaten by the people of China, utters a sweet plaintive note, when parted from its mate; and the coral ledges[7] of Nagosurie, are said to be a favorite resort of these industrious little victims of the sensual Chinese appetite.

The minstrel pitched his voice to harsh or plaintive tone, as he read of love or war: he rocked his body, he waved his hand; and men and women, youths and coolies, slid off their mats, and drawing near, with swaying heads, and moving hands, kept pace with limb and sympathetic look to the songs of their land, the sagas of Sumatra.

When he had ceased, I wished to see the manuscript from which he read. I saw an old scroll in Arabic script; and these were the chronicles of Browijoyo, Madjapahit and Palembang; but where was the story of the princess of the Passumah? The minstrel had it in his head alone, to which he pointed. Zaydee Komala is not yet dead; and wherefore should her *hakiyat*, history, be written. She wanders upon the white elephant in the Ulu;

she sails in the rambayah on the Moosie, whilst her *mantri*, minister, the rajah Tiang Alam, *Pillar of the World*, fights the foul djins of the sea, the Wolanda of Palembang.

What was all this story of seeming fact mingled with fable? I could not learn from Panyorang or pantun singer; but from all their words, I learned that the princess was not a Malay myth, although the widadiri and elephant might be. Somewhere in the forests there roamed one of the royal race of the princes of the Passumah.

The Panyorang rose, and motioned me to follow him. As we retired, the company fell upon the food we had left. My host led me into a small chamber, with richly varnished walls, and floor made of bamboo slats, fine polished and well jointed; in which for only furniture, I saw a thick, soft mat and a pillow, by which lay a loose cotton coat or kabyah, loose striped trowsers, and embroidered slippers; pointing to these, the Panyorang said, take a little sleep; and left me to enjoy the eastern siesta.

* * * * * * *

I have heard, said the younger Missionary to the commander, frequent mention of the pantuns and improvised songs of the Malays; but that the subjects of them were generally lewd and very puerile.

Such an opinion, it was said in reply, might be formed from what was generally seen and heard of Malays, in Singapore, Batavia, Pinang, and all other places where European influence was felt, and European habits prevailed. There the Malay was never called upon, except for impure dance and silly song. All Europeans had the same desire,—the ship owner and the captain, as well as the drunken sailor,—to bid the Malay man fight his beasts and his fowls; and the Malay woman, like Hindoo and Hawaian, to transcend the license of their pagan life; as in our own great marts of commerce, the countrymen and the stranger, were the chief patrons of the city vice.

But the highest races of the Malays of Sumatra, the Battahs, the people of the north-western coast, and of the Passumah, were a people that possessed much virtue; remarkable in the women, who in many a recorded instance, had defended their honor with kriss in hand. Among them, the history of wars and noble loves; of heroes, and fair and faithful women, were the common themes of their wandering minstrels. Sumatra, that is only thought of along with tigers, pirates, and pepper, is perhaps the last refuge of romance on earth.

The pantuns, or proverbial expressions in rhyme, are what their poets take most pride in producing. They generally show but very little logical connection; and, the same as in all their writings, there is a tedious repetition of names; but they abound in poetical descriptions and comparisons.

The rest of the incidents that occurred at the house of the Panyorang, were the subject of the narration of another day.

TWENTY-SECOND DAY.

As I lay in the siesta room, thinking over early dreams of the land I now lived in, I heard a low plaintive sound of women's voices, a wailing, mourning tone, that struck with touching pathos on my ear. Although I felt imprisoned till my host should return, I stepped a little forth from an outer door, to listen to the soft womanly chant, that seemed like some song of woe over a dead or dying child.

The wail changed to a lullaby tone, brisker, livelier and happier; that still drew me on nearer, to hear the notes of joy or woe, that broke on the siesta hour. I sat down beneath a cluster of the odorous *burung darah*, its blooms like their name, white doves on the wing. The fragrance of flower, the melody of voice, the strangeness of scene, flowed over my heart with stirring power: I bowed my head in revery, I heard the word, *anak*, my son; I looked up; and the majestic Panyorang stood before me.

Thinking of eastern etiquette and seclusion, I feared that I had stepped beyond the privilege of hospitality. My son is curious, said the old man; but his heart is white: does he come to smell the pigeon flower; or listen to the prayers of my women and children, who chant the *ngasar*, the afternoon prayer, to Allah?

I had thought I heard a lament for sickness, or a lament for death: it was not less pleasing to listen to a lament for sin, and a song of praise. The Panyorang said, follow, my son; you shall see as well as hear. He paused at the door of the room, from whence the sounds came forth; and I heard that solemn refrain of every moslem prayer; Oh God, the merciful, and the loving kind.

The Panyorang paused till the chant had ceased; and then he opened the door; and we stood in an oblong chamber, without ornament, besides its varnished walls, some lamps, a mirror, and eleven mats, upon all of which, but one, women of various ages were seated. Nemastiapa was there, and several matrons whom I had seen before; but there were younger forms and faces: three whom the Panyorang called his grandchildren; beautiful girls; beautiful as sun-browned children of Sumatra;—eyes with soft, tender and modest expression; and complexion of a mingled lustre of gold and bronze, soft and most pleasing to look upon.

The Panyorang bid them rise and called them by name; and he bade me take my vocabulary and pencil in hand.

Sareena, the gracious, was tall like a palm; and had large drooping eyelashes; Oombah, the swell of the sea, was plump, and merry in expression; Ledah manis, sweet lip, was so timid, that she hid her face, all the time that I turned my eyes towards her.

When he had repeated these names, with the ages of each, he looked around the room for some one else. Where was the *kambing utan*, the little wild rock deer. Afraid, said Nemastiapa: she fled when she heard the footsteps of the lord Captain, with my lord at the door: she had watched from the window: the wild rock deer is very mischievous.

The Panyorang called: a sliding sound was heard of the *charpoo*, the Malay lady's gold and bead embroidered slipper, with sole of soft, woody pith. A rustle of silk, and then I saw a pliant figure, small and graceful, moving with wave-like motion: the face of a maiden was before me, not so youthful, not so pretty and not so delicate in its outline, as the three I have named; but lively, curious, and beams of soul touched those plainer lines, such as I had seen in no Malay face before.

Her dress,—and I describe the others in hers, was the *kain sarong*, or skirt, of salmon colored silk, held in its folds by a *tali pendeng*, or girdle of gold, of pure gold, and commonly worn by Malay women of wealth, some weighing fifteen, and even twenty ounces: an oval plate, of *korangan*, filagree work, for which Sumatrans are famous, adorned it in front; the bust was veiled by a *choolee*, or scarlet bodice, bound by glistening gems; the *kabyah*, or outer robe, of flowered muslin, fell half way between the waist and feet: diamonds, not pendent, but stuck to the lobe of the ear, and long, diamond-headed pins, completed the toilette of Sahyoop, or Sahyeepah, the winged one, the grand-daughter of Panyorang Djaya Laksana. The Panyorang said that the antelope was not so beautiful as the palm tree, the wave, or the sweet lip; because she has the blood of Java. Her father, Wirojoyo, was of Cheribon, whither he had now gone with merchandise.

The old chieftain spoke for some time to the women about my ship, my country; and then he took pains to explain the use of my vocabulary. Again he asked me to say words and sentences in my own language, which he desired his grand-daughters to repeat; and all, like Seedap Malam, pronounced them well; but best of all by Sahyeepah; who was cunning and skilful, said Nemastiapa.

I asked the names of each article of dress, which Sahyeepah quickly gave me; and as all the others ceded to her in answering, a dialogue sprang up, between me and the skilful one alone: the

Panyorang, and the women, looking on with curious and admiring interest.

Had I a mother, sister, wife or daughter? these were now, as often with Malay and Javanese women, the first questions asked. Then my questioner spoke of *Wolanda*, Dutchmen; were they strong in my country, and did they invade the land, as in Pulo Percha; they were hateful and ugly: they treated the people of Islam like dogs; they were ugly as orang kubu.

The mention of orang kubu recalled to mind the creatures of the covered creek; and I spoke to the Panyorang about them. He stepped out of the room, making sign to me to follow. We

approached some outer sheds, *kandang*, or stables for buffalo. I saw coolies at work, some digging pits and trenches; others trimming and sharpening bamboo poles, and engaged in other labor for the erection of an addition to the kandang.

I heard some one cry *lakass*, quick and harsh, as though urging a beast; *yuh!* a grunt from a gruff voice in reply. An orang kubu, said the Panyorang; and I saw a dark brown form, tall as a middle-sized man, covered with hair, that looked soft and flowing; the arms, hands, legs and feet, seemed well formed like the Malays; the body was straight; and easily bore, on the right shoulder, the yoke of two heavy panniers, filled with material for the building that was going on.

The Panyorang gave me some of the same particulars about the orang kubu, that were told to me by the Dutch officer on the Soonsang, to which he added some of the fable, that surrounds every eastern, and especially Malay account of any thing.

These were *tai orang*, the refuse of men: they were the descendants of some slaves of Alexander, who had fled from their master. They could tell nothing of their forefathers; they could only speak some short grunting words; and one syllable only of Malay words they could repeat:—nassee, rice, being *nass* with them; and *yan* for orang. They were brutes, they had no worship, no marriage, no law, no clothing, no idea of its use; they were the accursed of Allah, companions of djins on earth; fit only to be beasts of burden; and the Malays hunted them and caught them in pits and tree tops; and made slaves of them, as of right, said the Panyorang, all beings ought to be, who are inferior to men.

The eyes of this Kubu were clearer, the nose fuller, and the lips were thinner than those of the common Malay, but the mouth was wide, lips protruding, and chin formed no part of the hairy face; yet it was pleasantly human in its expression; more so than the dirty, mottle-skinned lascars and coolies I had seen at Minto and Palembang.

Was this then some lower grade of human being, some connecting link, between man and beast, more human than orang utan, or chimpanze; and less so than Papuan or Hottentot? I could not say so from what I saw, nor from all the strange stories I heard. But that beings of well made human form, covered with hair, almost without speech, and living on raw food, dwell in the caves and tree tops of the forests of Sumatra, are facts that are well established.

The Panyorang said that the Sultan of Jambee had a great many Kubu slaves. They were to be found in the rich gold region of Korinchee, as well as in the gum benzoin forests, on the Batang Lekoh. Jambee and Kubu, had become leading objects of curiosity with me; and I questioned the Panyorang much about them.

The old Sultan of Jambee, Mohamed Pachroodin, and his brother, the Panyorang Ratoo Marta Ningrat, had made a contract with the Dutch company, which secured to the latter the monopoly of salt, and in which provision was made for the return of the fugitive slaves of either party; and stipulating for the establishment of a trading post at Moorah Kompeh, near the mouth of the Jambee River; but the son of Pachroodin, the present Sultan, Ratoo Abduhl Nasroodin, was opposed to the contract of his father, disliked the Dutch, and would have no trade or friendship wth them.

The river Jambee was navigable as far as the kraton of the Sultan, about seventy miles from the mouth, for vessels of three or four hundred tons burthen. The country abounded in gold, pepper, camphor, cinnamon, nutmegs, benzoin and other rich commodities, which the Sultan and the traders of his country wished to exchange in freedom with Americans or English; but the Dutch had planted some guns at Moora Kompeh; and although they could not get the trade themselves, they would not let it descend the river to go to Singapore; or let traders ascend to take it at Jambee. They were ravenous beasts, over-gorged with the plunder of *tanah Jawa*, the land of Java; yet they would not allow another to touch in Pulo Percha, what they could not devour. The Sultan of Jambee was independent, and any one might go to see him, who was not afraid of the Dutch at Moora Kompeh.

Jambee was on the way to Singapore. I wanted to go and see a Prince, who was not surrounded by the trammels of European power. I wanted to see the Malay, the ruling race of the Archipelago, in his highest state of independence; and I wanted to see more of the Kubu, and Gugur, the lowest of human kind in those islands, or in the world; and far more than to get gold and spices, did I want to find out, what were their claims to the family of man; and on which side of the line of demarkation between man and brute, did they stand.

I took my leave of the Panyorang Djaya Laksana. I have given the pleasantest picture of all that I observed of him and his family. I have not spoken of what I saw of lazy or dirty habits: more to be seen than among enlightened and wealthy Europeans, but far less than among poor ones. I have wished to introduce you to the Malay mind, taste and imagination; you have heard enough from others about their gambling and treachery, their filthy betel chewing, and their black teeth.

I saw something of this, at the house of the Panyorang, to spoil a good deal of interest; but I saw pleasant smiles of welcome all the time of my stay. I saw a row of pleasant faces on the verandah on leaving; and when I turned to depart, I heard the *selamat djalan*, safety on the way, sent from the mouth of

Sahyeepah, and as I stood in the rambayah, the Panyorang pointed to the flag that still floated from the cocoanut tree top; and said, Think of me, my son, in America.

* * * * * * *

The elder missionary felt an unsatisfied curiosity about the orang Kubu, and the orang Gugur, beings, whose existence gave rise to one of the most profoundly interesting questions for humanity. The commander had felt deeply interested in obtaining a thorough enlightenment, with regard to the habits and condition of these hairy men; he had resolved to visit the haunts of the Kubu on the Rawas and the Batang Lekoh. And with this resolve in view, he had not taken that pains to observe the few specimens of these beings to be found at Palembang, which he would have done, had he not had in view a farther and better opportunity to study them.

It would be useless to repeat, except as amusing fable, the extravagant stories related by Malays and Arabs, about many savage, aboriginal races, to be found in Sumatra, and disputing the jungle with the elephant, the tiger, and the innumerable family of monkeys; but it is singular, that on this great island, where nature has displayed herself most magnificent, beautiful and luxuriant in vegetation; most terrible and powerful in the brute creation, she should have made the original lords of this soil, the most abject on earth; and of doubtful superiority over many of man's wild vassals of the forest.

The Malays are not the aboriginals of Sumatra; although it is known as the chief seat of their race; for within a period commencing many hundred years after the beginning of our era, the first Mal-ayes, mountaineers, or Mal-ayans, wanderers, set foot on the great island, to which, owing to the course it lay, they designated as *barat sama utara*, N. N. West; and the latter words have been readily corrupted into Samatara, and Semantara, by natives; and to Sumatra by Europeans. Pulo Percha, the strip, or ribbon island, is a name now generally used by the common people; and Indalas is another name of the island to be met with in poetry.

Innumerable stories are told of giants, dragons, and nations of apes, who disputed with lower beasts the dominion of the soil, before the arrival of the great Polynesian wanderers: and Arab merchants, who probably traded on the coasts of Sumatra during the classic ages, seeking to guard their monopoly by cunning, which has been done later by force, carried to Europe those stories of fabulous monsters, who guarded the cinnamon and frankincense; which gave such an exaggerated value to those commodities in the estimation of the credulous western world; and led the historians and geographers of ancient Greece to people many islands of the eastern ocean with anthropophagi and hideous cyclopean forms.

The Greeks have been blamed for their proneness to invest the Eastern world with the fictions of eastern imagination. All accounts of the west, wore the simple garb of truth ; and even the fabled Hesperidean isles, were the abodes of a fair, simple and happy race; whilst the East, the cradle of humanity, was filled with the distortions of inventive brains, wrought out of the myths of Eastern imagination. But was the so-called fable of Ctesias about the dog-faced people of Budtan, who eat raw flesh and rubbed their bodies with oil, stranger than that of the hairy and chinless kubus, who rub themselves with gum?

The Greeks were perhaps too easily influenced by the Hindoos, in yielding credence to a belief in the existence of lower grades of mankind, connecting links between the human and brute creation, but however repulsive such an idea, and however much apparently disproven by ethnological research; yet the contemplation of such hideous, mindless abortions of humanity, as the beastly, herding Papuans, the wow-wows of Borneo, like the Cynocephali of the Macedonian traveller, the woolly Semangs of Malacca, and lower still the Kubus and Gugurs of Sumatra, is well calculated to humiliate the mind of the philosopher, and make him think of the possibility of the existence of varieties of the human form, where the existence of a reasoning soul is problematical.

* * * * * * *

When the commander returned to his vessel, he learned from his sailing-master many interesting particulars, confirming previous accounts about the Sultan and territory of Jambee. He had met with the master of the Arab ship Maimoon, who was formerly a sailor on board the Royalist, the yacht of Sir James Brooke, and was in his service, when rajah of Serawak.

This man had visited Jambee; and had spoken with the Sultan, who disliked Hollanders, and was friendly to the English of Singapore. An American ship would be welcomed the same as an English one; and as the monsoon was about to change, the Flirt might make the run down the Moosee and Soonsang, and ascend the Jambee, in less than four days. But it would be advisable to send a messenger with a friendly note, and some small complimentary gift before going there.

A good Malay scribe was wanted to write a proper message; and one had been wanted, for some time, to read Malay manuscript, history and verse, and to teach correctly the high Malay, for which the man Bahdoo was found to be entirely unfit. To obtain one, the commander had spoken to several officers of the garrison of Palembang, the same as he had done to obtain a servant at Minto.

He went ashore, and met the Major Blommestein, to whom he

mentioned his wish to engage a good Malay writer and scholar in his service. The Major would inquire. The commander went a second day, and the scribe he wanted was found; but he was surprised to see in the young man brought before him, the reader and pantun singer he had met at the house of the Panyorang. Yet it was not to be considered strange; the man wandered about to write and relate pantuns and stories for the rich: he had come to sing for the officers of the fort, and so the juro tulis, Kiagoos Lanang, was engaged to teach high Malay, to write messages to princes and chieftains, and to go if he wished to Singapore.

Bahdoo had brought one of his countrymen on board the schooner, a man from Padang, called Moonchwa; he was a foster brother of Bahdoo, and they wished so much to be together: he wanted but little pay, enough for daily rice and a new sarong; so the commander added Moonchwa to his two other Malay retainers.

The commander became intimate with many officers of the garrison of the fort at Palembang. He visited them in their quarters, and they spent a great deal of time on board his vessel; and Dutch officers were daily intermingled with natives of rank, coming to admire the beauty of the Flirt, but the Major Blommestein was most frequently associated with the commander. This officer was born in the East Indies; and had strong sympathies with the native races of the Archipelago: he was frank and intelligent, and spoke freely about his Government and the state of affairs in the East.

Some of these Malay men of rank, these Panyorangs whom you meet with, said the Major to the commander, are courteous and agreeable men; but the greater portion are lazy and vicious. Some cultivate a taste for letters: they all read the Koran, and have a respectable knowledge of Arabic, which is their classic language, as with all other Mahometans. They are of the sect of

Alides; but you must have observed that Islamism merely exists in form, and is mingled with a great deal of the old pagan superstition, so much like the mythology of the Greeks. The Malays of Palembang repeat the formal prayers of the Koran at the prescribed times, and observe the fast of the Ramazan very rigidly; but they seldom frequent their messigheet or mosque, which is chiefly attended by Arabs. They drink wine and beer freely with Europeans;—and the Malay gentleman—for there are many who would realize that character in the best European society—is a good liver, and a free thinker; and a very pleasant and hospitable entertainer.

POSITION OF THE WOMEN OF SUMATRA.

There are no social, nor any other kind of restrictions imposed upon the women: they are as free as the men, to go abroad publicly, to see and be seen, to transact business, to travel, to marry when and whom they choose, and more than all to become sovereigns in many states of Sumatra, and elsewhere in the Archipelago.

The *rayat*, or masses of the Malay people, have ever manifested a decided preference for female rule. Malay women have furnished instances for history, of a lofty patriotism. The uniform mildness and prosperity, attendant upon their sway, as contrasted with the cruelty and rapacity of the male rulers;—ever ready to sell their country for a few gewgaws of ornament and parade, has resulted in a decided preference in various portions of the Archipelago for the elevation of women, especially maidens, to the sovereignty; and this beautiful and chivalrous homage to women and virginity has been chiefly maintained by Boni in Celebes; and by Achin in Sumatra, that once proud state, which received an ambassador from a sovereign of England, and sent its hundred thousand warriors under Laksamana against Malacca; and is now the only truly independent state on the island.

Female divinities, for all that is good is feminine among Sumatrans, still people the forests and mountain recesses. Every deep-shaded waringin, or thick-tufted bamboo, every glen and cleft and cool recess, is tenanted by a widadiri, those celestial maidens, the nymph, the sylph, the dryad, and houri of the Malay.

Although the machinery of good and evil genii belong to a system of belief long abolished; yet they still exist in the legends of the land. In the superstition of the people, every person of note has some spiritual agency attending their birth; and whatever is surrounded with the slightest mystery, or whatever it is desired to invest with any especial interest, has been the object of the protection of the widadiri.

With stories of this kind, the chieftains who oppose us rally the people around them. The rajah Tiang Alam, who has stirred up the tribes of the Ampat Lawang in the territory of the Passumah against the Dutch Government, was of the condition of a slave not more than three years ago; yet by ingenious stories, making himself the protected of the good spirits of the country, and the protector of some pretended offspring of their old princes, he has gained the sympathies and support of the people; and been enabled to carry on a warfare that has been highly destructive to our interests in Sumatra, and threatened the stability of our hitherto strong position on the island.

One of the stories of Tiang Alam, is about a certain princess, called Zaydee, or Sahdeeah Komala; common names in Malay romance, and often given to wandering singers and dancers; for I have met with two Sahdeeahs at Palembang of that class. But the people firmly believe that some of the descendants of the old Madjapahit dynasty, and of the family of the late Sultan Badroodin, still wander in the fastnesses of the Ulu; and will be restored to the ancient throne by Tiang Alam, when he shall have driven us away.

I have often heard of this princess Zaydee Komala, and if the Malays did not mingle so much fable with every thing they relate, I should be inclined to think, from report, that she was a very interesting personage, and worthy of the homage so often accorded to their royal women; but from my own knowledge, I could not say whether this Zaydee is a pantun singer or a princess.

After leaving the Major, the commander spoke with Kiagoos Lanang about the lady of his song: she was indeed, he said, a real princess; and lived not far off; but a slave like him dare not approach her presence; and thus he had not seen her; but if the tuan, his master, should desire to behold the Flower of the Passumah, he would speak with a hadjy, who was a slave of the princess.

Some time afterwards, this hadjy, a very dark complexioned Malay Arab, whose name was Zenodeen, came on board the Flirt to signify the wish of Mantri, the Minister of the princess, who wished to see the American Commander, and speak with him about his mistress. A rambayah would be sent down the river; he must trust himself alone; and this visit to the wandering Malay young lady was thus related on board the Palmer, on the twenty-third day of her homeward voyage from Java.

TWENTY THIRD DAY.

AGAIN, with song and dipping blades, I sped along the waters of the Moosee, whither led, and to whom, I knew not; but urged by many stories of seeming fact and fiction; so strangely mingled, that I wished to see what ground there was for the pleasant Malay romance; or the Dutchman's plainer story.

The sun had set when I came in sight of two large rambayahs at anchor in the stream; each of size to carry one hundred men. They were covered with an atap awning roof; and curtains of dark cloth enclosed the sides around: a gong gave signal of our approach; a portion of curtain at the forward end of the largest barge, was raised up; I saw Zenodeen in gay scarlet dress, with a huge kriss in his girdle; and could hardly recognize the dirty hadjy I had seen before, in the armed and jewelled warrior I now beheld.

These first sights,—the warlike barges, and the armed pilgrim, made me think that I had been led into a pirate trap, where I should be held to ransom; but Zenodeen gave me little time to dwell on suspicions of evil design. A cloth-covered plank was placed for me to step on board the large rambayah; the hadjy led the way aft, through a number of oarsmen and women: we approached a scarlet curtain; he clapped his hands; it parted; and then I beheld a scene of curious pomp and beauty.

Amid many pendant lamps, like lighted lotus cups, softly shaded with an odorous incense cloud from burning benzoin; amid yellow and scarlet robes, of glittering gems, and many pretty bright, golden-hued faces, was one more soft and noble; of fine Arab type in many lines, of curving nose, thin lips, rounded chin, and proud setting of the neck; but softer ones, of Passumah poesy, marked the swelling brow with its downy border, at the base of the massive mount of glossy hair, that rose with magnificent sweep, crowning a noble domain of beauty, and dignified womanly grace, which had fittingly been named the Flawless Gem.

In words of most pleasant tone, she gave me the usual words of welcome: she spoke of my long voyage, coming so far without merchandise, alone to see the people of Pulo Percha; and did many men in my country feel good will to this land; and wish to give happiness to Malays? she had heard from the hadjy, that my country was very great, greater than Holland; and that I stood near the rajah of America when at home.

I had ceased to marvel at Malay magnification of my position and purposes after meeting with Dutch exaggeration of the objects of my presence in the Archipelago. So fanciful a personage, with such a pretty little ship, had never been seen in these seas before; and if the Dutch would have me to be a commodore in disguise, I could not be surprised that this Malay lady should suppose, that I was some high courtier, an American Mantri, or secretary of state, and confidential envoy of the rajah of America.

A tall and venerable man, with white beard, and robed in black and green, wished to know if American ships would not go up the Moosee and the Jambee rivers to buy spices, and cotton, which grew plentiful in the Passumah: the people would not sell to the Dutch; then would not American merchants come here, and make good trade, and wealth for themselves; the same as at Singapore? And of course, I told him that I should tell my

countrymen, who loved trade very much, all about what he said when I returned home This was Mantri Wira Menggala.

Zenodeen had received some sign of command; he clapped his hands, a space was cleared, and three girls came forward to improvise some words of compliment, about my visit; and at the same time, some vessels of the peculiar manufacture of Palembang, were placed before me, made of fine wood and of richest lacquer work; spherical, oval, and oblong, shaped and colored like fruit; and when I touched the fruit-like stems, I discovered lids and then receptacles full of jellied pulp of fruits, and spiced cakes of rice and cocoanut of great variety.

The minstrels were dressed as I had seen before, but I saw no adornment of flower wreaths, chaplets, and crowns of the kumbang melati. The glossy black hair, well combed back, left full to view the round, swelling forehead, bordered with a fringe of fine downy curls;—the small thin ear; and all of the mild and expressive face of the well-favored Malay female. One of these I now saw, struck me as having been seen before; but I could not remember where, and a glance of recognition seemed to flash from the eyes of the singing girl.

Of all that was sung, the greater part was lost to me this time; for I did not afterwards, as I had on the occasion of other singing, meet with any explaining interpreter. The smiles at certain parts, the nodding looks towards me, and a few understood words, told that compliment mingled largely in the song.

Then one sung alone, the one whose looks spoke of some past meeting, I knew not where. Her words, repeated slowly, and in the common Malay, I understood better. She sang something of Dutchmen, of officers with burning eyes; and faces, red and swollen with strong water, as a storm-setting sun. They uttered big words, they bellowed like devils, they struck poor slaves, helpless women, whose souls were gone, there was no heart of life left in them; as they lay in an evil abode; when Allah opened a door; his face was like a man; not like Wolanda, not like Arab, nor any seen before: like the grey cloud and blue sky, hanging over Dempoh.

At the first words of the song I recalled to mind the prisoners of the rakit. But the princess gazed with inquiring look; and the hadjy scowled, as the song went on. When it ceased, the princess spoke, and Zenodeen replied in words I could not understand. The singing girl fell prostrate, and seemed to implore protection from the anger of the hadjy.

What mystery was here: the hapless and innocent maidens, the shrinking victims of the night scene by the fort; now public players: the procuring hadjy then told of; and the disturbed and angry hadjy now before me. What foul play, left unrevealed until my presence brought it forth; and what part in this, had Zaydee Komala; and what was there true or feigned, in all this scene of hadjys and mantris, pantun singers and the princess? were thoughts that arose, whilst the singing girl plead, the hadjy explained and the princess frowned.

The hadjy retired; and the Mantri spoke again, he talked of battles in the Ampat Lawang between Tiang Alam, and the troops of the company; of men and forts in the interior, and of great stores of trade for American merchants, who would ascend the Moosee: to which I could only reply as before, that I would report his words on my return to America.

I had brought with me a Mexican topaz, large and of fine color, a piece of scarlet brocatelle, some vials of essences, and an engraving of Lady Blessington in a gilt frame: these were laid before the princess; she smiled on looking at the picture; it must be my wife, no; the wife of the rajah of America; not so; then it must be some princess I designed to take to my house, by and by; and as I did not wish to say that I had no knowledge of the original, I was willing for her to remain so near the truth, that it was the likeness of a princess whom I admired.

Wira Menggala received from the hands of the princess, what seemed at first to be a mangosteen,—with purple rind and a few thick leaves near the stem,—a real fruit to the eye, at a little distance; but nearer, I saw that it was a piece of the curious lacquered work of Palembang. The Mantri lifted up the stem and disclosed a beautiful flower of *korangan*, filigree work of gold, in which Sumatrans have given patterns to the most skilful artists of Paris. The flower was a blending on the same stem of jessamine cups, and of white-doves on the wing: the leaves were shaped like those of the tamarind, but of gossamer texture; a single leaf showing many hundred of the most minute gauze-like filaments and fibres, wrought out with the ductile gold.

This flower would be more fragrant than all the blooms of the forest: it was brightened by the sunshine of beauty,—and perfumed with friendship. It would dazzle among the flowers of America. I tried to say almost as much as this as I held the gift in my hand. The princess said that there were many flowers in the Passumah more beautiful than this;—the Dutchmen sought them, but they could not find them. They would be found by those who were not djins,—who had cleaner souls.

I rose to retire; the Mantri clapped his hands; after a while, a gong sounded; the princess said safety on the way, and safety to return, and visit the Ulu: when I stood in the rambayah to bear me back, a clang of gongs broke forth, and down the stream I sped again. We passed an ascending boat; and by the star-light, I thought I beheld a glistening epaulette.

TWENTY-FOURTH DAY.

WHEN on board my vessel, I found the Balinese Captain, who had many stories to tell, and some warnings to give. The Dutchmen at the fort were greatly disturbed by the daily levees of natives and Arabs, held on board my vessel:—my visits unarmed and alone; my reception by Malays of rank in a way never shown to any European before, had given rise to the most extravagant stories in the fort, that I had a concealed treasure of dollars and gems, which I was distributing with a profuse hand, to prepare the way for a more extended American influence in Sumatra.

The Balinese was puzzled himself to account for my rapid progress in winning the native confidence; and was, I dare say, annoyed to find that his ciceronage was in so short a time no longer needed. He did not, nor did any of the Dutchmen understand, that there were avenues of taste leading to the confidence of this people, even quicker than those of trade; and far less did he or they understand, that Malays, like all of the eastern world, were to be reached through their moral, rather than their intellectual convictions; and that confidence was to be won by bestowing it.

The Captain warned me, as he had done so often before, but I had ceased to pay any attention to his stories of Dutch jealousy and Malay treachery; which thus far had received no confirmation. And whilst he talked, one of the subjects of his warnings, the young Arab, Abdallah, the grandson of Scherriff Ali, came to see me; and with joy in his face, said that his grandfather and father had consented to let him go with me.

Since the first proposal of Abdallah to enter my service, I had received a great number of similar offers; but none so interesting as his. The sailing-master was receiving daily applications from Malays, who wished to join the vessel as sailors, having received not less than a hundred such, from men, who only asked for rice and three dollars a month, whilst they could earn four times that amount at Palembang. But the Malay is a genuine lover of adventure; and my ship and myself having been magnified by so many stories, promised some cruising of romantic interest; for which he was willing to forego greater profit ashore.

I had got, as I thought, the complement of natives I wanted, Moonchwa, Bahdoo, and Kiagoos Lanang, the cook, the valet, and the poet; but Abdallah urged, and I liked the youth; and I resolved to take the young Arab gentleman, as company for my cabin. He wished to have the parental consent at once confirmed; and took me in his tambangan to the house of the chief of the Arabs.

The Panyorang received me with warm and kindly interest: he had heard my name in the mouth of every man: spoken with friendship by Arabs, Malays and Chinese; but evil lurked under the tongue of the Dutchmen. I must go to Jambee, where all would be friends, Abdallah would be a faithful younger brother, and would help me to speak all my thoughts in the presence of princes.

Abdallah had retired to prepare for departing with me: after a while, he returned with a dejected look; his grandfather inquired the cause, then entered an inner chamber. I heard the voices of women, and a sobbing sound. The Panyorang came back, and said, the mother has become little-hearted, and cannot part with her last born, with Abdallah, who is a tender kid in his mother's eyes.

Whilst the Panyorang talked, the father of Abdallah arrived, Captain Aboubakr, with two of his sons, who assisted him on board the Djelanie. The Captain was a stout, handsome Arab, who manifested great pleasure on seeing me. He went to talk with his wife; his father joined him, but again the Panyorang returned, and shook his head, saying, it was hard to deal with women; he did not deceive me, but as he wished me, his son, to know that he spoke truth, he would break Arab custom, and let me hear his perverse daughter myself.

He led forth a female, dressed in garments of sober hue. A scarf like a Mexican riboso, covered her head, and was fastened under her chin, partially concealing features more oval than those of any female I had yet seen in Sumatra; the nose was aquiline, the mouth small, the lips thin, the teeth pure and white, and I saw a fine matronly face, that bore the marks of about forty years of age.

The voice of the Arab lady sounded deeper, more sonorous than the Malays. She was happy that her son, her youngest, her smallest, and her weakest one, had appeared so pleasing in the eyes of the American Tuan, that he would make her son his younger brother; but Abdallah was too weak to walk among strangers alone; he had not the teachings of the prophet, nor the customs of his people, very deep in his heart; he would neglect the *ngasar*, and the *mahrib*, the daily prayers in a strange land: and thus this mother, like all others in the world, Christian, Jew, and Moslem, feared chiefly on account of risk to the religion of her child.

Captain Aboubakr, said it was well;—that Abdallah should remain; he had an older son, one bold and skilful on the sea;

Hussein, his second born; and he pointed out one of the young men, who had come with him; but Hussein had not the expressive face of the younger brother; and I said that I would return to Palembang, when Abdallah had got the lessons of his mother deeper in his heart.

This was only one of many instances I met with and heard of, which confirmed the words of the Major in regard to the position of women in Sumatra,—even among Arab and Chinese, as well as Malay; though no women are so free as those of the latter; the rights of the Malay ladies are equal in every particular to those of the Malay lords.

I had seen interesting evidence of it, in the position and state that surrounded the young Zaydee Komala, and in the social freedom, and forward part taken by the women of the household of Panyorang Djaya Laksana; of one of those, of her womanly grace and intelligence, of her courage, enthusiasm, refinement, and tenderness; and of all that could constitute a noble and interesting woman, in any part of the world, I shall speak again, when we shall meet her amid other scenes, and taking a part that will show the exalted character of the Sumatran woman.

And that one, said the young lady on board the Palmer, is, I presume, the courageous visitant of your prison, of whom I heard such vague and contradictory rumors in Batavia; and even in China.

But the Commander observed, smiling, that he wished to give the greatest possible effect to the introduction of his Malay friends; and would not satisfy any fair lady's curiosity by anticipating their presentation in the due course of his story.

TWENTY-FIFTH DAY.

I prepared to depart. I had already far exceeded the stay I first designed, yet wishful to make it longer: to see more of the people; the panyorangs, and other nobles of Palembang; to roam in the gutta-percha, cinnamon and camphor forests; to rouse up the elephant and tiger that I had heard warring in the jungle, and to follow the hairy Kubu to his haunt; but I began to feel myself surrounded by the espionage of a power, that could see no good purpose outside of the pursuits of trade; and though not all powerful here, had the force and the ill will to put me in peril at any time.

Had I shown a liking for the coarse jokes, and the beer and tobacco fumes of the mess room; had I been content to interest and enlighten my mind by daily games of billiards, and by a nightly display of dollars on the card table; had I studied Palembang behind the guns of the fort, in idly watching the swarthy skins that plied the paddle on the river; and amused myself by kicking the yellow-skinned coolies, and calling them thieving and treacherous dogs, because they did not understand some uncouth jargon that I should bellow in their ears; had I sought thus to please, amuse and edify myself, I might have revelled on at Palembang in peace, till I had gambled away my ship; or given away my health to Dutch debauch in the East.

But I had done otherwise, and after a time, the Resident met me with a constrained look, the naval commander with a frowning brow; and all the officers of the garrison had become more or less shy; all except my friend, the Major, who met me as usual, with cordial manner, and words; and thus, at one time, spoke of the state of feeling towards me in the fort.

I had raised up a bitter enemy in the person of the Assistant Resident of Palembang. He was a mulatto, the son of the late General Storm S'Gravesande, and a negress of Surinam: a very dark man, was the Assistant;—with the woolly head, and marked features of the maternal side of his family. The Major reminded me of some remarks that I had made when dining with the Resident, about the condition of the African race in South Carolina; some simple statements about their moral and physical state; neither advocating nor condemning it, nor in any way reflecting upon people of color; yet the conversation afterward called forth from Storm most vindictive language, expressive of a very decided hate to Americans in general; which feeling at last, said the Major, settled down upon you in particular.

The Resident has placed the Captain commanding the topographical corps under arrest, for having shown you a map, indicating the military routes and posts in the interior; and he has become greatly alarmed at the daily levees of natives on board your vessel; and at the manner you are received by the chieftains of the surrounding country.

Born as I am and reared in the Archipelago, said the Major, I cannot view these things, these doings of yours, in the same light that those do who come from the land of my fathers. The instinctive jealousy of the Dutchmen about all that is English, whether of Old or New England, will grow only in the polders of the Netherlands, in sight of Doggerbank and the Thames. The prejudices of the fatherland do not flourish in Creole soil.

I have not ventured to remonstrate with the Resident about his suspicions; but I have endeavored to reason with my brother officers upon the absurdity of supposing, that a mighty and enlightened republic, like the United States of America, where every thing diplomatic is done so openly, because strength is always straightforward and open, should resort to the petty espionage once practised between states of old Europe.

My brother officers from Holland, I am sorry to say, are far from being equal to the standard of British officers in India, in point of education and general information; and this ignorance is accompanied with strong prejudices, strong as their steadfast character. Now one of these prejudices, strengthened by all Dutch journals, is that the government and people of the United States of America, are watching intently to get possession, not only of Cuba, but of Java, Sumatra, Borneo; and every other island, rich or valueless, which is the property of any one else.

These are absurdities; but you must expect to be disturbed by their influence, wherever Dutchmen have any sway or influence in these islands; therefore, if you wish to study the people of the Archipelago undisturbed, you must go farther north on the island; or to the north-eastern coast of Borneo.

I had resolved to go a little farther north, to the Sultanate of Jambee; but the remarks of the Major, and all that I had heard from others, led me to think that it would be my best policy to proceed directly to Singapore, and there arrange, according to my early plan, for my future cruisings in the Archipelago.

When I gave orders to make ready for departure, my sailing master had further news about Jambee to communicate: he had seen one of the petty officers of the fort, the adjutant Van Steenderen, who had been to Jambee, who spoke much of the wealth and curious interest about the place, and of the facility of the route thither.

My chief officer had become deeply interested in the account of the country; he wanted to go himself, to visit the land of the Korinchee, the Sultanate of Jambee, proceed farther north, through the territories of the Sultans of Siak, Indraghiri, and Achin; and then join me again at Singapore.

A little more knowledge of the topography of Sumatra, would have convinced us that such a land route was utterly impracticable, except with a good force of men, familiar with the swamp and the jungle; and that such a force could not reach Achin in less than four months; but the officer was adventurous, and sanguine of a gratifying success; and I became wishful to have my future movements in Sumatra determined by the observations of an intelligent man.

My second having resolved upon the adventurous embassy, made every preparation for the journey. It was necessary to obtain a guide, a tambangan and two coolies; the latter were easily procured; but there was difficulty in finding a man familiar with any land route to Jambee. Kiagoos Lanang spoke of the hadjy Zenodeen, who had a wife in Jambee; and as he now dreaded the anger of the Mantri Wira Menggala, on account of some transaction relating to the sale of Aleema, the pantun singer, and her sister, to the Dutch officers; he would be glad to offer his services for the bare means of reaching the abode of his wife.

The hadjy, who had undergone a great metamorphosis for the worse since last seen on board the rambayah of the princess, was retained as a guide; but when that matter was arranged, the coolies to work the tambangan objected to go; they were afraid of tigers, who often sprang from the banks of creeks, whose streams were narrow, into passing tambangans. Bahdoo and Moonchwa volunteered to join the expedition. I did not wish to part with them, but they begged to go; the master desired to have them; and I reluctantly consented to part with my Malay followers.

Some introduction or passport was required, and I instructed my Malay secretary to prepare a general letter, addressed to the chief sovereign princes of the north of Sumatra; and one in particular to the Sultan of Jambee; and with vocabulary in hand, I endeavored to communicate these words to Kiagoos Lanang, which was designed to be the substance of both.

"I ———, residing in the great land of America, send greetings to the lord Sultan who rules over the empire of Jambee. This writing will be brought into your presence, by the chief officer commanding my vessel; a man of truth and skill, in whose words and knowledge I have great confidence. He will speak of the great land from whence I come; of the wealth and power of America, and of the friendly dispositions of the American people towards his Highness of Jambee. He will inform my lord Sultan of my wish to visit the Kraton at Jambee, that I may present some gifts, and sentiments of friendship to his Highness. Therefore my lord Sultan will be pleased to give orders to his officers, that the bearer of this may be allowed to dwell for a time with peace and comfort in the territory of Jambee; and afterwards, when he shall have accomplished his desire, to be permitted to go his way without molestation."

Whilst engaged in my cabin with Kiagoos Lanang, and before the dictation of the letter was completed, the Balinese captain came on board to remind me of an engagement to attend a great Chinese wedding feast, that afternoon, which I had forgotten; for I was invited daily to many feasts by the natives of rank. The Balinese urged immediate departure with him in his boat. The Chinaman was very wealthy, and distinguished among his countrymen: he had made large preparations for a feast that would show the abundance and luxury of Palembang; and he had spoken to the Balinese about his great desire to have the American captain for a guest.

The master had wished to start that afternoon; but I requested him to delay his departure till early the next morning. I gave directions to the secretary to complete the letter with all the appropriate preamble and style, which I could not dictate, to be ready for my signature at an early hour in the evening, when I expected to return from the Chinese wedding.

TWENTY-SIXTH DAY.

Rows of little balloon tops and paper globes, pictured without, lighted within, and dancing about in the evening breeze, or swung to and fro, by the rising and falling stream, pointed out the wealthy Chinese rakit on the river; and the clang of gongs, and the ding dong of bells, told of the Chinese feast within. I met my merry, fat friend, Oey Soch Tchay, as I stepped from the tambangan: he was a relative of the host, whom I saw behind him, a thin intelligent-looking Chinaman, standing in the doorway of the rakit, bowing and smiling; and I was introduced to Oey Tsee Yang, who celebrated the marriage of a daughter.

The feasting room was large: two hundred persons, and more, moved about within it: and not Chinese alone; for mingled with the glossy heads and pigtails, were to be seen the Malay kabyah and golden kriss sheath; and even two or three Arab turbans. The profusion of colored lights, dancing amid clouds of burning frankincense, gave a softer shade to swarthy skins, and threw a mantle of peculiar Eastern pomp over the festive scene.

A number of Malay women, old and young, handsome and ugly, and all richly dressed, sat in a row upon mats on one side of the room, immediately behind a band of musicians, also seated on the floor, who struck little bells on boards like a dulcimer, touched the strings of the kechapee, tingled the triangle, and beat on the gandaarang a noisy thrum, whilst the women with lively good humor nodded and smiled to male friends, that moved about on the floor.

The doorway, and other open parts of the room, were crowded with the peering faces of coolies of the house, and servants of the guests. After I had entered, the master of the feast gave an order; a rush was made by outsiders, men and women, who quickly returned with small round tables, eight placed in two rows, and a ninth at the head: low stools were arranged, smoking bowls brought in, and Oey Tsee Yang approached, and invited me to a seat at the table, at the head of the room.

Choose your friends; he said. The Balinese explained, that certain especial guests presided at each table, and they chose their own company. I placed Oey Soch Tchay to my right; his friend Pood Djang next to him: on my left I placed a Chino-Malay, a stout middle-aged man, called Tchoon Long, who had come several times to speak with me on board the Flirt: next to him was Teo Chan Beng, whose singing Fair Night sat with the row of women, and two other Chinamen, the owners of ships and junks in the river, filled the circle of my table.

The Malays of rank, who would not eat with the Chinese, moved about among the tables, with a great deal of good humor, chatting with those who were seated. The master of the house walked among his promenading guests; young Chinamen, richly dressed, and evidently relatives of those seated, waited upon the tables; and whilst we eat, the musicians played livelier and louder strains; and before them stood up a group of men and women to perform the wayang.

The viands, mostly fowls, birds and fish, cooked into shreds, and mingled with rice, sago, tripang, beans, and fruits, were brought in course, one large bowl at a time, out of which each guest with a small porcelain ladle, filled the bowl or saucer in his hand; and then with chopsticks of ivory, silver tipped, made rapid disposition of rice and bean, grain by grain; and the minutest fragment of shredded meat, tripang, or fruit.

Between each dish the mild, warm, fragrant tchoo was poured by assiduous Ganymedes, in pigtails, into small, thimble-top goblets of excessive thinness, like the half of a bubble upon a tulip stem; and as Soch Tchay explained, it would seem that the Chinese of Palembang had made some study of the natural philosophy involved in the mode of taking, as well as in the manner of preparing their diet and drink. Every bowl and cup was reputed to have peculiar properties for giving a higher zest to the solids and fluids of food.

When the chief dish, the kimlo, the olla podrida of Chinamen was brought, Pood Djang, who was the wag of the company, first tasted of it; and giving a smack of approval, assured me that there was only a little of dog in it, but very young and very black; and young black dog was good. Not so, said Soch Tchay, frowning upon his friend at his joke; we eat no dog in Palembang: too great a plenty of chicken and bird. And I do not think that canine steaks or chops form any portion of "celestial" diet in that city.

A youth approached with a large golden goblet, a dish of especial compliment, accompanied by the host. This was *quah*, a thick pottage, which contained some of the famous bird-nest, the wax-like cells prepared by the little laweet in ocean caves, chiefly of Java. Memories of mutton chops! what was here! the bed where eggs were laid, and hatched, and which gaping fledglings had fouled many a day before, to be offered to my civilized stomach as the chief luxury of an oriental feast!

But Oey Tsee Yang explained; he had a piece of raw nest to show; clean, white, and waxy, of a dim shade like opium: this was from a nest just built: rich Chinamen did not eat of those, that had been soiled by a single egg; these new ones were very costly, worth more than their weight in silver, one dollar and a half an ounce; and the older kind, those stained by a brood of young, were worth one half that price. The Dutch gain great revenues, many hundred thousands of dollars, from the nest of the ocean swallow. The raw nest,—I tasted of it,—was almost tasteless on the tongue, like any unseasoned gelatine.

Poor little laweet, why was it robbed of the home so carefully wrought; made of the weedy gum sought in clefts of storm-washed coral, dissolved and wrought in the throat, disgorged, and then, with plastic bill, made into the spheric cell beneath the rocky eave of some deep wave-beaten cave, where the little young should lay; why was this,—the home of the myriad laweets of the Java shore, so cruelly stolen away?

Chinaman is made strong by bird-nest, said Oey Soch Tchay: it makes him fat, it makes him live a long time. I saw a quizzical look in the face of Pood Djang: he leaned back, and motioning to me to approach my ear, he whispered, casting a side wink at his friend Tchay; that bird-nest was good to give old man handsome face to please young wife.

The ronggengs postured, sang and raged in the wayang; and while tchoo was sipped, all eyes and ears were turned towards the music and the dance, all but those of Tchoon Long: he looked grave and thoughtful; he had none of the sensual, Chinese look, and his thick hair was not plaited into the long queue; but clubbed up behind. He asked me about my departure, and the port to which I designed to steer.

He had wished to speak to me often; but so many people had always surrounded me, when he approached. He went on to speak about a great man in Palembang, Ferdano Mantri Krama Djaya, the former vizier of the Sultan Badroodin; and had fought bravely against the Dutch, till the capture of his master, when he made peace, and became a steadfast friend of the Company.

The people loved him very much; the people of Palembang, and the people of Passumah. His body was tall and strong; his face was clean (open), and his heart was white (true): he fed two thousand poor men, women and children every day: they sang his praises; his fame was very great; and from the eastern sea to the western sea, the people of Pulo Percha said, how great and how good is Ferdano Mantri.

The Company did not like to hear this: they wanted no one to be great, but those whom they made great. They wished to make Ferdano Mantri very little, to make him their slave; but they had not strength enough to bend his proud neck. The *ular girang*, the great serpent could not seize the alang in the air: he lured him into his den.

Ferdano Mantri received presents and compliments from Resident de Brauw; who wished to see the good chief at the fort, to show him a beautiful fire ship, the Arjuno, which the rajah of Holland had sent to Pulo Percha. The confiding man came, some friends said beware; "what have I to fear," said the brave Mantri, "beneath the flag of the Company, which I have served with good faith and good service so many years."

He saw the great iron bowels of the ship: the mighty limbs whirling round and rising up, the fire and the smoke, the huge cannon, and the smaller things of war. He went into the chamber of the chief captain: he admired the carving and the varnish of the workmen of Holland. He came on deck to depart; the great dayongs were beating the water, the Arjuno walked down the stream; and the chief captain said, that the great man at Batavia wished to see Ferdano Mantri

Great and good man, beloved of the people of Palembang and the Passumah: the Dutch have put chains upon him at Krawang in Java. His children, his relations, and a hundred thousand people pray to Allah for his return. Prayers alone will not bring him back, but there are many hundred thousand rupees placed in safe hands at Singapore, to be paid to him, who will go with a ship, and some brave men, and bring Ferdano Mantri back to Palembang.

Tchoon Long had whispered these last words into my ear, although all the company at my table had moved beyond hearing; as he raised his head he looked intently at a burly Malay chieftain: he spoke of him; he was a Tumunggung, a chieftain of the third rank, called Nora Wangsa, a man with a bad heart, who spoke fair words to strangers; but was a spy for the Company, and would report all that I did or said to the Resident. This man had not been looking at the wayang; he had often come very near, and tried to hear our words.

Tchoon Long had seen both of my servants, Bahdoo and Moonchwa, at the house of Nora Wangsa. But why should the Tumunggung spy, since I had such great confidence in the Resident? I had taken into my cabin the servant and the oppas, of the house of De Brauw at Padang. I was startled at these statements of Tchoon Long; I asked him to explain. He then said, that Bahdoo was formerly a servant of De Brauw, and a policeman at Padang; and that Moonchwa was the valet of De Brauw, during his late expedition to the Ampat Lawang. Bahdoo and Moonchwa were plotting a bad deed.

I was astounded at this latter news; after a while, I moved to look at the play, and spoke to the Balinese captain about what I heard concerning my servants: he scouted at the story; said those half-breed Chinamen were the greatest thieves in the place:

this one wanted to rob or cheat me; or perhaps would be on board my vessel next day, to beg a little American pork and potatoes; as a present, in exchange for something promised by him, which he would forget to send. The Balinese captain knew that Bahdoo had been living for the last ten years at Minto.

I had paid little attention before, to the Captain's general denunciations of every one, Dutch, Malay or half-breed; but some of his remarks in this case striking me as very just, I felt disposed to doubt the stories of Tchoon Long; and when he came to speak to me again about Tumunggung, Moonchwa and Bahdoo, I turned from him and joined my Chinese friends.

Oey Tsee Yang was told of my wish to see the bride and her groom. None but the nearest male relatives were allowed such a privilege; he wished to do me all possible honor; and I should see his daughter. This was the third day of a festivity, that lasted as many days more; the ceremonial had been performed; the young people were joined together; but still were strangers to each other; they had a grievous ritual of fasting and silence to perform, before being left to their happiness alone.

I was led to a curtained doorway: the yellow folds were parted, and I passed at the threshold between two old women, seated on mats; then I saw before me, in the centre of the room, seated beneath rich canopies, the bride and her groom: she was covered with jewels; her head, ears, neck, arms and waist, was a mass of rich lace, ribbon, and silken fringe, obscuring a very pleasing half Malay, half Chinese face of good race.

The groom was dressed in a rich fantastic costume, not commonly worn; he was half Malay, and a handsome youth. They were a well matched, interesting-looking couple; but the pleasure of beholding them was greatly spoiled, by seeing their pained looks, as they sat still as the dead, and knowing that they had sat thus all day, without eating a mouthful, without stirring, without speaking, and not daring even to take a glance upward; for there the old women watched lynx-eyed, to prevent the slightest relaxation of the painful ritual;—like the sex every where, Christian, Moslem, or Pagan, conservative guardians of all ceremony, religious or social.

When I returned to the main room, the music and song was loud and lively. I drew near to the performers of the wayang; I now saw that Aleema, whom I had met at the fort, and on board the rambayah, was one of the number. I was a little disappointed. I had seen her at first, as the hapless innocent victim, next as a retainer of the princess, and now, as a hired ronggeng, at a Chinaman's house.

I spoke to Teo Chan Beng, who was a great musical and dramatic authority at Palembang. He had not seen the ronggeng, pointing to Aleema, before. She was a stranger in Palembang: she had fled from some one in the interior, and had lately entered the house of Tumunggung Nora Wangsa; who was patron, also, of another singing girl present, called Sahdeeah. He received a large portion of their gains at festivals, for the protection, he afforded them, as Chief. A Malay impresario.

When the wayang had ceased, the young girls, who sang, approached the chief guests, and presented them with portions of the wreaths of the small fragrant white flowers which had adorned their head and neck; and then received a gift in return. Aleema came to me; and as she removed some flowers from her hair, and arranged them to hand to me, she said in a whisper: "Hadjy is bad, will hurt Tuan, his servants are bad, saying bad things of Tuan at house of Tumunggung."

The young girl stepped quickly away, and the wayang began again. I could stay no longer. I felt a cold chill creep over my heart. Old stories of Malay treachery and assassination came to mind: I had not heeded the words of Tchoon Long, I had often met with treason in men, but would not believe that it existed in woman; and I was aroused by the warning of Aleema.

I broke away from the pressings to stay, of my host and his friends, and returned with the Balinese Captain on board my vessel. I had greatly overstayed the time I proposed. Midnight was past. Kiagoos Lanang was alone in the cabin; he met me with a letter in his hand, the one prepared for the mate. I had forgotten all about it, and the journey to Jambee; absorbed by thoughts of what I had just seen and heard, I paid little heed to the paper in his hand, except to glance at its general appearance; I began to think that the Malay missive would not be needed, as I was inclined to suggest to my officer to abandon his contemplated expedition; but he not being there when I came on board, I sat down at the request of my secretray to listen to what he had written.

I could not then read the Arab-Malay script, in which the letter was written; I knew not a single character of its alphabet; and even when read, I could only distinguish a few common Malay words among the high Court Malay of the communication. Kiagoos Lanang was very anxious to explain that he had followed my dictation exactly. Whilst thus engaged, the sailing master came on board: he had been calling upon some friends, mates of vessels in the river, to obtain two or three cutlasses and muskets, and a little ammunition for his defence on the journey.

I spoke of my suspicions; of what I had heard: he was incredulous; what could be the plot? to murder him on the way? that was not reasonable, as he would have no money, no presents, and nothing to pay for the trouble of killing him: did I apprehend the cutting out of my vessel by a piratical party, aided by traitors on board? Then my best plan was to get rid of my suspected servants by letting them go with him:—wait till the Bali barque was ready to start; or better still, propose to take some passengers, officers and soldiers, who were waiting for a vessel to go to Minto.

Thus we had no supposition of evil, except from the natives. I felt somewhat rallied again, and began to recall my good opinion of Bahdoo, whom I had treated very kindly, and taught to consider himself a man, an equal with any one on board my ship, and not a crouching slave. I had indeed, perhaps unwisely, bestowed too freely my Sumatran sympathies upon Bahdoo Moonchwa, and Kiagoos Lanang.

Whilst we talked, my cook and cabin waiter along with the hadjy, returned in the tambangan. I asked Bahdoo if he wished to rejoin me at Singapore: he said vehemently that he would go away with a little heart, if he thought he should not meet with his master again. I was moved by the fellow's earnestness, my suspicions were dispelled, and I began to feel loth to part with him; but my officer had set his heart upon going to Jambee, to start that morning; and other guides and aids could not then be obtained.

When getting ready to start, I observed something sinister in the looks of Moonchwa and the hadjy, as they whispered together. My suspicions were a little aroused, I thought of the helpless state of a man—one of my own race, who had been a faithful navigator and an intelligent companion, in my cabin, during a long and most interesting cruise. I thought of his helpless state, if deserted by the natives in the forest, swarming with wild beasts.

I proposed that a sailor, if willing, should go with the officer:—he would be heartily glad of such an addition to his company. The men in the forecastle were roused up:—the expedition was explained; this was the first time they had heard of it. A stout active young sailor, known on board as Yankee Jim, quickly volunteered to go; he had run away from his ship, on the coast of

Brazil, and crossed the continent to Peru: he was just made for a cruise in the brush, he said; and the brave, adventurous fellow was ready, kit and all, in twenty minutes, for the exploration of the jungles of Sumatra. If I had had only two dozen of such men, I should not now have been telling you this story.

The tambangan was ready; the provision, and the accoutrements for the journey, were on board. Bahdoo became faint-hearted; he did not wish to go; but Moonchwa urged him: and the Malays got into the little craft. I felt some emotion on parting with my faithful officer, and brave sailor. Should we meet on the deck of our gallant little ship again? God bless you, Captain. God bless you, old Flirt, said the sailor with choked words.

The tambangan shoved off; I entered my cabin with a heavy heart, and lay down on the transom, to take a little rest, without undressing, for it was near the dawn of day.

TWENTY-SEVENTH DAY.

I was aroused from my sleep on the transom by one of my people, saying that a man-of-war's boat was alongside. I sprang up the companion way, and saw the commander of the Pylades coming over the gangway, backed by a dozen marines. He hailed me gruffly, wanting to know where my mate had gone; which I did not think a matter with which he had any thing to do; but he would convince me, he said, that he had; and ordered me and my men, who had gathered on the quarter deck, to get down into his boat.

I asked him to tell the cause; and to show his warrant for what he did. He replied with coarse words. Yankee brigands should be strung up, without the trouble of showing cause. He roared out again with oaths at my men, to get into his boat. I bade them stay. The three Brazilians I had shipped at Pernambuco slunk away. Two men stood by me; and two lads, one of these the lonely keeper of the Flirt at Maceio; and the other, the black boy who had come to rouse me; a brave and faithful fellow, of whom I shall have much more to say, who now peered his head above the companion-way hatch, the old carbine in hand, levelled at the commander, and asking for the word to fire.

The lieutenant went away with my Brazilians, saying, he

10

would return soon to put me in irons, and my vessel under the guns of the fort. All this time, I was bewildered to know why was all this; and what cause of offence had been given to Dutch authorities by the departure of my sailing master to visit a prince, entirely independent of their authority.

Right or wrong, I was in the power of the Dutch; I was above the fort, and my force of hands reduced, yet feeble as that was, with a swift current, and the fresh breezes then blowing, if I had been at my first anchorage, I would have slipped my anchor, and with small spread of sail, have bid defiance to the swiftest pursuit from Palembang: but now I had to pass a battery that afforded no hope of escape; and why should I try? I would go and see the Resident; learn why I was molested; and surrender myself, if required, a prisoner to him.

Whilst on my way to the fort, I was met by a message from the commander-in-chief, desiring me to remain on board my vessel, until I should hear from him again. On my return, I found Tchoon Long in my cabin. Tuan will now see that I have spoken truth, he said. But how, I wished to know; what had the action of the Dutch lieutenant to do with the treachery of Bahdoo and Moonchwa?

Look yonder, said the Chino-Malay; and he pointed to a large rambayah, rapidly descending the stream, full of armed men; and with a glass I could distinguish my officer and sailor, fast bound in their midst. And what was the meaning of this? how had it happened? Adah! said Tchoon Long, European man was very proud and strong of heart; and would not hear council of colored skin.

I told Tuan last night, that Bahdoo and Moonchwa were bad; would do evil thing. Tuan speaks with Balinese captain; and closes ear to Tchoon Long. Why should your slave speak with double heart? He asked no profit, he asks none now. But, what was the evil plan of Bahdoo and Moonchwa? Tchoon Long did not, does not know; but this he knows; they went to the house of Tumunggung, to the house of the Assistant Resident many times, yesterday afternoon; to betray the commander, to betray his officer; how, he could not tell. And I could not conceive what was the nature of the betrayal, or why it should have been done; as I had made no secret of the departure of the mate for Jambee.

Tchoon Long said that Dutchmen hung quick; justice talked about the hanging afterwards. When Col. Poland commanded in Sumatra, a Chinese son came to offer himself to be hung in the place of his father. As you like hanging so much, said the Colonel, you shall hang with him; and father and son dangled on the same gallows. Col. de Brauw will hang as quickly. Tuan come ashore, among the people of Ferdano Mantri to-night, they will take Tuan down the river; they will get a prahu on the Banyoo Assin; take Tuan to Singapore; and then he can return with a fire-ship, and many of his countrymen, to release Ferdano Mantri, and regain his vessel and men at Palembang.

I could not imagine a cause, why I should resort to any desperate measures to escape with my person, and abandon my vessel. I still unjustly suspected Tchoon Long. Whilst I talked with him, a large tambangan came alongside, manned by eight stout Malays, and two young Arabs heavily armed, and as these two stepped on deck, I recognized a man I had seen at the house of Panyorang Scherriff Ali, called Seyd Rachman Alkhaaf, the commander of a small vessel, and his companion was Seyd Ali Saghaaf bin Bafadal, who had visited me on board the schooner, and received a present of some Turkish tobacco.

Rachman had heard from the Panyorang, that the Tumunggung was plotting something bad, against the American Captain. He did not know what it was yesterday; but he saw this morning. Rachman and Saghaaf desired me to get into their tambangan, and go to the Arab quarter. Tchoon Long now spoke, and said I would be safer with the friends of Ferdano Mantri.

I could not yet see a reason to join Arab or Malay. Whilst talking in the cabin, we heard a shout from the Malays in the tambangan. Ali Saghaaf was first on deck, and I saw him leap over the schooner's hammock nettings into the large tambangan, that was shooting by the quarter. Tchoon Long and Rachman looked wild and fearful, as they saw their tambangans speeding away; and saw marines, who had lain concealed, as their boat approached, pouring over the schooner's sides. Sandals and upper robes flew off, and they leaped into the stream. The marines on deck cried out, others in a boat pursued. Arab and half-breed struck out lustily towards the swift current of mid channel. Fire! said a brutal voice, I knew. A volley from marines; but when the smoke cleared away, I still saw Arab and half-breed, rapidly gaining the left bank of the Moosie.

Whilst still looking at this exciting scene, I heard a hoarse, harsh voice, cry out with fury, in bad English; "Ha'll down that flag, you dam Yankee insurrectionnaire." I turned round; and confronted the coarse face of the lieutenant commanding the Pylades, red with passion, and behind him, scowled and leered the foul dark face of the Assistant Resident of Palembang.

Again the Dutch officer roared out his insulting order; pointing to the ensign that fluttered with the breeze, on the flagstaff astern. I had no desire to show a useless pride or defiance in my helpless state; but the savage fury of the man, and the memory of his past taunts, made me unmindful of the risk of provoking him to greater brutality. I said that having been accustomed to give orders to lieutenants, I bade him haul down the flag himself.

"Lieutenant!" said he, with fury; "I will show you, I command here." He drew his sword. I stood by the cabin companion-way hatch; I seized a portion of its sliding top;—I dropped it after a moment's thought, folded my arms, and made no attempt to parry his lunge; but his sword arm was seized by a dark hand, and then I saw the friendly face of the Shabandar. Again the lieutenant drew back; the Assistant Resident stood before him, and said that he must take his prisoner alive before the Resident.

The fury of the drunken officer,—he was partly intoxicated, must expend itself. He rushed towards the flag-staff, he pulled at the signal halyards, but the flag was fast. Why, I then knew not, but the trusty black boy had driven a few tacks into staff and bunting; he seized a drooping corner, hauled upon it till it came from the staff, and flung it overboard astern, where it hung by a shred, trailing in the water, and was afterwards brought on board.

This did not satisfy the furious man; he rushed down into the cabin; there was a brass gold-plated eagle, that was on the blue velvet of the curtain board of my berth, where it had been placed when the vessel was a man-of-war; he tore it from the velvet; he came on deck; and with insulting words about the "American bird of plunder," flung it into the water in the presence of thousands of natives, now assembled around the schooner in various river craft.

The drunken man seemed to become sober after these exploits. The Assistant Resident expressed great regret, that he was compelled to desire me to accompany him as a prisoner on shore. I had addressed a letter to the Sultan of Jambee, proposing a scheme to destroy the Dutch. I said, that I had certainly dictated and signed a letter, addressed to the Malay prince he mentioned; but there surely must be some other cause than the contents of that letter for these high-handed proceedings.

Into the boat," said the lieutenant, rising up again into fury; 'you shall be shot in two hours from this time." I paid no more heed to the drunken man. The Assistant Resident bade me direct my cabin boy to select a few articles of dress, and some bed-clothes for my use. Pirez, or the Peri, as called by my men, went below; he delayed a little, apparently looking for something. I was reckless in those troublous moments about what he got for change of toilette. I bade him hasten again and again, with harsh voice; but little did I think he was doing me one of the most grateful services of my life; of which I shall tell you another time.

Pirez flung up carelessly, through the sky-light, on to the quarter deck, some bed-clothes, and a pillow, which along with a small trunk, were handed by marines into the boat of the Assistant Resident, who desired me to follow. My remaining trusty followers were ordered into the boat of the lieutenant; who, as he pulled off towards his vessel, said he would have me shot that afternoon, or he would throw away his epaulettes.

As the boat of the Assistant Resident shoved off from the schooner, I heard the heave and paul of the windlass, and the hoarse rustle of the chain through the hawser hole,—getting up the anchor to move her under the guns of the fort. I saw through the stern lights coarse Dutch faces in my cabin, and some peering over the bulwarks. My beautiful ocean home was despoiled and plundered; but as I sped through the crowded craft of natives, among whom I had lately moved so proudly, I felt then my humbled, helpless state too much, to think of the despoiling and loss of my beautiful Flirt.

TWENTY-EIGHTH DAY.

SABBATH ON BOARD THE PALMER.

TWENTY-NINTH DAY.

I PASSED the same portal as a prisoner, which a few days before I had entered as a distinguished guest; but the spirit which had entertained, was no less hostile than that which imprisoned; for the latter did no more than carry out the work of espionage, devised by the former.

Captain Kress, commandant of the garrison of the fort, met me and my captors at the gate; he asked in a harsh, gruff voice, if any weapons or papers were among the baggage, which some coolies were bearing along behind me. There was a great change in the tone of this infantry captain, who had received me so blandly, often before. It was the insulting one of a tyrant of small soul, feeling triumph over a disarmed foe. I felt reckless at that moment, and even something of the spirit of banter. The day's experience of excitement and brutality, made the surliness of this man fall upon me without force. I told the captain, that I had the chief armament of my cabin in my trunk; and a few private papers about my person, which I hoped to be allowed to retain.

The Dutch officer looked at me with an evil scowl upon his face. It was a grave offence, a proof of my piratical character, to attempt to enter prison with concealed weapons, which ought to have been handed to the magistrate who arrested me. The

Assistant Resident, who was reflected upon by this remark, said that he had examined the trunk before leaving the vessel, and was sure that it contained no weapon of any kind; he could not understand the prisoner's motive for saying so: he had discovered no weapon whatever on board, except an old rusty carbine.

Captain Kress would examine the baggage himself: he ordered the trunk to be opened. Pirez had forgotten to give me the key, and a sneer was added to the scowl on the face of the officer, as I fumbled anxiously in my pockets. Captain Kress did not need keys when overhauling the traps of pirates; the lock of my trunk was forced, the lid wrenched open; and the contents taken out, and fingered and scrutinized with the keen eye of an old jailer,—adept in the arts of prisoners, who often hide papers and tools, in the hem of a garment, or the sole of a shoe.

Piece after piece, of clothing and articles of toilette are brought forth; and gazed at with curious eyes, by Dutch soldiers and Malay coolies, who stand grouped around the trunk. The bottom of it is reached, and yet nothing in the shape of contraband of war yet found. Captain Kress scowls darker and uglier than before; he is about to speak, but checks himself, and his face lightens up; the searching soldier has discovered something—a crack, a sliding piece at one end; he pushes, he prizes, he presses, at last it opens, and several pieces of coal, rock, and other mineral tumble out, and there is something in a dirty, rusty linen cloth. It is heavy, he unfolds, iron appears, and behold a pistol, a real revolver pistol.

All stand back at the sight of this. Dutch soldiers, coolies and magistrate, all, except the prisoner and Captain Kress. The latter takes the weapon in his hand, with severe solemnity of look. He handles it carefully, and rather daintily: carefully, perhaps, owing to a fear of some hidden spring in the formidable six-shooter, of which he had heard, but never before had seen,—and daintily, on account of its being in a very filthy and rusty condition. He draws back the hammer, and the chambered breech moves slightly; he wants to pull trigger, and see how it works, the man of arms has become interested. But the revolving tubes have not moved into right position for the hammer to strike. He tries various ways, but the thing won't work. He knits his brows, then turns towards the prisoner, his countenance relaxes: he says not a word, but it is plain to be seen, that he would descend awhile from his official severity, and ask the prisoner to explain the working of the weapon.

I took the revolver in my hand. It was one of the smallest of the manufacture of Colt, and had been given to me at Pernambuco. I had amused myself awhile with it shortly after leaving Brazil, shooting at sea birds. I laid it aside for awhile, and when I wished to use it again, I found it so much impeded with rust, as not to be fit for use. I took it apart, and after much labor of cleaning, restored it again to its former condition. Another short neglect, rendered it useless again, and then I abandoned all further attempts to keep it in order, and preserved it alone for show. The presentation of it, had served to quell an unruly demonstration on board my vessel, when off the Cape of Good Hope; but I had not had since, any other such occasion to parade it.

I removed the breech from the mandril upon which it turned, to show the spring and catch, and principle of working, but the hammer made only a partial movement. I saw that the pistol was hopelessly rusty and ruined. I told Captain Kress that such was its condition, that I had not attempted to fire it, for a long time; and expected not to have any use for it, or any other pistol, while I remained in the Archipelago.

"What then did you mean, sir," said he, resuming his sternness, "when you said that the chief armament of your cabin was to be found in your baggage." I explained, that I had another weapon, a short, breech-loading carbine, which had been accidentally left on board my vessel. I did not have a single fire-arm of any description, nor did one belong to my vessel when I left home; and no other but the two mentioned, had been held by me, or belonged to the vessel, whilst I had owned and sailed her.

I then stated, that while on the coast of Brazil, I had shot with the pistol, a small sea bird on the wing, and this good hit had established my skill as a marksman among my crew. But another time, whilst ascending the Soonsang, I had fired with the carbine at a large alligator, and missed: I did not disturb him on his log. In the opinion of my men, the failure was the fault of the carbine, and not of my hand or eye. With the pistol I could not have missed, even at the same distance. I was a sure shot with that in hand,—so thought my men; and therefore I considered it the chief defence of my cabin against riot on board.

The commandant eyed me with a mingled look of scrutiny and incredulity. He turned to the examining soldier and said, "Any powder, ball, or caps?" A few caps, green with verdigris, but not a grain of powder, not a single ball. He looked puzzled, and frowned more than before, and turned his head aside, as in deep thought, then suddenly fixed a searching gaze upon me. He seemed to debate in his mind, whether I had been playing with him or not. He spoke in an undertone with the Assistant Resident, then turned quickly upon me and said, "Those papers, produce them." I hesitated, I wished to explain;—no parley, I must produce them at once.

I drew forth a little silk bag, hung around my neck, in which during the excitement of the day I had put a few relics of dear ties, some fragments of home; and chief of these was a slip of paper worn and stained, on which was a dim red print of the hand and foot of a child and these words: "The hand and foot of my Lucy sent from home in South Carolina, to show me how much my child had grown."

Captain Kress took the slip from my hand; he read the words; he scrutinized the print like the plan of a fortress; he looked at the creases and lines of the small fat foot, the plump, round, baby palm, and the little taper fingers. That harsh face relaxed: perhaps there were memories of a home by the Schelde, and of some precious baby feet and hands, beating against his heart.

Captain Kress handed the slip of paper with the print, to me, and the pistol to the assistant Resident. He said a word to the guard, they moved forward, and led me to the prison cells of the fort.

THIRTIETH DAY.

I WAS placed in the hospital ward of the fort, in a small room, about thirteen feet long, by ten wide. What a change from my good little ship, from my commodious cabin, with its many pleasant comforts, from the prospect of an untrammelled range among lovely isles, and shining tranquil seas, and from many cherished hopes and purposes. What a change from all this, to four narrow, dreary walls, a damp tile floor, a grated aperture for light and air, a sentry at the door, and in the hands of dull, gloomy Dutch despotism.

The sun had gone down, darkness had set in, and a soldier entered my room with a rude lamp in his hand, a small burning wick of white pith floating in a tin cup, filled with cocoa-nut oil, and he had some rice, beans, a yam, and a little fish curry for my evening meal. This man's face had a pleasant expression. Whilst arranging the articles he had brought, he gave me a look that said he had something to say; but the sentinel was standing in the doorway, and observing us closely. A sound of voices was heard in the outer court, which drew off the attention of the sentinel for a moment, and instantly, the soldier whispered to me in French: "There are friends about; lie down soon, but don't undress. Trust in me, I am a Frenchman."

There was comfort in the voice of the Frenchman, whom the sentinel called Bois, and shortly after he left I had fully recovered my composure of mind, as the Resident and the Assistant Resident were announced. Col. de Brauw met me with an expression of regret, that he should have been compelled to change his late character of my host to that of my jailer; a change brought about by my own doing. He had understood that I wished to speak with him; and had come to hear what I had to say.

I had wished to speak with him when free on board my vessel: now I had no longer to deal with the Resident of Palembang, but with the supreme authority of Netherland India, which would have to deal with my Government.

The Resident assumed a very friendly tone. What could I have hoped to have effected with the Sultan of Jambee? He was a vicious Malay slave, who would have robbed and assassinated me, as soon as I had come within his power. I answered nothing; and the Resident and Assistant Resident left me.

The guard was relieved, and the man placed at my door, was disposed to converse. An oppas came, he whispered to the sentinel; and after a little parley, a small basket was handed to me:—sent by one I may never see again; and whom I thank at this moment. There was a dainty feast inside, a roasted bird, fried plantains, some mangosteens and dookoos, most refreshing at that time; and a bottle of wine, with which I allowed the sentinel to make free; and this made us very good friends, whilst he was on guard.

He told me, that my sailing master, and the sailor who went with him, were confined in an opposite quarter of the fort; the rest of my sailors were on board the Pylades. The commander of the gun brig was desperate against me. He had urged the Resident to have me shot; the Assistant Resident was said to be willing; but Major Blommestien had stood up for me against the lieutenant, who had sworn that he would tear off his epaulettes, if I was not shot. There was a whispering about among the officers, that the trouble with the lieutenant was about some wandering young Malay woman of rank. He had made many excursions on the river to meet with her, but in vain, and had become furious on learning that the American Captain had been received with so much state and attention.

Whilst we talked, footsteps approached; the sentinel challenged; the door of my room was opened, and Col. de Brauw walked in alone. He came to say a few words to me as a friend; and not as a magistrate. His manner was very frank and cordial. I began to be touched by it, and conversed freely with him. He asked for some explanations about my voyage, and my object in coming to the East, which I gave.

He spoke of Dutch power in Sumatra; the precariousness of its position in the territory of Palembang, which would have been seriously affected, had such a letter as mine, with its overtures of friendship, reached any of the interior princes; so readily inflamed to acts of hostility. I wondered indeed; it would be thought too ridiculous in my country, to suppose that the power of Holland could be jeopardized in Sumatra by the proffers of friendship to a Malay chieftain, by a man with an unarmed vessel, and seven empty-handed followers like myself.

Col. de Brauw thought that the American Government would be equally jealous, and watchful of any attempt, however feeble, to tamper with the Indian tribes on the Hudson River. Yes, on the Hudson River, and oftentimes, while in the Archipelago, I heard remarks, equally expressive of the grossest ignorance about America. I could not point out the Resident's sad deficiency in geographical knowledge; and allowed him to think, that the case he supposed, was parallel to that of a man, who should attempt a friendly intercourse with independent princes in the interior of Sumatra without consulting the authorities of the fort of Palembang; who exercise from that point about the same jurisdiction over Sumatra, that the British Government does over Spain at Gibraltar.

During all this time, I supposed that my great offence consisted in attempting to form an acquaintanceship with the chieftains in the interior of Sumatra, without consulting the officials of Holland in India. I had some idea upon entering the Archipelago, of an outrageous assumption of a governmental control where there was no territorial foothold; but as yet had not seen nor heard any evidence to warrant it; and felt that I had a right to send a message to the Sultan of Jambee without consulting the Dutch; yet, knowing that there was some such assumption, I felt also at the time, that they would wish to thwart me in the sending of such message, and thus, though my messenger made his preparations, and went away in an open manner, with men late in the service of the Government; yet I took no pains to make an official announcement of my design at the fort, and for this infringement of assumed rights and claims, I supposed that my vessel was seized, and I was imprisoned.

After my arrest, I realized more forcibly the arbitrary, military dominion of the Dutch in the East, and recalled to mind the massacres of Amboyna and Batavia, the summary hangings of natives, and incarceration of Europeans without a shadow of law. I was led to suppose that the Resident of Palembang, as guardian of the extravagant assumptions of sovereignty of the Netherlands in Sumatra, was compelled to arrest me for the mere fact of trying to become acquainted with a distinguished native, without leave; and had been forced to harsh measures by reason of the violent hostility towards me of many of his officers.

I was led to feel during this interview that De Brauw entertained kindly feelings towards me. I had paid no attention to the denunciations of a drunken officer, I had doubted in the face of many evidences to the contrary, that the Resident had had, formerly or lately, any relations with Bahdoo and Moonchwa, and I had not paid much heed to the story about Ferdano Mantri; though I observed that the Resident was much startled when I made allusion to that chieftain, and eagerly asked, who had ever spoken to me about him; yet he made such explanation about the position and suspected treachery of this distinguished native, as satisfied my mind at the time.

We did not discuss the nature or contents of the letter that I had designed to send to the Sultan of Jambee. The character of this prince and the difficulties that lay in the route, to his kraton and fort, were spoken of by De Brauw. Had the letter been produced and read to me, that was a year afterwards brought forward, in a court of justice, as the one dictated by me, how different would have been what afterwards took place; and how different would have been my conversation with De Brauw.

I began to think that he was indeed a friend, and had saved me from the violence of the naval commander, and other officers, and would be compelled to send me to Batavia, a measure he could not avoid. We exchanged many friendly remarks, and as he rose to depart, I pointed to a Mexican serape, a very rare one, of the best Saltillo manufacture; that had been much admired by a member of his family. I begged that he would accept of it. He could not, situated as we were, accept of any thing of so much consequence—some trifling memento he would be happy to receive. I had a few Mexican silver reliquiæ, composing an Indian chaplet of small medals, and curious charms, among which was a heart, this the Resident took in his hand, and said, "qu'il soit un cœur," let it be a heart, the memento of friendship between us.

Let it be a heart, said the kind friend, Col. de Brauw, who came to visit me in prison; and on the same night, the Resident of Palembang wrote to the Governor General of Netherland India, that the commander of the Flirt was a dangerous man,—that during his visit at Palembang, "the police was ordered to keep a vigilant eye upon him," that he "wanted to act the part of James Brook," that Moonchwa and Bahdoo, his servants, and Kiagoos Lanang, a young man of rank, his master of the Malay language, had early given information, some time before the departure of the mate of the Flirt, that this American might have caused "disastrous results among a people prone to rebellion, and remarkably superstitious;" and therefore he considered that the acts of "this stranger should be regarded as treason, and punished with death."

That despatch afterwards fell into the hands of him who gave the silver heart.

Whilst the Resident was leaving, during the opening and closing of my door, I heard my name whispered. I looked up, and by my dim lamplight, could discern a human face, peering through an aperture near the tile roof, and after a while could make out the features of the friendly French soldier. The sentinel had begun to pace to and fro in the passage before the door, and each time he turned his back, the soldier whispered from above. I must lie down apparently to sleep, and put out my light;—then a rope ladder would be let down to me;—I must clamber up silently;—he could easily pass me outside the fort;—there I would find the Balinese Captain, the adjutant Van Steenderen, and the sailing master of the Maimoon, and some native friends, who would take me down the river that night. He and Van Steenderen both wanted to desert, and would go with me. I would soon get another ship at Singapore, and could give them employment.

I did not want to escape. I had at one time felt some apprehensions for my personal safety, on account of the fury of the naval commander, but otherwise, I could not imagine any reason for my attempting to break prison like a felon. But there was another reason for not wanting to go. It was plain that the friends who wished to assist me, and to escape with me, expected that I would appear as a man of wealth and influence when I reached any place where the authorities of the United States were to be found, and that I then could reward them for any sacrifice made in my behalf. I declined with many regrets to attempt to go. The soldier deemed me mad; he urged, I would not consent to make the attempt. He drew in his head, and at a late hour I laid down to sleep, well wearied with the excitements of the day.

THIRTY-FIRST DAY.

On the morning of the third day of my imprisonment, I was aroused by the Balinese Captain, hailing me through the grating of my door. He had obtained permission from Captain Kress, to speak with me a few minutes. He came to express his surprise and the disappointment he had felt on learning that I did not wish to escape. My life was really in danger. The Major and the topographical Captain had both assured him so, and had thrown out hints that I would do well to escape. He would sail the next day, and lay to for me off the mouth of the Banyoo Assin, if I would agree to get out that night. He knew a foster brother of the Demang of Soonsang, and a devoted follower of Ferdano Mantri, who were eager to help me, and would take me to a safe retreat till I could get on board his vessel.

Whilst I thanked the Balinese Captain for his desire to serve me, I still could not see the necessity for what he urged me to do. I had many enemies, no doubt, in the fort, but the commander in chief was friendly; and I doubted not but that he would make such a representation to the Governor General of what had taken place, that I would soon be at liberty again, after paying a fine perhaps, for my infringement of a police regulation.

The Balinese was surprised to hear me talk so. I was not accused of any mere finable misdemeanor, but of "high treason," as the Assistant Resident says to every body, and punishable with death. I was deceiving myself most lamentably in supposing the Resident was friendly, or even open and candid with me. The topographical Captain had said, "Tell the American commander not to put any trust in De Brauw, who is greatly excited about something said in relation to Ferdano Mantri, and never wants the commander to leave prison alive;" and put no trust in any Dutchman, said the Balinese. He had been cheated out of a great deal of freight money; he had been insulted, and he wanted to have revenge upon the Resident, and a great many of the officers of the fort. He would go with me any where, sacrifice his ship, time and money to help me in any scheme, by which he would have a chance to be revenged on De Brauw, Kress, and other officers he named.

I had now still less reason to wish to escape, even if it were true, that I was accused of a capital crime. I did not wish to escape for the sake of aiding soldiers to desert, and the Balinese Captain to gratify his revenge. Whilst we spoke, a native servant, the same who had brought me food and wine the first day, in addition to the prison fare, now came with another small basket full of dainties, and was readily admitted into my room. As he removed the articles from his basket and arranged them for me, he slipped a piece of paper into my hand, and as he went out and for a few moments engaged the sentinel in conversation, I had an opportunity to read these words: "Every word of your conversation with De Brauw has been made the subject matter of a verbal process, drawn up by Storm. The Resident hates you for many reasons, he hates every thing American; but it is your knowledge of the Ferdano Mantri affair, that excites him so much against you. He will do all in his power to have you put to death. Your case is aggravated by the circumstance of your mate firing upon the Tumungung who went to arrest him. Escape if you can."

I recognized the handwriting of one whom I thought was true

and good-hearted. I began to feel disposed to think of escaping. I said so to the Balinese who still stood outside my door. He was rejoiced at my change of mind, and he left me, saying that some one would be at the hole in the tile roof again that night.

But there was no occasion to go to the hole in the roof. An officer came to inform me that a war steamer, which had arrived from Batavia, would return immediately. I must depart within an hour. Plans of escape from Palembang were hopeless, but there was full hope of soon being free again, and these words were cut into the plaster of my prison wall: "I will return," and whilst cutting the last letter, the Assistant Resident came with a guard of soldiers, to conduct me on board the steamer.

The mulatto Assistant led the way from the fort to the boat landing, through a lane of troops. We entered a barge, and were rapidly pulled through a throng of small native craft on the river. I observed a hand raised in a tambangan, and got a glimpse of the faces of Abdallah, the grandson of Panyorang Scheriff Ali, and of Seyd Rachman Alkhaaf. A minute afterwards, I was upon the deck of the steam sloop of war, Arjuno.

The commander ordered me to be placed in a state-room below. As I descended the companion-way, my hand was seized with a friendly grasp. The light was dim below, and it was not easy to discern any face, but the friendly voice of the Shahbandar was heard whispering a few friendly and comforting words. In a few moments the surging and buffeting of paddle wheels were heard, and the Arjuno was rapidly speeding away from the floating town of Palembang.

A marine, with cutlass in hand, stood at my little state-room door. He was talkative, said that a midshipman had been murdered in the berth I occupied, a few days previous. The midshipman had a Javanese servant, whom he had kicked and called outrageous names on one occasion. The Javanese feel very keenly any personal indignity, and this one took a fearful vengeance, of which there was some bloody evidence, left on the rail of the berth, that I had to occupy. No one on board would sleep in it since the murder had occurred, but the friendly marine hoped that no thoughts of the matter would disturb my slumbers.

It was night when we came to anchor at Minto. I obtained leave to take a walk with the marine; and when on the quarter deck I received a pressure of the hand from the good-hearted Havermeester, and the friendly intelligent Doctor. The latter, who was an old friend of the commander of the war steamer, obtained leave to talk with me alone; and as we stood by one of the gangways looking at my vessel lashed alongside, we dwelt upon the contrast between the present and our former meeting on the quarter deck of the Flirt in the roadstead of Minto.

The Doctor was deeply grieved, not only on account of meeting me under such changed circumstances, but on account of the folly which he believed the officers of his government at Palembang had committed. I was the victim of that absurd spirit of jealousy towards all foreigners, of which it was time for his countrymen in the East to get rid. The spirit of the old illiberal spice-destroying company still seems to exist, although the Dutch monarchy, in assuming complete sovereignty over the Archipelago, inaugurated a more liberal and wiser policy. It was his opinion, that I owed all my troubles to an absurdly exaggerated idea of the object of my presence in the East. He had understood my motives and my tastes, and had endeavored to combat some of the extravagancies that had continued to be manufactured about me, since my first arrival at Minto. I had gone to Palembang with an exaggerated character, the authorities there and natives of rank had fallen in with the idea—and he would not be surprised if it were a fact, that I had got my head turned, and with princely consequence wished to enter into a warlike alliance with the Sultan of Jambee.

He listened to my account of the matter, and when I spoke of my confident hopes of speedy liberation at Batavia, where I would have no personal hostility, and no ignorant military prejudice to combat with, and where I should find an American consul, who would see that I had fair play; he shook his head with a doubtful expression of countenance. He advised me to prepare my mind for more serious consequences. The Resident of Minto and the Resident of Palembang were both known to be singularly anti-American in their feelings. They were noted alarmists on the subject of the American spirit of annexation, about to stretch across the Pacific, from the Sandwich to the Malayan Archipelago. The destructive and expensive warfare waged in the Palembang territory, would make the government very severe upon the attempt of any foreigner to establish without their leave any kind of relation, however harmless, with the natives; for it does not recognize the sovereign independence of any prince in Sumatra; even those who are not immediately controlled by the presence of its authority. The Government of Netherland India is now presided over by a very severe man, a gloomy, religious fanatic, and a cold-hearted financier, just sent out to regulate the Indian treasury; and of him you may expect the severest possible construction of the representations of De Brauw. And hope nothing from any representative of your country at Batavia; no consul or other official agent is recognized in Netherland India, and the two or three Americans who live in Batavia, are all Dutch burghers, hold property, and would not dare to open their mouths in your behalf. Your chief hope is in the appearance at Batavia of your commodore commanding the East India squadron, and he will soon hear of your condition by the mail steamer, which passes here on its way to Singapore.

I felt that the Doctor spoke sincerely, and I began to feel, perhaps oppressively, a gravity in my situation, and this I felt the more, the day following my conversation with him. Whilst the Arjuno was traversing the Java sea, I was talking with the officer of the watch on deck. I saw marines standing in the gangways, starboard and larboard, and two accompanied me in my walk. What was the meaning of this unusual display of vigilance? The commander had received some especial instructions at Minto, to guard me like a man charged with a capital offence, who might attempt to jump overboard whilst passing the small islands, strewn on the way to Batavia.

Beautiful isles! with leaf and flower clustering down to the kissing wavelets of Java's placid sea. How I had looked upon them with loving and longing eye, wishing to court their deep shade and sweet solitude, when I had glided happily by them in my own pleasant little ship; but what were those longings now as I hurried past in this grimy ship of war, in the grip of men, who counted my tastes all folly, my curiosity dangerous, and my sympathies treason.

My longing eye gazed wistfully at the Watcher and the Brothers, as some who hear me once had done. The Arjuno safely passing those Brower shoals, which wrecked the Palmer, and broke your quiet revery amid these tranquil waters, and mine soon was to be broken in upon; and in as unlooked for a way by the arresting hand of Brower the sheriff of Batavia.

The ascending slopes, the terraced hills of Java, burst upon the sight. The towering shade of Dapoor and Edam, and of the last of the thousand isles has sunk below the ocean line, and a thick forest of masts rises up to view. Yonder flies the common emblem of a score of nations, copyists of republican France, the tricolored, horizontal stripes of Holland, floating above ramparts, and in the roadstead of Batavia.

THIRTY-SECOND DAY.

I SAT one weary day, within my narrow cage, to meet the gaze of curious men. The next day, I was put on board another man-of-war, the corvette Boreas, the guard-ship of the port. As I walked along the gun-deck to the berth assigned to me, I saw my sailor Jim, with hands manacled and chained to a gun. The brave fellow said some words of cheer, and something about weathering our captors. Further words were interrupted by a blow from a marine, and as I was hurried away by the two marines on either side of me, I saw my brave sailor vainly struggling to loose his manacled hands, to return the blows of the brutal and cowardly Dutchman.

I felt my imprisoned state very severely on board the Boreas. I was thrust into a close, dark, foul smelling den on the berth deck. When night came, an overspreading cloud of hammocks covered every beam: one hundred and twenty reeking bodies within the space for twenty, sent up a rank, animal steam. I choked, I begged for air; but I sat for many days in the fetid steams, down in the hold of the Boreas.

On the fourth day, I was marched into the cabin of the commander, into the presence of a short, stout gentleman, with a mild and benevolent-looking face, who asked me many questions about my late voyage, which I answered; and many more about what I had seen, said, and heard, in Sumatra, which I refused to answer.

I had sent for a countryman, an attorney, some kind of counsel; but no one had come near me. I wanted the fair play and open justice I expected to meet with in a Christian and enlightened country.

But my questioner said it was the law of Netherland India to be questioned by the prosecution, before receiving counsel of any kind. I thought that it was an unjust and inquisitorial law. I would remain silent. One more question my interrogator urged me to answer, and he held up a bundle of papers, among which I had a momentary glimpse of one, marked with strange characters. Had I dictated and sent this letter to the Sultan of Jambee? I had ordered a letter to be prepared and sent to that Prince. I thought, and he thought, that the document he held in his hand, was the letter sent by me. How different, as when De Brauw spoke with me, might have been the after proceedings, had that letter then been read to me; or the paper been put into my hand.

The next day, on a Sunday morning, an order came to remove me to prison on shore,—to a prison in the sultry grave of Europeans, into a dismal cell, where faint rays of blessed light, and a stifled breath of still more blessed air, struggled through close woven bars; and yet this picture seemed pleasanter than the nauseous berth, the bad fare, and the hideous society of the guard-ship.

I was placed in a boat between two marines; and eight oars, plied by stout arms, sped us swiftly through the throng of ships lying at anchor in the roads. At the landing near the Custom-House steps, I was politely greeted by a man wearing a gold-laced cap; he was in the early prime of life, with fresh complexion, and good-humored expression of countenance. With a smiling face he said, pointing to a small covered wagon, that he would have the honor to accompany me to my new lodgings. This invitation sounded smoother than the gruff order just lately heard, to get down into a boat; but as perhaps this shore suavity was to be followed by a harder lot than had been met with in prison afloat, it was not easy to appreciate the good-hearted politeness of Jan Brower, the *duurwarder* and sheriff of the Court of Justice of Batavia.

The ground was deserted when I had landed; no one stood near me but Brower. On entering the van, I paused for a moment on the steps, and looked around. I saw in the verandah of a tiffin house, or tavern, a young man, a well-dressed sailor, like the mate of a ship, who had such a look of home in his face, that I hailed him to know if he were an American. "Yes, by the Lord! what's to pay, countryman?" was the hearty and cheery reply, and I hurriedly shouted out some words, the unjust imprisonment of myself and crew, to tell of it to an American Commodore or Consul. At my first word the wagon started, the young man ran to catch up, I heard the words aye, aye; the horses were whipped into a brisker pace, and I lost sight of the American.

There was chance for but a slight glimpse of the "queen city of the East," whilst hurried along the banks of canals, and beneath the deep shade of long rows of trees of rare foliage and flowers;—huge bouquets, swaying to the breeze, and loading it with a rich burden of sweets; but I saw enough, and was not in too gloomy a mood to feel, that I had never seen such a city of fair villas, as stood on the site of the old Jacatra, the foundation of Pieter Both, the metropolis of Netherland India.

We stopped at a small gate, in a crumbling wall, that is to be seen no longer. Brower led the way, and a barefooted native, with a drawn sword in his hand, brought up the rear. Blue coats, yellow leather belts, and glistening bayonets thronged around a doorway. We entered a small whitewashed room, bare of every thing, but some police truncheons, three heavy, leather arm-chairs; and a desk covered with black cloth—The little room looked very chill and gloomy, amid all the sunshine of Java; and while waiting to see a jailer, with hard-lined, dungeon-like face, I saw a little ruddy man, a very Santa Klaus of early fancies, bounce into the room; Brower introduced Mynheer Pieters, who gave me a hearty shake of the hand; and pouring out Belgian French very rapidly, said that he had heard of me, as being a very bad subject; he always liked bad subjects; they were the best of customers at his hotel; and to have an American, he had a great liking for them too; the first he had ever had; it was an era in his establishment.

The little man's good humor, and volubility and jollity, were not at all cheering, in the midst of bayonets, truncheons, thick walls, and heavy, iron-studded doors. There seemed to be a Jack Ketch jocularity about him, that I did not relish. I felt, as I looked into the little, cold, watchful gray eyes, that he would in the same tone, apologize for any rough adjustment of a halter; and compliment me upon being one of the best-looking subjects that he had ever hung.

Sheriff Brower bid me adieu; and Mynheer Pieters requested me to have the kindness to take a look at my apartment. We passed some rows of doors, with little gratings, behind which dirty, bearded faces, stared at me. We stopped at one of the doors; Pieters looked around, and called some one. A tall, lank, low-browed, hard-lined, livid-faced man, the one I had looked for at first, appeared. He singled out from a huge bunch of quaint old keys, the one needed for the door, where we had stopped; and we entered a small, high-walled court, with a row of four grated doors, along one side.

I saw bearded faces, and half-naked figures, at three of the doors, and Mynheer Pieters introduced them as I approached. At the end door, on the right, stood a low, slender figure, with a very yellow beardless young face, dressed only in a long cotton sarong; and this was a native schoolmaster. At the end door, on the left, stood a tall, thin young man, pockmarked; with yellow skin, and scant of dress like the other; and this was a native merchant.

At one of the middle doors, I saw a man of another type. A fine, open, fresh, Caucasian face. A tall, military figure; but bare as the natives; and a broad chest, an arm of fine muscle, and

a well set neck, were fully exposed to view by this half nude prison costume. Mynheer Pieters bowed low, as he approached this man; he stood silent as in the presence of a superior, whilst this personage thus spoke to me:

Prisoners need no introductions; especially from this old-pensioned adjutant, Pieters, who dares to turn a key upon me, his old master. I am a captain like yourself; but a sword's man, instead of a rope's man. They say you are a pirate; but you do not look like one, and if so, it may not prevent you from being a good comrade in jail. You are to tenant this little den of Pieters alongside of me, and if Baron Van Norden, late captain of infantry in the Netherland's army, can be of service, command him during your stay in the Prison of Weltevreden.

THIRTY-THIRD DAY.

It was dusk when I was locked up; and I saw little of what was around me; and soon gave way to sleep which no hopes nor fears could ever take from me; and in the morning, I found none of the prison horrors I had looked for, no den of torment in some Castle keep; but I could not boast of the comforts of my abode. I had a room, ten feet wide, by thirteen long, with coarse, plaster walls; scraped, cut, and gouged, by weary prisoners before me; the floor was of tile, and wet all the time, from the oozings of the prison moat that washed the outer wall; but I was provided with Chinese clogs; rude, wooden soles, with a leather strap for the instep, that raised me one inch and a quarter from my wet floor.

From a grating in my rear wall, I could get a whiff of Java breeze, and a glimpse of a bayonet, passing along the edge of the green, slimy moat, and beyond this I could see a piece of marsh ground, in the centre of which stood a gallows for the use of the prison. The prospect from the grating in front was not of so wide a range; but somewhat like, in the bayonet, the dreary prison court, in the centre of which stood a platform, for the application of the bastinado to men, who showed too much discontent for the comforts of the prison life.

I had a wooden bench and platform to serve for seat, bed, table, and washstand, and all other purposes of furniture. I had a stone pitcher and bowl, and had been furnished with a horn spoon, and a tin platter; for which I found an early use on the first morning of my stay in Weltevreden.

At seven o'clock, I heard the grating of rusty bolts, and then saw the dead-man's face of the turnkey in the doorway. Behind him, came a tall, stout native, with light brown skin; he had a heavy iron collar, fast rivetted on his neck; and wore no other garment, but a pair of short, blue, coarse cotton drawers. He entered my cell, with a large wooden tray poised on the palm of his right hand; and then placed on my platform, alongside of where I had slept, a small bowl of brown rice, some fish curry, and some red pepper pods and beans.

Whilst eyeing my small mess of meagre food, I heard the voice of the Baron, who appeared before me, robed like the Jupiter of Phidias. Rice, fish, and red pepper diet, would save me from Java fever; but before I had eaten, he would have me go to the door of our small court, and take a look at the prison. At feeding time, and the relieving of guards, there was a short privilege for prisoners, to step to the doorways of their several courts; and then could see their neighbors at other doorways of the several wards or blocks of the prison.

I had heard during the night, fearful shrieks, and howls, and sounds like the dying rattle in a strong man's throat. I heard them again, followed by a grating and lumbering sound, as I stepped to the gate of the outer court. One of our madmen; said the Baron, confined in a room of the first block, to the right of the jailer's house, as you enter.

This is a strange, and fearful maniac. He has not left his room, foul like a wild beast's den, for one moment in eight years. He is hairy and hideous like an orang utan; and naked, except some foul shreds only, of the garments which he wore when he entered, hanging to bands around his neck and waist. He raves most terrible thoughts, of evil designs upon him; and barricades at night his door, with marvellous, clock-like regularity,—removing with the same punctuality the barricades in the morning,—the lumbering and grating of which you have just heard; as he removed the platform upon which he sleeps, from his door.

But the strangest feature of his madness, is an extraordinary concealment of his face. Nobody has seen it exposed to view, since he entered his den. He has the filthy blackened fragment of an old straw hat, which he holds before his face at all times. When he paces his floor, he shifts the dirty mask from hand to hand, so as to keep the side turned towards the door, always hidden; when he eats, he conceals his face with the hat; and when he sleeps, the same everlasting screen is found firmly pressed with his clasped hands, upon the hideous, wilted, maniac face.

I cannot tell you his history, nobody knows; the government put him here, that has so many dark ways of dealing with people who may give cause for fear or trouble; and all talent and freedom of expression soon qualify a man for these walls, wherein are to be found better material for the formation of a government, than the one that put them here; and strange as it may seem, a large part of the headwork of the government is carried on here.

You see in the gateway of the block next to that of the madman, a short, stout-built man, about fifty years of age, who was lately condemned to two years of prison. His broad, heavy, sallow face, show lines of a highly gifted mind. He was the private secretary of a late governor-general, and a chief magistrate of the island of Banca. The Resident, as we call him, is daily consulted in matters pertaining to the courts, and the affairs of executive administration; and the strong head, for the sake of an extra pittance in prison, willingly uses his brains for the advantage of those weaker ones, wielding the sword and the purse, who have encaged him.

The slender, deadly pale, and haggard-looking man, who stands near to the Resident, is the most skilful artist with pencil and engraving tools, in Netherland India. He was the government draughtsman, and has been lodged here for ten years, on account of draughting some papers for his own especial use. But he works in his cell, the same as in the topographical bureau, and is at present engaged upon a new map of Japan for the Government, which contains the recent observations of Dr. Meunicher, who accompanied our embassy to Jeddo.

You see another man, standing in the gateway of block No 3., and the block companion of the Resident and Topographer. That broad Tartar forehead, and fine-shaped nose, is of Russian origin; and it might seem strange to see him here, since my Government has courted every thing Russian so much, since the time, our late William courted the Anna Paulowna of Rusland; but alas for this man, with all his Russian prestige, he caused my Government some loss of guilders, which merits jail so much in Dutch eyes; and from which no Russian Dowager could save him. Yet he works in his cell for some government functionary; and every day, a liveried slave brings a roll of documents to the Russian secretary.

Whilst the Baron was speaking, a tall, thin, haggard man passed before us. This was another madman, allowed the privilege of walking in the main court. He had been the most eminent lawyer in Netherland India. He prosecuted a case for the recovery of some two millions of guilders from the Government. He was seized with a little fever; and in spite of his own, and the protestations of his friends, was pronounced a subject for hospital treatment and confinement; and plentiful blood-letting soon sent him a raving lunatic, to be confined in jail.

He had a strange whim of playing upon words, with childish comparisons of sounds and meanings. He would converse sometimes with great ability and display of learning; at other times, according to the phases of the moon, he dwelt only upon the most incoherent fancies; but ever ended every discourse with one perpetual refrain: "*there is no law in India.*"

The crazy man passed us again. The Baron spoke to him; the lunatic scanned me with a lengthened stare; and when my name and country were mentioned, he shook my hand heartily, and expressing himself in good English, was delighted to see one from the land, where the African race abounded. He had been studying the tubular, cellular, and capillary distinctions between hair and wool; which my countrymen could not do without bitterness, hence the name amer, mara, bitter, which we have to put into genever, your gin, but how unfit for a can,—the milk cup of a child;—you make amer,—with a can;—that is brutal, like our council,—but "there is no law in India."

The learned lunatic walked away, muttering about the brutality of putting bitters into a child's milk can. He occupied a chamber in block No. 2, the first one on the left, on entering the prison. There was one more tenant of the block, in a chamber next to the crazy lawyer. He was a bankrupt merchant, confined for a bad disposition of assets. He had failed with ample funds in the hands of friends outside, who smuggled liquors and wines to him in prison, of which block No. 4,—the one in which I was confined,—got ample share, from the defaulting merchant.

In our block, said the Baron, we have but a small share of the governmental talent of the prison. However, my next door neighbor, the little schoolmaster, the son of an Englishman of

Bencoolen, is a rare scholar in the language, literature, manners, customs, and antiquities of the Javanese and Malays; but the government sets but little value on all that; nay, look upon it as the next thing to treason, to teach such stuff; and have fastened up the poor little scholar, to prevent his teaching or writing books; and keep him busy, drawing up contracts with the natives for coffee and pepper.

You have a great rogue, in the trader next to you; but he has travelled with his packs into every corner of Java; he knows the routes, throughout the native states of Surakarta, and Yugyakarta, better than any man in Batavia; and many an exploring party, has received their instructions for the route from your neighbor the trader.

Before passing from our block, I will say a word about myself, and show what part I play in the governmental talent of the prison. I was four years, commander of the small military post of Lahat on the Lamatang River, one of the Western branches of the Moosie, in the territory of Palembang. I thought I had given satisfaction to my government, which I think was the case; but I had displeased De Brauw, the same cold traitor, who sent us both here.

The royal adjutant who rules our Dutchmen at Palembang, could be heard against any one, when the late Governor-general Rochussen ruled at Batavia; but a new man has come out, who sat on the same benches, where I had learning beaten into me, in the High School of Utrecht; and I hope soon to have a backer against the Resident of Palembang, in the person of an old schoolmate, the new Governor-general, Duymaer Van Twist.

We were speaking of this coincidence of experience, and discussing the character of the Resident of Palembang. The lugubrious face of the turnkey appeared. His hand wielded a huge key; and from the lank, wilted, dead face, there came a voice, that bade us fall back,—get in,—Hold, you *smeerlop*, roared the Baron, with voice of command; you gallows-cheating dragoon;—touch your cap, and speak as an old foraging lancer should, to gentlemen.

Blixem,—growled the turnkey;—giving the Baron a shove,—butt against me; and as we staggered into our quarters, rusty bolts rolled gratingly into their sockets.

The Baron, after some mutterings of anger; spoke, with returning good humor, about the fortune of war: the jailer, once a petty officer; a non-commissioned adjutant, had served under him; and Beckers, an old dragoon, in a regiment of lancers, who had often curried the horse of the Captain, after being invalided by the bite of a serpent, which gave him his dead snake skin, had been made lieutenant-jailer.

My fellow prisoner spoke of the mean economy of the government, in giving to such refuse of the army, the direction of so large a prison, containing so many gentlemen, who had filled high military and civil stations. But the same government that wants a jailer for its chief prison, who will accept of 600 recepissen (about $200), wishes to feed gentlemen prisoners with twenty cents a day, which furnished the rice and fish curry that now invited our prison appetites.

Whilst we eat our coarse meal together, the Baron continued his description of our fellow-prisoners; along with a running commentary upon the governmental talent, that took so large a part in the direction of the affairs of Netherland India, at the jail head-quarters of Weltevreden.

The late administrator of the army of Java, was in the next block, to our left. A venerable military officer of high rank, who had enjoyed the favor of the late king; and was decorated with the royal orders of William of Nassau; and of the Lion of the Netherlands; but the new king, who "knew not Joseph," listened to councillors, who were hostile to the distinguished old servant of his father; and permits the gray hairs of Col. Joseph Timmermans to remain in one of the felon cells of Weltevreden.

The Colonel, by which title, he is best known in prison, was at the head of the civil direction of the affairs of the army of the Netherlands in Java, during the five years war, between 1825 and 1830, against Deepo Negoro, and Sintot; those celebrated Princes of Yugyakerta, and though he holds no longer any official portfolio of war, though he can serve his country no longer openly, and is stripped of his honors, still the gray-headed, outraged old veteran, serves in his cell with his great experience, the military administration of Java.

You wonder that the Colonel, the Resident, and others confined here, should render service for any consideration to a government, that holds them like felons. They felt as you do, at first. The military chief entered prison like a stern, indignant old Roman. He trusted that when his countrymen heard of the indignity that had fallen upon his decorated gray hairs, that they would lay siege to the Palace, and the Chambers of Deputies at the Hague, and demand his triumphant restoration.

But time wore on: day after day, of many months and years of the deadly gloom of jail; the dirt, the coarse fare, the brutal keepers, the weakening, wilting heat of Java;—all common wants uncared for, and all lack of soothing, soon sapped the pride of heart; and then memory fades in this eternal heat, in close, damp cells; the old brain wandered at times; the diseased old body, sick, craved some comforts of its keepers, and by and by, had lost sight of pride, and was willing to work with plodding patience for men, on whom the faded pride once spat upon.

This is the course of every one, who stay a time,—the course to madness, or hopeless imbecility, that steals with fatal certainty over all,—the old after the third or fourth year, and men at our time, in a little while more. I have been here but one year, and even now I feel a drooping of soul, a wasting of my former strong self, that appals me; and I seek refuge in strong drink, the refuge of all.

You think that helps the shattering of the mind. But what shall stay up the weary, fainting agony of a man, worn out with daily hope or apprehension. There is no certain and open course of law; the decision of one court, that might give liberty and property to.day, may be reversed to-morrow, by a secret tribunal, which you have never seen; decreeing death and confiscation You must seek refuge in drink, till madness comes to your help; and you cry out with the lawyer, "There is no law in India."

Whilst combatting the gloomy and hopeless views of prison life, of the Baron, and as I endeavored to rally him from the sombre state into which he had fallen, we heard a shrill, painful, feminine laughter. Another mad creature in prison: a little more of the daily music, mingled with the yells of the mask maniac; and the occasional shrieks from the bastinado,—that is better accompanied with brandy than philosophy, said the Baron.

You will hear that laughter half the night, if you are not a sound sleeper. It comes from the daughter of a very pretty woman of Pulo Nias, so famous for fair women; and of an English officer of Bencoolen: when this daughter was quite young, and she is not more than twenty-five now, the beautiful Creole received the protection of the President of the Netherlands Trading Company, who is now about to retire to Europe with an enormous fortune. With the loss of a child, she lost her reason, and the protector put her here, paying the Government the price of our luxurious board.

I do not know her name, nor that of her father. Mynheer Pieters says that he does not know them himself. She is lodged in the servants' ward, in the rear of the cell of mad Grunewald. I have not seen her, but am told that although she has a sharp, fitful maniac look, yet her face is pretty, her figure exceedingly graceful, and has most magnificent glossy brown hair, flowing down to her feet, when uncombed; in the care of which, she spends her time, all day.

This delicate creature, this lonely woman tenant of the prison, is waited upon by the same iron-collared convicts, who bring us our rice and fish. Those coolies with the scant blue pantaloon, the penitential dress, are all condemned pirates and assassins. That stout fellow, who brought our breakfast, was a Dyak pirate, and convicted of lopping off several human heads, and government has made him waiter for life, at the Hotel of Weltevreden.

Why don't they hang such chaps? Their lives are valuable· good hands for mines, and public works, as well as to wait on government guests; only hang Dutchmen, and other white subjects, who should happen to amuse themselves with throat-cutting; it would have a bad effect upon the native mind, to see Europeans doing drudgery; it is better to hang them, or make poor crazy wretches of them, lock them up, and feed them at the cost of six cents a day.

We expect an addition to our corps of waiters, a Javanese young gentleman, just condemned to a life of light employment, for having taken the life of a midshipman on board the steamship Arjuno. You say that you slept in the berth of the murdered man. You may again take the place of the unfortunate naval officer, in the matter of waiting. I hope that the exploits of the cooly, in the ward-room of the steamship, may not be repeated in block No. 4 of the Prison of Weltevreden.

You think that there is something horrible in all this; the mingling of state prisoners, or suspected gentlemen like yourself, along with many vile, half-bred felons, whom you see here; the mad raving amid the sane; and the employment of convicted cut-throats, to wait upon gentlemen prisoners of state, and upon a lonely, delicate, crazy lady.

You have probably thought of preparing an indignation article for some morning newspaper, the usual vent of an Englishman, and I believe of you Americans, also. You will find one little journal here, the Javaasche Courant, that has all its matter, leaders and correspondence revised at the palace of Ryswick; and you will find a public opinion regulated by various governmental grades and amounts of guilders; the public opinion of all government clients.

You must have patience, for my countrymen move very slowly. Our justice will think of you two or three months hence; will inquire into your case a few months later; a year hence, you may be acquitted by the court of justice; you wait for months to see the door open to let you out; and by and by you learn that some other court has condemned you a month ago to three, five, or ten years. Such has been the fate of numbers here; if it be yours, and you lose patience and hope, try a little brandy.

Wines and liquors are not allowed in prison; but more excluded by the thirsty guard ever watchful for drinkables, that are more confiscated by them, than by any force of law. My bankrupt friend, in the open, or debtor's ward, receives supplies of comforting liquids from adroit friends outside; and he, with some of the same adroitness passes a portion to me, and it is about the hour I should hear from my bankrupt Bacchus.

The Baron approached the wall of our little court, that separated us from block No. 2, the ward of the mad lawyer, and bankrupt merchant. He stooped low down, with ear inclined to listen. No expected sound; he paced to and fro our narrow, wet, high-walled enclosure. The fine face looked anxious; the handsome features frowned: the Baron muttered, cursed, and lost his temper and politeness.

It was noon-time; hot, stifling air filled the cells, and the narrow court; the trader and schoolmaster were asleep in their cells; the sentinel had leaned his musket against the grating of our outer door, and had sat down, with face turned to the wall, to get a bit of shade from the coping stones above. The stillness was very great, broken now and then, by a mad laugh, or a soft note from a burung kukur, under the verandah of the jailer.

The surly mood of my fellow-prisoner had increased: he paced restlessly, and listened at the wall from time to time—I heard a low grating sound. The face of the Baron lighted up; he stepped with stealthy and nervous step to the wall, bidding me in a whisper to keep a look out on the sentinel. He stooped down to a drain that ran before our doors, carrying off the moisture of the cells and the yard, and passed beneath the wall: he thrust his hand into the filth of the drain; his arm passed as far as he could reach, under the wall; and after groping awhile, withdrew it with triumphant look, with a bamboo, like a walking stick in his hand.

He beckoned me to follow him, and when beyond observation, he pointed with great glee to a plug in the small end of the bamboo; he pulled it out, and after cleaning and wiping it offered the open end to me, which sent forth a decided smell of brandy. I did not need any; never had, at any time in life. Better begin to think you do now; said the Baron, as he tipped up the bamboo, and took a long draught, from the long goblet.

My comrade pronounced his bamboo, the staff of life; and leaned lovingly upon it, till the pith and sap began to fail, as the Baron observed; and then the staff proved a broken reed to his tottering steps, and left the trusting man prostrate on the wet floor of his cell. I raised him up, and put him on his sleeping platform. He sang joyously; he raved amusingly of the *schelms*, *kladdakers*, and *smeerlops*, the rogues, scamps and beasts, and Pieters the prince of rogues; who entered the cell, as I tried to persuade the Baron to sleep.

How had he got the drink, the little red-faced jailer asked with great energy. He must not seek information of me; although to prevent such sad havoc on so fine a man as this, I might have done well to have informed, and prevented it. The half-breeds knew nothing, and Mynheer Pieters locked up the Baron, and then left, with a threat to report to Mynheer Van Rees, the Resident of Batavia.

Whilst the Baron prolonged his maudlin chant; and hickuped his abuse of the two adjutants; the royal, and the petty one; the bastard Belgian, and the bastard of the Hague; thieves of honors, and drink; and princes of rogues and jail birds at Palembang and Weltevreden: whilst thus he sang and raved, I sat down in my cell, and passed the rest of the afternoon alone musing upon my situation, and the experience of my first day in the Prison of Weltevreden.

In answer to the inquiry of the lady of the Elder Missionary, the late prisoner of Weltevreden said, that an afternoon meal, a dinner, at 4 o'clock, was served out to the prisoners; the same rice and fish as in the morning, with the addition of a small piece of pork, from which a thick soup, with more rice and beans, had been prepared. There were other prisoners in the block, described by the Baron; and four large blocks, beyond these, the gloomiest, closest and filthiest portion of the prison, which held from fifty to a hundred soldiers, common felons, and men condemned to death or life imprisonment. The prison was called the civil and military prison of Weltevreden. The imprisonment was not severe, as compared with many European and American prisons; for with their close and silent systems, a man would sink down within a month, in the climate of Java. As it was,—the cries of maniacs sounding daily in the ears, the wet floors of the cells, the hot, stifling air, and the uncertainty of law in Java, made the Prison of Weltevreden tolerably uncomfortable.

THIRTY-FOURTH DAY.

I WAS roused up early, on the morning after my first night in the prison of Weltevreden, by a loud tattoo, the reveille of the troops stationed at Batavia, whose barracks were ranged behind and adjoining the prison. I heard the measured tramp of feet, entering the main court of the prison, then some loud, quick, and long rolling words of command; the tramp stopped, another loud, and long rolling sound of voice; the butts of muskets thundered on the ground; and I could see through the grating in the doorway, that led into the main court, a file of soldiers, formed in line near the platform where the bastinado was applied.

An officer in the uniform of a colonel, and who held a paper in his hand, conversed with the jailer—the turnkey appeared with his keys; he went towards the gloomy cells, accompanied by four soldiers, and returned with two men, stripped to a pair of short drawers; both soldiers, the one short and fleshy; and the other very spare made. They were bade to lay themselves, face downwards, on the platform; their feet were made fast in stocks; and a soldier, at the arm of each man, held him firmly upon the platform.

Two huge-built Africans wielded thick rattans, whose leaded ends sprang to and fro, with lengthened sweep, as they swung them in the air, with nervous play of hand, eager to hit something more solid than to be striking at space. The officer spoke in command; the negroes stepped forward, and drew the garment of the prostrate men below their loins, the rattans were raised, and fell with a dull, deadly sound upon human flesh.

The stout man groaned, and the thin man shrieked; again and again, the torturing rods fell upon the quivering flesh; and as I counted the strokes, I could count the raised ridges, the bloody wales, that corded the flesh of the unfortunate men. They had received four and twenty murderous blows; a man in civil dress, a surgeon, stepped forward, looked at the work of the blacks, he spoke to the officer, who spoke again in command; the feet and hands were loosened, the stout man stood up, the thin one lay still; they turned up his face, it was ghastly pale, the surgeon felt the thin man's pulse; he had only fainted; two iron-collared convicts took him by the arms and feet, and bore him off to his cell; after this, there was another hoarse rattle of voice, muskets clattered; and whilst listening to the retiring tramp, the bolts grated in the doorway, the dead snake face of the dragoon appeared, and after him, the Dyak pirate, bringing my rice and fish for the morning.

The bastinado had taken away my appetite; and while I sat in my cell, thinking with gloomy thoughts upon the courtyard scene, the Baron entered. He hailed me with a groaned good morning; his head was tied up, his eyes were bloodshot; I spoke of what I had seen; such savage blows upon a man of small frame; but I thought that he had suffered as much from the brandy loaded bamboo, his "staff of life," as the poor wretches had from lead-loaded canes.

He laughed at my loss of appetite; another bamboo would put him all right again; some things were cured by the cause, fire was good for burns, iron rust for spear wounds; see the case of the Greek hero at Troy; but bastinado bruises were not cured by a little more of the cane. My stomach would be stronger, by and by; bastinado was the morning recreation of the prison; he had felt too much invalided to turn out, but had I not seen the other gratings, all crowded with dirty beards and eyes? Why, nine tenths of the fashionable world would give the price of an opera season ticket for these grating privileges; and of our block in particular; for besides the bastinado in the main court, we of this ward alone, can enjoy the hangings that come off, about once a month in the marsh, of which you have such fine prospect, through the bars of your rear wall window.

His humor and flow of spirits began to rally me, and with amusing philosophic comment, we went to work with our fingers upon our rice and fish rations. We were scooping out the bottoms of our bowls, when I heard a soft, clear voice, cry out, *Papa Koptyne*, Papa Captain. My little girl, said the Baron, she was sick yesterday, and did not come. She is too late, and cannot get in now. I looked out, and saw a little face, jumping up to the grating, in the doorway of the main court, and crying out, Papa, Papa Captain.

The Baron went to the grating and spoke to the sentinel, who growled a dissent to what was said. The Baron turned to me, to ask if I had any small coins; I handed him one: the sentinel received it, and immediately stepped away from his post to call the turnkey; that functionary needed a coaxing coin as well as the sentinel. The great door grated on its hinges, and in jumped a very pretty, graceful, bright-eyed creature, a little native girl, between ten and eleven years of age, and followed by a stout, coarse Malay woman in servile dress.

The face of the child was like amber, or a beautiful blending of burnished gold and olive, tinting the fine lines of high Sumatran race. A slender little figure was dressed in a yellow sarong, and a white kabyah; her little feet were bare, and she held in her hand some bunches of fruits, which she laid down on the ground, as she ran forward, with outstretched arms to embrace the Baron.

The little girl drew back, she frowned, and muttered in Malay, that her papa captain was bad; she smelt strong water, and she saw the fire of it, burning in his eyes; she would not kiss such a bad, ugly papa captain. The Baron approached her with coaxing look and words, but the indignant little maiden ran away, and as he chased, she slipped with swift foot from side to side, and when the baffled and panting Baron gave up the chase, she sat down and laughed merrily in a corner.

My moral reformer, said he to me, when he had recovered his breath; she lectures me like a curate; but she is to me like my own child. A poor little foundling:—A very curious story I have to tell about her; and whilst we eat some of the fruit she has brought, I will give you the history of my little Umbah.

The Baron picked up the fruits that had been thrown down; there were some mangosteens, dookoos, and rambutans. We burst open with our fingers the purple globe-shaped rind of the mangosteen, it being soft, like a green walnut hull, when fresh pulled, and becoming hard as wood after a couple of days. The delicate white pulp, in five clove-shaped compartments, was thrilling to the palate and nostril, like the blending of honey, cream, roses, and all that is best and finest of sweet and acid, in the best of fruits; of melon, peach and cheremoya; such is the custard pulp of this imperial luxury of the oriental orchard.

One can afford to eat rice and fish with our fingers, with such dessert, said the Baron with smothered words, and mouth half-buried in one of the fruity hemispheres just burst open. I should be underground now, were it not for mangosteens; they are the only things that can make true the saying, of raising an appetite under the ribs of death. I have been twice at my last gasp, broken down by long marches in the swamps of Sumatra; my bamboo failed, but a taste of mangosteen raised me up from the grave.

I thought he had better stick to mangosteen and drop the bamboo: not so, said the Baron; they had their appropriate spheres, the one to cure fever, and the other low spirits. But fever and mangosteen reminds me of the story that I promised you. By this time the little girl had stolen into the cell, and taking a place, at an end of the platform farthest from us, sat in her own eastern way, watching me with earnest eyes; as the Baron talked on, making frequent mention of her name.

HISTORY OF UMBAH.

I was at one time, on a march with a company of men, in the territory of the Ampat Lawang, in Sumatra. We were in pursuit of some plundering marauders from the country of the Rentjon Tingga; who made forays upon those dusuns, or villages, whose people were well affected towards the garrison at Lahat. We approached a dusun, late in the afternoon, where I wished to halt, being feverish, and unable to go any farther.

We heard shouts and shrieks, as we drew near, and saw thick clouds of smoke rising up: I felt roused; and gave the word to go forward with quickened pace. As we entered, some marauding lancers of the mountains were running out; the place was sacked, every house was in flames; and dead bodies of men, women, and children were strewn around. We gave the brigands a volley as they fled, and charged in pursuit.

I was now very faint, and in the confusion and smoke, fell without being noticed by my men. I struck my head against a stone, and lay senseless for a time; and when I returned to consciousness, I still lay helpless, and raging with fever; no help was near, my men were gone, would suppose me killed; they would not return that way. I began to think of the future world, and as I groaned for mercy and a little water, I heard a cry, a sad, plaintive baby cry.

A baby alone with me, amid these burnt ruins; the wailing little voice rose up again on the air, it roused me, I got up on my feet, and staggered towards the sound. It came from near the chief dwelling of the place, as I judged from the size of the ruin. I approached a group of bananas; the cry sounded louder, but the smoke prevented me from seeing, and whilst staggering, with eyes closed from time to time, I heard the cry right under my feet, and then saw a baby, upon which I had almost stumbled, lying upon its back.

A little girl baby, not more than six or eight months old. Poor little thing, I forgot my fever for a time; I took it up in my arms, and wiped the blinding tears out of its little bright eyes; and as I fondled, and rocked it in my arms, it ceased its crying, and turned its face, sobbing, towards my breast. What was to be done now? a baby could not be much help for a sick man; nor a sick man for a baby. I felt fever and faintness coming over me. I could die alone, but could not listen to the moans of a dying child.

I began to think of crawling away; and thought somehow, as I had been forced to leave many a dying comrade, to leave the little innocent to the mercy of God. My body raged, and my head swam: but this abandonment seemed too horrible. I would try to crawl beyond the smoke, and try to find water, that I knew must be near. I had not staggered many paces, when I saw fruits on the ground,—almost such a lot as we have before us,—with mangosteens among them.

I had just strength enough left to burst one of the purple rinds; the fragrance inspirited me; the delicious pulp went straight to my heart, and, as I quaffed down this rich cordial of nature, my strength came, and raised me right up; and baby was not forgotten, for at each pulp draught I took, I moistened a little gaping mouth, close by my breast.

I was not well, I was not fully strong; but the noble fruit had restored much of my strength; and all my hope and energy. I followed the track of my men; I knew they would not camp far off; and would waste no time in running after the nimble scamps, who were already in the mountain. I was not mistaken; I came up with their encampment, after two hours weary marching: about to lie down in despair in the dark, I heard the company's dog, found my men, fainted away, and lay in a tent, delirious for a couple of days.

I had said a word about the child before dropping down; and had handed it to the wife of my servant, to take care of. The little girl was brought safe to Lahat. She grew fat and strong: she soon ran after me; a real "child of the regiment," began to call me, Papa Captain. I came to Batavia; my troubles commenced; after a time, entered prison, where the little foundling of the Passumah comes to scold me about the use of the bamboo; and to bring me mangosteens.

I had given her an elegant European name; but my servants have called her Umbah, the wave; and perhaps suits the little Malay better than Mathilde or Louise. She was probably the daughter of the Kapala, or chief of the dusun that was sacked. She had some rich trinkets of gold and pearl around her neck;

and had a heavy band of gold round her right wrist. But without those little trinkets of aristocracy, the fine lines of her face, of the highest Sumatran Malay type, would show that she was of high race.

She comes to see me every day, accompanied by one or both of my old servants, who still cling to me in misfortune; and now, whilst I am stripped of every thing, they work for their own living, and furnish me with all the comforts they can obtain for me. Umbah, who has the freedom of the prison, at certain hours, brings me a daily addition of fruits and flowers, to the coarse ration of the jail.

I spoke to Umbah; she came towards me with open face and confiding manner. I spoke of Lahat, and the land of Passumah: she remembered the Lamatang, the top of Gunung Dempoh, and tho rambahya on the Moosie; her mother lived in the Ulu; and when her Papa Captain had left the house of care (rumah susah), as Malays call a prison, he would take her in a prahu to Lahat; and then she would ride upon an elephant to go and meet her mother at the foot of Dempoh.

I had lost my vocabulary, and all the rest of my papers; fallen, as I then thought, into the hands of my captors; and I needed the aid of the Baron, to understand Umbah. He had a Dutch and Malay vocabulary, and with my knowledge of the former, I tried to talk with the little Malay maiden, whilst her papa captain went to look through the grating at some military prisoners just brought into the main court.

Umbah could not read nor write; but she had in her head many pantuns, and stories of the wayang: a hadjy began to teach her the Arab letters and the koran; and her papa captain had taught her letters in a book of the orang Wolanda; but she did not like the hadjy; and her papa captain was so often crazy with strong water, that she had but a very little piece of the koran and Wolanda book in her head: she would like so much to have more.

I discovered that she knew the Roman alphabet: with my help, she joined some letters together in syllables, and with repeated efforts made out some simple Malay words in the book. She was delighted, she wanted to be able to read books, like the European ladies of Batavia, when she had grown up to be a woman. Then she would become rich; and buy a beautiful horse, and a fine sword for her papa captain, he would be happy, and he would drink strong water no more.

I was charmed with the quickness of perception, assiduity, patience and ambition of the little Malay; and still more with her hopeful, earnest, and affectionate heart. The gloom of the prison was chased away by the light of her presence. My late troubled experience was forgotten in the interest of her story; and I began to feel a pleasure in the contemplation of the development of this little Malay mind, that made me, for the time, unmindful of the discomfort of the close cell, the wet floor, and the coarse fare that had sickened my soul the day before.

As we conned over some words of the vocabulary, we heard the voice of the Baron, in loud, obstreperous and drunken tones, vociferating all the coarse and emphatic words of the language of Holland; so pithy and foul in its slang and blasphemy. I stepped forth, and saw my cell neighbor stripped to his waist, and flourishing a fresh bamboo in his right hand; whilst with his left, he held the half-breed trader by the throat, backed up against the gateway of the main court, and was about to dose him, as he said, with the outside of his bamboo.

I saw, through the grating, the red face of the jailer, seeming to make struggling exertion to force the door, which opened inside; but was held closed by the pressure of the choking trader, held against it by the infuriated Baron. But, strange sight for a prison scene, I saw the turnkey inside, squatted on the ground with back against the door, and heels dug into the ground, struggling to keep the jailer out; and looking up with drunken leering glee at the belaboring of the trader by the Baron.

I ran to keep the peace, and to help the chief authority of the jail. I seized the uplifted bamboo, and drew back the Baron. Mynheer Pieters entered: he kicked his lieutenant, who struggled on all-fours to get upon his feet: the trader made piteous appeal and protestation; the Baron cursed louder and lustier than before,—little Umbah cried out, pattered with her feet, and beat the air with her hands; whilst myself and the great stolid face of the grinning, listless Dutch sentinel, stood for a time, wondering spectators of this scene in the prison of Weltevreden.

After a quarter of an hour of the mingled din, of Dutch and Malay outcries, I began to learn that the turnkey occasionally tasted of the small end of the Baron's bamboo; he had been seen to totter after these leanings upon the "staff of life:" the governor had suspected the Baron, and instructed the half-breed spy in our ward to watch; he, whilst supposed to be sleeping, had seen through a crevice in his cell door, the bamboo obtained through the drain—had seen the turnkey enter, at a signal made by the Baron; and then he, in a concerted manner, had thrown over the wall, a note attached to a stone, and gave the information which brought the jailer.

The turnkey had been denouncing the trader as a spy; who had been suspected before, and when the head jailer was seen to approach, the Baron had no doubt about the informant, and began to belabor him as I have described.

If I had not seen the glistening bayonets, the gloomy sentinels, in front and rear, and all around; who with frowning looks, bid me stay within a narrow limit of high-walled barriers, and iron-barred doors; and in a close, wet resting-place, I should have thought that I was in some riotous quarter of the city of Batavia, where drunken riots were the common scenes of the day.

I was in a large and dreary prison, filled with military officers and common soldiers, with gentlemen and coolies, with state prisoners and the meanest of felons; with suspected and convicted men; with maniacs;—men and women, all jumbled together;—guarded by a troop of stolid brutes of soldiers; and directed by a vulgar, pensioned petty officer, and still more vulgar, bestial old dragoon.

I had wondered at a great many things; at the bold language of the Baron, at the repulse of the dragoon; and their after guzzling companionship. I wondered at such riotous disturbance of the peace of the prison, so lightly passed over, when appeased, by the authorities of the prison, but I began to perceive something of the many influences that affected the discipline and direction of the jail.

The Baron had many friends, with position and power. The President of the Court of justice at Batavia, had been his fellow schoolmate at Utrecht; and the new Governor-General was expected to extend to him executive favor, on account of similar scholastic reminiscences; and many of the officers, who were quartered around the prison, and controlled a great deal its internal economy, were haters of De Brauw, and his connection at Batavia, and were sympathizers with the Baron.

The consciousness of these influences made the jailer obsequious at times; but as there were others, equally powerful, who would expect greater severity and closer discipline; he manœuvred as he best could, to wink at all excess, where winking was safe, in order to please the military influence; and yet keep the disorders of his charge concealed from the civil influence that appointed and paid him, which he failed to do at times, as on this occasion.

I had entered the cell of the Baron, to quiet Umbah, whilst the din of voices was still prolonged. It was suddenly hushed; I looked and saw the benevolent face of him who had questioned me on board the Boreas. The jailer with face very pale, stood before me, and said the Fiskaal wished to see me in my room. The turnkey had slunk away; the Baron stood with defiant air, and folded arms in the centre of our little court; and the trader, with fawning, suppliant look, was making explanation to the Fiskaal and pointing to me; but that functionary bade him enter his cell, motioned to the Baron to enter his, and ordered the jailer to lock the doors.

The officer of justice said that it was his unpleasant duty to search my person and cell, for any papers that I might have secreted. I had no personal effects with me, nothing but a few sheets and a pillow for my sleeping accommodation. My baggage had been left on board my own vessel, and the Boreas. I was then suffering for want of a change of linen. The benevolent functionary was indignant at the neglect, and would send an order to the commander of the guard-ship to have my effects sent ashore.

The oppas, and the secretary or translator, who accompanied the Fiskaal, began to inspect my cell: one began to handle and examine the mattress on my platform, the other had my pillow in his hand, which was closed with a running cord like a sailor's sack; he had opened the mouth, and was thrusting his hand into some stuffing moss, with which it seemed to be filled, when the magistrate made a motion with his hand to desist, and asked me to give my word of honor, that I had no papers, concealed about my person or in my room, which I did, and the inspection ceased.

The Fiskaal went to speak with the Baron, and bade the jailer, who stood at my door, cap in hand, to lead me to the Chamber of Instruction, to await his coming. At the doorway of the main court, I found Umbah seated on the ground, her hands covering her face and sobbing bitterly; her papa captain was shut up, the servant had not come to take her home, and she was afraid to go out alone to-day, to pass some drunken soldiers, who stood at the great gate; she was not always afraid of them; but afraid of the drunken dragoon, who would come into the court, when the Fiskaal, and jailer and myself were gone.

I told Umbah to follow me; the jailer bade her go away, to go out of the prison; she cowered with fear; I took her by the hand, intending to ask the Fiskaal, to allow his servant to accompany her beyond the precincts of the prison: the jailer seized another hand, the child clung to me; the Officer of Justice appeared, the jailer began to explain, he was requested to be silent, and Umbah followed me to the Chamber of Instruction.

THE HALL OF INSTRUCTION.

I entered the little room, where Sheriff Brower had introduced me to Mynheer Pieters. A functionary in black sat at the desk with a large bundle of papers before him; the Fiskaal and the translator occupied the other two leather-covered armchairs, and a seat was placed for me. The formality of asking name, age, birthplace and so forth, was gone through; and then the Fiskaal addressed to me some questions about the conduct of my fellow-prisoners and the discipline of the prison.

I had hoped to learn what was the foundation for the charge alleged against me, which had led the authorities of Holland at Palembang to seize me, my crew and vessel; and which caused the authorities of Holland at Batavia to subject me to confinement in a vile prison, without allowing me an opportunity to communicate with any countryman or counsel of any kind, and I did not expect to be called upon to act the part of an informer; a vocation as unfamiliar and detestable in my country, as was the crime with the commission of which I was charged.

The Fiskaal was authorized to seek instruction or information from every source in order to subserve justice, and the proper administration of the laws: I must not think that every question was put to me in the spirit of espionage; or that the course of law was inquisitorial in Netherland India, because I had not been allowed to consult with legal counsel; why should I need any advice, to prepare my answers, if I felt a conviction of my innocence, and that a simple statement of facts would establish it.

I felt surprised that I should be subjected to any interrogation whatever. I was arrested for having caused to be written, and sent, a letter addressed to the sultan of Jambee. I had acknowledged, did now acknowledge the dictation and signing of such a letter. Let the tribunals of justice of Netherland India adjudicate upon that fact; nothing else, no hostile speech, or action, nothing else in the remotest way opposed to the sovereignty of the Netherland government, had been alleged against me; then why these interrogations, which I must regard as unjust, and inquisitorial in the highest degree.

The Fiskaal spoke of my sudden intimacy with an officer of the government, the Havermeester of Minto; I had given him a miniature; and he had supplied me with government stores; and otherwise aided me at the time of my departure. It was said that I held conversations hostile to the government of the country with a Chinaman at Minto; with one of that turbulent race who had given the government so much trouble in Banca and Borneo;

and it was alleged I had agreed to receive a dozen deserting Belgian soldiers on board my vessel.

Then at Palembang I had after the first days of my stay kept company with the natives; and went off upon several expeditions without consulting my guests at the fort, who believed that I held intercourse with their enemies, and although a hostile solution to all this strange conduct, was manifest in the letter to the sultan of Jambee; yet still there was much that was mysterious, that affected the conduct of officers, and native vassals of the government; and the justiciary of the country desired to be informed of the whole matter.

I then said; if the justiciary of Netherland India wished to be fully enlightened about all that had taken place between me and officers and vassals of the government; let those persons, including the Residents of Palembang and Banca; their assistants, the Havermeesters of both places; my late Malay servant; a naval commander, and several officers of the garrison of Palembang; let them be brought to Batavia, and confronted with me in an open court, and then I would speak.

It would probably be seen that I had been furnished with private police from the household of the two Residents to be my confidential servants; that the stories about deserters, and treasonable conversation, had been manufactured out of innocent occurrences, by these spies imposed upon me; and that throughout my stay at Minto and Palembang a most disgraceful spirit of jealousy had been shown, and espionage had been practised towards a stranger, and had thrown upon the hands of the government a very troublesome affair, that must necessarily involve it in unpleasant relations with the government of the oppressed party.

The Fiskaal asked me with some surprise, if I was not hazarding some remarks when I spoke of private police; men in the employment of the two Residents of Palembang and Banca, having been imposed upon me as confidential servants. I expressed my convictions that such was the case; spoke of the motives for the hostility of the assistant Resident and naval commander at Palembang. The Fiskaal said it was a strange affair; he must see into the root of the matter; he had been acting upon the report of the Residents of Palembang and Banca.

The Fiskaal promised to send me some things that I wanted from my vessel, and bade the jailer lead me back to my cell. As I stepped out of the Chamber of Instruction my hand was seized by little fingers, and Umbah was by my side; she had sat crouched behind the door, and I had forgotten her during the long and pre-occupying interrogation and conversation that had been taking place.

Poor little Umbah trembled as she walked beside me; and began to weep bitterly, when we entered my prison ward, and she saw that her papa captain was locked up. He was sober and sad now, and the little foundling did not scold as she had done, when he was riotous and unrestrained; she put her lips between the bars of his window, and wept over her dear papa captain, who was so good till bad men gave him strong water; then he forgot his little Umbah, and made himself sick, and made her heart sad.

The Baron felt that there was no lowness of spirits so painful as the state he imposed upon himself by attempting a cure. He caused grief to his best friends; he retarded his liberation; he forgot that he was a gentleman and an officer; he colluded with a swindler to bestialize himself; and then drank and rioted with a vile turnkey. He would reform; he would for the sake of Umbah, if nothing else. I must help him; and there by the prison bars he promised reformation; he spoke to Umbah in an altered tone; her little face shone with hope and joy; and it seemed that one might be more useful and happy in a prison, than wandering uselessly through the world at our will.

The servant who accompanied Umbah came; the wife of the old follower of the Baron, a stout little Javanese woman called Tayrah: she had been reared in the camp, and was a bold and resolute personage. As she talked with her master, the turnkey bade her hasten, as he wanted to close the gate: she called him some offensive name; and then took Umbah by the hand; who had said adieu to her papa captain, and uncle captain, as she called me. As Tayrah passed out, the turnkey took hold of her rudely by the arm; she let go the hand of Umbah; and instantly I saw a little blade, gleaming before the face of the brutal turnkey who slunk back, muttered some doms and blixems. Umbah laughed and merrily kissed her hand to me, and darted off with her resolute protectress, and I retired to my cell to muse over the events of my second day in the prison of Weltevreden.

* * * * * * * *

On the morning of the third day of the confinement of the commander of the Flirt in the prison of Weltevreden, he received a visit from the commercial agent of the United States at Batavia. The agent had not called upon the commander sooner, because he had heard such atrocious stories of piracy charged upon the commander; of sales of arms to rebel chiefs; of scuttling defenceless vessels in various parts of the Archipelago; and such rumors of the most daring buccaneering, that he had said to the Resident of Batavia, when conversing about the Americans in prison, "Hang them, there are too many such filibustering fanatics in America; hang them at once." Some further information and a visit to the Flirt had led him to doubt the truth of the extravagant stories he had heard. He resolved to call, and now he was astonished to see an unsailor-like landsman, in the stead of the rugged buccaneer he had expected to confront. He knew something of the anti-American feelings of the Resident of Banca; he did not doubt that most absurd jealous fears had been excited, and that the spies who had been placed about the commander had overdone their part. The agent did not believe that the present governor-general of Netherland India, would approve of the extraordinary display of zeal on the part of Resident De Brauw. It would be advisable to address a plain statement of facts, a memorial to the governor-general:—the agent was on the eve of departure for America; he would remain if he thought his presence could be of any service to his countryman; but as his official position was not recognized, he could make no effective interference. The agent took his leave and was seen no more in the prison.

THIRTY-FIFTH DAY.

SABBATH ON BOARD THE PALMER.

THIRTY-SIXTH DAY.

A BETTER state of discipline was observed in Weltevreden; the Baron was restricted from our little court yard privileges, the passage of the drain under the wall was closely grated to check for ever the growth of any more bamboos. Umbah came and conned a Malay lesson in which her teacher learned as he taught; the daily rice and fish came in the morning and afternoon; the mad lady laughed; the maniac howled and told the hour by the making and undoing of his barricades; and the lunatic lawyer paced the main court, muttering about the lack of law in India; on the fourth day of my stay in the prison of Weltevreden.

On the morning of the fifth day, the good-humored face of Sheriff Brower, appeared at the cell door, of him, whom he had lately introduced to the prison. He had an order from the Fiskaal, to conduct me on board my vessel, so that I might assist at an inspection of it and obtain such articles as I needed.

Another drive through the city of gardens and villas; a guarded boat was in readiness at the steps of the "boom," the custom house; and in half an hour after leaving, I trod once more the decks of my gallant little craft:—a sad sight for me to see upon her decks the bloated scowling Dutch faces that leered in surly watchfulness; but sadder sight awaited me below.

The beautiful cabin, the work of art and pride; and the tasteful hall of state, of a floating home of beauty, was sacked and plundered, and vilely befouled; the brocatelle was rent from curtain and cushion; the mirrors smashed; gilding torn off; the floor blotched and streaked with the drippings of coarse feasting; the air rank, with beer, tobacco, gin, and grease defilement; and heavy breeched vandals, sweltering in drunken riot, lay lumpishly on the transom, and glowered at the late lord of this cabin home.

Official scrutiny pried into recesses that had been better probed and searched by the hand of private plunder:—canisters, boxes and bottles were emptied in quest of powder; planks were ripped up and spaces between timbers were searched for shot and small arms; ballast was pitched to and fro; sails were spread out; sailors' kits were emptied; and my already well ransacked, culled and picked baggage, was shook and handled; but not a fragment of war-making material, or of piracy was to be found.

And the needful things I sought also were not to be found:—boots, shirts, hats, trinkets, stationery, and some comforting cordials, were as scarce as powder, cannon, blunderbusses, and bullets; the latter had only existed in Dutch minds; but some of the former were to be seen figuring on Dutch forms; and the cordial bottles were all like the sapless bamboos of the Baron.

The verbal process was drawn up; the good condition of the vessel verified;—she was afloat; her contents all in order; kept by the proper guardians of the law;—kept never to be returned; no arms or evidence of hostile design, to be found as yet;—might be found by and by, in some hollow spar, or the shank of an anchor; so the verbal process was signed; I got some of the remnants of a once ample wardrobe, and was led back to my cabin ashore.

The events of the sixth day, were the visit of a Dutch Baron, and an English merchant, agents for Prince Henry of Holland, the brother of the present king: they were his agents for the working of some tin mines, in the little island of Billiton. The prince was bankrupt, and he had received from the government of his royal brother the appanage of the island to afford him an opportunity to pay off his debts with its plentiful supply of tin; as princes are expected to pay up as well as peasants in Holland. The agents wanted a small vessel to carry rice, coolies and ore between Billiton and Batavia. The Flirt was just the size they wanted, and it was expected that the commander would soon be at liberty; he no doubt was tired of cruising; would he not sell it at a moderate price, as the prince could not afford a large one? I would not then part with my vessel, not for all of Billiton, for all the hopes of future solvency of the bankrupt prince.

On the seventh day Sheriff Brower appeared again at the prison of Weltevreden; he had a paper in his hand, and this time his good honest face was shining with smiles, as he took my hand with some warmth; he had a long document for me, and what did it say? among other things, that the Resident of Palembang had seized and sent to Batavia, certain persons without communicating with any officers of justice, but had held correspondence with the governor-general alone, who "has the power to order the imprisonment of such persons as he may think proper, by a warrant signed by himself personally; yet notwithstanding this, and considering many other points enumerated, "this affair had not been managed by the ordinary course of law," and the court of justice of Batavia ordered the enlargement of the commander, mate, and crew of the Flirt.

Free and soon to be afloat once more. The bitter past was all forgotten. In sight of freedom, blessed freedom, the interests of the prison ceased to charm—no more sights of the bastinado, nor startling sounds in the night watches, of hoarse voices and heavy feet; and shrieks, and howls and laughs, and drunken revelry from cells within and barracks without; rice and fish wooed the appetite in vain; the close damp cell, the prison cell of Weltevreden had lost its romance, and I turned my back upon all this with a very complacent eye.

But I meet at the gate a little form, little hands bearing bunches of fruit, and a little mouth says, Uncle captain, where are you going? Who shall teach me my lesson now, who shall help papa captain to be good? The liberated prisoner began to regret his liberty: little lost flower of the Sumatran mountains, poor little foundling of Passumah, he could have staid in prison for the sake of this motherless child to teach and to save; but he thought of another one, far away, and he went with wetted eyes from out of the prison of Weltevreden.

I went to the house of a relative of the American agent,—then acting in his stead. A company were at dinner; and among others, I was introduced to a fine looking man in early prime of life, who was one of the judges of the Court that ordered my liberation. He gave some explanations about the regulation of the judiciary in Netherland India. He was member of the local court of justice of Batavia,—other Residencies had similar courts; but this was the chief one; and many of the remote possessions of the Government in Sumatra, and Borneo, were subjected to its jurisdiction in all criminal matters. It was the duty of the Resident of Palembang to have communicated my case at once to the Fiskaal, or prosecuting officer of the Court of Justice of Batavia, instead of which, he had entered into correspondence about the matter with the Executive alone. The Court had declared my detention illegal; and he doubted not but that the High Court of Netherland India, a superior tribunal of nine judges appointed by the crown, would not interfere with this decision; and he had not heard that the Attorney General had entered any opposition.

I was an object of very especial curiosity in the city of Batavia; I had lately furnished so much material for the gossip of the place; I was feasted, I visited the notable things of the city; the parks, the palace, the opera; thus spent some rejoicing hours, whilst awaiting the restoration of the papers of my vessel, after receiving which I would go on board the Flirt, get some needful supplies, and quickly make sail direct for Singapore.

But in the midst of my rejoicing, I was called upon by the Dutch baron, who had wished to purchase the Flirt on account of the Prince Henry of Holland. This baron had travelled much in the United States, and expressed great friendliness towards Americans: he did not like to see me, he said, deceiving myself; my enlargement was only temporary on account of the informality of the seizure by the Resident of Palembang. The Attorney General had sent a requisition to the Court of Justice demanding an order of re-arrest against the commander and crew of the Flirt; the Court was then deliberating; would certainly grant the order; and I might expect to see the Sheriff at any moment, coming to conduct me back to prison.

There were others at the hotel, who joined the baron in his view of the case; they all recommended a speedy flight. There was little hope, they said, for me: I had two powerful enemies; the Residents of Palembang, and Banca; they must be supported in their action towards me; my liberation was their condemnation; the Attorney General, a dyspeptic, ruthless old man, was determined to support De Brauw, and to have the dictator and bearer of a certain letter addressed to the sultan of Jambee, punished with death.

If the act of enlargement was final, and not to be followed by other process, the commander would certainly have received his ship papers, and other property seized by the government. This had not been the case. The Court of Justice had demanded the surrender of the Flirt into their hands, in order to restore the vessel to its owner; but the demand was refused, and the vessel was still held by order of the admiral of the port; acting in accordance with the instructions from the high prosecutor of the government.

In view of all these facts a flight was strongly urged, flight on board a fishing prahu, which would reach the straits of Sunda during the night; there the fugitive might await, within many close islet hiding-places, the passing of some China bound ship. I would soon find the commodore commanding the squadron of the United States in the East Indies, and could return with him to Batavia; to demand the restoration of my vessel, and indemnity for the false imprisonment, and losses I had sustained.

One of the advisers would order a prahu to be ready at a certain point, another would get some necessary provisions and equipment, and the baron would take the fugitive in his carriage to the place of embarkation. But I had not consented to this flight. Why should I run away, and by so doing, convict myself of the false charge of attempting to incite insurrection against a power friendly with my own government; and at the same time abandon a fine vessel and valuable property? There seemed to be powerful reasons not to think of flight; and yet there were some weighty ones, to weigh the other way.

A return to prison was imminent; and before innocence was established, a delay of many months might elapse, enough time in the foul atmosphere of a jail in a tropic climate to destroy the constitution of one, whose health was already affected. It would be easier to establish innocence with the counsel and protection of countrymen, backed with power and official authority, than in the hands of a despotic government, surrounded by hostile influences, and denied the aid of counsel.

In the midst of this debate, a new adviser appeared, a stout, powerful-built man, with a dark bronzed face, and a firm, bold look; who addressed me in the pleasant vernacular of home; and in the rough, hearty dialect of the sea.

Look out, said the bluff sea captain, as he led me aside, there are more sharks about here than afloat in the bay. I've been a cruiser in these seas, among Dutch and Malay, and have run into this port off and on, for the last sixteen years, and it's an even tie of treacherous rascality, between the run-a-mucks, and the Van Breeks. These fellows want you to run away so as to get your vessel: the agents of their beggarly Prince Henry have interest enough to get hold of it, as soon as you are gone. Yours is a hard case I know, but the scamps dare not hurt you; they know that Uncle Sam has a few big keels in these seas; and enough of paixhans to blow every burgher of this Dutch settlement into the middle of next week. Stand 'em out; and I'll stand by you; and here's the hand of Gorham Bassett of the ship Rambler, just from the old Bay State.

I was indeed well disposed to stand by the counsel and experience of this frank-spoken countryman. We sat down to dinner, to talk of home memories, of Empire, Bay, and Palmetto States. Another American captain and his lady had joined us; the four talked of voyages and adventures; we had met with mutual friends; we were drawn together by a fast-increasing interest; we were wandering back o'er oceans, amid happy scenes on the banks of the Hudson and the Chesapeake, when Sheriff Brower appeared, and with a sad face this time.

Another paper in his hand, a warrant for the re-arrest of the late lodger in Weltevreden, not to return to that prison; a cell in the Stad or City Jail awaited him. The kind heart of the lady betrayed emotion: the two captains were indignant, but it was no fault of honest Brower. If his prisoner wished to stay a little longer with his friends, and would give his word to be at the prison before the hour of nine that evening, the sheriff would leave him. I gave my word, and Brower departed.

After dinner, a drive, to get some last quaffings of ocean breeze; among the beautiful grounds of Cramat,—around Koningsplein, and through the square of Waterloo, where the lion of the Netherlands was seen, rampant upon a small column with a green bush growing out of its head, nourished by the fecundating, moist air of Java, which covers rocks with luxuriant vegetation; and the sprouting antlers give the look of a rampant goat to the stone beast, that commemorates the victory of Waterloo, gained by William of Nassau!

Some glimpses of the bay, some parting looks at the despoiled little craft that lay hampered beneath the guns of the rude Boreas of Batavia. A last shake of the hands of friends at the hotel, and then Captain Bassett went with the prisoner in quest of his new lodgings.

We took the wrong route; we lost our way; then we retraced our steps, and a little after the appointed time, we knocked at the gate of the City Prison. The sentinel, a Javanese soldier, bade us go away; the hour was past for visiting:—but it was a prisoner who wished to enter;—the sentinel had nothing to do with that, we must go away; the Captain was about to knock again at the gate, a bayonet was presented, and was instantly knocked out of the hands of the feeble native soldier, by the sturdy Captain, who thundered at the gate, and roared out to wake the sleeping keeper, at that pitch of voice wherewith oftentimes, he startled a sluggish crew on t'gallant yards in a gale of wind.

The heavy gate rolled on its hinges; a tall, dark half-breed came forth in night-cap, with lamp in hand, and stood before the Captain and the prisoner; at the same time a tramp of feet was heard behind, soldiers appeared, a file of the guard, brought by the discomfited sentinel, who had fled on losing his firelock. The sergeant of the guard wished to know of the alarmed keeper what was the matter; and the alarmed keeper wished to know of the sergeant of the guard, what indeed was the matter.

The Captain, who with his companion had not been observed, stepped forth from the obscurity of the wall, and growled out in mingled bad Dutch and Malay: —*Blixem*, you *kladdakers;* nothing at all the matter, *trada apapa*, except my friend here has been beating the gamelan, on the gateway of this old hotel, for the last hour, trying to get in; he has a room here; open your establishment, and let us see your accommodations.

The half-breed muttered with inquiring look, something about Brower and American captain; All right, *betul;* said Bassett, here is your man, and giving me a shove forward, walked in with me. The gate was closed upon the staring and bewildered sergeant of the guard, and the astonished jailer led the way to show the apartment of his guest, so unceremoniously introduced at so late an hour.

The keeper opened several doors, and went through passages, and passed sentinels, and tenfold more gloomy indications of prison than at Weltevreden. The air was foul and suffocating, within these walls; and even the best air in that old pestilential quarter of the old town of Batavia was bad enough. We came to a side door in a dimly lighted passage; we entered a gallery, which ran along by six gloomy cell doors; we stopped at the first one, the jailer opened, and showed the lodging designed for his new guest.

A narrow den, a foul sweltering oven; ten feet in length and eight in width, half filled by a coarse platform, its only furniture. No light or air, but from one double-barred grating in front. The cell stank, the air was dead and still; I sat down with sickened feeling, on the platform; the foulness and heat of that place was fearful. The Captain raged at this murdering Dutch villany; his countryman should not be put in there;—but the prisoner must go in, and the jailer could not now let him out without an order from the Fiskaal; the Captain bade the keeper let him out quick, crying out to me as he left, that he would have me out, or be put in there also before twelve hours had passed away.

The door was closed, the dead air felt deadlier and stiller, one quaff alone of the breezy air of the morning was prayed for; and then water, not thought of when the keeper was in the cell, water, water, I called for between those bars, but the brutal sentinel paid no heed; a little water, and a little air, were the craving wants of a dreadful night passed in the Stad prison of Batavia.

And where was the Captain of the Rambler? He had gone, driving furiously towards the house of the Fiskaal. He roused the oppas at the door, and bade him wake the sleeping functionary. The affrighted native could not think of such a thing, Tuan must be mad; Tuan was indeed mad; he roared at the quaking copper skin, who glared with his eyes, who dropped his jaw, who shook and groaned, and was being shaken by the mad Tuan, when a candle, a night shirt, and the benevolent face of the Fiskaal appeared.

Had he given the order to confine the commander of the Flirt in the Stadhuis jail? the vilest den of the old deadly quarter of the city, where none but Chinese, and native cut-throats and thieves were confined? Was that a fit place for the detention of an American gentleman, merely suspected of a crime, which it was an absurdity to suppose he had committed? The Fiskaal had not given the order for removal to the Stad prison; he had now nothing to do with his disposition in prison; a judge commissary of the Court of Justice of Batavia, acting in accordance with the instruction of the Attorney General of Netherland India, had given the order. The Fiskaal had hoped that the prosecution would be dropped, after the liberation of the American captain; he could see no grounds for the Government to proceed upon; and should recommend to the Court of Justice, the final enlargement of the Commander and crew of the Flirt.

But, meanwhile, the prisoner might die of stench and suffocation. The Captain would not lie in the den he had just left, during four and twenty hours, for all the coffee in Java. He inquired the way to the house of the judge commissary; and after another furious drive, was again rousing sleeping guardians, and disturbing the repose of a slumbering Dutchman. A head sprinkled with gray, and a pale and sinister face came to the door; and a thick Dutch voice, speaking in bad English, wished to know, what business brought a man thundering at doors, kicking servants, and waking up an affrighted family in such a drunken, brigand-like way.

Softly there, Mr. Judge; said the puffing and blowing, yet self-restrained Bassett. I am sorry to make you turn out of your nice, wide berth, with plenty of fresh air; I regret the kicks given to the boy at the door which ought to have been given elsewhere; and I did not mean to scare you or your family, but I do talk loud, when I get excited, and I am a little so now. You have locked up a friend of mine, in a hole not fit for a beast; I want him out, this very night, and put where he can have a chance for his life.

And was this the errand of a man, who dared to break the rest of a judge; to ask him to disturb himself about the comforts of a pirate, lodged but too well already? That's just my errand, said Bassett, and pirate or no pirate, I want an order to have that man removed to better quarters, or I don't leave you, Mr. Judge. I'm a fixture, and I give you the word of Gorham Bassett for that.

The judge, as he stood in his night garments, stared hard at the broad, heavy-built American; he looked with an appreciating eye, at two ponderous fists, and massive arms, thick with muscle springing out of the chest of a war horse; perhaps he counted over his coolies, the oppas, and his own force to put the ugly-looking fixture out of doors, but he evidently did not think his combined forces equal to the task, and spoke in a milder tone to the disturber of his rest.

What he had done, was in accordance with a requisition emanating from the high prosecuting office of the Government. He would consult with him, the next day. But that would not satisfy the Captain of the Rambler; he wanted an order then, he knew that the judge had the power to give it. The judge remonstrated; it was absurd, at such an hour, the sheriff would not turn out, the keeper of the jail would not open a door:—the Captain wanted the order, he would look after the sheriff, and see to the opening of the prison.

The judge became indignant, to be dictated to in such a manner, on such a matter, in his own house, at that time of night: he would send for a file of men, of the city guard, and have the intruder lodged in jail himself. All ready for the guard, or the jail either, were words uttered doggedly in reply. Gorham Bassett had sworn to have that man out of the infernal black hole into which he had been stuck; or go in himself. The judge, and the Government should have two American cases on hand; and then look out for young America when he heard of all this, on board the Susquehanna.

The judge bit his lips; he muttered something about American audacity; he walked nervously to and fro; he stood before the Captain, and confronted a fixed unblenching face; there was not a shadow of back out, of compromise, or put off, in those dark, bronzed features. It was a hard case for judicial pride, and Dutch obstinacy, to give up to this dogged sea captain, but some American commodore might present a harder one, and something must be done.

Some rays of dawning day began to stream across a starry Javan sky, when the scowling judge, handed to the resolute Captain a document of writing, with which he issued forth from the dwelling of beleagured justice, and once more roused the still streets of Batavia;—horses' hoofs resounding, and carriage wheels rattling and rumbling, on the way to the house of the sheriff of Batavia.

The prisoner had groaned on his platform all night, or sought at times, to get some quaffs of air through his grating; but it came foul and rank, from a close yard, devoted to vilest use. The odor within was a deadlike smell, rising up from his coarse couch, like the rank fetor of the decaying matter of a slaughter house; and after a night of suffocating misery, as some few rays of morning began to stream through the grating, in the cell door, the prisoner began to discern on his platform, some dark streaks of putrefying blood.

The honest face of Brower once more appeared, and brave

Bassett was shaking the exhausted and haggard prisoner by the hand. The sheriff was indignant at the sight of the cell. He was not aware that such quarters had been designed for his prisoner, or he would have protested himself. He spoke of the good heart of the Fiskaal, who wished to liberate the American Captain altogether, but this judge commissary, who now had charge of the "instruction," or preliminary investigation of the case, was an avowed friend of Resident De Brauw.

The sheriff explained the cause of the blood on the platform. A young man, about twenty years of age, had been suspected of crime; he was lodged in this cell, whilst awaiting a trial. His case was overlooked; eight months passed away. The prisoner loved a young lady, with strong attachment; he hoped soon to be with her again; and this hope sustained his spirits; but time rolled on, many months had passed away; his case seemed hopeless, and the father of the girl, wished her to marry some one else. The lover heard of this, he clamored for a trial; he became delirious; attention was called to his case; it was discovered that there were no grounds for prosecution; an order for his liberation was handed to Sheriff Brower, who came, and found a dead body on this platform. The young man had attempted to cut his throat with a piece of glass; but shrinking from that task, he had strangled himself with his handkerchief. It was his blood upon my sleeping place, which the neglectful jailer had not yet cleansed away.

Harsh and unmusical they would have been to Dutch ears, the words that rolled out with hissing sound between the gritting teeth of Captain Bassett. Short work with the Stad prison, and the city of Batavia, if the Captain had been commodore, and lay off in the harbor, with a steam frigate, and a few sixty-four pounders; there would have been no more blunderings of a government of suspicious and sordid men; there would have been no complicated "case of the Flirt," nor "Prison of Weltevreden."

RETURN TO WELTEVREDEN.

But back to the prison of Weltevreden, Sheriff Brower leads his prisoner, back to the barracks, to the country retreat of Adjutant Pieters. The red-faced jailer was happy to welcome his late lodger back again. The little cell in the little court was vacant still. It was wet and close, and the air passed through it with sluggish sultriness; but there was some air, without privy or charnel smell; and there was company, the Baron, the trader, the schoolmaster, and little Umbah.

Honest-hearted Baron, he stood in the gateway to welcome his cell neighbor: he too had been in closer durance, suffering dreadully for the want of a bamboo; and Umbah had been gone, she could not enter prison whilst his cell had been closed: the mad lawyer passed by, was glad to see the American captain back again; and though still affirming there was no law in India; yet there was a pleasant welcome back to the prison of Weltevreden.

One night of horrors had made a dreary house of care look bright; it was not a change from a beautiful little ship, and a happy, free sea life, to that of loss of property, and the restraint of confining walls. That feeling was past. It was now joy to change from a cell of death, rank with decaying drippings of self-slaughter, to one where the air came freely; and human companionship was near at hand.

But the night of horrors had done some hurtful work, on the health of the returned prisoner. When the sheriff and jailer, and his brave defender had left, he sank down on his platform, and passed a feverish day and night. The kind-hearted Baron sat up with ministering hands. The invalid found repose as day began to dawn, and when he awoke bright rays of light were streaming like golden shafts through his grating; and little bright eyes were shining on him, from the golden face of Umbah.

She had mangosteens in her hand; mangosteens for her uncle Captain. Purple rinds were burst, rich pulp was quaffed; and the sick uncle Captain was refreshed and revived, like the papa Captain, who when feverish and faint, had seen little bright eyes and restoring fruit at the same time. Umbah's cure would have sufficed, but the generous Bassett had sent cordials, and tasteful provisions, for the entry of which another order had been obtained.

The invalid was soon restored by a ministering little presence, and the fruity medicine. The lessons in Malay, of reading and writing, were begun again. The half-breed schoolmaster helped both to trace the straight *alif*, the many curved *sim*, the looped *lam*, the cup-like *nun;* and all the intricate sinuosities of the Arab script. The student and traveller traced them not more quickly than the foundling Malay child.

He had a love to learn of all that belonged to the East; which no alarms could disturb; no weight of woe could destroy. Instruments of oppression were sought for knowledge; sentinels and marines, when they would talk, were made to tell of their country, of the fleet or the fort, to which they belonged; and no place had been so wretched, but he had thought as much about its history as its horrors.

In Weltevreden, there was nothing that a free man should wish for; unless one should be found, that would covet a close cell, with a wet, paved floor, the fare of eastern slaves, the companionship of mongrel felons; and howls of torture and madness resounding daily in the ears. All this, and other striking features of a prison life, may be curious and interesting to tell; but soul and body sickening to him who felt them.

There was one, however, in Weltevreden, who felt them not too much, to stop his love of study, instead of seeking refuge in stimulant or unavailing complaint; and by so doing, he preserved his health and the even temper of his mind. He was not unmindful of liberty, he deplored the loss of a beautiful ship, the interruption of a delightful cruise; and more than all, he bitterly deplored the loss of a choice gathering of notes for history, poetry, science; and the art and romance of a curious people; a rare lot of Malay manuscript fallen into the hands of his captors.

All his choice papers; many manuscripts given by Panyorang Osman, some by Panyorang Scheriff Ali, by Demang Sapedin, by the Panghulu of Palembang and others; as he had parted with all that he could spare from his vessel for evey scrap of knowledge about Sumatra. All this was left in his cabin; perhaps destroyed by the plundering keepers; or in the hands of his judges never to be returned.

Thus he thought, and often so painfully after his capture; and he sought with the material around him in prison, to make up some little of the loss. There were other masses of papers, the gathering of past years, mere personal memoranda, in the hands of his jailers: he could part with them without pain; but his Sumatran collection,—loss more felt, almost than loss of liberty; but it was a loss sooner restored. Strange experience had that man then and *afterwards in the recovery of lost papers*, from out of the hands of his Dutch captors.

How his Sumatran notes were found, he thus told on board the Palmer on the thirty-seventh day of her homeward voyage from Java.

THIRTY-SEVENTH DAY.

I HAD lain in prison two weeks, and had not heard a word about my men. My late navigator had been brought to Weltevreden, and placed in the block No. 3 of the prison, in company with the Resident, the Topographer, and the Russian secretary. I heard news of preparation for the reception of my sailors, and on the afternoon of the same day, I heard the unsubdued voice of sturdy Jim, raised in song, mingled with the cursings of Dutch soldiers, the clatter of bayonets; as the prisoners and escort entered the main court of the prison.

I looked out through the bars, at my men, as they stood in the court, waiting for the opening of doors: some joyous greetings were exchanged with rough glad faces, even with the deserting Brazilians; past weakness and neglect of duty forgotten; and the difference between the cabin and the forecastle being overlooked in a common lot. One more forward than the rest, the poor, half-savage, faithful Pirez, ran up to the grating and after some quick words of salutation, asked if I had found any thing in my pillow. Before I had time to speak, a soldier of the guard pulled the faithful fellow away, and with a brutal kick, urged him on towards his quarters in the prison.

I must now speak of Pirez more fully; as he acts an interesting part, in my after experience in prison. I found him at

13*

Pernambuco, where he sculled a little boat, and oftentimes, he alone, had glided me along through the channels between Recife, Boa Vista, and Olinda. I had been struck with the strange ugliness of the boy; and stranger jargon of his speech; said to be known to no one but his African mother.

His thick lips, and wide mouth—a very wide one, stretched out far beyond forehead and chin; little yellow eyes seemed straining to start out of a dirty yellow skin; blotched and mottled like the back of a toad. The narrow, pointed, pear-shaped head, was dotted with scattering stunted tufts of coarsest and kinkiest of wool; the body, short, fat, and shapeless, the legs bowing out, heels large, and great teeth ever grinning. Such was the Peri, as called by the crew of the Flirt.

Speech was more brutal than form; a thick, ruttling voice that came forth with grunting jerks; a wild jargon of Portugese and some African dialect. People sought to speak with him in vain; they made signs in bargaining for his boat; but oftener the hideous and unintelligible boatman was passed by, whilst I became a frequent patron, and tested largely those powers of pantomime, that became famous in Sumatra.

One day, I wanted him and his boat; and I saw him pushing off from the landing, with a passenger, an old black woman, his mother, and she was about to give place to me; but learning that her destination was near the same point as mine, I insisted that he should take us both. The woman, a pleasant-looking old African, with some likeness, but none of the hideousness of her son, spoke some Portuguese and Spanish which I could understand.

She talked of her rude son; as true and honest, as he was rough and ugly. His father, a Cape de Verde Portuguese, was one of the bravest men she had known or seen. He was a sailor, and had saved her life on board a slaver, when she was dead sick, and about to be thrown overboard as worthless cargo. She wanted to do nothing else, but give him all her life after that. He took her to Brazil; where he left her from time to time, on many a long cruise, whilst she worked for him and their children ashore.

He went to Mozambique, to Goa, Malacca, Macao; and then had sailed many a time with an adventurous captain, between Arabia and Sumatra; and who was he? who but the uncle, the mysterious wanderer, and story-teller of the East. The father of Pirez had sailed with him many years, and was lost or killed, she knew not how, in his service.

This was fresh cause for interest in Pirez. I always sought his boat, he lingered daily, more and more about my vessel; and when ready to sail, he wanted to go with me; and his mother being quite willing, I took him, more as a servant than a sailor; and though he liked the ropes, and to run out on the yards, with the best and boldest on board; yet his chief duty was in my cabin; and he enjoyed a confidence which Bahdoo had not superseded.

I learned to understand all the words, or articulated grunts, and signs of this wild creature. No one else had learned to talk with him on board. I took a fancy to teach him to read and write, during idle hours at sea, for which he had much aptitude. He had the daily handling of my literary labors, in putting away papers, left loosely on my table, and he learned to know the place for note, memoranda, or letter, by being able to read their contents.

And now you will be prepared to listen to what I have to tell you about my pillow. As soon as Pirez had spoken in his wild way, at the grating, I stepped into my cell, I took up my pillow, and with trembling hands I undid the cord, as the oppas had done a few days before; but thrust my hand down deeper, pulled out the stuffing, and felt something hard; you can guess what it was, better than I could then. In a compact roll, well packed round with moss stuffing of the cushions of my cabin, were my much prized papers.

Before my arrest at Palembang, I had never supposed that the authorities would venture upon so high-handed a measure, and had had no thought of trying to make any disposition of personal valuables or private papers; which lay loosely in lockers, and on my table, when the invading marines poured in upon my deck; and when I gave the order to Pirez to pack up the few things I was allowed to take, I had no idea of a chance to save any thing of valuables or papers.

I did long to say a word to the boy, to give him one look, as he went below; but he did not need it; whilst I complained of his delay, he had quickly seized papers, he believed to be the most especial, the most important to conceal from my captors; those that told about Dutch and Malays, also some interesting Mexican reliques; he packed the pillow case, and trusting to good fortune, flung it carelessly up through the skylight on deck.

The same faithful hands had driven the tacks into the ensign, that was afterwards torn from its staff by the hands of a drunken Dutch naval commander; and that flag was not lost;—hardly less strange was its preservation and reappearance, than the recovery of the lost papers; but I shall tell of that farther on in my story.

After rejoicing over the recovery of my papers, I rejoiced over my escape, when the Fiskaal came to examine my cell; an escape from the stain of dishonor in the eyes of that functionary, for had the hands of the oppas gone a little deeper, at the moment I gave my word I had no papers in my cell, I should have made an enemy where I afterwards found a just and kind man, an able and intelligent friend.

But that visit reminded me that I might receive many more, from less gentlemanly inquisitors; and I made speedy disposition of my papers; in small packages that were delivered to Captain Bassett, and other American captains, who came to see me; and of all the scraps I accumulated, and memoranda I made during my long stay in prison, I sent from time to time by various hands, I know not to this day, if one package ever safely reached home in America.

The prisoner knew not, when he spoke with his friends on board the Palmer; but he could have told them afterwards, that of all that the faithful Pirez saved, and all of a collection of rare notes, gathered in prison, all fell into faithful hands, those of Bassett, Bursley of the Izaak Walton, Smith of the Raja Walie, and the worthy Shaw of Singapore; some wandering round by China, some by California, and some by Australia; yet all brought safely to hand, the untouched trust of the prisoner of Weltevreden.

The brave Bassett went with the coming of the faithful Pirez. Daily had the kind, bold-hearted captain, invaded the prison with pockets stuffed, and hands filled with good things for me, and for little Umbah, and the Baron, who had become sharers of his kindly regards. He had sympathized with the tastes of the latter, and one day came with a little bamboo in his pocket.

The guard wished to fumble pockets, and feel coat laps, as he did with all incomers; but away flew bayonet, and soldier fled, as at the gateway of the Stad. The jailer ran to the Resident of the city, and to judges to complain; and the colonel at the barracks, demanded an order for the arrest of this knocker down of soldiers, this bullier of judges, this prison invader, this great filibustering Bassett.

The judiciary and magistracy of Batavia, knew too well this man; they did not want to have him on their hands; worse than a score of such "pirates," as they had already caged. Give him a wide berth, no order for the colonel; and jailer is desired to withhold his complaint. Give the captain a free run, and only watch, and have guard enough not to let him carry the prisoner out.

Brave Bassett came to go away; the Rambler has her hold filled with the berry of Java (fragrant promoter of sick liver and sick headaches); and he came for the last time, to visit his friends in prison. He could go away with comfort now; he had seen me through the worst; now more comfortably lodged, having promise of a speedy trial; feeling safe in a happy issue from the kindly disposition of the Fiskaal, and from the avowed opinions of judges of the Court of Justice.

Bassett took a message to deliver to the commodore, commanding the American squadron in the East India seas; he promised to rouse up American functionaries, wherever found, in behalf of the commander and crew of the Flirt. But we looked long, in vain, for the coming of the commodore, who never came; though we doubted not the brave Bassett was true to the promise he gave, when he bid adieu, in the prison of Weltevreden.

He kept it; said the Boatswain on board the Palmer; we heard of the Flirt and her folks, being all foul among the Dutchies at Batavia, when I was with the fleet at Hong Kong. The people on board the Susquehanna, from first luff down to captain of chain gang, were charged to the muzzle with fight; they wanted to go right off, and have a brush with Dutchy's tubs, if he didn't let go the Flirt and pay up handsome for his frolic. But the old man didn't pass the word to get up anchor; the Susquehanna lay quietly grinning at Hong Kong rocks, and Chinaman Joshes; day after day, week after week she lay; by and by, we heard more stories about Flirt and yourself; hardest sort of a case; but old Susquehanna, didn't move, and the old man walking the decks, surly as sick thunder. One of the ward-room mess, said that the commodore wanted to give the Dutch lubbers a broadside of fits; but he couldn't move; he'd got a small scrap of paper, and six lines, from the Department fogy at home, that said, don't move out of sight of Hong Kong till further orders; and all on account of some fuss with a beggarly Brazilian plenipo, and one of our people going minister to Rio, who charged the old man, with having charged the Brazilian for his board, when on board the Susquehanna, going to Brazil. There, Uncle Sam's big ship was stuck; or steaming back and forth to Macao, burning coal at forty dollars a ton; and Uncle Sam's people, and flag, and honor, and interests, were getting jugged, trod on, befouled, and swamped; but the big ship couldn't budge, waiting for another order from another fogy, which she did for a year and more.

By gracious king! said the Boatswain, warming up, our people has got grit enough, real Kennebec grit; we have lots of Bassetts afloat, enough for a thousand commodores, that would make every beggarly nation, in the world, think a thousand times, before they dared to lay a crooked finger upon an American citizen or an American flag; but we have an everlasting lot of sharks at Washington, all the time, and of all stripes; whether whig or t'other, 'tis all the same, a scramble for votes and plunder. What do they care about honor abroad? they are only thinking of keeping on the soft side of the pork-raisers, nigger-drivers, and timber-choppers who put them where they are. You go home, and ask them to back you up in asking damages of the Dutch; and they'll wait to see whether the pork-raisers, nigger-drivers, and timber-choppers, care any thing about it first; if so, and you can get up a breeze among the people, all well; and you'll sail in. But just get foul of the sharks at Washington; and their bloodsucking, piratical papers, will give you worse fits than you ever got from the Dutch. I would rather go abroad, any time, with a British passport, than one from my own government; and I am not the first one that has said it.

THIRTY-EIGHTH DAY.

Many days were passed away, looking for help that never came. Many times had I been summoned to the Chamber of Instruction, to appear before the harsh judge, made harsher by the rough handling of the hero of the Rambler. The hopes of quick trial, and of leave to go in peace, were daily made less, by this commissary judge, working like a lawyer of small scope with the quirks of the law, to give some form and proportion to a baseless case.

The prisoner was led forth at all hours; at early dawn, at noon, at night, often in the midst of a meal, or repose, the rusty bolts rolled and grated; and the livid snake face of the lock up dragoon, called the hungry or unrested man to come to the little black hall, to meet the frowning commissary, who, with quick questions about matters spoken of a week, two weeks before, sought to entrap a weary and unaided man, having no counsel but in his own head, and no strength but in his own heart.

And through what winding ways, this judge of the Chamber, the Star tribunal of Netherland India law,—through what winding ways, with hints, and threats, and made-up tales, he strove to worm out some words of weakness that might be dressed up into a phantom of crime. Such tales of what some servant, sailor, or other one had said; such cajolery about the clemency of Dutch rule in the East; and such warnings of its power, and threats of its vengeance; and such insulting demands to confess, he knew not what.

Let them be brought before me, said the prisoner; the men, who speak of evil words and deeds, that they have heard and seen. Let them come; governors and soldiers, servants and sailors, and tell their tale before the face of him they speak against. But this would be too great expense, trouble and derangement for the government to do. Then the prisoner would be silent; if justice rules, they will be brought, and he will speak; but if power rules under a form of law, then further words are vain.

The judge threatened; and spoke of crime seeking safety in silence. With him, it was a sign of guilt to ask fair play and open justice; he would be thwarted in the working of so many nicely contrived entrapments, that afford such triumphs to small legal minds, versed alone in the letter, and knowing nothing of the spirit of law. This judge had no screws or racks for a silent victim; he surely would have used them; he must consult a court, men who controlled him; and they looked with a better eye upon the prisoner.

It was decreed that accusers and accused should meet; and should be heard, face to face. The government, whose strength lay in meting out justice to all, should lend its ships of war, its army; nay stop the functions of every servant in its pay, to have justice quick and faithful, for the meanest of its subjects; and how much more for a stranger, whose health, whose property, whose time was wasting, and made painful by slow and uncertain justice, the greatest wrong of all he had to undergo.

Back to Palembang, went the Arjuno; the decoying trap of the Sumatran chief, the blood-stained prison of a confiding guest, back it went to bring the decoyer and false host; and more besides; the mulatto of Surinam; the naval captor of the Flirt, the friendly Shahbandar; the courteous Major; the examining Kress, the topographical Captain, wishful to sell the secrets of his service for a carbine; and with these to bring the suspicious Resident, the courteous Doctor, and related Havermeester of Minto.

And why should I indeed wish for the presence of these men in Batavia? The private spies of one were my betrayers; I had another's hate, for coming from a land where that man's race were slaves; a third, with a brutal nature and drunken delusion, beheld in me a rival; a fourth, hating me for being thwarted in an ungentlemanly covetousness; and all feeling some Dutch ill will, and jealousy of America; and yet I would have them all to come; and give the better chance that the whole of a dark story might be known at home.

But no tale shall be told by many of these men, no tale of truth or fiction, of what they saw, or what they were persuaded to see. The Arjuno speeds in vain up the Moosie; she stems not the stream so swiftly as those have gone down, whom she goes to bring; they shall tell nothing of the Flirt or her commander; their story mingled with the melody of the rambahya song, and went with a gurgle down the Moosie.

It is the King's birthday. There are rejoicings at Batavia and Palembang; and wherever the Dutch flag floats, they celebrate the birth of a coarse bad man; the hero of many a vile deed of night in the Binnenhof, and by the Koekamp in the Bois de la Haye; the grandson of him called William the worst. Hahnshche bier and schiedam flow freely even in Weltevreden; and there is hope and rejoicing among prisoners of state and manacled felons; two prisoners shall go free on the King's birthday.

And who shall they be? The Colonel and the Baron? or

Resident and Topographer; or perhaps the Commander and mate of the Flirt? The patriotism of strong drink rises up in song; the man has beer who will have the bastinado on the morrow; the convict clanks his chains with maudlin joy on the nineteenth day of February; for then a king was born; and on this day, there is a jubilee of gin in the prison of Weltevreden.

There is revelry in the rakits on the waters of the Moosie; men are zealous to be drunk, drinking hard, and singing loud; and "Willem's bluid" is mingled largely with patriotic beer in the barracks of Palembang. The red-headed lieutenant and the adjutant, brave with schiedam once more, would honor the birthday of William the Third by exploits like his own; and go in quest of hadjys again who have helpless women to sell.

But they have better escort than a picket of men this time. There is the bloated lieutenant of the sea, for this is a fitting expedition for him; and for the mulatto of Surinam; but what is the haughty chief doing here, the cold-hearted De Brauw, and the courtly Blommestein; the rude yet soldierly Kress; the worthy Shahbander, the hospitable Van Ochsee; Böckel, the Secretary; and Poolman, van Hemskerk and Schmidt; all aroused by the inspiring swill of schiedam, are going to do fitting honor to the birthday of the debauchee of the Hague.

They are going in a barge, to cross the Moosie; they are thirteen in all, besides the steersman; the trusty helmsman of the Resident; but where is he? the barge is ready, he is not to be found, and there is no one to steer; a skilful hand is needed in the swift current of the stream; and one is standing near, a half-breed, well skilled with the dayong, oar or rudder on the waters of the Moosie; and the Resident accepts the service of the master of the barque from Bali, to steer them safely across the stream.

It was on the day after the birthday of the King of Holland, on the 20th of February, 1852, that this excursion took place; this day happening to be the feast of the Chinese New Year, the Chap-Go-Meh; a day of great license and debauch among Chinamen in Sumatra. As the officers of the garrison wished to take a part in this revelry, the Resident had deferred the leave of frolic for the royal anniversary until the following day, when an excursion was proposed among the Chinese, and certain Malay campongs. The Resident had business in view in connection with this excursion; he had already received instructions to obtain every particle of evidence relating to the visit of the Flirt, and the intercourse of her commander with the natives of all ranks. He designed to visit in particular the houses of those Chinamen, who had entertained the American commander; and he took with him those officers, who had been the most in his company, and could testify to the greater portion of his conversation during his stay at Palembang. These officers were to be called upon for their testimony; they were the principal witnesses for the government. They had noted down words, said in friendly and confidential moments, the same as certain officers of the Arjuno and the Boreas; as part of the service of every Dutch military and naval officer in Netherland India, is that of a spy for his government.

The absence of the regular steersman of the cutter or barge, was probably accidental, as also the presence of the Balinese Captain, who stood ready to take his place. But no doubt the half-breed thought at once of gratifying his revenge for the insults that had been heaped upon him by these Europeans. He was at home, like a fish in the water; the river was swollen, the wind was blowing fresh; it would require skill to cross, and there was no safety, but in a faithful, as well as a skilful hand.

Plenteous gin had made the European officers affable with the half-breed; debauchery is democratic; and soldierly pride and magisterial dignity, reeling with beer, were willing to follow the Creole to a Chinese serai. They followed the dancing lantern lights, and the ding dong of bells, that had guided the American commander on the last evening of his freedom at Palembang. They visit the rakits of Tchoo-Kee-Lin, the chief of the Chinamen, of Oey Soch Tchay, and of Oey Tsee Yang; the latter shows the seat of his late American guest, and mentions all that he had observed him do, and with whom he had spoken. Tumungung Nora Wangsa has related the conversations with Tchoon Long, the Resident always startles at the mention of the name of Ferdano Mantri; the Chino Malay is sought for, and found, and with him they proceed to return to the Fort. Plentiful tchoo having been added to gin, made the barge unsteady with reeling epaulettes. The two half-breeds were seen to speak together, before they left the shore; they were seen to exchange looks on reaching the mid-current of the stream; the waters were rolling fast, and the barge for a time was held firmly with her head to the stream; her sail fluttered in the wind, she began to pay off, she is broaching too, broadside to the stream; some one rushed towards the Balinese, but ere his hand could be stayed, the waters of the Moosie were sweeping over the barge.

When the first surge had entered the boat, the half-breeds were out, and breasting their way towards the native campongs on the left bank of the river. Many of the Dutchmen, who were in a little state cabin, were seen no more; some uplifted arms, and epaulettes were seen for a time, but the wâters soon roll over, and all were gone but three; two dark faces stemmed away towards the fort, and a last struggling arm was seized by a native swimmer. The Resident, the Assistant Resident, and the Shabandar, were all who returned to the fort of Palembang, and there were no witnesses to return with the Arjuno to Batavia.

Some brave and courteous men, and some rude and brutal soldiers were food for the caymans. Some portion of the remains of Major Van Blommestein, afterwards found far down the stream, were only recognizable by a fragment of uniform and button attached; and a skull with an obliterated face was found, but some remnants of deep red hair, told that this was part of the once stern Kress. There are other details of this event, that need not be dwelt on here, which are recorded in the Javaasche Courant, the official journal of Batavia, also in the English journals of Singapore, of the 9th March, 1852.

* * * * * * *

The drowning of the ten officers at Palembang; the suspicions resting upon the Balinese Captain, and the half-breed Chinaman; their former relations with the commander of the Flirt; all these circumstances gave rise to many extravagant rumors and suppositions at the time; and caused the American prisoners at Weltevreden to be subjected to a more rigid surveillance. Wild stories of strange-looking piratical craft, having been seen lurking among the islands of the Straits of Sunda, were in the mouths of all the gossipers of Batavia; there were rumors of an armed expedition, hovering near the coast of Java, watching an opportunity to carry off from Krawang, the chieftain Ferdano Mantri, and a prisoner of Weltevreden.

The chieftain was confined more closely in Poorwacarta; and the prisoner was for a time subjected to closer discipline in his cell. He could see no one, he had no books to read and no means to write. He suffered with bad air and bad food; he had no relief from cheerful companionship, and the little child whom he had taught, and from whom he had learned, could come no more with a pretty smiling face, and with refreshing, health preserving mangosteens.

He began to feel more fully, the desolation of four close, bare walls; of a wet tile floor, of a rude platform, of rusty iron bars. He wanted to be tried; but his judges wanted to find out the foundation for the wild rumors they had listened to. The Arjuno went back again to Palembang, with peremptory orders to bring the Resident, with all his surviving officers, and all natives that could be secured, who had spoken with the commander of the Flirt. Two other steamers, the Phœnix and the Borneo, were sent to visit Engano, to cruise in the Straits of Sunda, in those of Gaspar Straits, to visit Bali, Linga, and many more islands said to have been visited by the Flirt, before she touched at Minto.

The Flying Dutchman that had so often disturbed the dreams of sailors in the times of Drake and Tromp, had emigrated to America, and had appeared with the stars and stripes at the gaff of the Flirt, among the islands of Mynheer in the East. He had been seen at anchor, among a pirate fleet in some bay of Bali; or scuttling a ship in Gaspar Straits; selling cargoes of arms to the people of Jambee, Siak, and Indraghiri; and doing many other piratical feats; and as the Pylades had captured him, and the Arjuno had brought him safely to jail, it remained for the Phœnix and the Borneo to look up the evidences of his exploits in various quarters, since no witnesses from Palembang could be obtained; and thus the naval forces of Netherland India were in very active service throughout the Archipelago in 1852.

The efforts that were made by the Netherland India Government, to hunt up evidence against the people of the Flirt, were strangely disproportioned to the cause of the exertion. No man in Netherland India had seen more than nine feeble men; and not a cannon, nor keg of powder, on board the little schooner;

and yet, why had she caused such alarm at Palembang; and so much "disturbed the peace of Netherland India;" as Col. De Brauw said in his despatch to the Governor General. It was not the little Flirt; but there was a shadow of something behind her; a largely looming shadow of a presence, coming to disturb a peaceful monopoly of more than two hundred years. The shadow of a power fast coming, was there; that would know why great empires of land, and forest and mineral wealth, were to remain embargoed by a petty power, that had only the force to menace, and not the means to develop and control.

THIRTY-NINTH DAY.

For a time it was a hard struggle even with some help of philosophy of soul, and a good constitution, to bear up against hope deferred, uncertainty of law, badgering in the judgment seat, bad quarters, bad air, worse food, and nothing to do. This,—the hardest fate of all for a prisoner, to have nothing to do, but to prey upon himself; to dream of home, of bright firesides, of shady groves, of sunny fields, and glistening spring streams; and then of love-in its best and brightest garb, of love without motive, love without thought of gain; beside it in the quiet home, beside it in the fields, and by the sea shore; and then to think of lapse of time, of the gulf of space; of the good forgotten, and evil only growing by absence; to feel the world rolling over us, alive in a grave; no one heeding, no one coming; not a voice through those bars, but the voice of demons, aye, demons of cells, who come alone to lonely men, and blow, foul staining breaths, on mirrors of home, blotting out love, and hope, and peace from the self-eating heart.

But there was work for the prisoner to do; something to rouse the self-preying soul; work for his jailers, work for the Government; that had put all its talent into prison.

The Government wanted many millions of bricks, to build some store-houses, some barracks, and some more walls and cells in the prison of Weltevreden. The government, like all other governments, gave its good jobs for public service or public plunder to favorites of the governing ones, without much regard to the interest of the governed.

The contract for bricks was given to the grandson of a stout supporter of the Netherland India monopoly. A terrible man, by the way, was that grandfather, who took large contracts to slay men; a marshal of the great contractor, Napoleon;—the Marshal Daendels, of whom the imperial warrior said, that if he had two Daendels in his army, he must hang one; so terrible for hanging his own people, as well as for slaying the enemy, was that old Dutch marshal.

He was sent during the imperial sway of his commander in chief, to be Governor General of the late Dutch empire in the East, now merged into the empire of the French. He gave out contracts to build forts and roads. He said to one, make ten millions of bricks, and to build a fort within six months, and if not finished, the man should hang on the top of his work. He bade the people of Java, to make a road the whole length of the island, from Anjer to Banjoowangie, on which he might roll his carriages and his cannon, and for every portion not finished in a given time, he hung those who directed the labor; such a fort-builder and road-maker was the terrible Marshal Daendels.

But this was not all; whilst he demanded the labor of the men, and hung when not promptly performed, he demanded the favors of the women; and was as ruthless when thwarted in the favor of the one, as by a failure in the labor of the other. He burst through the wilderness of Java, with his great military road; and he burst into many a Javan home, with his great soldierly lust. At every relay on his highway march, there was a virgin sacrifice offered to this Blue Beard, this great devouring Dutch Moloch of Java.

And a grandson of this man, this marshal of Napoleon, this chief devil of the Javanese, had a contract for bricks; but had none of the grandfather's way of getting the job done. Bricks were no longer to be made, as in the old man's time, when the clay of Java might have been mixed with Javan virgins' tears, and worked with the fettered feet of Javan princes. The grandson must content himself with the sweat of Chinese coolies, and the working feet of Javanese buffaloes.

Hand-working and beast-tramping were too slow for the wants of the Government, but what was to be done? there was no marshal now, to demand the unwilling labor of five thousand men; for just so many were wanted to do the work as fast as required; and these could not be got, nor paid when obtained. The government need of bricks was talked of in Batavia. A great many Dutch labor-saving ideas were suggested; but all, very little faster than Chinese feet and buffalo hoofs.

There was one, who had travelled in America; he had heard of machines in that country, that turned out their thousand of brick, whilst a buffalo could turn round. Where was the American that could tell the contractor something about such a brick-making machine? Two men then lived in Java, wanderers from the land of notions, who could tell something, give some idea of a plan; but they had been thirty years absent from home; thirty years behindhand with the progress of their country; and the American burghers of Batavia could not start any ideas for making bricks any faster than their Dutch fellow-subjects.

But these are not all the Americans in Java; we have some caged in Weltevreden. The contractor and his friends speak whisperingly about them. They must be cautious how they mix up treason with bricks. The marshal's grandson has a friend, a fine, generous, brave young fellow, whose father was the noted friend of Americans, at a time when there was no heavy export duty on coffee, and the roadstead of Batavia was often filled with American sails; that father, though not in trade, kept open house for Americans, whom he loved to see; and now the son had often called on the American prisoners in Weltevreden, and had been active to soften their condition.

The contractor spoke with his young friend about the American prisoners; were they all ruffianly sailors, captain and crew? or was there a gentleman among them, one having some knowledge of the art and science of his country? The young friend thought there was more than one; men who seemed to know a little of books as well as of ropes. The one he knew best, was the commander; he spoke of him in the kindness of his generous young heart, with some partiality. The contractor became interested, he wanted to see him; he had a friend in the court of justice, and obtained permission to visit the prison of Weltevreden.

The contractor and his friend came together; they found a prisoner much sick and worn out; the young friend brought some smuggled trifles to refresh him, and spoke words of hope and encouragement; and the contractor spoke of the machine that was wanted. The prisoner knew but little of such things; he did not say so; for a hope dawned on his mind; his memory was busy with what he had seen in his visits to workshops, and at fairs of mechanics at home; thoughts were busy, and he felt in a mood to attempt impossibilities; it would be something to do, and he might raise up means and friends outside, by the attempt.

The prisoner said, that he had seen such a machine as was wanted; one that would save the labor of hundreds of men; he believed that such a one could be made in Java, that Javanese mechanics had skill enough to follow a good plan, and he could make that plan. The contractor was taken aback, this was far more than he had dreamed of;—to get some idea of the nature and cost of one, to be sent for, was all that he had hoped for; but to have one made in Batavia, why, it would be a colonial invention, and he would get an octroi or patent from the Government.

The prisoner was pressed with eager questions. Could he indeed do such a thing? make a brick machine? He would try. The contractor was in ecstasies; he would give ten thousand recipessen (about $3,000), for such a plan;—for a good drawing from which a machine might be made. The prisoner boldly pledged himself to produce the plan; his young friend and prison comforter became his guarantee; and the contract for the brick machine was made in the prison of Weltevreden.

The contractor and his friend had influence to obtain from the Court of Justice, many relaxations of the surveillance and discipline that had been imposed on the commander of the Flirt. He now saw his prison friends again, the Baron, the Trader, the Schoolmaster, and the interesting little Umbah. He received paper, pencils, and instruments, all that he wanted; and was busily and happily at work for the Government of Netherland India, like the Resident, the Colonel, the Baron, the Topographer, the Russian, and the rest of the talent which that government had locked up in jail.

But in the case of the brick machine, the fact as to who was the planner, was to be concealed from the authorities. The payment for the plan would depend on the preservation of secrecy; as no octroi could be obtained for the work of a foreigner, much less a prisoner, and such a prisoner; treason would be suspected in a machine from him, that might turn out to be when made some self-acting catapult to pelt the Dutch out of Java, instead of a peaceful grinder and moulder of clay.

The draftsman affected to be occupied with various small sketches for his patrons; but during the siesta hour, and other undisturbed periods, he was busy with combinations of clay-workers and brick-moulders. It was perhaps a rashly undertaken task for one who had dealt so little in bricks, who had never seen a brick machine, except to gaze at it as a curiosity, who had never bought a brick, nor sold a brick, nor ever thought particularly about bricks before.

He had a confused picture in his brain of revolving cogs, of a huge clay hopper, and then of little sliding boxes and scrapers, and of brown bricks shoved out on a platform, like brown bread from a Dutch oven. But this picture was like some few notes of a rare song, that chime on the ear, that flit through the air; but the untaught throat can make no melody of it; nor could the draftsman get his cogs, moulds, and scrapers, into feasible shape for making bricks.

He spoiled sheet after sheet of good drawing-board; he made cogs to revolve horizontal and perpendicular; he made bricks to slide out, to be shoved out, to drop out; but still the way was not clear how they got in, got started; or how they came out at all. He devoured every page of a few old Dutch books, having some meagre details of mechanics; now more harmonious to him than the graceful postures and pantun songs of Pleasant Night of the Ulu.

He strove in vain for a time, to work out a principle into the details of a working plan; and oftentimes he paused to think that he might be like a forger of his own chains; or like the maker of the brazen bull of Phalaris for roasting men; or the French chopper off of heads; the first use of his machine, might be to make bricks to strengthen his jail.

But he thought of the guilders, he thought of home, and all the bright world outside; and ideas began to dawn, the idea of the brick machine; and the idea to get out, before his own skill had strengthened his jail. He had got a hopper reared up, and revolving buckets to feed it, some troughs leading the clay into an endless chain of moulds, and buffaloes hitched to levers like arms of a cotton press; when the contractor called to see the progress of the work.

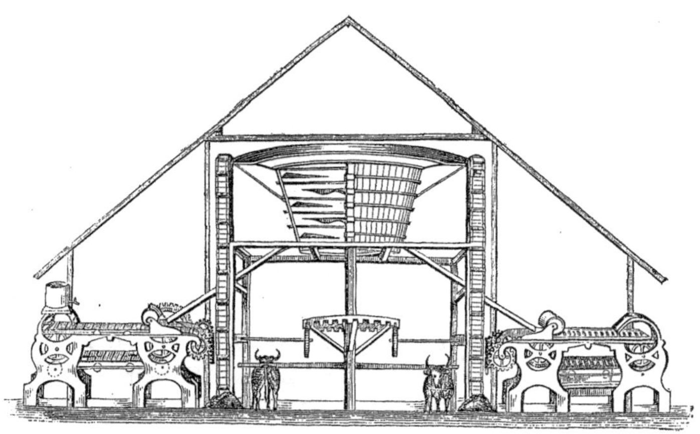

The grandson of Napoleon's marshal was in raptures, he did not know why; he knew little of mechanics; but he saw a machine, though little knowing where the clay went in, and where the bricks came out. The young friend was proud to see the work done, as though it were the achievement of a brother; his guarantee was made good; and in the joy of his generous heart he drew forth a gold watch of costly make, which is worn by that draftsman to this day.

The grandson of the marshal, had a copy of the plan made by a skilful Chinese artist; who though so little inventive, are so famed for copying painting, plan, or writing, with the minute fidelity of the copying sun. Plan and papers were laid before the grave Council of India, Van Nes, Hogendorp, Ruloffs, and Visscher, the four advisers of his Excellency, the Minister of State, and Governor General of Netherland India, Mynheer Albertus Jacob Duymaer Van Twist.

The skill of Tromp, the chief of Dutch engineers in the East, and chief examiner of the Government patent office at Batavia, was called in to judge the work of the grandson of the glorious marshal of road-making memory. His triumphs of war, in forts, roads and rapes, were counted dim by the side of the grandson's triumph in peace; who would pour out bricks, and rear forts, and jails with so little cost of guilders, blood and virtue.

The octroi was obtained, "*voor een machine tot het vervaardigen van muursteenen en dakpannen*," for a brick and tile machine, granted to the grandson of Napoleon's marshal, for the exclusive making of bricks, throughout Java, Sumatra, Borneo, and Papua, whenever bricks should be needed there by Dutch burghers, throughout in fact all of Netherland India, which in the eyes of that Governor, Council, and the Government at the Hague, is all land south of the equator, and all east of the Cape of Good Hope, in the Indian Ocean.

The contractor got his octroi, quicker than the inventor got his money. He had to wait for the most of it, till a machine and bricks were made; but the money did come, after a long lapse of prison life; it came in good time, when the prison walls began to grow thicker and to rise higher, when hope of help from home, and hope of justice began to fail; then the brick machine that was helping to strengthen the prison, did good service for the prisoner of Weltevreden.

But this was not the only plan of machine that was made, nor the only octroi granted by the Government of Netherland India, for the work of the "high traitor," they held in their civil and military jail. They had no good means to cut joints, tenons, and knees for ship timber; nor any contrivance with fine saws to rip up in veneering flakes, the sandalwood, camphor, and other fine woods of the Archipelago.

The late commander of the Flirt was more at home in ship timbers, than in bricks; he had less difficulty with the arrangement of round and upright saw blades, than in the arranging of brick moulds and clay scrapers; he arranged gear to make sloping cuts for knees; and curving ones for fellies; and the plan was octroied; for they had need of great improvement in ships and cart wheels in Netherland India.

The labors of the prisoner did not cease with his plans to fashion useful things out of the earth and the forest, for his jailers; they had work for him in the water; not in the grand old ocean to guide some ship he had made, over its broad bosom, to search for what had slipped the eye of Hanno, Columbus, De Gama, Cook, La Peyrouse, and Van Dieman; no, they wanted him to make a steam washing machine.

This prisoner might think no more of vying with those old navigators of Carthage, Spain, Portugal, England, France, and Holland. He had launched his last keel, he had buffeted his last wave with the bows of the Flirt; but he might still win glory and gold, with steam, soap, dashers, driers, and mangles; in providing a means for the speedy cleansing of the linen of the great unwashed army and navy of Netherland India.

Boilers were contrived, with pipes leading into vats, pipes with punctured ends like garden cans from whence the hot steam was to issue, into the cold water bubbling and clattering, like jostled plates of metal; dashers were produced, like the fuller's buffeting pedals, a drying drum, then mangling rollers for smoothing the Dutchmen's shirts; and even crimpers and fluters for Dutch dames' collars and caps; thus the steam washing machine was made; and another octroi was granted to two Hebrew German merchants of Batavia, who hold their patent to this day.

These labors extended over a lengthened period of the stay of the prisoner in Weltevreden, about the half of a year; and during the time, he had seen many changes, many strange scenes, many new faces. He had seen the Baron reformed; and Umbah reading Malay; he had gained the privilege of a walk in the court; and had talked with the Colonel about the army, with the Resident about the jurisprudence; and with the mad lawyer, about the absence of all law in Netherland India.

He had talked with the Dyak pirate about Borneo; and he had seen a later fellow prisoner, a director of mines of coal near Banyarmassin, from whom he had obtained copies of the great tortuous river of Banjer or Barito; and from other sources, he mapped the Kahajan, the Moorung, the Kuteh, the Kapooas, the Sambas, and other waters, and of the interior of the great continent island of the Archipelago.

He saw prisoners and visitors from without, from Celebes, the Moluccas, Timor, Papua, and from all parts of the Archipelago. He used all his small chances, to take notes, sketches, and plans; and why? to prepare some plan of invasion? to get afloat once more, and to start for Jambee with some machine in the Flirt, that should save the work of hands and guns, and knock down Dutchmen, as he had turned out bricks?

There were Dutchmen willing to believe such things as that; Dutchmen in the Government, and Dutchmen in the courts of Netherland India. They got some hint of his doings, and paid him a domiciliary visit of justice; although they found nothing, but some rude and rejected tracings; yet they saw little else but treason in river and coast lines; and in sketchings of cogs, buckets, saw teeth, flowers, brick moulds, kriss blades, mangosteens, wash tubs, and Malay women.

They curtailed his liberty again; his walks in the court, his talks with the prisoners; he was called often to the Hall of Instruction, to that weary little black hall, whither he went; and elsewhere before judges in Batavia; altogether two and fifty times did he appear before a judicial tribunal, during his strange fluctuating life, of hopes and fears, of teaching and learning, of inventing and laboring; and of misery and plenty; and of bitter sorrow and pleasant interest in the prison of Weltevreden.

The weary prisoner denied his former use of books, paper, pencils, and pens, made charts and vocabularies on his bare walls. He studied a little of language from every sentinel, and every convict, that would talk to him through his bars; learning of Dyak language habits and piracy from his waiter; and much about the common life of the masses of these islands from other waiters and soldiers; a piece of charcoal transmitted what he learned to his broad pages of plaster; and by and by, when scrawled all full in columns from top to bottom, the cells were whitewashed, and that gave him a new supply of stationery.

Yes, with charcoal, and on his bare walls, he wrought out many a fancy, many a thought; they fled with the whitewash brush; but the record on the wall for a time, helped memory the better to hold them till now. And those thoughts and fancies were all wrought out and treasured for the instruction or entertainment, and none for the hurt of his fellow-man; and his jailers might have seen this, and spared him some misery, and themselves some shame.

"Hang him or let him go free," were wise words, said by one old judge; but he spoke in vain to his younger colleagues, like the Samnite Senator to his compatriots, when they had caught the Romans in the Caudine forks. "Let them go untouched, and make a great people your fast friends;" said the Samnite. "Let him go, restored to all he had; and make the citizen of a great people, your praiser among them;" said the Batavian judge.

But the other judges, councillors, and Government of Batavia, would fain try the timid policy of the younger Samnites; pursue a middle course, use the yoke and the prison, delighting to torment; but not having nerve to kill. And did not the one reap a harvest of war and utter ruin for this wavering, unworthy policy for a nation? and what has the Government of Netherland India reaped, by the policy it pursued?

It may have reaped only this; a slight unveiling, perhaps the slight awakening of an interest, nothing more, among the great people of America, to inquire into the monopoly of Holland in the East. And that inquiry may not be stilled, till the monopoly of nations that cannot be controlled, of lands that cannot be tilled, of mines that cannot be worked, and of spices that cannot be gathered, shall have ceased in the East Indian Archipelago.

The Romans went under the yoke; the prisoner is in his prison; and he is weak and weary, and wanting many things at this time. He has made machines for bricks; but he needs a few dry ones for his floor; he has set many saws in whirling motion; but not one will cut through those iron-studded doors; and he has contrived a plan for washing an army in a day; but he sadly needs some washing; and even some linen to be washed.

He has now money to buy; but he cannot have all he wants; some proper hands to prepare some of the under garments of civilized life; he was not fastidious, he knew rough life and rough fare; but it was harsher than coarse fare, to go with unwashed linen; or to roam his cell like the Phidian Jupiter,—or like his neighbor the Baron, who had been fifteen years a soldier; and had a good tough Dutch skin.

His young friend, the solace of his prison, came to his aid; he had a relative in one of the judges of the Court, the one the prisoner had met, during his first hours of liberty in Batavia; the young man plead with his relative; the judge came to see the prisoner; he spoke with him kindly, he had wished him to go free, long time ago. He spoke with the jailer to relax agian, despite the orders of the Attorney General; the prisoner received many comforts; and he should not wash clothes in his yard any more; but should have the service of a washerman.

Washing, sewing, cooking, waiting, and the most of domestic work done by women in the western world, is performed by men in the East. In the Archipelago, as in Hindustan and China, men milliners cut and make the dresses of European and native ladies; chambermen make up the beds instead of chambermaids; and male hands dash and rub and soap soiled linen; wringing, drying, starching, and ironing, and doing all the duty of a washerwoman.

Women have not much to do of housework in Java, they do the most of the responsible labor of men,—except the fighting, the gambling, opium smoking and drinking of arrack; they set up shop, a toko, and like grass widows of Paris, do all the small counter transfers of trade, the small peddling of wares, and changing of coin; gain little freeholds and cabins of their own; and often generously support some returning, recreant lord, content to live ingloriously on the gains of woman's saving and skill.

A washerman came to the prison, to help the washing-machine maker wash his own clothes. This orang chuchee, this washerman, had another privileged client in prison; the two made some bulk of clothes to carry; and Chuchee's wife came to help; but not always; there came another to bear the burden of one prisoner's clothes, a help that bore away the burden of many a prison care; and sent him garments once that helped him to walk forth from those prison walls.

Who was that help, that aided the Chuchee, that cheered the prison, that bore away clothes and cares? A help without hire, a liberator without ransom; who was that help, that came to Weltevreden? The story was told by one when fresh from its walls, by him who was helped, when grateful memories of the helper were fresh, warm in his heart, not warmer than now; but brighter and livelier, as he bounded homeward on rolling waters.

The warm words of his fancies then, the fancies that danced with the waves, are fitter for the theme, than the heavy thoughts of these after years, made weary by much hard tilting with harsh souled men. Let us listen to the story, along with the missionaries and their spouses, the young lady, the nurse, the baby, the Boatswain, the Captain and his lady, on board the Palmer, on her homeward voyage from Java.

FORTIETH DAY.

I HAD passed five months in prison; the first of these, full of startling change; from a yacht to a fort; two valets in a dainty cabin; two marines guarding me in a kennel in a ship's hold; and then passing from a bloody berth to a bloody cell; from a steamship to a guardship, and from amid sailor cursings to maniac ravings. I had passed through a painful ebb and flow of hope; two days I had been free, then back to my cell; worried with examinations before a prosecution where I had no aid of counsel; asking for trial, asking for confrontation with my accusers; but justice delaying; and Providence interposing, making my complex case still more complicated, and then at last getting up an interest in the companionship of my prison, in the Baron, Umbah, and my neighbor felons; and thus passed the first month in Weltevreden.

I had become well used to the fare, to the rice and curry; I found indeed my stomach strengthening; for it had been a little ailing in years past, as it is with nearly all at home in America, feeding on fats and sweet and pasty compounds; I no longer awoke with the accustomed clammy tongue and dizzy head, that followed the richer fare of home. Rice, the chief grain food of two thirds of the people of the earth, when cooked dry and soft, as in the East, is an open, porous mass in the stomach, allowing the ready action of digesting juices, far better for the sedentary, women, pensmen, artists; than the more concentrated farinaceous grains. I must thank the Dutch for forcing me to appreciate the health-preserving diet of rice and fruits.

I had become used to a wet floor, an oozing sweat from the moat; I had dreaded cramps and aching joints, the fate of others in the cells; but they never came. I kept always on my stilt-like clogs; and took as much care to dress, with what I had, as when among society outside. The prisoners who abandoned themselves to a half nude state, to an unkept face, to unshod feet; seeking ease and an escape from the heat; seemed to suffer the more. Their feet swelled, their bodies became blotched and festered with exposure; and Java fever, that scourge which had given to Batavia the name of the grave of Europeans, was almost daily thinning out the prison.

I had obtained the privilege of a walk in the main court, half an hour in the morning, and half an hour in the afternoon. I had become acquainted with the Resident, the Topographer, and the Colonel, at their several gratings; I had talked with the mad lawyer, I had studied Dutch and Sumatra with the Baron; the Malay and Arabic writing with Umbah and the Schoolmaster; and thus passed away my second month in prison.

I had counted my stay by days, then by weeks; but now I began to count by months; and hopes of liberty or escape, that had at first seemed painful, when a week ahead, now seemed more tolerable, if likely to happen in a month to come. The pain of the prison had not become less, but I had begun to enter into a world within these confining walls; and I found opportunities there, better, perhaps, than if I had been some well comforted guest in a hotel outside, for obtaining a thorough knowledge of the people, and resources of the East Indian Archipelago.

I seemed to be forgotten; there was but little incident in connection with my judges and jailers, after the drowning of the witnesses at Palembang. I learned afterwards of the busy search for evidence, but during the time, I heard nothing of what was doing in my case; heard no word from home, from Commodore, or Americans any where, in reply to all the messages that I sent forth, and so it was, that with studies and machine making I passed very quietly all of the third month in prison.

At the commencement of the fourth, my late crew were set free. The men were liberated in order to make witnesses of them; and it had been supposed from some peevish words of a few, that they would testify against their commander; but never was prosecution more disappointed in a set of witnesses, than the attorney-general and Government in my sailors. They were all true, even the Brazilians; not one word, but what most triumphantly vindicated me; as I had an opportunity to learn from the record of their testimony at a later day.

But prison life had made sad havoc on the stout frames of my men; they were lodged in closer cells, had fared even coarser than I had done; and being without any store of thought, or occupation of the mind, the body had wasted and wilted away in the damps and heat of the prison. Two had already gone to the hospital, stricken down with Java fever, before the order came for the release of all; and as I never heard of those two again, I believe that they found a grave on Javan soil.

The stout Jim was a woful sight; that hardy bullet of a man, with rugged face, and thick muscle; as I had seen him enter the prison three months before. He now drooped his haggard face; he walked with wavering step; and his voice could barely be heard; and yet, poor fellow, hopeful and stanch to the last, proffering words of cheer and encouragement to me, that was so well. I would stand by the ship, would I not? The Dutch would have their turn, and we our "innings," some day.

I never felt the prison till I saw my men go out of it; more my men now, since we had suffered together, than when a crew on board the Flirt. Great children they were, in the matter of self-control, that knew not their right hand from their left, whom I had only known before at the cold distance of command at sea, to work and to correct, to feed and to physic them; but in the prison, the barrier between the cabin and the forecastle had been broken down;—by me, and not by them. I had sent them counsel, and equal shares of all the luxuries that came to my hand; and when free, they all wished to stay and await the day of my liberation, hoping that we would all sail in the good little Flirt again.

But they could not stay ashore in Batavia. No stranger can stay in Java without the permission of the Dutch Government; no person can go there to reside, without providing two bondsmen, to be his security to a large amount; and as my sailors proved to be of no value as witnesses, the Government wanted to be rid of them; yet would afford them no means to enable them to go away, if they had wished to leave.

At this juncture, the generous young friend of Americans, came forward to take my men to his house; he had already taken two under his roof; but the Government forbade his offering this shelter and comfort to American seamen; they were removed by the police, and all my men were sent on board the guard ship. There they remained in a worse condition than in prison; they prayed to be sent back to their cells in Weltevreden; by and by, as they lost health, and all hope of sailing with me again, they wanted to ship, and get to sea again; but no shipmaster would take such emaciated men; the Government would not pay their passage to Singapore, where a United States Consul might take care of them; and thus these men lingered at Batavia; the victims of a government and jurisprudence, that had blundered into a case they did not know how to dispose of.

There is no doubt, that for a time, the Government of Netherland India, would have rejoiced to have got rid of us, by our escaping; or in any other way, that would make us appear self-convicted of the crime that they alleged; whereby the action of their officers at Palembang would be sustained, and the Government would be relieved from all liability to a reclamation for damages. But the men would not go away; and I would not try to escape. Dutch justice stood waiting for something to turn up; and that was the state of affairs during my fourth month in prison.

During the fifth, a stricter discipline had tightened upon me, in consequence of the discovery of my mapping and sketching. I had been subjected to most extraordinary fluctuations of treatment, since the first day of my arrest. For a time in the fort of Palembang, I was guarded by a sentinel, who had to watch every movement I made; the following day the sentinel paced to and fro, and allowed any person to speak with me. On board the Arjuno, I was closely watched to prevent my attempting suicide; but allowed to converse as I pleased; on board the Boreas, the orders were to arrest any one, who attempted to speak to me; but I had every opportunity to drown, to choke myself, or cut my throat, which ever way I felt inclined. I was carried in a vàn with guarded secrecy to Weltevreden; but went and hunted up the Stad prison, in an open carriage, along with a friend. Then there had been a continued tightening and relaxing of my confinement; then a sudden stirring up of my judges; examinations and worryings in the little black star chamber; followed by a long dead calm. The simple fact was, that Government and judges did not know what to do. They had been put by the excess of zeal and treachery combined of their officers at Palembang, upon the high horse of treason, "*hoofd verraad*," and did not know how to ride him, or how to get down. A trial for such a stately crime, was a novelty in Netherland India. They had been accustomed to hang men at once, who had become troublesome to the Government; and then send a report of the matter to the Hague. They had without any molestation, or after reclamations, massacred a number of Englishmen at Amboyna; then, in the time of Valckenier, they had made a second St. Bartholomew's day in Batavia; slaughtered in cold blood ten thousand Chinese men, women, and children, without a shadow of the excuse of the Turkish Sultan for slaying his janissaries. There was no fear of reclamations on the part of a Chinese emperor, who can afford to sell one hundred thousand people every year, to labor or to die as slaves.

Thus the monopolists and taskmasters of these Eastern islands, had hung and quartered on several occasions, without the troublesome and expensive inconveniences of a trial; but there was that shadow behind the Flirt, an ominous shadow, that had flitted from time to time, across the Archipelagian waters; it might be of some very ferocious, it might be of some very gentle, placable monster, but evidently one that could devour the Archipelago in a trice; and it would be well not to rouse it, by devouring the little Flirt and her people in too unceremonious a manner; and so they fluctuated between the fear of letting me go to stir up disturbance by my denouncing tongue; and the fear of destroying me, which might stir up worse.

One of these tightening fits had come over my jailers, during the close of the fifth month. I was denied the walk in the yard. I was out of employment, except the scrawling and sketching upon my walls. I was beginning to feel the oppression of my prison very much. Hope in my Government, hope in friends; and with the common weakness of mortality, hope in God began to fail. I felt nothing but a dark and dogged resolution to defy my jailers to the last; but this dark state, was that deepening gloom that precedes the dawn.

Three stirring events were about to break in upon the dreary monotony of my prison life; and to make all its after experience a drama of intense interest and strange variety. These events were, a visit, the celebration of a day, and the advent of a ship of war. And as first in order of time, and first in interest, I will tell you of the visit.

FORTY-FIRST DAY.

THE VISIT.

It was one of the last days of the fifth month of my stay in prison; and on the first day of July, at the hour of noon, the siesta hour, when all doors were locked; keepers and prisoners generally were asleep, sentinels were dozing; and I was stepping over my narrow cell floor, back and forth, with unsteady and clattering footsteps in my Chinese clogs. As I looked through the bars of my window, I saw the grating in the doorway that leads into the main court, darkened from time to time, by a peering woman's face.

I was surprised to see any one, but the sentinel, in the main court at that hour; but sometimes Chuchee, the washerman, or his wife, had come a little while before the hour of admission, and were allowed, if a good-natured sentinel was on guard, to pass the outer gate, and enter the main court; where they would sit, quietly chewing their siri, or betel nut, until the cell doors were opened for the entrance of visitors, and the attending coolies; and this was now the case, as I observed, very soon, the livid face of the turnkey at the door of the court; and behind him came the lank, shrivelled figure of the wife of Chuchee, followed by two young females, who carried between them the basket of clothes.

For a time, I did not observe these helps, who stood outside of my cell, whilst the hideous face of the turnkey stared in at my door, watching the old crone, as she sorted out my portion of clothes. He asked gruffly, who these women were, that had followed her into the block; what did they want? They were two young women, from the country near Samarang, staying a while in Batavia with their brother, who was now with them; but the guard would not let him pass the outer gate. They were curious to see the prison, and had come with her to help her; they had good letters to the Kapalla campong (the native portion of Batavia, being divided into campongs, over which a Kapalla, or native alderman, presides); they were not nyahees; but people of good character; and would not give Tuan Tutup, Mister Lock-up, as the natives called the turnkey, any cause for complaint.

The turnkey went off to open some other doors, growling to the old woman as he turned away, for her to clear out quick, as he would be there in a minute to close the door.

As soon as he had turned his back; and whilst the old woman was stooped down, arranging the basket, my doorway was darkened; I saw a pleasant face that I had seen before; but a coarse dress, hair tied up in a common knot, ears, neck, and arms without ornament, and other indications of the coarse toilette of the inferior class of Javanese women, prevented me, for a time, from recognizing the graceful and intelligent grand-daughter, the kambing utan, the antelope of Panyorang Djaya Laksana.

Her hand on her lips, and an expressive look, checked some exclamations of surprise. The old woman had arranged her basket, and stepped to the door. The other person, whom I had not seen, stepped forward; a stout, handsome, matronly young woman, of pure Javanese type of features; she took one handle of the basket, and she and the old woman moved off; and, when they had turned their backs, I learned from a few words rapidly uttered by the remaining one, that after my arrest, the Panyorang had felt great distress about me; but he had believed that I was betuah, invulnerable, that the Dutch satans could not hurt me; he wanted to help, but Allah only could help; he had prayed to Allah; then Wirojoyo came, and took his daughter back to Cheribon; the Panyorang said, to send him much news of the American tuan, when in Java. Wirojoyo had come to Batavia; his two daughters and a son with him; they had heard of the American tuan in the house of care; they wanted to see him, but were afraid; every body spoke with little hearts about the Tuan; afraid of the Company. Wirojoyo was afraid to ask at the gate; he and his daughters had often passed by, and looked sadly at the prison walls; they spoke with an old woman that came out; she saw the American tuan, she washed for him; they then put on dress like little people, affected poverty; and made friendly face to the old woman; they pretended also to have big eyes; curiosity to see the house of care; and offered to help; their hearts were very little, trembling with fear, as they passed the gate, and saw the fierce soldiers, like tigers; but Allah was good, and great indeed, they had seen the American tuan; and the Panyorang would have heart joy, so much, so much, to know that Tuan was well. Papa Wirojoyo would help the Tuan; and what could Sayeepa, and her sister and brother do?

I had begun to speak in reply, when I heard the beast voice of the turnkey calling out some offensive words to my visitor; she started with affright, and fled; he rushed forward, and seized the terrified young woman. I had reached him, almost as soon as he had laid hands upon her; and yet I found hands upon him, even quicker than mine. The Baron seized the ex-dragoon by his shaggy hair, applied his foot to his back, and laid the brutal turnkey sprawling in the court-yard, whilst my visitor fled, with her sister, out of prison.

The outcry of the belabored Tutup, roused the prison from its noonday torpor; the stolid sentinel having no orders to interpose, or shoot any body, looked on the scene with quiet glee. The jailer appeared; and listened to the groans and charges of his lugubrious subordinate.

Mynheer Pieters seemed to think that Baron Van Norden had carried his audacity, and his presumption upon judicial and governmental favor too far. The American Captain had no favor to presume upon; and he had taken a step that would qualify him for irons and a close cell in one of the back blocks. Mynheer Pieters was determined to know if he was the jailer, or a prisoner; also if the Baron had received the commission to hold the keys of Weltevreden. He would have this question decided at once by Mynheer Van Rees, the Resident of Batavia.

The turnkey slunk away; and the jailer bustled off to the Stadhuis to make his report, leaving myself and the Baron at liberty in the court-yard.

The Baron laughed heartily for a time;—then spoke somewhat seriously. It was lucky for us, that these brutes did not have supreme control of the jail; but were obliged to get the orders of the Resident before making a change in the condition of a prisoner; were it not so, this old adjutant and dragoon would give us irons, the bastinado, and the close jug very frequently.

This is probably one of the most loosely managed prisons in the world. The Resident, the chief magistrate of the city, has, according to law, the chief direction of it. But the attorney-general has an influence superior to him; and the jailer would not venture to liberate a prisoner, even with an order from the High Court in the hands of the Sheriff, unless he had a private note from the chief prosecutor that all was right. The Court of Justice or Low Court of Batavia, has something to do with the payment of Pieters; and, of course, he must pay court to that important branch of his patrons.

The result is, that you see almost as many different prison-treatments as there are prisoners. One has friends, and another one has enemies, who have influence with one or more of these patrons; and his condition varies accordingly; and then he sometimes has a friend in one court, and an enemy in another, and he fluctuates as you have done, between a close cell, bad fare, and ugly looks; and an open court, with promenades, and a good deal of smiling obsequiousness. Several men have been driven to despair and strychnine; and others have gone mad with license and debauch within these prison walls; just according as he stood personally with Government or Justiciary. By the way, this place has rather a singular name: on this site once stood the villa of a burgher of the time of Van Imhoff—Weltevreden signifies good comfort, or contentment, in Dutch.

But let us turn to a pleasanter theme than the Prison of Weltevreden. I was struck with the graceful appearance of those two young women, who came with your washerwoman to-day; especially the one who stopped behind to talk with you. Though dressed like the nyahees of soldiers, they looked more like fitting inmates for the kraton of the emperor of Surakerta, than for this prison. Relatives of that old woman, from the interior near Bogor; perhaps so; but I doubt it; and the smaller one looks half Malay, and of a type I have seen in the Passumah.

Now, what training of Europe could give greater style, more dignity of bearing, and ease of movement; and such a graceful adjustment of a coarse dress, as these two young women exhibit;

and as you see in almost every woman in Sumatra and Java, that is elevated above the common coolie class. They are equal to the finest standard of European aristocracy in person and habits. They are not more remarkable for their grace and elegance, than for their cleanliness; in one particular especially; the right hand which is used for eating, for saluting, and for embroidering flowers on their fine clothes, is never allowed to touch a vessel, or raw food in cooking, or any other defilement; but is preserved by the Javanese woman, as sacredly cleanly as a sacramental chalice.

These two are evidently of a higher race, than their dress would indicate; but such disguisements are the common practice of every native woman of any quality above the lowest class. Any comeliness of person, or elegance of garments would expose her at once to deliberate, open brutalities by our civilized brethren; against which the Malay or Javanese woman has no protection, but her own personal courage, and nerve to use pointed steel; which, by the way, is common enough, and saves them to a great extent from one universal assault upon their virtue; for which Netherland India law affords not a shadow of protection.

This oriental grace, and symmetry of person, I have spoken of, is certainly not monopolized by the women of the Archipelago; there are the same fine moulded limbs on the banks of the Indus; but nowhere in Continental India, or in all Asia, will you meet with such courtly grace; and nowhere, except among the better classes of the European race, can you meet with such goodness of temper, such fidelity, vivacity, and domestic affection. They will at times show great violence of temper; but chiefly on account of jealousy, and they are quickly appeased;—it may be said also against them, that they readily form new attachments; but they are devoted to their actual husband or lover; and are ever ready to make all those sacrifices for the man they love, which are only heard of in works of romance in Europe.

The Javanese women, in particular, make the best of wives, for men who do not require any very intellectual companionship, which is the case with the most of our Dutchmen; and I should judge such to be the case with the rest of the European race; as I think I am safe in saying that of nearly every one, the exception is a rarity I have not yet met with; and so I will say, every Dutch, English, and American trader, who has come here in his youth to amass a fortune out of coffee and pepper has, during his early struggles, found a devoted friend in a faithful Javanese woman.

Intelligent ladies of Europe wonder at this preference of the society of simple, half civilized creatures, as they think, to their more elevated companionship; but there is no cause for wonder in a knowledge of the facts. The Javanese woman has no caprice, no weak nerves, no pride of family, no exactions of any thing, especially due to her wealth, connection, or any thing else; no flirtations, no intrigues, so common among our European women here; she is the devoted slave; yet pleasant, talkative, witty, cheering companion of him she loves; and how does the European trader repay this sacrifice of self, this devotion to him?

After that the trader, who has formed these relations, has accumulated a fortune, he is then generally of a mature age; he is ambitious to make a display in the home country; he wants a position there, a wife that will grace his fortune. But what is to be done with the faithful friend, and mother of many creole children? She is provided for as a mad woman in this prison; or, she is furnished with a servant's half pay; and her children grow up out of the pale of Christianity in the campongs; now this is true of nearly all, and many of your own countrymen among the number, that have made fortunes in Java; I have seen their creole children playing among the Mahometans; whilst the Christian father is receiving honors with his new bride at home. Do you wonder, then, that the creole of these islands should hate and curse the race of his father?

Sometimes a soldier commits a foolish piece of justice; when promoted, and retiring on half pay, he will marry the faithful companion of his marches, and the mother of his children, though become old and ugly. I have many stains on my soul; I have led but a useless life; and am now in the condition of a degraded felon; but it seems to me, that it would require a much greater experience of evil,—a more thorough hardening of heart, than any known to my soldier life: and I should need the society of some devils to keep me in countenance, before I could put a good face upon the heartless abandonment so commonly committed by European traders in the East.

The lady of the Elder Missionary remarked on this occasion, that she had heard such a statement confirmed in every particular, during her stay in Batavia.

FORTY-SECOND DAY.

SABBATH ON BOARD THE PALMER.

FORTY-THIRD DAY.

The Baron had become engaged in the discussion of another subject; we heard the rattle of wheels; saw in the court, the running to and fro of oppassers with long scarlet kabyahs, leather belts and sabres; and the usual accompaniments of an official visit. The Baron stood with arms akimbo, in posture of defiance, expecting the Resident or Fiskaal; but another man appeared, the good-hearted young judge; and the Baron lowered his arms and assumed a more courteous attitude.

This judge was now the examining commissary, in the place of the one who had so harshly dealt with me. It had become his duty to hear the complaints made by prisoners, or made against them; he had heard some very strong charges against us, from the jailer; and now had come to hear us speak for ourselves.

The Baron, as usual, was chief spokesman; he could make a good speech in the vernacular of Amsterdam, Rotterdam and Dort. He put forth more defence for me than for himself; he expressed some indignation that a stranger and a gentleman should be subjected to the brutalities of speech and behavior of the villainous old lancer, who opened and shut the doors. His speech told better than the explanations of the jailer or the turnkey. In the midst of the pleadings and contention, the young friend of Americans appeared; came apparently by accident, to pay a visit to me; but had been led to do so on account of having heard of the prison visit of his kinsman, the judge. This powerful advocate gave such an explanation of his knowledge of my habits and occupations, as completely turned the fluctuating tide of judicial favor in our behalf.

The judge sat down with his relative in my cell; and spoke with me in friendly tone. He had been greatly amused on being let into the secret of my machine making; but this was not in my presence, nor supposed to be known to me. His voice had always been in my favor, in all the deliberations of his court upon my case, but his favorable opinion had been hitherto based on the belief, that there were no sufficient grounds for the prosecution to go to work upon. He would now give the matter a closer investigation after this personal acquaintance with the principal defendant. He went away, after giving order to the jailer, to allow me all the privileges of the most favored prisoner; a promenade in the main court, morning and evening; and to allow the free ingress of visitors to see me.

That evening was a season of holiday for myself and the Baron. It was an evening marked, also, by a total eclipse of the moon, and a peculiar exhibition of the superstition of the Chinese. As the white disc became broken by the dark shadow, we heard a confused clamor of bells, drums, gongs, kettles, and hideous human voices; the bedlam roar rose up higher from the campongs, that surrounded the prison, as the bloody shadow increased; and when the fair moon was completely engulfed in the jaws of the celestial monster of Chinese imagination, the calm, starry night was made frantic with a tempest of unearthly roars, shrieks, and a warring clangor of every harsh, loud sounding thing.

Stupid people;—said the Dyak pirate, as he entered our block with lamps for the night. Yes, observed the Baron, these Chinamen, who are the shrewdest business men in the world, for we have scores of them in Batavia, who have accumulated many millions of guilders, are certainly among the most stupid specimens of humanity; and are even looked upon with contempt by this savage Dyak. These yells, to scare the monster away from the moon, are on a par of good sense with their writing prayers on gilt paper, and burning them in the belief, that the written request will reach heaven in smoke. What a small amount of brains is needed to make a nation of good traders.

Among other privileges obtained by the intercession of my young friend, was permission for Pirez to remain one month ashore, to call upon me morning and afternoon, and discharge little commissions for me in the city. My faithful savage was overjoyed to wait upon me once more; he had grown fat on prison fare and prison discipline; and he and myself, the highest and lowest of the Flirt's company; the chief thinker, and the one of no thought at all, had borne prison life the best; but the black tough skin and sleepy head, had borne it better than philosophy.

On the third morning after being allowed the liberty of the prison, Pirez appeared at my cell door with a rather extraordinary appearance of increased bulk of body; he gave me to understand, that he had something very curious to show me, by and by. He spoke with the huge Dyak, who came with the breakfast. Pirez had, from his first entrance as a prisoner, been a noted character in the jail; and was now intimate and on good terms with all its officials. I had made several little distributions of presents to the iron collared convicts; and they made a return of good will to my man.

He was active and mysterious this morning; and the gleeful Baron seemed to have some knowledge of the object of his manœuvres. When the breakfast had been served, and the turnkey had retired to his room, I saw Pirez watching intently at the egress of the drain under the wall; where the Baron had sought his invigorating staff of life. The grating that had partially blocked it up, had been removed from the other side. Once more a bamboo appeared; but this one was six inches in diameter; it was pushed through the opening, and as some one shoved on the end without, Pirez hauled on his inside; till he drew forth some forty odd feet of bamboo, almost the length of our small court. This surely was not a mammoth brandy bottle.

Pirez lashed a small ring to the end of this spar; then uncoiled a small cord from round his waist, that had been hidden by his dress; he rove this cord through the ring, like signal halyards; and then the stalwart boatman of Pernambuco reared up the pole against a *ketapan*, a species of almond tree that grew in the centre of our court; he quickly mounted the tree, and with the help of the Baron at the foot, he drew up the pole, so that it overtopped the ketapan some twenty feet clear; and with the butt resting in a crotch, there made it well and fast, and then slid down.

I was astounded and mystified with these preparations. Pirez entered my cell; he seemed to be in agony with the encumbrance of a great superfluity of clothing; he removed a thin, loose, jacket; and showed folds of red and white stuff wrapped around his chest and waist; he uncoiled, and I beheld stripes, then stars; I recognized the ensign of the Flirt; and this was the Fourth of July.

THE CELEBRATION.

One of the sailors of the Pylades, left on board the Flirt, to guard her, had saved the ensign from the water, after being torn from the staff and cast overboard by the commander of the gun-brig. The sailor had made use of the flag in his hammock; it had served as curtain, coverlet, and other useful purposes to this Dutchman, for many days, till passing from ship to ship, he was drafted on board the Boreas, about the time that my men returned from Weltevreden. They heard of their old banner; they resolved to rescue it, at all hazards; but no great sacrifices were needed. The Dutchman was willing to sell it for thirty rupees.

Poor fellows, they had not so much money among them; not six dollars in cash at the time:—but, one parting with a finger ring, another with a fancy tobacco-box, and one Brazilian with a pair of ear-rings; they made up the requisite sum, and purchased the flag;—they recovered, as they felt, some of the honor of their noble little ship; a signal to them of an ultimate retribution upon their oppressors. The flag of America, that had been vilely treated by the Dutch and sold for thirty pieces of silver, was to be elevated on the soil of Java.

My men had hoped to surprise me with a display of the flag at some future day. Fourth of July approached; they saw Pirez, and heard of his permission to visit me. It occurred to their minds, that it would be a treat to me, to learn of its recovery on that day. The still feeble Jim suggested a bold idea to Pirez, who was eager to carry it out; he had spoken with the Dyak, who had passed through the drain the bamboo, used as a scantling in some repairs on the house of the jailer; and he wanted to run up the flag, if only for one minute, to wave a defiance to Dutchmen.

This was an extravagant feat; it seems so, to think of now; an unwise kind of bravado, well calculated to compromise me,—to aggravate my situation. But I did not take that view of the matter in prison. I was highly gratified at the sight of the flag; it seemed a precursor of hope, of far off hopes, lying beyond those

prison walls. I wanted just one moment's exultation, one thrill of triumph, to relieve the stagnation of my heart; and so I resolved, at all hazards, to raise up that flag above the walls of the prison of Weltevreden.

Pirez only needed a look, to bend the ensign on to the halyards; not with him for the gratification of any Fourth of July glorification; he knew nothing about it; he thought only of the chance for a crow over the beer-drinking burghers of Batavia; he had learned to feel with his shipmates, that a Dutchman was a good butt for game, in peace or war. The stars and stripes ran up the bamboo; floated above the ketapan tree, and many feet above the highest wall of Weltevreden.

There they floated, full one hour, from 8 o'clock till 9 o'clock in the morning, in sight of thousands of the troops of the surrounding barracks, and of the people of Batavia, assembled in Waterloo plain. The jailer had gone to the Resident to make his usual morning report; the turnkey had been tampered with by the Baron, with a portion of a smuggled bottle of liquor, and he had retired to one of the back wards, to attend to some especial duty; so as not to be supposed to have known any thing of what had taken place; and the stolid sentinel, who generally had no other idea of the object of his presence in prison, except to shoot down any one attempting to escape, stared lazily at the floating bunting. The officers and soldiers in the barracks, and the people in the plain, stared in stupid wonderment; they could not make up their minds as to what it all meant; and no one seemed moved to endeavor to find out.

I could observe from my rear grating the road by which the jailer returned; and the way to the government palace. A crowd began to assemble in the marsh, the field of execution; an orderly was seen to gallop across the plain. I heard the turn out of the guard at the main gate to receive an officer; and at the same time saw Mynheer Pieters coursing at a furious pace towards the prison.

It was time to think of a capitulation; the flag was hauled down, and rapidly disposed again around the body of Pirez. Tu-tup came into our court, demanding, with feigned fury, the hauling down of the vanished flag; at the same time the jailer appeared. Some military officers entered along with him; a number of curious people had slipped in amid the excitement at the gate; and our little court was crowded, when the good judge commissary appeared.

The Baron met his comrades in arms, and I the judge. The former were soon persuaded out of their indignation, and became disposed to laugh at the celebration of the American great day of Independence in prison. The latter was sorry; the matter would compromise him, on account of the relaxation he had ordered. He would probably be compelled to have me placed in much closer confinement; and to prohibit all further visits to my cell, without special permission from himself.

But where was the flag? It certainly should never be hoisted again on the soil of Java. It was not in my cell; nor in that of the Baron; nor in any other in our block. Four oppassers were ordered to make immediate search; as they ransacked our mattresses and trunks, some one, probably the spying trader, had spoken of Pirez; he had brought it, and he had taken it away; but where was he? Gone, upon the opening of the court gate by the turnkey. An orderly is quickly in his saddle, and coursing over the plain towards the house of the young friend of Americans.

The judge left, after stating that the subject of a greater restriction of my confinement, would necessarily have to be laid before the Court, the second day after this, their next regular day of meeting; and he regretted what he knew must inevitably be the consequence. I made the acquaintance of several cavalry and infantry officers, who were not at all displeased at this frolic of the flag, by the alleged ally of Ferdano Mantri and the Sultan of Jambee, which would be told at the expense of De Brauw.

The orderly galloped in vain after Pirez; the faithful fellow had counted upon a quick and hot pursuit, and a close search. He was not long in reaching the house of his patron; he had became familiar, as a prying monkey, with all its out of the way nooks and corners; the flag was soon stowed away, and when the orderly arrived, my cabin boy stood ready at the gate, to hold the horse of the trooper. Pirez was a simple, honest fellow, but he possessed the instincts of stratagem of the savage, and at the same time, greater coolness, than his whiter shipmates.

The flag was sought for in vain; that day and many more; and was not disturbed in its hiding-place, till some months afterwards. Pirez took it, according to my directions, to place it in the hands of an Australian gentleman; a warm friend to me; of America; and a friend to the greater extension of American influence in the East Indian Archipelago.

A REMOVAL.

The Court held its deliberation on the sixth day of July. I was led to suppose from the remarks of the judge commissary, and from some rumors from without, that I might expect to be removed to a cell by myself; probably in the Stad Prison again. I passed the evening of that day in a state of unpleasant suspense, but the day went by and the morning of another day came, and still no change.

About noon of this day, the fussy, little red-faced jailer, came into our court. He had an order for my removal; and where? I never would go back to that Stad Prison, unless dragged there by force. The little jailer laughed; he had no orders to send me to the Stad; coolies were now preparing an apartment, in near neighborship with him. I was to be removed from the bad company of my block, and placed in a commodious room in the debtors' ward; where I would have the free range of a court, and could see as much company at certain hours, as I pleased.

What was the meaning of this? Mynheer Pieters could not explain. The Baron and myself were confounded; but I was not backward in accepting of the new lodgings. I had not much to pack up. I turned with pleasant musing to take a last look at my labors on the walls. The Baron presumed that the Americans had taken Java; or that my steam washing-machine had been cleansing the eyes of the Governor General; or the Sultan of Jambee had made some powerful demonstration in behalf of his ally. Whatever the influence, I was certainly in luck. I must not feel elevated above the ragamuffin society of block No. 4. I would find Baron van Norden always the same; and Umbah should come and study Arabic and English, the Bible or Koran; and poetry or treason, with her uncle captain; as much as he pleased.

I took possession of a fine establishment; the best in the prison; a room about fourteen feet long, by twelve wide; a tile floor, but not quite so damp as the apartment I had just left. I had a good strong iron bedstead, a small teak table, two split bamboo chairs, and a wash bowl. I certainly felt rich, as I tried the luxury of a seat with a back to it. I sat down in one chair, and put my feet on the other; and leaning back complacently, surveyed my enlarged domain and newly acquired possessions.

I was musing upon the probable causes of this change. The

grandson of the marshal of Napoleon had given one of the judges an interest in the brick machine. There was a speculating judge in the Court of Justice of Batavia; he had a friend in whose affairs he was pecuniarily interested, who was about to import a large quantity of water-coolers from Boston. It had been whispered by my young friend, that I could make something; a double case with space between, and a lamp furnace on top, to produce a strong evaporation:—a great improvement on the Bostonian article.

Severity was calculated to cool down invention; a little relaxation would thaw it into most successful development. The Resident of Palembang, the Mulatto of Surinam, and other zealous anti-Americans, were probably satisfied with my being five months in jail. The Court and Government must be easing off; by and by, I would be lodged in the house of Mynheer Pieters; and when I had got very tired of the climate of Java, I might run off at my leisure; some afternoon when the jailer, judges and Governor General were at dinner, and not expected to see me. In the midst of my musings I thought I heard the boom of a gun; then more; thirteen quite quick, with American rapidity; followed by thirteen rather slower booms from the Dutch fort.

Whilst musing upon the cause of this cannonade, a panting messenger, a servant of the young friend of Americans, enters the debtors' ward; he has a note in his hand, which Mynheer Pieters takes, and hands to me with great suavity of manner. It had not been read more than five minutes, when another messenger arrived, the servant of the friend who took charge of the flag; the note of this one was still in my hand, when the servant of him, with whom I had dined on leaving prison, came with a third note; and all three said, "An American man-of-war was signalized in the offing this morning at 10 o'clock, and proves to be the sloop of war, St. Mary's."

ARRIVAL OF AN AMERICAN MAN-OF-WAR.

The stars and stripes hoisted above the walls of Weltevreden, were about to put me into some close felon's cell; but the stars and stripes, floating above twenty-eight long, heavy paixhans, had procured me an improvement in my lodgings. Had I heard those cannon an hour earlier, I should not have moved. It might have been interesting, to the commander of an American ship of war, to have seen how the authorities of Netherland India were disposed to lodge a citizen of the United States, suspected of having done something, when they were not influenced by the approach and presence of that man-of-war.

I heard all the circumstances connected with the arrival of the St. Mary's; the coming ashore of the Commander and first lieutenant; and many little particulars of their conversation at the hotel where they put up, from the polite Mynheer Pieters.

The Commander and first lieutenant came to see me. It was pleasant to see the epaulettes, the brass buttons, the eagles and the anchors; and a little talk made me think, that I should obtain help from the wearers of them. The Commander was determined to see me out of this place. He expressed himself still more determined after taking a look at my old quarters; at the block where the men had been lodged; and after paying a visit to the cell of my officer, who, from the fact of being a subject of the Queen of Great Britain; though in American service, did not share in the advantages attending the arrival of the American ship of war.

The Commander, in the midst of his indignation, on listening to my statement of the case against my jailers, spoke however of their politeness, of his reception, and so forth. The Admiral had received him with marked courtesy. Politeness was very cheap, it was true; but so much had not been expected from Dutchmen. Then the attentions at the hotel; the Rotterdamsche hotel, I said. How did I know? no matter. The proprietor had said; I repeated what proprietor and Admiral had said. The Commander was as much astonished at my particular knowledge of his recent words and movements, as the burghers in Waterloo plain, on the morning of the Fourth of July, at the sight of the old ensign of the Flirt.

I could explain in a few words. The jailer had gone with his report to the Resident, which is a minute account of every visit, speech, and movement, that could possibly be observed by ever so many prying eyes in prison; he happened at the Stadhuis, when the police report of the movements ashore of the American officers came; he had the opportunity and the curiosity to look over it; and now that I was in favor, he felt interested in giving me the particulars on his return home. You who listen to me, and any one else who has resided in Batavia, know well that every hotel proprietor of the city, is an official spy upon his guests.

The Commander was disposed to believe that official politeness at Batavia, covers perhaps a great deal of the meanest of espionage. He now seemed to have formed a resolution, more than before, that I should be a very little while longer the victim of exaggerated fears, spyings, and jealousy. He had known little or nothing of the case; he had come from the Pacific, with some educated Japanese from America on board—a present to offer to the Syogun of Japan, to induce him to open his ports to our whale ships, clocks and hardware. The Commander had delivered these coaxers to a treaty, on board the flag ship of the American Commodore in the waters of China. The Commodore spoke of my case; he was bound, hard and fast, by an order from the Secretary of War, on account of some old affair; the St. Mary's could call and see what the Dutch were about; and now, said the Commander, I am going to have you out.

But Dutch politeness had more attentions to offer to our naval officers. The Governor General sent a carriage, with two of his aides from his palace at Buitenzorg; which is thirty miles distant from Batavia. It was proper to go and receive the hospitalities of the head of the government at once; notwithstanding the unadjusted cause of grievance that stood between an American naval Commander and a Dutch Governor. Buffaloes and wretched human vassals of the polite lords of Java, dragged the carriage and our naval officers up the bold steeps on the way to Bogor. They arrive and are received with an excess of politeness by the Governor General, Mynheer Duymaer Van Twist.

In the grounds surrounding the elevated palace of Buitenzorg, the Commander of the St. Mary's found all the productions of the temperate zone. The apples and plums of home; and tulips and hyacinths outvying the dainty flower cups and petals of Harlaem; he found breeding tanks for rare fishes; and tanks of marble for baths; he found curious beasts and birds, many large serpents and baboons; Javanese statuary, relics of the old empires of the island; he saw other evidences of the skill of Dutch hands in plundering, and gardening; he tasted of their skill in the preparation of the bountiful food of Java; he enjoyed an unlimited lavish of politeness; and thus three days were spent very agreeably by the Commander of the St. Mary's at the Dutch palace at Buitenzorg.

I was not forgotten; of course not. The Governor General had a great deal to say, about my curious voyage; he thought as strangely of it, as did the Resident of Banca. The Governor

General would never have thought of undertaking such a wild voyage. The Commander also thought it was a curious one; what business had any one to go to the East; or any where else, on business which the most of people could not understand. The connection of my cruise with "high treason," and the Sultan of Jambee, was not very clear, but the cruise was a very curious one; and although I had written a long letter to explain it, the Commander and Van Twist could not fully understand the object of my sailing in the Flirt.

The translation of a letter, said to have been addressed to a Sumatran prince, was shown to the Commander. This one spoke of powder, bullets, and blunderbusses; of *lelahs*, or Sumatran blunderbusses, and several ships of war; to be presented on the part of the United States of America to his Highness; and this letter, this offer, was the chief, nay sole foundation for the charge of high treason.

The common sense of the Commander, nothwithstanding the excess of politeness of his host, was aroused at this. If the Governor General could suppose that the United States was cognizant of, and consenting to such an offer, it was an insult to the old ally of Holland; if, on the other hand, the Commander of the Flirt had done so, of his own will, it must be regarded as the act of a madman. No American, no European in his senses could have dictated *that* letter.

The letter was certainly more incomprehensible than the cruise. But there were other circumstances to be considered; associations with disaffected native chiefs in Sumatra; with other people hostile to the Government; studies of the languages of the Archipelago; what business had I to study Malay, Javanese or Dutch, without the permission of the Dutch Government? and so many maps, and plans of something made in prison.

I had too great a passion for languages and geography to be a peaceful man; and then more than all, I had hoisted the American flag on the Fourth of July.

The Commander of the St. Mary's did not see as much treason as the Governor General in these charges. There was a very prevalent habit among the American people, to learn as much as possible about all nooks and corners of this earth, and even of the moon. They pursued geographical studies to a very dangerous extent; and had some taste for philology; though the fancy to study Dutch, was not very prevalent. Moreover, there was a great disposition among them, to distinguish the Fourth of July by the burning of powder, and the fluttering of bunting; and if this disposition broke out, even in a prison, it must be regarded as the effect of American education; of an instinctive, inveterate habit of bidding defiance to bondage in every shape.

The Governer General was glad to be assured from an official source, that the Flirt no longer belonged to the navy; and that her commander had no connection with the naval service of the United States. The Governor General was disposed to take a very lenient view of the case. There had been unexpected delays; the sudden death of all the principal witnesses had greatly retarded the progress of justice; and had led to a minute research for evidence of all the circumstances of the cruisings of the Flirt in the Archipelago. No hostile steps, except those that were about to be taken in the direction of the Sultanate of Jambee, had as yet been discovered. The Governor General would interpose with the executive influence, and the American Commander might expect to see his countrymen at liberty within a few days. An official of the Governor, one of his aides, or a secretary, hinted that if the prisoners were set at liberty, during the stay of the St. Mary's in port, it might seem like yielding to a threat. For the sake then of saving Dutch pride, the Commander would do well not to determine upon remaining, till he saw his countryman out of prison. He would hear of his liberation almost as soon as he should reach Singapore, to make his report to the Commodore.

During the absence of the Commander at Buitenzorg, I received visits from the rest of the officers; second and third lieutenants, purser, master, and passed midshipmen of the St. Mary's. One lieutenant, in particular, I must remember; an outspoken, dauntless American; another Bassett, who wanted to have me taken out of prison without parley; considered the St Mary's equal to the task of bombarding the town if necessary. I rank him with Bassett and Drake in my memory; but I must say, that he was somewhat abrupt in his way, like the former, and did not appreciate Dutch politeness.

Again the Commander and the first lieutenant paid a visit to the prison. The propriety of a concession to Dutch pride was discussed. American pride must give way in this case. The Governor General was very polite; and had actually expressed himself as feeling lenient towards me; he had stated that my case would be disposed of in a very short time; an official had said confidentially, in fifteen days. There was no doubt about it; the Commander believed that it would be just so; and I was anxious to feel persuaded that such would be the case, although I had my doubts; yet I acquiesced in the propriety of the departure of the St. Mary's, whilst I remained in prison; especially as I had not that naval authority attributed to me by the Dutch, to enable me to retain her, to put her alongside of the Boreas, and to wake up the Dutchmen that were defiling the Flirt.

The Boatswain on board the Palmer said that the St. Mary's had been on a long cruise, was homeward bound; and that might be one cause for not wanting to hold on any longer at Batavia. He had heard this visit spoken of at Hongkong; also whilst he staid at Batavia; and there the general opinion was, among the foreign residents, that the Dutch laughed over their pipes about the matter; saying that in this, as in a good many other cases, a good deal of American bluster had turned out to be a bag of wind. They considered that the Commander of the St. Mary's, and the Commander of the Flirt, had been thoroughly bamboozled.

FORTY-FOURTH DAY.

The fifteen days expired, and no word was heard about liberation; or that any thing was being done in my case. During these days of anxious hope, and all the time since the coming of the St. Mary's, my usual labors in the prison had been laid aside; I had been arranging plans for my movements when free; had written out a list of stores for the Flirt; transmitted plans for some repairs of the vessel to my officer; and had sent orders to my men, to make ready for duty on board the schooner again; but the period fixed for liberation passed away; many days; and as the hope of getting out of prison began to wane, I turned to my old interests and labors within.

I might have been a very wretched prisoner; drooping down on that we[illegible]r; sickening on coarse fare; and filling my cell with moans, and with curses against my jailers; for the imprisonment was hard for one who had always known the comforts of America, and the freedom of its great mountains, valleys and wild woods. But it is not my wish to tell any tale of woe; rather to say, that the prison was turned to good account; and it may not be that you, or others who may hear my story, will, by reason of the advantage that I gained, think any differently of the right or wrong of my imprisonment; or of the justice, or injustice of my jailers.

I had been removed to a larger cell; the size perhaps would give it the rank of a room. I had a little more liberty of movement; but there were some associations connected with my new lodging, which were not observed at first, and which were calculated to diminish very much an appreciation of the advantages of the removal. The turnkey was my neighbor on the left, and on my right was the maniac; who told the hour by the barricading of his door; and daily and nightly masked his face with the fragment of a hat.

For several days; during all the time of the visit of the St. Mary's, he had remained very quiet; giving no sign of his existence but the usual barricading sounds, to which I had become accustomed, and to which I paid no heed; not even thinking of his neighborhood.

One night my sleep was broken by a fearful howl, with horrid moans, and strange rattlings of the throat. Some fainter sounds like these, I had heard before; but now they were painfully close, within six feet of where I lay. They seemed like the sounds of intense anguish, of struggles, of dying agony. I called loudly for the turnkey; it was pleasant to see his hideous live face; he laughed at my alarm; the madman had been a little sick and quiet; but now he was getting strong again, and bellowed in his usual tone.

I wanted to see him, even then; my rest was broken, and my curiosity was excited. Tutup accompanied me with his lamp. The bars of the window of the cell of the maniac were covered with a piece of coarse cloth, which the crazy man kept jealously closed at all points. The turnkey raised up a corner, and let his lamp pour in a stream of a light; and I applied my eye to another raised aperture, and beheld my fearful neighbor.

A terrible looking human being, was in that cell. A man of

small frame, without covering, except some filthy tatters of decayed cloth, hanging from a belt round his waist and what seemed to be a cord or iron collar round his neck; these foul shreds of garment concealed but little of a squalid, hairy body, of a shrunken and livid skin; but there was a blackened, filthy fragment of straw plaited work, in an upraised hand, that shut out from view what must have been a horrible face, to fit so horrible a body.

Nothing but a bare platform for his sleeping place, and nothing for covering. He slept very little, and walked in his cell very much at night; he had been walking, but stood still whilst we looked at him. He asked in a thick, and almost indistinct voice, what did the rogues, the foul beasts want; he was profuse in vile epithets; did we want to rob him of three hundred thousand guilders; and then go and laugh with his brother at Buitenzorg? We were thieves and drunkards, leagued with his brother and the Council of Justice; we were beasts, seeking his hurt, robbing him of——— a woman's name he mentioned; and of three hundred thousand guilders.

This was his daily raving, about a brother who lived at Buitenzorg; who had married an heiress with three hundred thousand guilders, to whom the madman had been engaged; and this was indeed the cause of his insanity. Surely the brother and his wife had a right to suit themselves as they pleased; and were not to blame for the madness of this man; but they ought to have made better provision than this den, and wild-beast condition, for the former brother, and lover; although I must say, that this Dutch madman raved more about the loss of the guilders than the lady.

This was a neighborhood, that you would suppose would have made me clamorous for another change of lodging; but there were advantages that made tolerable the howls of a crazy man, and of a crazy woman too; there were greater chances for freedom, when the free granting of it should become doubtful; greater chances to see more of human faces; and besides, some mad cries and the sight of poor harmless wretches, were not worse neighborship of sight and sound, than the gallows in the marsh, the bastinado block in the court; and the howls of sound men, who had their live, healthy flesh ridged and bloodied with loaded canes.

There were greater chances to see more of human faces; and

those who wished to visit my cell, could come more freely and stay much longer. Many strangers, foreign and native, could at certain hours pass the outer gate (where a new building with an archway passage now stands), and walk into the debtors ward, and the main court; and speak with the prisoners in these wards; and there were visitors I hoped to see, who would have feared to enter my old quarters.

One day, a young Javanese, whose dress showed some rank, entered the court; he sauntered about with curious look; stopping to exchange some words with the mad lawyer, then made a halt at the door of the bankrupt merchant; chatted awhile with Tutup, who stood by the gate of my old block; took a glance through the several gratings, at the Colonel, the military prisoners, the Resident, the Topographer, and the Russian; then sauntered back towards my ward, along with Tutup, who had followed him, to show him, as he often did to well-dressed visitors, the lions of the prison; not failing on these occasions to throw out some hints about the smallness of his pay.

The visitor took a long stare at the man, who raved about beasts, guilders and a lost lover; after seeing him, he seemed to have his curiosity satisfied, presuming that there was nothing more of interest to be seen; but Tutup had not shown him his greatest lion, the American animal, who took precedence in the estimation of Tutup, over the barricading time-piece, and him who had devoted the rest of his life to the very sound and truthful assertion, that there is no law, but the law of might, in India.

The turnkey had become very polite to me in my new lodgings; he had wiped out the memory of past brutalities; indeed, a certain neighborly good feeling had sprung up between us. He had told the story of many of his old griefs, when a dragoon; and he made it appear that Dutch dragooning in the East was not a very happy life; and could not be stood there, no more than elsewhere, except by a man, who had a very thick head and a very tough skin. And then my sympathies had been moved by the smallness of his pay, which was not much more than doubled by black mail; to which I contributed a few modest guilders.

Tuan Tutup introduced the Javanese young gentleman, who was the son of a Raden, he said; one of the small chiefs of the island. The worthy dragoon knew that I was curious about the language of the natives, and a great many useless things, which led him to regard me as very little stronger in the brain department, than my right-hand neighbor. He was willing, however, to help me gratify my whim, for the sake of the guilders, that I did not want; and so left the visitor to talk with me about Java.

My visitor was a young man, about twenty-five years of age, dressed in a rich sarong covered with prints of turtle and deer; he wore a short silk jacket instead of the kabyah; his long hair was bound in a knot, and fastened behind with a comb, in the style of European women, which is the custom of the men of Java; his features were pure Javanese, which are more elongated than the Malay, and more expressive of candor and mildness. His complexion was a mingled bronze and cream, bright and soft; his movement easy, his manner dignified; and his countenance expressing a polite, and careless curiosity, till the turnkey had turned his back.

My visitor then approached with a friendly smile; he took one of my hands between both of his. He was Diporo Kasumo, the son of Wirojoyo; and grandson of Panyorang Osman Jaya Laksana. He had come with his sisters, Sahyeepah and Sareena, to the gateway of the house; they had all come like little people, at that time. The daughters of Java have fear of the satans, the soldiers and other Dutchmen; they fear to wear the tali pendeng

and best battek cloth; fine dress, which might add to the comeliness of the person. The hearts of his poor sisters had become very small indeed; the heart of Sahyeepah is not always weak; but strong and wise; it was little then, when in the hands of an evil man; but his elder brother was strong in the arms, and strong in heart; the djin had no power to hurt her. Then beating hearts made quick steps; Sahyeepah could only speak when safe in the campong; the house of care was full of djins; but their elder brother was there; him, whom the Panyorang loved; they had a message to give him, they had words to say; but their hearts were too little to go again. Then they see the old woman; and Chuchee speaks. Their elder brother has more room in the house of care; no Tutup locks him up, and no djin with a bayonet stands by his door. Sahyeepah remembers our elder brother, and his wise words on the Moosie. Sahyeepah is skilful; has the heart of the daughter of Europe; knows the science of Arabs, and Malays, their history, and the *Koran*. The words of our elder brother on the Moosie were good and true; they are treasures in the heart of the Panyorang; they are treasures in the heart of Sahyeepah; other hearts are not so large; but they will hear and find treasure too. Our sisters had wish again to enter the house of care; they came with the younger brother; adoh! their hearts are little at sight of red faces, fiery eyes, and bayonets; they go back to the campong; they come again, but our sisters have fear of bad men. Sahyeepah has no fear of a tiger; she has fear of a Dutchman. Diporo Kasumo then will come alone, and not with the garments of a coolie; but with the dress of the son of Wirojoyo, a demang of Cheribon.

Diporo ceased speaking, and drew from beneath his sarong a piece of polished bamboo, about six inches long and two in diameter, ornamented with an ivory rim at both ends, which were closed;

and I saw that it was contrived into a cigar case; but when he had handed it to me, and I had examined it closely, I observed fine scratches on the surface, some words of Arab script, and a letter to me from Panyorang Laksana.

This is a common mode of writing, in the interior of Sumatra; on pieces of bamboo tube; many of the Passumah tribes who use the angular Rentjon script, employ no other material for the preservation of their pantuns and chronicles; they use a leaf of peculiar shape, with many dents and points for their private correspondence, which when folded up, cannot be opened without tearing the leaf. But the Panyorang, who knew the use of European material for writing, had only resorted to the polished bamboo, as a compliment to me, on account of the interest I took in all genuine Malay customs; and besides, a message upon an article of common use about the person, and legible only upon close inspection, was more likely to escape official scrutiny than if written on paper, and protected with a seal.

I was then a student of Malay writing; but not so far advanced as to be enabled to decipher the bamboo, without the help of Diporo. It is a good sample of a great many Malay letters, that I have read and translated; and shall repeat it, with all its formula of compliment, multiplicity of epithets, and repetitions of names.

"A TRUSTY MESSAGE.

"Now these are the words of Panyorang Osman Jaya Laksana, dweller on the Moosie, and the Ogan Ileer, and a chief by the help of the great Lord of Hosts over many children of Pulo Percha; a message from a clean heart, a straight hand, a gray head, from a father to his son; who is faithful, wise, devout, brave, who loves the children of Pulo Percha, who comes from the lands beneath the wind, from the great land of America; now in the hands of the djins of Wolanda, at their kraton in the land of Java. Therefore this is to say, that Panyorang Osman Jaya Laksana has felt great grief of heart, that it has been the will of the Almighty and Loving One, to tie the feet of his son, to close his mouth, to shut up his hand. Panyorang Laksana has grief, no fear; his son is betuah, and Allah wa taala is good. Moreover the heart of Panyorang Laksana is one with the heart of his son; will Bookit Sebookinking change its place? the heart of Panyorang Laksana will never change. Wirojoyo has come in his prahu to Pulo Percha; Wirojoyo has gone back to the land of Java; the wild rock deer, the morning light in the heart of her grandfather has gone, Sahyeepah has a heart of Europe, with a face of Java; the words of the prophet, great is his name and to be ever praised, are in her heart, in her head, and drop from her tongue. Sahyeepah remembers the good words of her brother from the great land beneath the winds. Sahyeepah will go with Wirojoyo and bear this message. Allah wa taala, grant that it shall come into his presence; and he shall be well. Panyorang Laksana will rejoice, Nemastiapa, Sareena, Chayah, Umbah, Widjahyah, Wira Menggala will rejoice.

Wirojoyo and Sahyeepah will tell much news of Tuan Besaar, his officers, and of many things at Palembang. Salutation and heart's wish, to our son, many, many years. Written this day of good fortune, the thirteenth Dyoomadi'l àchir 1268 of the Flight, (15th April, 1852)."

The friendship of the noble old Sumatran Chieftain, and the interest shown by all his family, led me to look upon my visitor with some warmth of regard; the presence of his sister, the letter of his grandfather, had filled my prison with brightness and hope. Diporo Kasumo was indeed a younger brother. After a

16*

perusal of the letter, I took the hand of the young Javanese, as he had done mine; he raised the other, and looking upwards with Javanese reverence, said, the great Lord of Hosts Eternal is good; his might and mercy be with our elder brother.

The turnkey came to interrupt our conversation. He was glad, that I had been so much pleased with the son of the Raden. The Javanese were not all stupid; said the old dragoon to me confidentially in Dutch; there were some who had a little sense; this seemed to be one of them. I returned the confidence of the turnkey by whispering that I had, as he knew, a desperate fancy to learn the Javanese language; the Schoolmaster in my old block, who was not a Javanese, had made me pay very dearly for what he had taught me of Arabic, Malay, and Javanese. I had learned more in a short conversation with the young Raden, than in half a dozen lessons with the Schoolmaster; and if this young man could be persuaded to pay occasional visits to the prison, as he had done to day, and call on me, I should learn very fast; and as it was certain that the Raden would be offended to have any pay offered to him; I could do something else with those spare guilders; and I looked earnestly at Tutup.

This worthy functionary entered into a lively sympathy with my tastes; he became quite alive to the progress of my studies in the Javanese language; and put on all the Dutch politeness that his old dragooning habits would permit, when he accompanied Diporo to the outer gate; and as far as I could see them, the hideous Tutup was talking very earnestly with the visitor, expatiating upon the many interests of the prison that had not yet been seen; the mad lady, a real white skin, and young too, not generally to be seen by visitors; but Tutup would gratify Mynheer Raden with a sight; also a Javanese soldier, that was to be hung; a musician of one of the band, to be shot; and two mornings after this, three men were to receive the bastinado. The Raden was not proof against this bill of attractions, as Tutup came to tell me with great glee. However, he had in his zeal to serve me made three out of only one, that was to receive the bastinado; but I could explain that the triple flogging was postponed; and that would secure him for another day.

About this time, the Baron was liberated from prison. He had not calculated in vain upon the fact of having been a student at the same Institution in Utrecht, where the Governor General and President of the Court of Justice had received their education. The prejudices and hostile influences of one man had unjustly lodged him in a prison; and the partialities of two others had with equal injustice taken him out. It was an injustice to others in prison, lodged there upon the same indefinite charge of a maladministration of affairs, who were not lucky enough to have an old schoolmate in power.

The Baron was a brave, honest, good-hearted man, with some bad, soldierlike habits, which had left him in such a condition that the boon of freedom was almost a misfortune to him. He had lain in prison two days after the jailer had received the order for his discharge; because that order was written upon a stamped paper worth one hundred and ten guilders; a pardon for a man about to be hung being worth five hundred; and so in proportion to the crime; the petitions costing the same, whether answered or not; and the good-hearted Baron, so ready to help others, and to share freely every thing he received in prison; money, provisions, or drinkables, had not wherewith to pay off the incumbrance, which his old schoolmate, with one hundred and fifty thousand guilders a year, thought proper to send along with his liberty.

A fellow prisoner heard of the strait of the Baron, and sent him the needed sum; and as much more, to help him to a good appearance when outside. After his liberation, the Baron came almost daily to visit his old neighbor in Block No. 4:—and Umbah, the dear child, came also with gifts of mangosteens and many little luxuries; which would not excite the greediness of the brutal guard, ever ready to seize upon every thing dainty or drinkable which happened to be in the hands of a woman or a child.

Umbah had been watched over with great care, by a noble-hearted protector, during her early years, until prison life had begun to produce its sad effects upon him. She had a good honest nurse; and with the watchfulness and care of this woman, and some little instruction from the Baron, the little foundling had grown up with all the grace and playfulness of a Malay child, and at the same time had acquired much of the character of the European. She had also been reared in a camp, was cool and resolute; though she showed some little timidity, on my first day in prison; but in general knew how to avoid the soldiers; and upon any rude attempt to stop or to teaze her at the gate, would show a high Sumatran fierceness in her little face, that made great brutes with bayonets in their hands, stand back; who knew that Malay maidens carry steel; and are quick to use it.

She oftentimes took under her protection timid women, the wives, relatives or friends of prisoners, who on their first visit, would be afraid of the guard, and loiter in the road outside. Umbah would see them, would bid them follow her; and many grown up women had felt themselves safe with the escort of the little foundling of Passumah; as occurred a few days after the visit of Diporo Kasumo.

FORTY-FIFTH DAY.

In the midst of my machine making; being engaged upon the saw-mill, when I moved into my new quarters, I also continued my studies with Umbah; having better opportunity to do so, and learning myself as I taught her. I felt a pleasant stimulus in practising the Arabic letters; and in writing Malay pantuns and verses of the Koran, to learn in advance of my scholar. We sat unmolested, except by the uncouth noises of the prison; during an hour in the forenoon, and two in the afternoon.

My interest in the child was all the greater; that she was a motherless one. She spoke, as orphans often do, about a mother they have never seen; who becomes a bright being with wings, stealing upon their dreams or waking fancies. They have seen that bright mother; they are sure of it; she sat by their couch one night; they heard music, and the air was full of fragrance; and they remember a lady with flowers in her hair, who sang sweet songs and talked about God by their bedside, till they fell asleep. Such was one revery I had heard from a child in a Christian land. This was the revery of the little Malay.

She had a kukur, that said *mari-lah*, Umbah! Umbah come; and the bird had once flown in the woods, near the foot of Dempoh; there, Kayroom had caught it; Mamma had spoken with the bird, had said, Umbah come, all the day. She saw her when she was little, near the woods of Lahat; she sat in a waringin tree, her face was shining like the eye of day; her hair was twined with the flowers, white-doves-on-the-wing. Umbah went to her, Mamma smiled, her face grew little; the gold changed to white, and then she had wings, and flew away to Gunung Dempoh. When Umbah was a woman she would go back to Lahat; and look for her Mamma, who was held by some djins, and could not come to her.

And Malays, old and young, like this child, see visions of beings upon the earth, and in the air; they have a vividness of fancy, that soon changes any imagination that is dwelt upon into fact, to them. But I found the European common sense, that Umbah had acquired from her foster father, quite disposed to listen to my reasonings upon her visions.

She looked upon pictures of her mother in a bright space, where spirits lived; they were with Him who had made sun, moon, stars and earth; and Umbah knew more about the God of her foster father; than the Allah of her nurse. Her mother was above the earth, and would live for ever; she would not live in trees, nor tell birds to speak to her child; she spoke in the heart of Umbah; and if Umbah learned many things, to make her wise and good, her mother would often come into her heart, and fill it with music, and she would, by and by, hear stories of the other world.

How the Malay child listened, and wished for the music every day in her heart; and by and by, she did a nice little piece of work for her papa captain, with which he had been so much pleased; and then she took a little money, some copper doits to a poor sick woman, who called her a little princess; and then one time she had been very spiteful with her old nurse, and called her a bad name, giving much pain; and then she had been persuaded to go and kiss and ask forgiveness; and nurse was happy; and Umbah was happy; and having no idleness like little girls in the campongs, to make her weary, she was joyous, she sang; and young as she was, that Malay child began to understand what was meant by music in the heart.

After she had begun to understand about music in the heart; she began to learn from many stories, how that certain kind of evil spirits, never to be seen, could live in the heart too. She wanted her own way sometimes, she had done some foolish things, she had wanted to do them again after once being sorry; that was the work of a real djin in her heart; they would grow very strong when she had nothing to do; she had seen them strong in the heart of her papa captain when the fire was in his eyes; he was good, he was brave, Umbah knew it; but he did no labor, he wrote with no pen, looked in no book; the djins came, he had nothing to do; his heart was empty, he wanted to fill it, and they would fill it; and then he felt good, for a little while, only a little; and then he was sick; there was no music; and so Umbah began to see something of the mystery of evil.

Such was my pupil and my teacher, during many months in prison. Many strange things passed over me during those months which have not been, which need not be told now. What will you care for lengthy stories of the workings of Dutch justice with me; to know all the circumstances of the two-and-fifty times that I appeared before a functionary of Dutch jurisprudence, to be examined and cross-examined by a tedious intermediary of an interpreter; and all the brow-beating and worrying during a space of one year and more? It is not so much my purpose to tell you of all that I underwent; as of all that I saw and learned during my stay in the prison of Weltevreden.

It was a great college for the study of humanity in some of

its most interesting forms and characters. Children of these isles were books and professors both; filling my soul with a new and a lightsome lore. There were some coarse, heavy Dutch tomes and teachers; judges, jailers, soldiers, convicts and madmen; these were the drudgery of my studies; the pleasanter themes were in the bright pages of Umbah; and yet these were but elementary; there was a volume of richer lore, a deeper study of the Malay and Javanese soul. You shall now read it with me, as I turn back to think over my studies in the College of Weltevreden.

Umbah entered the main court, one day; turning round after passing the gate, and beckoning to some persons to come forward. Two young women in Javanese dress appeared, who stepped along timidly, under the escort of the little girl. Beckers approached; the women stopped, and were about to fly; the turnkey called to them to enter, with an assuring voice; they had been told before coming, that he would not molest them. It was Sahyeepah and her sister who came to pay me a visit.

Umbah was at home, and did the honors; she placed the two chairs for the visitors, sat down herself in her own oriental way, on the top of my little table, a favorite perch for her, and left me to accommodate myself on the top of my trunk. My visitors were better dressed than when I had seen them at my former lodging; yet still the costume of one showed a great contrast to the rich apparel I had seen in Sumatra.

Sahyeepah spoke; her voice had sounded pleasantly at the house of her grandfather; but so much more so now that I understood so clearly what she said. Her brother, Diporo Kasumo, had gone away quickly to Cheribon; some news that had been received from an uncle, required his sudden going; if he had been here, he would have come with his sisters; and her father could not leave his prahu, which was a large vessel of several hundred tons, managed by thirty six men, and was commanded by his son-in-law, the husband of the sister of Sahyeepah; but who was, at that time, attending to some business in Samarang.

The sister became engaged with Umbah, in looking at some sketches, pictures and maps that lay on a shelf; and Sahyeepah talked with me in a lower tone about Sumatra. When Panyorang Osman had heard, that Kiagoos Lanang had a place by the side of our brother in his ship, he had sent a faithful messenger to warn his son, to have nothing to do with him: Kiagoos Lanang had been with the Company, upon an expedition into Ampat Lawang; he was skilful in all the customs of the country; he knew the laws; sang pantuns; and recited history; he was wonderfully skilful; and Panyorang Osman sent for him to come to his house, to give pleasure to his son; but if our brother had asked, did Kiagoos Lanang possess a white heart, and a clean face; the Panyorang would have said no; he sent the messenger to say so; but he came too late; our brother was in the hands of the djins of Palembang.

Kiagoos Lanang said with a big mouth, to the people of Palembang, that he had received money from the Company to write a false letter for the Sultan of Jambee. The people of Palembang speak of it to this day. Kiagoos Lanang said, that when the American Captain was at the marriage feast of the Chinaman, his servants, Bahdoo and Moonchwa, went to the houses of Karanga Kerta Negara, and Tumungung Nora Wangsa; two chieftains in the service of the Company; the servants were sent to the house of the Mantri, who stood by the side of Tuan Besar; a man with a black skin, the Assistant Resident, who gave them instructions to tell them what Kiagoos Lanang should write; they went to the house of the Assistant Resident twice, before the letter was finished.

Panyorang Osman had felt great grief for his son who had fallen into the hands of the djins of the Company; but he felt greater that the hands of children of Pulo Percha should have helped to put his son into the house of care.

It was well, I said; that it is so; her brother had come to know the tongue and the heart of the people of Pulo Percha. Allah had sent him to the house of care; his eyes had become strong, his ears were opened wide; he saw deep into the wickedness of the Company; and deep into the hearts of the people of Pulo Percha, and of the land of Java. Without this trouble, he would not have known the great and good friends that he possessed. Allah would take him out of the hands of the satans of Batavia; Sahyeepah need have no fear.

Sahyeepah spoke of her grandmother, of Nemastiapa, of her cousins, Chayah, Sareena and Umbah; the namesake present, turned round on hearing her name mentioned; were we speaking about her? She had a map in her hand, a map of the globe in hemispheres, drawn with some care, and colored; but without the parallel and meridian lines, which were calculated to confuse the unmathematical Malay mind, and one so young as Umbah; the map was zoological and botanical; as some particular beast, bird and plant, that belonged to each region was drawn upon it. Umbah was proud of her knowledge, and eager to point out to Sahyeepah, as she had been showing to her sister, the land of the kangaroo, of the lion, and of the eagle, or America.

The names of every country were written in Arabic; also various notes and explanations upon spaces in the different oceans, upon the deserts of Africa, the steppes of Asia, and the prairies of America. Each one was read; Umbah explaining; and Sahyeepah and her sister looking on; they learned about a cold ocean, where the water turned to rock; and where fish as large as prahus, sported among the floating mountains of crystal; they saw Pulo Percha, and Palembang, and the river Moosie; and followed the way they had come, along by Banca, Lucepara, and other islands, they knew in the Java sea; then they watched the little fingers of Umbah, as she pointed out the track of the ship of her Uncle Captain; leading them through the Straits of Sunda, across the great waters, where those great fish were to be found, then round the extreme point of the land of lions, across another great stretch of water; and so on to the land of eagles.

What expressions of delight and wonder at this glimpse of the world. How Panyorang Osman had been delighted at the rude pen sketch; the Malay mind, prone to adventure, seems to have an innate desire for a knowledge of the surface of the earth; they have among their writings some extravagant poetic notions of geography, like what is found in the dwipas of the Hindoos; having but little knowledge of lands, besides China, Siam, and the country of Adjem, or Persia; they believe that the Dutch control nearly all the land of the West; and that the English, Portuguese, and Americans live perpetually on the waves, wandering about for trade or plunder.

The Panyorang and his granddaughter had some such rude ideas about geography; though so well versed in the Koran; and in the history and poetry of their country. Knowledge on this subject seemed to break in upon them like strains of new music; knowledge coming with all the picturing and stories, that would gain for it an entrance into the minds of children; and the Panyorang, his granddaughter Sahyeepah, and Umbah, were three children very much alike; they stood about equal at the threshold of civilized lore; perhaps the little foundling, the farther advanced of the three; and I was moved by a desire, more than ever created before by interests of this world, to teach them.

I do not speak of the sister of Sahyeepah; a half sister rather, a daughter of a Javanese mother; who was also the mother of Diporo. The sister looked on with quiet, simple good nature, chiefly occupied in preparing her betel nut, siri leaf, lime, and gambier, or cardamus; which she chewed with the sleepy contentment of an inveterate tobacco chewer, or smoker at home. The vermilion saliva that oozed out of her mouth, and, as it dried, formed dark streaks upon her lips, was certainly not quite so offensive,—having a pleasanter color; as the mahogany ooze from the tobacco-leaf, copperas and molasses, chewed at home. She was a wife and a young mother; and cared as little about dirty streaks of siri on her lips, as some young American wives do about a tobacco pipe between theirs by the home fireside; and caring just as little about geography, when the dressing of baby happened to be the chief care.

Perhaps the sister did not feel so much interest in the teacher, as the other two; there was nothing said that would betray any feeling of any one in that way. Sahyeepah had brought a message from her grandfather; a part of which her brother had brought, and he might have brought it all; but perhaps the skilfulness and good memory of Sahyeepah were more relied upon; and so she came, that I might receive the message more fully, having also a great curiosity, despite her fears, to see a prison; or perhaps she had listened with great interest to some stories told in broken Malay; as ladies in other countries are often pleased with persons, who speak their language in broken words; and she had wished to hear the same person again, and the stories continued; and came on that account to see him.

There was one who speculated thus; but Sahyeepah, the simple child of nature, spoke only to the friend of her grandfather; she had been interested in his words, when she had seen him before; she was now interested; she had a lively curiosity and a love for knowledge, which all Malays possess to a greater extent than other Orientals; she listened eagerly, like the people of Sumatra, to chronicles of Malay states; she could repeat some herself, many young women of Sumatra can; she was eager to follow the footsteps of the Malay race; and she was more Malay than Javanese; leaning to the race of the grandfather who claimed an admixture with the sacred race of Mahomet, of which Sumatrans are so proud. She had been getting a glimpse of great lands and seas beyond Pulo Percha; a great world of wonder for every young, curious, well developed mind of any race; she wanted to know more; and who would not have been eager to have told her more? all they knew. She would study the world I had made on paper; she could not in prison; but she could take it away to bring back again, and another one should be made for Umbah.

We were roused by a start and an exclamation of terror from the sister; and the next moment I saw my ugly Peri standing in the doorway. He was hideous enough to frighten a timid lady any where; but the people of the Archipelago have a peculiar horror of the negro race, to such an extent, that the Dutch Government endeavored to profit by this dread, in the subjugation of the different islands. Great numbers of Africans were sent from the Dutch possessions of St. George d' Elmina, and several companies of black troops formed; but this Africanization of the Netherland Indian army was suddenly stopped by the British Government, which would not allow negroes to be kidnapped and sold for killing Malays, any more than for working sugar and cotton plantations. The few Papuans; the name that Malays give to all black skins and woolly heads, that were brought to the Archipelago, inspired more horror than the sight of the orang-utan; hence the start at the sight of my poor, honest, brave-hearted, faithful Pirez.

This dark, distorted young monster was diffident and confused; he stood in the doorway, turning his woolly plaid cap in his hand; grinning, and looking disposed to retreat. I bade him come in; as he entered, the sisters cowered with looks of fear; but Umbah, the little heroine, the valiant escort, had seen this black djin, this rakshasha before; she went up to him; saying, nobody was afraid of Peri, any more than of Bassett; and gave a dab with her little fist at the monster; which he endeavored to dodge with awkward, grinning good humor.

You will perhaps wonder, that nearly six months after the departure of the brave Commander of the Rambler, Umbah should make such familiar use of his name; as though she had been playing with him the day before; such was indeed the case, with the Bassett that she spoke of; a little chunky, sturdy, black and white dog, that had belonged to one Captain Dückers of the Navy, confined on account of a duel, in the same block with the Colonel, when I first came to prison. During my early promenades I had become acquainted with him; shortly afterwards he was pardoned out; and on leaving, he presented to me his little dog, then called Pompey; which he gave me the more particularly, as it was one of a litter obtained from an American ship; and though not born on the soil, was essentially a native American dog.

Pompey was a well-made, brave little fellow; he manifested after belonging to me a decided antipathy to a stump-tailed dog of the turnkey, and towards Dutch soldiers, in which display of hostility, he was certainly encouraged by Umbah. She had made for him a collar, to which she sometimes attached a patchwork of silk, that bore a striking resemblance to a miniature American flag; this had given umbrage, on one occasion, to a great red-faced, red-headed, Dutch sentinel; he told Umbah to take it off the dog; she was not disposed to comply; he made a rush to seize her; but the nimble little nymph slipped away; the more easily, as Pompey had seized the soldier by his leg, and made a considerable rent in his trowsers; the Dutchman turned furiously;

Pompey faced him; several bayonet thrusts were made, which the dog continued to dodge; whilst the trooper was making another charge, he received an assault in the rear, a stone thrown by Umbah, whc then beat a rapid retreat; Pompey joining his mistress, amid roars of laughter, that came from the gratings of the several blocks. After this event, the Baron decided that the name of Pompey should be changed to that of Bassett, in remembrance of, and out of compliment to the gallant Captain of the Rambler.

Umbah was on equally as good terms with Peri as with Bassett; she made various demonstrations to prove that he was a very harmless, good-natured animal, except when roused in defence of his friends; and I made such remarks, as induced my visitors to look upon my faithful follower, with curiosity, unmingled with alarm. And when about to depart, I had so well set forth his bravery and trustiness, as made them willing to accept his escort, along with Umbah and Bassett, back to the campong.

FORTY-SIXTH DAY.

In the afternoon of the same day that I had received the visit of Sahyeepah and her sister, I was called upon by a Catholic priest of Batavia; one of his colleagues made a weekly round of the prison, and celebrated mass, and preached twice a month, in the little hall of instruction; it was not a government regulation, but a voluntary act on the part of the Catholic clergy; who were the only ones that ever paid any visits of mercy and charity, during my stay in prison.

A man was condemned to be hung; a native soldier, of the Bughis race of Ceylon; he had been removed from the military quarter, and on this afternoon, was placed in a cell in the debtors' ward, where he was to be closely guarded for three days, previous to execution. This condemned cell was nearly opposite to mine, adjoining that of the mad lawyer. The priest wished to speak with the condemned man; and although the Government forbids all missionary operations beyond the precincts of Batavia, and some other European towns of the Archipelago, yet has no objections to the consolation, or conversion of dying men; who will have no opportunity in this world, to make any pernicious use of their Christian enlightenment; and so the priest was allowed free intercourse with the man whose moments of life were numbered.

It was a late hour, when ordinary visitors were not allowed to enter; and I obtained leave to accompany the priest on his visit of mercy. A sergeant sat in the doorway; and another sergeant sat in the cell, with the condemned man; who was not to be left alone, or unobserved for one instant. He was a stout, well-made man, in early prime of life, perhaps thirty years of age. His complexion was like that of the Javanese, which is a shade deeper than the Malay of Sumatra. He had the broad forehead, round head, and bold expression of the Bughis race; one of the bravest, and most industrious in the Archipelago; and so justly famed for their enlarged commercial enterprise.

This man was condemned to be hung for a deliberate act of murder; he had expressed a desire to speak with the panghulu, or Mussulman priest; but not being satisfied with his visit, he had signified a wish to see a Christian teacher. He had met with a Christian missionary of Amboyna; one of the native converts of that island, who had given him a few exceedingly rude notions of Christianity, which were mingled with some strange notions about the transmigration of souls, a belief entertained by a large portion of the people of the Archipelago; especially of Celebes, and of the Molucca group. He wished to know if the "prophet Jesus" would help him to pass out of his body, without pain when strangled; and would if he prayed to him, place him in the same class of bodies, along with one, a young woman, whom he had loved, and who had been killed by a tiger.

The priest spoke of man, after his death, after his heart had ceased to beat, and his body had grown cold; he had nothing more to do on this earth; he went to meet God, who had caused him to live, who had made his soul; who had sent His Son, God like himself, to suffer great torment; to die on this earth; so that evil, and pain, might not always have power over the hearts of men. To slay our fellow man to gratify our own bad wishes, was a terrible bad deed; and caused by the spirit of evil; he had felt its power, making him do wrong often in spite of good thoughts not to do so; if the condemned man now felt great grief for what he had done; and would believe in Christ, that Son of God, who suffered to save him from the pain of evil doing; if he would believe in Him, he would die in peace, and go to a world where pain and evil were never felt. But this Bughis soldier understood nothing of all this.

He believed that when his spirit was forced out of his body at the gallows, it would then take flight across the seas, and return to the haunts that it loved best; perhaps to enter the body of a tiger, or a bird of paradise; or perhaps to pass into the body of a new-born child; and thus have an opportunity to act a better part in life again, by the help of his past experience. If for the present, he passed into the body of an animal, it was on account of some anger, some machinations of djins, which he wished to circumvent; but this animal condition was only a purgatory, which would prepare him for a triumphant career at last, in human form. The Bughis soldier was steadfast in the belief in his idea of purgatory; and the priest had to leave him after a fruitless visit, as the panghulu had done. On leaving, my clerical visitor presented me with a copy of the New Testament, in the Malay language.

I felt desirous to talk with the soldier, myself; he was an interesting-looking man; I wished to hear something of his history; also more about that curious notion of the passage of the soul into a beast, or another human form; and I thought to try and satisfy some of the inquiries of his mind. The solicitation of the turnkey obtained for me permission to visit the condemned cell at a late hour; and this was granted the more readily by the application of a few guilders to the palms of the sergeants.

The criminal did not appear in the least dejected on account of his approaching fate; yet notwithstanding his confidence in his continuation upon the earth in another state of being, he seemed to regret some memories of what belonged to the present; some memories of an early love, the chief thought and anxiety of this murderer. I had spoken to him of his home, his family, his country, and his pursuits; he had drawn near to me, and both the sergeants preferring the cool air outside, and heedless of the regulation, left us to talk undisturbed by their presence. All the memories and interests of the barbarian soul of the Bughis, had been stirred up by words that took him to his early play, and hunting grounds, and beneath the waringin groves, where he first had loved.

His name was Wongso; and the son of a small chieftain in the service of Arong Datu, queen of Boni, a kingdom of Celebes. This princess made vigorous war against the English in 1814; and afterwards against the Dutch under Van der Cappelen. The sovereignty of Boni is the ruling state among the nations of Celebes; its sovereigns are elected by the chieftains of the country; and since the time of the Portuguese, when an act of cowardice and treason was committed by one of their kings, they have almost invariably elected a queen, in preference to kings; for at the time of the elevation of Arong Datu, she had an elder brother, and a man of great experience in war.

Young Wongso played with Nawah, a granddaughter of Arong Datu; he spoke of her as man speaks every where of his fondest memory of womanly loveliness. He had when arrived at the age of manhood, taken part in some hostilities against Goa, the rival state of Boni; when he returned, he could take Nawah to his own campong; he would own a ship, like many of his countrymen, and take rich freights to Batavia and to Singapore.

He came back, a warrior; he could give the bridal gift her father asked; but he must not see his love, till the women had prepared a feast; nor before the panghulu had spoken the consecrating words. Wongso was impatient; he knew that his lover went with a company of young women, and servants, to a certain shaded creek to bathe; he went to watch; though he placed his life in danger. Nawah wandered a little way from her company, she ascended the creek bank; she was looking for rare wild flowers; she stopped, she stooped to gather a bloom. Wongso was near; he heard a fearful squall, a bound, and then beheld his Nawah borne away in the jaws of a tiger.

He rushed forward with wild outcries, the tiger bounding through the thicket, and Wongso following. The beast was not full grown; he had too heavy a burden for his strength, he bounded with difficulty; Wongso gained upon him, he pressed on and shouted, till the cowardly creature let go his prey, as he will often do, when resolutely met or pursued; and the lover regained the body of his bride; but life was gone, and no doubt had fled at the first grip of the cruel beast.

To be devoured by a tiger is a common fate in the Archipelago; not less than two such deaths occur every week in the neighborhood of Palembang, according to Dutch official report; and many such take place in the vicinity of the British settlement of Singapore. Tigers have been known to spring upon wayfarers within an hour's walk of the city of Batavia; and Baron Van Norden affirmed, that this terrible beast had, on several occasions, at Lahat leaped sheer over an enclosure, ten feet high, into a court-yard, and bounded off with a coolie, who was at work inside.

His tigership manifests a decided preference for the native brown skins. If a European and Malay or Javanese happen to be together, he will invariably spring upon the native; but he is said by some to prefer a good fat monkey to either; whilst others contend for his greater partiality to man. Yet no effort has ever been made by the people of the Archipelago, of Sumatra in particular, to make war upon this fearful enemy of their race; they will attack, and endeavor to kill, any individual tiger, who has slain a relative or friend, looking upon such a tiger as a murderer, and their private enemy; but they will make no indiscriminate war upon the blood-thirsty felines, for fear that they might perchance kill an ancestor; tigers being spoken of with great respect; and commonly called *neneh*, or ancestors, by the

Malays. Europeans being on good terms with the tigers, do not choose to interfere in behalf of the natives.

Wongso buried Nawah; he had eaten all his heart, had given all his soul for her; and there was no more joy of life for Wongso. He hated life, and hated men; he went away from Boni; he joined some pirates of Saleyer; he helped to kill the crew of a Chinese junk; after a time, he was captured by a cruiser of the Dutch Company; they would not put him to death, though a pirate; he would make a good soldier; he served in the campaign against Bali; he returned with his company to Java; then a Dutch corporal struck him; and he cut his throat; for which deed he must hang, because a soldier. Had he been out of the army, he would probably have been sent to the prison as a waiter.

Wongso did not speak of deeds of blood with the dogged indifference, or hardened ferocity of the more civilized assassin. He did not feel that he had done very terrible things; he had put to death some dogs of Chinamen, and slain the man who had dishonored him with a blow; he felt very keenly that sense of honor, felt by men of other races, who hardly consider the robbery of a man, or any lack of honesty, a stain upon honor; but conceive a tarnish on character from the slightest hostile touch, or a crooked word, which only blood can cleanse away. Wongso entertained orthodox notions, in accordance with the European code of honor. And his notions about the future condition and final disposition of his soul; if barbarous and absurd; if so widely at variance with orthodox Christian belief; yet he believed them earnestly, and felt, however strangely, that the life to be realized beyond this one, was now his chief concern.

We talked about Celebes; about Kings, Queens, and Chieftains; about great wars, ships, temples; and all that man could be and do; about love, and far-reaching schemes; about friendship, courage and honor; and all that man could think and feel; we talked about the earth, the forests, the water; and all that man controlled or used; then about the sun, moon, stars; the pathways traced on the sea by skymarks in the heavens; the sure knowledge beforehand, of the darkenings of the great lights of day and night; and other things to show, how far beyond this earth, how far above the brutes the mind of man did reach.

We had talked with simplest words; the innermost recess of the barbarian soul of Wongso was entered; ideas, for which even his language had no words, began to dawn; he had been met on his own ground, with his own rude fashion of thought; he stepped out to a wider circle; he went on himself; he felt that he was not taught, he was only awakened. He was not told that his belief was absurd; nor told any thing, equally absurd to him; but he felt a growth, a greater worth of soul; his thought went on, stretched out into the mystery of being, into a consciousness of immortality; and he began to feel that it was inconsistent that a man's soul should enter into the existence of a tiger.

It had grown late, I was obliged to retire; but Wongso begged that I would come and talk with him, the next evening; his last on this side of his grave. The following day, my mind was busy with thoughts about this oriental belief in the change of body of souls.

A belief, said the lady of the elder missionary, interrupting the narrator, the idea of which, western philosophers no doubt got from the Archipelago; and not these islanders from the western philosophers; it is a belief that one might think was congenial to the primitive and poetic minds of the people of those islands; and there are many minds, in the midst of our civilization and enlightenment, who cherish the idea of an anterior state of being on this earth; the many mysterious thrills and indistinct memories, so often awakened, like echoes from a hidden world within, from a state of being gone by; seem to tell the soul of some other condition of being it has passed through, and would make plausible to some the Malay metempsychosis.

But the elder missionary hoped that the narrator had not been alone interested in speculations upon this belief. This would be explained in the continuation of the story of Wongso.

When the time of visiting was over, and the gates were closed for the night, I again obtained leave to talk with the condemned man. He met me with an anxious look; he had been thinking of life and death, all day; and death seemed more fearful now, than before we had talked about the value of man's soul; he thought of the men whose blood he had shed; their cry and agony was in his ear; their shortened life, their defrauded being, seemed to stand to his charge; and he was afraid to meet them in death; where perhaps they might have power over him; where perhaps the Ruler of life might meet him, and make him a slave to those he had robbed; he had conjured up a hell, and he was terribly afraid of it.

But he was led on to think; by the progress alone, almost, of his newly developed reasoning; that even if he could restore the life, the peace, and the property he had taken away, he would still have the bad heart, to do more evil of the same kind; it did not seem to require any tedious, trained exercise of reason, to arrive at that conclusion; he felt it, even with his feeble oriental mind; then he began to conceive wants, and feel wants, that began to startle my own thoughts, and to baffle my own reason, to satisfy; and I was led to think of helps, perhaps like many a one else, that I never thought of applying to for myself.

We had reasoned about a soul; he had been led to feel that he had a soul; and that it was in a bad condition for his present idea of a future existence. He seemed to appeal to me, to help him further on; but the civilized was as helpless as the uncivilized. What more could I do for Wongso? Nothing, nothing. He had been led to think, to feel, that immortality and a future, elevated state of being, was a better belief than that he should go into another bad mortal like himself, or a tiger; but what hope of happiness was there with this immortality? I knew not; though I had listened to many proclamations of what was the best foundation for that hope. There was no one to proclaim it now; a few hours only remained to Wongso; and there was no more hope of helps or counsel from man, than what he had with him; and I felt that all further reasoning was in vain. But there was the authority from whence men derived the foundation of a hope of future bliss; the Testament, that had been given to me by the priest; the Malay Testament, which I had prized so much, as an aid in my future studies of the Malay language; might there not be something in it, that would satisfy the heart of Wongso?

I certainly had no idea of disturbing the mind of the doomed man, with discussions of the mysteries of the scheme of Christian salvation; and I went for the Testament, as a kind of refuge from the responsibility that I had imposed upon myself, of satisfying the mind of this awakened man, in some way. I first glanced at some passages, that spoke of the evil nature of man, the deceitful, desperate nature of sin; what was sin, and its wages; the power of sin, and man's need of help to contend against it; then the history of the birth of Christ was read—His sermon on the mount; His remarkable life, so different from any other man before or since; His power, His miracles, His meekness, and ardent love for man; His suffering, His death, and resurrection; then I read some of the words of the followers of Christ; their testimony as to all the facts of the Saviour's life, the testimony of ages and ages, the belief of all the most powerful nations of the European race, perhaps the great cause of their strength, and superiority over the disbelieving portion of the world.

Wongso cared not to know about all the after proofs, and substantiations of the existence and mission of Christ; he wanted to hear more about what He said and did. I read His life from another evangelist; then the words by which He called little children; the weary and heavy laden; the sinners in their sins; hopeless, helpess bad men, like Wongso. I was treading paths that were strange to myself. I had wanted to lighten up a curious receptacle of uncivilized darkness, but there was a far different light dawning, than what I had conceived of shedding upon it. The night was far advanced, far on into the morning of the last day of Wongso. I had been urged, nay, ordered to leave; but he clung to me; and the sergeants were persuaded to let me stay; they had to keep awake; this talking helped to drive away their drowsiness; and one became interested, and relieved me at times by reading to his fellow-soldier.

Wongso begged us to read again, and again. I had come with some enthusiasm to rouse up a dull, barbarian mind, an apathetic, semi-pagan, Mahometan soul; but the savage showed an ardor, an eagerness to find a something to satisfy his soul, in launching into the future, that shamed my weariness. He wanted to hear, more, more; and all about Christ, that called bad men to come unto Him with broken hearts. The sergeant who read, became roused up; he wept, he wished the good dominie he had so often listened to when a boy, were here; he proposed that we should do, what he had often done before he became a soldier; that we should pray; and the soldier and the two prisoners knelt down; and the soldier raised up his voice, appealing to a throne of grace, for mercy upon his own sinfulness, and praying that the man whom he was guarding unto his death in this world, might be raised up unto eternal life in another and a better one.

Wongso wept, as the sergeant wept; he continued to weep; he thought not of his soon being raised on a gallows for his crimes; but of One, who had been raised up ignominiously, for what such as he had done. It was a terrible scene, the agitation, the weeping of that murderer. But he was becoming calmer; was his animal nerve giving way? was this a reaction of mental excitement? perhaps so; but Wongso said that he believed in Christ; not the "prophet Jesus;" but Him, who died for sinners; and now Wongso was not afraid to die.

The sergeant said something about baptism; a necessary stamp of Christianity; that could not be complied with now. Wongso had heard of it, and his mind was disturbed; but still lost no hope; nor felt that all would be lost, if he died without it. The sergeant had read, and I had read, that many earnest Christians believed that unconsecrated, and even hands of sinful and unregenerated men, might, in extremity, perform for a dying fellow-being the formula of this sacrament. If it was not so; yet still the unsatisfied point in the mind of Wongso, would be relieved. A bowl of water was obtained, was poured on to the head of Wongso; and he was baptized by a fellow sinner, in the name of the Holy, Almighty and Everlasting Trinity.

It was now nearly daybreak; at six o'clock, the sun rose; and at seven, the guard would come for the prisoner. I left the Testament with the sergeant; Wongso wished to hear something read to the last. I said some parting words, he wept again; but seemed to possess a joy, that I did not understand. All that I had done, was to help to ease the mind of an unfortunate man. He had given some directions that were to be communicated to the judge advocate, that all the little property he possessed should be given to the family of the man he had murdered; he gave eleven rupees to the sergeant to buy two Testaments in the Malay language; the same, as the one from which I had read, to be given to two of his comrades in prison, who could read. He begged of me to go and talk to them. The time came to part; I asked him to raise up his right hand to heaven the moment before they pinioned him, under the gallows, as a sign that his heart felt strong to the last; and with profound emotion I parted with Wongso.

A solemn roll of the drum; and harsh voices of command, roused up the prison at sunrise. A guard entered the court; the sergeants delivered up their charge; and I saw one wipe his eyes, with his sleeve, as he turned away from the man, whose moments were counted. The turnkey afforded me an opportunity to see through the grating, that overlooked the field of death. Long lines of troops were formed into a hollow square, the bayonets glistened in the sun, the horses of a commanding officer and his staff pranced about the field, loud voices resounded; and there was great stir and pride of warlike array.

In the centre of all this, was the gloomy gallows; a man, in a dark robe, the judge advocate, stood with a roll, the death warrant in his hand; he read it to Wongso, who stood near him; then a man in uniform, a military sheriff, took the regimental coat, and cap, from off Wongso; he was degraded as a soldier upon earth; and was given up to the hangman; then Wongso mounted steps; and before the cords were passed around him, he made the sign, he raised up his right hand towards heaven, affirming, at his last moments on earth, that he was a steadfast soldier of the Cross.

I saw no more; I could not look upon the horrible mode of Dutch hanging. It is not enough to kill a man; but he must realize the most excruciating agony that is possible to be felt by the body of man, before he is strangled. I cannot give the details, but look into their laws upon death; a man to be hung is so foully bound, that ere his neck is broken his bowels are torn, I heard a signal tap, a solemn roll of the drum; a man had gone to the land of souls; and then the band struck up a lively tune as the troops marched back to their quarters.

The elder missionary after some comments upon the probable salvation of Wongso; and the fitness of the instrumentality employed; went on to say, that the mind of the western world seemed to have been beating in vain against the externals of Oriental prejudice; we had been continually battling with our common sense against their absurdities, without the pains to consider these absurdities, which were comprehension to them; we missionaries, I am afraid, have acted like the people seeking gain; we have sat down at the outskirts, the outports of the Oriental mind and character; where we have been content to erect the stiff forms of our own rigid, common-sense temperate clime, waiting for the dreamy, imaginative Oriental to come round to us. He has not come; he has felt nothing at the hands of the European, but a harsh manifestation of supremacy of skill and intellectual power, his sympathetic nature has revolted at this; the avenues, which reach him, through his moral convictions, have been closed; and the millions and hundreds of millions in the East pass away, uninfluenced to the slightest extent by European dominion and enlightenment.

Surely, the souls of men should be esteemed worth something, even to a trader; but certain millions of pounds of pepper in Sumatra, are more zealously sought after and considered, than the millions of Malays on the island; and yet the Malay seems to have a destiny, that will affect all the relations of trade, in the great treasure ground of commerce. He advances; we have abundant evidence that he is taking possession of every outpost and highway, that lies between the Pacific and the Indian Ocean, in the great trading centre of the world; he flourishes in a region in which the European wastes away, after the second generation, a third being rarely ever perpetuated; the European, who can never colonize the Archipelago, but must always look forward to the Malay, as the chief instrument in the production of what he so much covets; might it not be, even to the interest of his pocket, to stoop to closer relations, to enter with some fraternal touch into the sympathies of those, who must be the perpetual producers of spices and other precious things of the commerce of the East.

What is the glory of a so-called merchant prince, who has gathered a great hoard of money? who has reared a huge pile of brick and stone, who has filled it with mere pamperings of the body; who has fenced himself around, and sat down, content to gaze for the rest of his days at his sordid substance, made out of advantageous barter with simple pepper growers, coffee planters, and gum gatherers; who are herding in the forest, and brutified with the vile belief, that their soul will pass into a tiger; whilst the intelligent European, who is glorying in the substance wrung out of their feeble hands for a small, and often hurtful exchange, is looking forward complacently in a cushioned pew, in some church, partly of his building, to the heaven that his hired preacher promises him.

The world is not to be all Caucasian; it needs the contrast of stronger and weaker brethren; of the practical and the intellectual; with the sympathetic and imaginative; the Caucasian ceases to be such within the tropics; his superiority is only a little more oxygen, that belongs to his temperate latitude. That man is a vulger egotist, who exults in the accidental advantage of his greater strength over his weaker brother; the fancies and dreams of the one, should have a place as well as the bold conceptions of the other; flowers fill the eye, as much as great trees, and repay as much by their cultivation. The European should cultivate the friendship of the Malay! whilst seeking out routes for trade, he should look for pathways into the sympathies of his soul, and call forth all his pleasant fancies and dreams; or shall he be always met with the sordid selfishnes of the trader; and be left to his viciousness and piracy, instead of encouraged to bring forth the pantuns and songs of his land!

FORTY-SEVENTH DAY.

The seventh month of my stay in prison had come; and with it, the arrival of Resident De Brauw and his Assistant. The Phoenix and the Borneo had sought in vain for evidence against me, throughout the Archipelago. To have a witness, some one besides my Malay servants, some one, who could testify to something; it was necessary to send for the Royal Adjutant; the proud Governor of Palembang. He must have met his late guest and prisoner with chagrined feelings; after dooming him to death, still to find him, after a lapse of more than half a year, disturbing his government; and disturbing him in his quiet at Palembang, far more than any number of successfully transmitted letters to all the Sultans of Sumatra could have done.

We met at the Stadhuis, whither I was carried by the friendly Sheriff Brower; we met for confrontation, the late guest and host; the prisoner of Weltevreden, and the witness De Brauw. There was no occasion for much courtesy of feeling; perhaps a spirit of vindictiveness ruled at the time, and charity was all forgotten. De Brauw was led to believe, that the brutality of a naval Commander, and the natural treachery of some of his own Malay police, were not held in such low estimation as the part he had acted; he was led to believe that he was looked upon as a false-hearted man, notwithstanding the romantic incident of the silver heart; and it so happened that he stood before a judge, the good judge, who permitted him to hear all this.

The mulatto Assistant had an evil-looking face, traced deep with treachery; yet he was but a small man, this son of the negress of Surinam; though so useful to the Dutch Government at Palembang. It could not be made manifest, how far he had been serviceable in the production of a certain hostile letter addressed to a Sumatran prince; but enough was said, to assure him that more than one of those who spoke with him during the confrontation, believed that he had taken a large share in the dictation; and the assurance seemed to give a deeper shade to his dark face.

The crew of the Flirt were re-examined. Some time was spent in trying to find an interpreter; who could understand Pirez. They found a Portuguese, who had lived on the western coast of Africa. Great efforts were made, not by the examining judge, but by an underling of the Attorney General, to draw out the boy:—he had been so much near me; he must know a great deal of what I had said and done. He had been badgered for a time, in vain; but he was getting weary; he seemed about to yield; and had something to tell, that would gratify the inquisitors; he had heard his master say, one night at Palembang, a dark night, standing by the starboard shrouds, on board the Flirt; yes, standing by the starboard shrouds; that,—well what was it?—that his master said that his Dutch visitors wanted to drink too much beer; more than he cared to supply.

All this examining was carried on in a loose and irregular way; the usual mode is, that a commissary judge takes the place of a grand jury at home, to examine accused and witnesses, to determine the probabilities of guilt; and the result would be, a report whether the case should be brought into judicature, made the subject of a public trial, or not; but in my case, the chief solicitor of the government, not the Fiskaal attached to the Court of Justice, took an active part to ferret out some little circumstance, some little peg upon which to rest the charge of "high treason;" first made by De Brauw in his despatch to the Governor General, and afterwards maintained by the Government of Netherland India.

Notwithstanding the zeal, and the prolonged efforts of the Government officers; the Court of Justice of Batavia, after numberless examinations, after a long deliberation, arrived at the conclusion, that there were "no grounds for prosecution in the case," no foundation for a trial; that the accused should be immediately set at liberty, and restored to his property; and this decision was recorded, and a copy served upon me, on the 25th August 1852. In this decision, the Court of Justice had been assisted by the Fiskaal, or prosecutor, who in a requisition, a document of the date of the 18th of the month, fully set forth that there were no grounds for the charge of misdemeanor, as alleged against the late commander of the Flirt.

I thought that I would surely go free; and to return no more this time. I had packed up the slight baggage of my prison; and was awaiting the carriage of my young friend; when Brower came with an unwelcome look, with a decree from the High Court, the tribunal of appointees of the Crown, that deliberates in secret, and gives no man a chance to speak for himself; which reversed the decision of the Court of Justice, and decreed my continued detention in prison. The friendly Fiskaal was removed, and the underling of the Attorney General, a clerk of his bureau, was appointed instead of the former lenient prosecutor; some changes were made in the Court of Justice; and it was moreover decreed that the inquisition that had been going on for seven months, should be all gone over again.

The examinations were held at intervals, during a period of four months more. What I was questioned about, what others had to say concerning my case, during all this time; during this relabor of such well-wrought ground, is now a matter of wonderment to think of; how all the petty details of past life and habits, were hunted out of some imagined admissions, out of some old papers, and many people's fancies; how the politics and social state of America were brought forth; the proneness of its people to association, to adventure, to study, and to do as they pleased, how all this questioning, about every thing, but the matter in point, whether I dictated and sent a certain seditious letter to the Sultan of Jambee, or not; how all this grew daily into great volumes of judicial docket, is still a wonderment to my thought; and may be looked upon by some after inquirer, as a remarkable monument of labor, stupidity, espionage and perversion of justice in Netherland India.

But I shall pass over the circumstances of these questionings; pass over a description of the attempted brow-beating exploits of a lawyer; and of all that was done to meet them. The arrogance and craft of the one; or the caution and tact of the other, will add nothing to the interest, which it is desired to call forth; an interest in a race of which there were some opportunities to gain a deeper and more startling knowledge, during the intervals of the harassing of the law and of law's delays in Weltevreden.

Sahyeepah came to the prison with her sister to return the map she had taken away; she had studied all the colored compartments, knew all the names of countries, as linked with beast or bird; had read all the notes; and was prepared to give her grandfather great gladness with her knowledge, when she returned to Sumatra. But such love for study was rare in any woman, in any region of the world; and still more to seek to pursue it in a prison; there surely must have been some interest beyond the study, to such a mind, to a tropic-born heathen girl, to a Malay young woman's soul; and something there was, no doubt, disturbing the artless thought of one and puzzling the mind of the other. But a desire to learn European wisdom, had been a ruling thought before the Flirt went to Palembang; for this was no common mind, a remarkable one to be met with among Caucasian, as well as Malay.

I had taken rambles far upon many strange paths into the native Oriental mind; I had entered many curious regions of fancy and feelings; and I, who had often regretted that the world was so small, so quickly explored, so thoroughly known, wishing at one time for young adventure's sake, that its girth were one hundred thousand miles, instead of twenty-five; I now began to feel that there were rarer fields of exploration in the unmeasured, unexplored human soul; in many strange varieties of race, than all that might meet the eye in a limitless space of mere earth and sea.

I had contemplated with some interest a quick and marvellous Malay mind, and a fervent young Malay heart; but I had become wrought up by late scenes, touched with sympathies for a race, and moved to the maintenance of a character, that inspired me with a feeling to save myself; if not before the rest of the world, at least from any sign of weakness before them. Some enthusiasm, the offspring of a strange experience, caused me to meet the love of learning of Sahyeepah, as the sole ground upon which we might stand together; and further events, a further growth of the thought in the one, and observation in the other, made it desirable to maintain the relative position, the teacher and pupil, the master and disciple, in which we had met.

And Sahyeepah came and sat down in prison, and listened to talk of many things; beginning with some of the absurdities of the dreams of her own race, and then advancing to the region of reason; and thus on to an enlarged consciousness of soul. It was not so strange for her to listen to all this now; as it was for the other to so unfold himself in such a place, to such a person; all had been strange to her, the first word, the first thought, coming from what seemed to her and her people, a superior and wonder-working race; and her object in coming to listen, was childlike curiosity and wonder; whilst the other, though not seeking this encounter, now sought in the curious interest of it, a study of a remarkable Oriental character, the analysis, never to be realized in the midst of civilization, of a woman's nature; and some antidote against the lethargy and stagnation of some prison hours.

We went over some of the same ground, that had been gone over with Wongso; and in regard to the worth of the human soul, the granddaughter of Panyorang Laksana, conceived as quickly, some enlarged and Christian conceptions, as the Celebes soldier; but she felt no anxiety, expressed no curiosity with regard to any future disposition of soul; and none for a time was discussed.

Curiosity was led on from the map to various other studies; the Book that had proven of so much consolation to Wongso; a Malay story, the romance of Ghralaam; some chapters of the Bidyasari; a Malay translation of the Ramaina; some chronicles of Madjapahit; the exploits of Panji; a Javanese metric legend of the wars of Browijoyo; and a collection of Malay pantuns in manuscript; these afforded themes, of such novelty and interest, as won the curiosity, and some labor of study, from Umbah, Sahyeepah, and their fellow-student in Weltevreden.

Sahyeepah came a second time with her sister, then with her brother, who had returned from Cheribon; and then I saw the father. Wirojoyo was a man of some little rank in Java; he had been a demang of a dessa, or small town near Samarang; he had been suspected in earlier years, of favoring the cause of Deepo Negoro, who threatened the existence of Dutch dominion in Java, at one time; at a later period, he had been again suspected of a hostile disposition to the Government, and of selling arms to the insurgent people of Bali; and this led to a deposition from the authority and emoluments of his native rank. He engaged in commerce; he owned several prahus; and was an active successful man in trade. He was married for the third time, the mothers of Diporo Kasumo, Sareena, and Sahyeepah, being both dead. Wirojoyo was a quiet, honest, incurious character; submissive and truthful like the rest of his countrymen; and the son and daughter by the first, the Javanese wife, resembled him; but Sahyeepah, the child of the Sumatran mother, was curious, sensitive, proud, high-toned, like the old Sumatran aristocrat, her grandfather

Wirojoyo and his Javanese son and daughter came, and smiled with good-humored indifference at what was talked about, and studied along with Sahyeepah in prison. They had liked me at first, because their old relative in Sumatra had taken such an interest; by and by, their Javanese sympathies were touched, and then they liked me on my own account. It was a curious thing to have a European, one of the race of their masters, for a friend; it was a matter of novel interest to have him commune with them; to have him as they thought come down to them; and then they to go up to him; to hear no talk but of their pleasantest fancies and sympathies; no want for their service, but rather to serve them. They clothed me with the extravagant attire of their active fancies; there was nothing too strange for me to propose, too curious to happen. It was not too great a wonderment to these oriental minds, that their daughter and sister should like a man, and show it; it was perfectly consistent with their customs that she should go abroad, even more freely than in European countries; and so, after the novelty of the first adventures to the prison, the after visits became matter of everyday incident; and Wirojoyo and his Javanese son and daughter seemed only to think, that when the house of care should open its gates for the American Tuan; there would be rejoicing on the Moosie and the Ogan; but what part their curious, studious, enthusiastic daughter and sister might take in that rejoicing, never entered their unmanœvering, unspeculating, simple Javanese minds.

And Sahyeepah, the unsophisticated child of Sumatra, untrained and unskilled in the art of civilization, though so graced with the finest manifestations of humanity; she knew nothing of possible compromise of position; she was of an age it is true to feel the full extent of all of woman's relations in life; and they are supposed to be so quickly realized in the East; but not so much, when undisturbed, as in the sentiment-stimulated souls of women of the West. The Malay young woman, whilst left to herself in the quiet of her paternal home, dreams of no adventure beyond the achievements in dyeing and embroidery within the walls of that home; and it did seem that Sahyeepah had dreamed of none that had relation to an interest in another sex, beyond this; she had listened to stirring tales of the ancestry of her grandfather, Arab and Malay; she had listened to his hate of the Dutch, and wild hope of restoration of the royal race of the sacred city, of the once mighty Menangkabau; she had heard read in her grandfather's house, so many legends and pantuns, that spoke of renown and power to come for the Malay people; of royal women who ruled, of princesses, young maidens like herself, reverenced, and obeyed by a whole people; she had thought of these things, her grandfather had watched her dreamings; and some of my words, when in Sumatra, touched some of the secret dreams of the ambitious grandfather and the enthusiastic grand-daughter.

This unsophisticated daughter of Sumatra was perhaps ambitious too; a feeling that has been shown by many Malay women; and rarely ever by a single Malay man; never to the extent of any heroic exertion or sacrifice; but the women of the Archipelago have shown it to the extent of disdaining the common weaknesses of their sex; or rather overlooking them,—not feeling their force, not having been acted upon by any nature of their own race, who could awaken an interest superior to this strange enthusiasm, as in the case of Sahyeepah.

She had no thought of compromise of womanly position; and her feelings had evidently been too indeterminate to disturb her, or to make her think that there was a relation in life to be cared for; she had had thoughts and curious dreams of a pomp and royal state, that had belonged to some one of her ancestors,—of its restoration again; and perhaps in her person; when the Dutch should be driven out of Sumatra; and then she would ride upon a white elephant, and thousands of people would touch their foreheads to the ground before her;—then whilst dreaming of this, she had heard words about European skill and power, from one whom she and her grandfather thought of a superior race to the one they feared and hated; they had listened with wonderment, they had longed to hear more, they wanted to believe that the visit of that

American ship and her commander was not a dream; they followed him in sympathy; and then one did in person, even to a prison.

Sahyeepah came with her father, brother, and sister; but they could not come as often as she wished, nor stay to hear talk about things for which the poor people of Java could have no use. By and by, an old nurse of Sahyeepah, called Ayum, came from Cheribon, and accompanied her young mistress; and they always had the escort of Pirez; and sometimes of Umbah and Bassett. The jailer was easy in his prison discipline towards me, for several months after the visit of the "St. Mary's;" he had been curious about the visits of the Javanese family; and he had evidently been much questioned about them at head-quarters; but the curious dyed cloths in which I had taken an interest, for articles of dress,—the sewing that was done for me; and all the commonplace, business appearances that were put upon these native visitings, fully satisfied the jailer and his employers.

The turnkey was completely bought over to my interest; though I knew that the brutal old dragoon watched me as keenly as ever, for any false move on my part,—the report of which would insure him reward and favor from those he served. But in the matter of little privileges which a turnkey controlled; and all that he could sell, were entirely at my disposal; he fully understood when he might show up his chief lion to visitors, and when not to do so; he was careful not to have my Javanese calls intruded upon; he would sometimes open a door, and make a satisfactory explanation to an obstinate sentinel at an unseasonable hour; he managed the introduction of visitors with all the tact and profit to himself, of a well-skilled flunkey, who manages the avenues, —the ante-chamber leading to an employer's presence.

There was a class of visitors, the Malay and Chinese peddlers, who came at certain hours, and could sell certain small permitted articles to the prisoners; these did not occupy any of Tutup's care; except to levy a heavy black mail upon tobacco, whenever any new trader unfamiliar with the tariffs of the prison, made an unwise outward show of a stock of that article. One of these, a Javanese, came one day, and interrupted some study with Umbah and Sahyeepah. Nothing was wanted; and the peddler was told to go away; still he importuned more than usual, to have me only look at something he had to show; he said he had very curious articles of the manufacture of Poorwacarta in Krawang; Sahyeepah spoke, at the mention of this; what did they make in Krawang, that was not made in all Java?—they made most marvellous little boxes from buffalo horn;—but I had no use for such a thing;—still I would find this one very curious, if I would only look at it. The importunity of the man made me look at him; he did not seem like a peddler, and he looked at me, as though he had something to communicate. I went near him; he had his finger upon a letter among his wares; he put it into the little box; which I bought; and he immediately left the prison.

When my company had gone, I inspected the contents of my purchase. A message of deepest interest, from a man whom I wished to see above all others in Java. It is not necessary that I should say what was that message, or from whom it came; my only object in alluding to it, was to mention the cause that gave rise to an incident of peculiar adventure and heroism,—the details of which will introduce you a little into the heart of the great island of Java; as far as the imperial residence of Solo or Surakarta—a vestige of the once great empires of Madjapahit and Matarem.

I had a great desire to find a faithful messenger, who would carry a message to the Javanese imperial city. There was Pirez, faithful and courageous enough; but the Government would never give him a passport to go into the interior; and his fear-inspiring physiognomy would attract too much attention, if he attempted a clandestine expedition; the rest of my sailors were still more unfitted; the Baron was disposed to do most extraordinary things for me; but he was wholly unsuited to aid me now, to do this, I sounded the temper and adventurous spirit of Wirojoyo and his son; but I learned from them, without making any allusion to a message which I had to send, that to accomplish a visit to the great city, without the escort and facilities furnished by Government to visitors going into the interior, would require one month of time, the employment of six coolies well armed, two horses, and the expenditure of one thousand five hundred rupees; and then he must be a bold man to face all the dangers of the route without the government protection. The risk of such a journey would never be incurred by Wirojoyo or Diporo Kasumo.

I sought in vain for a messenger, whilst all the particulars of the route to Surakarta became the chief study for the time. Umbah was soon tired of the study of the geography of Java, but Sahyeepah never flagged in attention to all that related to the imperial island, that once wielded an absolute sway over all the rest of the Archipelago. She was familiar with the early dynasties of Susuhunans or emperors; and could chant some of their exploits in the heroic lines of the Bratah Yudha, the great epic of Java; she often heard of the glories of the Kraton of Surakarta, no mean relic of the Madjapahit splendor; as it contained not less than two hundred thousand people within its lofty walls. She had longed to see the Kraton; but I reminded her that she must never hope to see it, unless with some rich and powerful protector. That was true, she thought; a poor weak woman, would be assaulted by robbers and evil men, or devoured by tigers;

and if escaping all these, would be made a slave by some of the people of the Susuhunan.

I manifested a profound regret in contemplating all these difficulties; and why should I care, why should I regret so much? I could not tell Sahyeepah; but by and by, she heard from her father and her brother, of my earnest and particular inquiries of them; her courageous and enthusiastic soul was moved; you hardly need be told in what way; and what she was about to say and propose; as you have a better knowledge of her extraordinary character than I had then. She spoke of my inquiries of her father and her brother; of the deep interest shown before her. What was wanted at Surakarta? What message to send, what commission to execute? Sahyeepah would do it. But where were the robbers, tigers, and slave-makers she would meet on the road? She did not see them now; she would go vilely clad, and take her old servant and a boy; and they would travel as poor peddlers. I listened as to the wild whims of adventure of a child. The father would, no doubt, as soon entertain the idea of her swimming back to Sumatra; and so I shook my head at all the volunteer heroism of Sahyeepah.

She came one day with a look of fixed purpose; Allah had spoken to her in the night-time; she had heard her name called; she had trembled till her soul was almost gone; and she had heard a voice say, that she had a great work to do for Tuan. She felt the heart to do it; she feared no more the tigers, robbers, and other evil men; she had heard of a renowned *suwanggee*, a magician, who lived near Gunung Gedeh; she would get from him some charmed things, that would secure her against all danger.

It is common to hear among the Malays and Javanese, of communings with spirits. I have heard several simple, earnest characters, assert such experience with the utmost earnestness and particularity of detail; it is easy to be believed of highly imaginative, simple, uncultivated minds in tropic regions; but Sumatra is noted for instances of remarkable spiritual manifestations to women, remarkable in the estimation of the Sumatran people, who, in one instance, built a great broadway, straight up to the top of a high mountain, some ten or twelve thousand feet high, because a certain supposed communicant with the spirit land, had declared with much enthusiasm, that the body, the relics of a certain holy personage were buried on the summit of the mount; and many other instances are recorded in authentic history of the effect of spiritual manifestations in Sumatra.

Sahyeepah was of a character to become one of these noted spirit mediums; an earnest, enthusiastic, imaginative creature, with all the devotion of a perfect woman, yet only a child in point of cultivated reason. She urged her desire to undertake the hazardous expedition; and urged so resolutely, that I began to think it possible, that the interesting young enthusiast was perhaps the surest, and no doubt the safest messenger to send. But it seemed impossible to suppose that the father would consent, that his daughter should undertake such a wild adventure. Wirojoyo came, he had heard of the resolution of his daughter; it was the will of Allah, Sahyeepah was marvellous beyond all her people; she could accomplish what one hundred men would not do; his daughter would obtain charms from the renowned suwanggee; his son, the American Tuan, would soon be free; and he was willing to let Sahyeepah go.

Wirojoyo and Diporo Kasumo, were both impressed with the idea, of some supernatural commission being imparted to Sahyeepah; they no longer imagined risk to her, in undertaking a fearful journey of several hundreds of miles; whilst they would be filled with alarm if her sister Sareena should walk half a mile in the campongs alone. There seemed to be no longer any opposition for me to make; except my want of faith in the charms, and supernatural influences to protect a young girl against so many risks to which she would be exposed; but if the wonderful art of the suwanggee and of the spiritual manifestations did not inspire any faith in their efficiency; yet I doubted not that some poor lonely woman, would be the safest bearer of a message, through such a region;—and better protected by her poverty and loneliness, than by any safeguards she could take;—she needed no passport; and would be subjected to none of the interruptions and official stoppages to which men would be exposed; and so it was resolved that Sahyeepah should go to Surakarta.

Preparations were made for the journey; a little native built cart, and a Java pony were got ready,—coarse dresses prepared like those worn by women who peddle little articles of ornament, and charms for the credulous;—a small stock of these were obtained; and Sahyeepah, Ayum, and a little boy, called Ambon, were ready for the journey. I prepared my message, and had been puzzled how to contrive for its greatest safety; how the most effectually to conceal it in the event of a search. Sahyeepah had an idea; the message was written on the finest tissue paper; she rolled it into a ball, the size of a pea; she placed it on the head of a large pin, like a little skewer, used by the common people for fastening their hair; the head of the pin had an eye, by which the paper top was securely fastened; then with a liquid preparation, one of the lacquers of Palembang, the head, after being oiled, was coated over with the lacquer, layer after layer; which, as it stiffened, was pressed into a resemblance to the horn head of another pin; and was painted red like it;

and thus Sahyeepah was all prepared to carry my message to Surakarta.

I parted from my remarkable pupil. Diporo Kasumo accompanied his sister to the confines of the Residency of Batavia, where he had to stop for the want of a passport; and it was not advisable that he should go any farther. He left his sister at Bogor, to pursue her way with Ayum, the boy, and her own courageous heart; and before we shall hear her account of her journey, I shall tell you meanwhile of some incidents that took place with me during her absence.

FORTY-EIGHT DAY.

SABBATH ON BOARD THE PALMER.

FORTY-NINTH DAY.

THE Baron had received, with his liberty, the restoration of his sword, and his rank in the army; he had been discharged from prison, as a guiltless man, who had been deprived of his liberty nearly two years, without any foundation of crime, or misdemeanor, whatever. The Executive did not pardon the Baron; but declared the decision of the Court of Justice, that had condemned him, as null and void. So much; said he to me, one day, for having sat on the same school bench with a man in power; but, though the restoration to liberty, rank, and an unimpeached character, was simply a portion of what was due to an injured man in this case; yet it illustrates, as much as my own strangely protracted proceedings, the insignificancy of the judiciary; and the irresponsibility and arbitrary position of the chief of the military despotism that controls the possessions of Holland in the East Indies.

The Baron continued to be my most constant visitor, and adviser in prison, and my faithful ally outside. The well-dressed, elegant-looking officer, that came to see me, presented a marked contrast to the half-nude, reckless, riotous, carousing prison neighbor; and after showing to you the effect that a prison can produce upon a fine man, I am anxious to present him before you in his restored and natural state. But the prison life had broken up his career; he could not join again his comrades in arms, and had tendered his resignation. He had no longer any voca-

18*

tion in Netherland India; he had no wife, no near relations in Holland; and wished to retire to America.

He was talking with me, the day after the departure of Sahyeepah; he had come to consult about Umbah. She was now within a few months of being twelve years of age, the dawn of womanhood in these islands; he could not take care of her much longer, he did not think himself fit even now. He could not and he would not take her to Europe; the delicate Oriental did not bear transplanting to the rude north-west. I now occupied a relationship towards the interesting foundling; and I had been her teacher; and must take a part in the family consultation, concerning her future settlement in life.

Sometimes, said the Baron, it has seemed to me, that you were developing ideas and tastes, that may prove a source of discontentment and unhappiness. You think that the old Dutch spirit, that destroyed spice groves in all but one spot, in order to get the greatest possible advantage from the small quantity produced, might very well have dictated my words; but Umbah must remain a Malay woman; and as you would deplore the possibility of her becoming the mistress of an European; she cannot look forward to any other lot, than to fall into the hands of a Malay or Javanese lord; and of what use will geography, the knowledge of books, the use of the pen, the science of numbers, and some inkling of philosophy be to her in such a relation?

These acquirements might be of no more use, no more called into play, than in the case of nineteen twentieths of the young females of our race, who generally make such little application of a long, scholastic experience in the matrimonial state; that is to say, there is no evidence of the application of geography in housekeeping, of natural philosophy in cookery; or of any heavy demand being made upon the science of numbers in keeping accounts with shopkeepers; yet after all, the training of study, the discipline of arts and letters however slight, renders more simple, easy and purposeful, the exercise of every duty; and thus, it is the merest truism to say of Umbah, that she will not make the battek cloth; and prepare the kimlo, and the sambol goreng, any the worse for knowing more of civilized learning than her uncivilized lord.

Umbah has learned by the little exercise of her Malay mind, she has gone through, to look with horror upon the use of strong drink; to despise a chewer of opium, to consider a man, who does little else but train chickens, lizards, and cockroaches to combat, as many Malays do, to show for amusement and profit, as of no more use on earth, than a trained dancing dog; or one of their own self-destroying beasts and reptiles; she has got by all this reading and worrying of her little head, some idea that a Malay has a soul; and that she has one; and there is no fear that she will surrender up any control of her being to any one; European or native, who is not a companion of her spiritual nature. There was no reason to fear that our resolute, thinking, little foster child must necessarily fall so soon into the hands of a master; she was of a character, to be her own mistress; and the only important consideration was, to provide for her a suitable home asylum, a family protection, the association of influences that would help to sustain her fine womanly instincts. This course was decided upon; to find a suitable European family, over which an intelligent and refined lady presided; such a one, I may say here, was found; and when I last heard from Umbah, she was under the roof of a Christian family; and pursuing the studies she had commenced in the prison of Weltevreden.

The Baron always brought a great deal of gossip from the city; and among other matters on this occasion, he could tell me something of the history of the crazy lady, who was confined in a room in the court, immediately behind mine. I had often seen her from the grating of my back wall; and had often spoken to her; but she had only replied with peevish mutterings; and would continue many hours in succession, seated on her door-step, and engaged in her usual occupation of combing her hair.

He had learned that her name was Virgina Small, and he wished to see what effect would be produced by repeating her name to her; and speaking of some matters of her early history, which he supposed might affect her. By standing upon my table, we could have a good view through the bars of the small window of my back wall, into the court behind; and the room of the crazy young woman, was not more than thirty feet distant from my window. She had not yet come to her door; although it was the usual hour, about sunset. A few rays of departing beams still gilded the tops of the tamarind and almond-trees, that overlooked the court. The Baron called out softly; Virgina, Virgina.

A movement was heard in the chamber of the crazy one, the door opened quickly, and a pale face was thrust out; she looked around wildly; her shrunken hand grasped nervously the door-post, as she uttered in piteous voice, Louis, Louis; where are you? do you call Virgina? The Baron was hardly prepared for this; he was stirred up a little; and then he mingled with some low words of anger, the name of one, who had been her protector. He spoke again, with accents of tenderness. Where is baby; where is Mawar? poor little Mawar; Virgina, where is our Mawar?

She had not looked towards my window before; she now stepped forth into the small space before her door; she seemed to search for the one who had spoken to her; speaking in low tone, as it were to herself; Louis wants Mawar, where is Mawar? and then she laughed and looked piteous in turns; and mumbled something about Mawar, a Chinaman, and the big canal.

The Baron seemed to have heard enough; he jumped down from the table, and paced my floor, with quick, nervous step. He spoke of an honorable, wealthy and distinguished gentleman, once a protector of this young woman; he had retired to Europe, overcharged with wealth and honors; he would solace his declining days with a companion and domestic peace in the fatherland; he would not wish to have the home circle he contemplated, interrupted by any voice, that should cry out, father, from the campongs of Batavia; and so, Mawar, little Mawar;—listen to that name, old man, went perhaps, as Virgina seemed to say, with some ruffian Chinaman, to the big canal; and yet the crazy woman rouses at the name spoken in some old tones of love, and says; Louis, where are you? Wherever you are, indeed, come before death overtakes you, and take her out of this jail,—she who once clung to you, still clinging in her madness, despite the stealing and murder of her child.

Whilst the Baron continued to talk, we still heard the inquiring voice of the crazy woman. He thought, as I had been led to believe, that this was an easily curable case of insanity; one of those which so frequently occur in early maternity. Representations were made to the Court of Justice; and I think that she is now cared for with a proper nurse, and in a more comfortable establishment.

This reminds me to give you some little account of the chief attendant of the crazy young woman, whilst in Weltevreden; the huge Dyak pirate, the same who had always waited upon me; he was a monster in size, and in dark, ugly features; but there was a simple, good nature in the expression of his countenance, that did not correspond with the character of pirate, for which crimes he had been doomed to perpetual imprisonment. I had felt an interest to talk with him,—he being a native of the vast insular continent of Borneo, stretching nine hundred miles from north to south; and eight hundred from east to west,—a great empire of fertile soil, of rich mines; and gorgeous forests, teeming with life; of rare birds, strange beasts, and wild men; untouched as yet by civilization, otherwise than in the way of trade; except at one small point, by the regenerating hand of Brooke.

The Dyaks, the aborigines of Borneo, exhibit in general the traits of a frank and docile nature, which appear in strong contrast

with the crafty, restless character of the Malays, who have taken possession of all the coast of the great island; and are overrunning it, like the rest of the Archipelago, with their language. However, nothwithstanding the general fine traits in the character of the Dyaks, several of their tribes are led on by a horrible superstition, to an atrocious system of assassination. The good-natured Dyak, who is frank and hospitable at one time, will, on another occasion, go in quest of his fellow-man, in order to cut off his head, believing that whoever holds the head during life, and has it buried with him in his grave, will hold as a slave in another world, the soul of the beheaded one. My waiter had entertained this belief, when in Borneo, and on the occasion of getting married, he joined a party on a head hunting expedition, wishful to get one to present to his bride. He had been captured during the expedition by a Dutch cruiser; had been drafted into the Dutch army; had deserted, and engaged in some act of piracy; was recaptured, and sent to Weltevreden to wait on his fellow-men there, without losing his head; and Conan, as he was called, was led to believe, after some conversations with me, that the decapitation of his fellow-men was a very bad practice.

Conan, was a Kahajan Dyak, from the southern portion of Borneo; born at Kota Moowara Rawa on the Kahajan River; he told many singular incidents of his Bornese life; about piracy, and some adventures with orang utan; one of the stories relating to the wild men having been confirmed, as to the facts of the incident, by the Baron and others, I shall endeavor to relate it in the words of Conan, as a further illustration of the wild beings in human form, that roam through the jungles of the Archipelago.

ABDUCTION BY AN ORANG UTAN OF BORNEO.

This happened to Conan when he carried a firelock for the

Company. His Commander Tuan Lieutenant, was marching with a troop of soldiers and some coolies from Kota Marabahan on the Banjer River, to a post on the Murung. The Commander had a child with him; a daughter, the substance of his heart, the bright light of his eye; the child of a Malay mother, who was dead; and Ledah, the little girl, was like Umbah, the joy of Tuan, who comes to the house of care. The servants of Ledah were with her, to wait on her, and watch that she got no hurt.

The sun was hot one day, and Tuan Lieutenant said, halt, under some waringin trees, near a stream of water. The soldiers and coolies ate rice, they drank arrack,—Conan too; and all lay down to sleep, while the sun was hot. But Ledah, silly child, did not sleep; she had big eyes to look into the deep shade of waringin trees; she heard sounds, they were little beasts in the forests; Ledah thought they were beautiful children of the country of the Bekumpay, that is full of devils only; but Ledah must know; must see with her eyes; women must know every thing, Conan says it.

Tuan Lieutenant, and servants of Ledah sleep; she takes off the charpoo, and walks softly with little bare feet, away from the encampment. Ledah walks down where the earth was hollow, the waringin shade is thick; there is a dim light down in the hollow; but Ledah sees beautiful flowers; she fills her hands; the air is still and hot under the shade, she takes off her kabyah and fills it with flowers. Ledah has gathered a great many, and she sits down, at the foot of a great tree, to make some garlands to give to her father when he awakes.

Great eyes are staring at Ledah; eyes of a wild man. He creeps nearer, softly along the ground like a tiger; the wild man does not eat Malays, or Dyaks; but wild men carry off Malay and Dyak girls when they walk outside the campongs. The wild man has come behind the waringin tree; the pretty child is twining her flowers; she is thinking of her papa; he won't be angry because she ran away from her nurse, when she brings such nice flowers; he will take his Ledah in his lap; and she will twine her wreaths round his neck. Aachh! the wild man cries; Ledah is seized; arms of a beast, strong and hairy are around her; and she sees great eyes burning in a hairy, beast face.

Ledah does not faint; she is a Malay girl; and screams as Malay girl can; her screams fill the hollow glen, they pierce through the forest, they ring in the ears of the sleepers on the creek bank,—in the ears of the father, who cries aloud for his child. Some heard the voice of Ledah very quick; Conan heard the first scream; he ran, all the soldiers and coolies ran; all ran to where they heard the voice of Ledah,—the substance of the heart of the father, and the joy of the company; they have entered the forest; and hear cries in a tree,—high up in a great tree-top, they see their favorite in the grasp of a great, hideous orang utan, who springs from limb to limb,—body of little Ledah no trouble.

Orang utan are strong; far stronger than Malay or Dyak; they carry a big Dyak in one arm, easy like a child; and easily this one, leaped along with Ledah. The soldiers could shoot him; but where would be Ledah? Conan ran to one tree; other soldiers and coolies ran to other trees; some climbed up, and all shouted; and the father shouting out; a thouand rupees, to him who will save his child alive. The orang utan is pressed; he approaches the creek bank; the orang utan always takes to water, when pursued. There is a great tree, it has high limbs, that overhang the water; the orang utan has sprung into this; and Ledah is bleeding,—her arms and feet are torn,—her voice is still; she is surely dead; but Conan is in the tree; he sees her struggle again, he climbs swift as the orang utan; others are climbing, coolies are on the edge of the stream; they see above them, on a limb, high up and far over the water, they see the monster, and Ledah; Conan is near; the wild man cries, aachh! looks down, raises up, and springs; Conan after, plunge into the water,—others have plunged, the creek is full, they have hold of Ledah, the monster bites strong and fierce, he dives, he escapes; but Ledah is safe, and in the arms of her father.

This abduction of the little girl, was a story of which I heard some particulars from officers at Palembang and Minto, and from several persons at Batavia. I heard many different accounts; but have preferred to give you the version of an eye witness. There are many well authenticated instances of the abduction of young girls, who have strayed beyond the safe limits of their village. Ledah recovered from the effects of her fearful excursion in the tree-tops; and is said to be married, and now living near Amboyna.

Conan not only entertained me with stories; but became one of my pupils;—when the gates were closed at noon, Conan would come; and sometimes at night, he had a chance to get out of his block, and come into mine unobserved; for he was not confined to a cell at night; the fast-riveted iron bands being considered sufficient protection against any attempt at escape of a native; whenever he could thus get away, he would come and sit on the doorstep of my room, and with the docility of Umbah, would listen with simple credulity to whatever was told to him. He had a comrade, a Javanese robber, called Gedeh; another great childlike creature, docile and good-natured, who had warred against a portion of his fellow-beings, from superstition, and with sheer brute unconsciousness of crime.

These encaged wild creatures, had begun to take pleasure in listening, first to the stories, and then to a little reasoning of civilization. In a short while, they did not seem so far off from it; and they wished to come nearer; nearer to the knowledge of the European; and all their brethren would wish to come nearer, even to civilization; if civilization would study their weak natures, and go nearer to them. But I have more to say on this subject, when I speak of the chief representative of the ruling races of the Archipelago. The Java Malay enthusiast who went on a bold journey to Surakarta.

FIFTIETH DAY.

It was in the beginning of the eleventh month of my stay in prison, that Sahyeepah went upon her adventurous journey; and her return was expected within six weeks at the farthest, from the time of her starting.

This eleventh month is made notable to me, by the occurrence of three events, of very different, though of equally imposing character; and the more notable to me, and the more vividly remembered, on account of having occurred, so quickly following after each other.

There are many little particulars connected with my prison life, of which I have made no mention; there were many visits, many anecdotes about fellow-prisoners; many curious characters coming in, and going out; many little matters occurring between me, the jailer and his family; with my sailors, judges, friends; some changes in living, diet, health; and all the detail of a prison life, daily full of incident, to which I have not even alluded. But one of these unmentioned particulars of my prison experience, I will now speak of; and that was the annoyance from reptiles,—of numberless frogs in the court, of lizards in my cell. The latter are not unfamiliar in well-kept houses, even in Batavia; they run upon the wall and the ceiling after flies; and sometimes their feet lose their power of holding on; and oftentimes drop into beds, where there are no overhangings, as was in my case, and startle a sleeper, with their cold, glassy bodies on his breast. But I was roused one night, by a more alarming visitant than a lizard.

I awoke from a painful dream, and perceived an oppressive, sickening odor in my room; I raised up; there was a fluttering in a cage, from a little crimson-streaked dove, that I had; there was a sliding sound; and by the starlight of a Javan sky, that shed some faint rays through the bars of my window, I could see a large serpent on the floor.

Any one who has lived in a log cabin in the upper districts of South Carolina or Georgia; or perhaps anywhere in the Southern back woods of America, would not be surprised at the sight of a snake in his room; there are even tolerated house snakes in Georgia, on account of being such good mousers; snakes are met with in very strange places in a backwoods home; and oftentimes have to be turned out of a bed before a man can turn in himself; but they are small snakes of harmless bite. I might have heeded them no more than the lizards; but this was one of the great, venomous reptiles of Java.

He could not get the bird; he raised his head, he moved it around, seeming to survey the room; I could see his glittering eyes; he slid a little towards me; he raised his head again with dancing motion, as though smelling in the air; he slid nearer; his head was within five feet of mine; and I thought he was going to spring. My right hand was upon a *gooling*, a tightly stuffed little bolster, that is universally used in the Archipelago, to place between the knees; a means of coolness to the limbs;—which I hurled with fear inspired energy at the monster; there was a horrible hissing, a beating of the floor; the serpent wound round the bolster, quickly coiling and uncoiling, and biting at it for a few moments; and then the great constrictor slid away, leaving behind a suffocating, nauseous odor; which with some apprehension of his return, made me pass an uneasy night.

Conan, when he came with my breakfast, told me that such visits were not uncommon in some of the blocks next to the moat; this was the great *ular sawah*, that came from the canal through the drains; it had entered my room through a hole in a corner, which was made by a singular burrowing creature, a species of Java mole. I discovered outside a distinct trail fully five inches across, and the serpent must have been nine feet in length. This was the first of the events, that marked my eleventh month in prison.

The third night after this occurrence, was very sultry, even for Java; it was impossible to sleep; there was oppression and sickening languor in the air; and it was exhaustion to attempt any relief; the enfeebled brain filled the hot night air with foul shapes; the demons that come to the Javan mind, and even to any mind, that is sweltering in the heat of Java. The drapery of the night sky droops its glittering folds down closer to the earth, shutting out the winds, and shutting in the heat. There are murmurings in the air, like the tremulous signal sounds of a Thug; and waf-waffings of the great vampire bats with musky wings, fanning deadly odors upon a heat-enfeebled sleeper; who reaches feebly forth with unnerved limbs to cast off the thrall of Javan nightmare.

I heard a murmur of sound; it was not the rustle in the almond-tree tops, from the breath of a rising breeze; the murmur became a rumble, a march of dread sound, that rolled from the east to the west; it rolled on louder, it rushed upon the city, and then the earth heaved, walls shook, tiles rattled from the roofs; the heaving rocked and sickened me, like a rolling at sea; and the whole length of Java, and many distant isles, were shaken by a great earthquake.

There are twenty-one volcanoes on the island; smoking, flaming, and belching forth, at frequent intervals, the hot liquid matter of the earth's bowels. The great Tomboro on the island of Sumbawa, has burst forth at times, with heavings, that have shaken the farthest verge of the Archipelago. The sea has risen up in the Moluccas, and carried vessels many miles inland; it was so this time; and Arjuno or Merapi were making a grand pyrotechnic display on the hot night, that I was tossed about on the floor of my cell;—and this was the second notable thing, that marked the eleventh month of my stay in Weltevreden.

You have learned, that one Fiskaal, well disposed towards me, was removed; and another one, a clerk in the office of the chief prosecutor of the Government, appointed in his stead. You have learned also, that some changes were made on the bench of the Court of Justice, that witnesses were brought from Sumatra; all that remained; the chief ones in fact; that the Residents of Palembang and Banca; that the Havermeesters of these two places, an assistant Resident, some naval and military officers, my sailors, and my treacherous servants in the pay of the Government, had all been examined; the whole instruction, or preliminary investigation gone over again; pressed by an active, unscrupulous Fiskaal this time; followed up by a strenuous requisition, demanding that I should be tried and punished for high treason. And the Court of Justice deliberated upon all this; looked over the piles of docket, of reports, correspondence, and private papers, that had accumulated during the progress of the case; they had my whole history, late cruise, and smallest transaction during my stay in the Archipelago, all before them; and on the twenty-second of December, 1852, they recorded their solemn decision, that there were "no grounds" whatever, for the charge of "hight reason," alleged against the Commander and mate of the Flirt; refusing to bring the case into a public court; and ordering the immediate liberaton, and restoration of the property of the prisoners; and this was the third notable event, during the eleventh month of my stay in prison.

Thus, this Court had thrice ordered my liberation; the first time, on account of the illegality of the manner of my arrest; and a second, and a third time, had declared solemnly, that there was no foundation for the crime alleged against me; and now again, this decree of liberation was opposed by the chief prosecutor of the Government, and he obtained another decree from the secret high tribunal, peremptorily ordering the Court of Justice, to hold a public trial of the Commander and the mate of the Flirt, in the Stadhuis of Batavia; and this event, this order of re-arrest, which I did not learn till some time afterwards, during the twelfth month of my stay in prison; this was the order, that was handed to me by Sheriff Brower, and cast me from brightest hope, into darkest gloom, on the same evening that the Palmer struck on Brower's shoals

Shortly after this, I heard of you, and saw some of my friends who now listen to me. You found me busy with my notes, making preparation for the grand trial that was to take place the following month. The Arjuno and the Borneo had sailed again, to bring a second time all the civil, military and naval officers of the Government, that had any knowledge of my case; and besides these, to bring every native chieftain; and Arab, Malay, or Chinaman, with whom I had spoken; there was the stir and rumor of a grand preparation; of such a trial, as had never been seen under Dutch East Indian rule; a trial, that would afford an opportunity to bring out many appearances against me, even if I could not be convicted of high treason; that would show some excuse for the protracted, blundering management of the case; that would impress America, with the idea of the deliberation and fairness of Dutch justice; but above all, that would afford an opportunity to strengthen the prestige of Dutch power in the native mind; that had seen the flag of a great nation trampled upon; its citizens cast ignominiously into prison; and then had heard of one of their ships of war coming to their rescue, and going ingloriously away; they had seen and heard all this; and now they should see the citizen of that great power, arraigned before their judges, questioned, browbeaten, and perhaps condemned and begging for his life.

I did not think much of this, during the excitement of that period; there was another matter that weighed upon my mind. The eleventh month had passed away; and no tidings of Sahyeepah. As the days of the twelfth rolled on, the father, and brother, and sister came to see me, with anxious looks; looking for assurance and hope in my words. I had plenty to give them; although I began to lose it fast myself. I felt a keen self-reproach for having consented to such an adventure, by such a person, on my account. There was no longer the excitement of the circumstance that led to it; her own enthusiasm, and the ready acquiescence of the simple relatives. Wirojoyo, and his son and daughter, like simple, credulous, confiding children of Java, seemed to look up to me, to some powers I possessed, they knew not what, for the restoration of the absent one. And as time rolled on; the seventh week having gone, since the departure of Sahyeepah, I began to realize the first view, that Wirojoyo had taken of the expedition; the great distance,—about four hundred miles; the steep mountains to ascend; the rivers to cross; the almost impassable roads to labor through in some places; and then the tigers and serpents swarming in the jungle, and along the path; the robbers; and worse than all, the evil men, who ever lurk in every land, to rob what is more precious than treasure or life, from every defenceless woman.

The twelfth month had passed away; some days of the thirteenth; and the time was near at hand for the great trial. I had to summon memory, resolution, hope, patience, and the pride of country, to enable me to meet the array of opposing influences, that, I supposed, an unscrupulous power was about to bring and to wield against me. I felt no shrinking to meet all that; but I shrank from meeting Wirojoyo, who came with desolate, and tearful face, to tell me that there were no tidings of his child.

FIFTY-FIRST DAY.

My trial commenced on the anniversary of my entrance into the prison of Weltevreden. Twelve months of diligent preparation on the part of the prosecution; and twelve months of diligent study on my part for the acquisition of the very knowledge; the pursuit of which, was, in truth, the real cause of the hostility of the power that had seized and held me. It sought to punish me for spying out the land; and yet had placed me in the midst of the best, and most zealous of instructors,—eager to teach me all its means of strength, and all its sources of weakness. In seeking to punish me for entertaining feelings of hostility to the Government, I had been placed in the rankest atmosphere of treason in Netherland India; and now, the consummation of all this was to be shown, in a public display of executive domination, of judicial incapacity, of a confusion of all laws, and in a most imbecile decision of justice.

The forces of the Government were marshalled at the Stadhuis; a grim old fabric, consecrated to injustice by Speelman, Valckeneir and Daendels, the chief hall of which was still garnished with the pincers, thumbscrews, and the brodequins for crushing tender feet; the relics of less responsible times. In that hall were assembled four judges; a president and three associates; and there was the chief prosecutor of the Government and his aids; there was the Resident, and Havermeester of Banca; there was the Assistant Resident of Palembang; the chief did not come, the Government had some reasons for allowing him to stay away; the Shahbander, the Topographical Captain, two lieutenants of the army, three officers of the navy, Bois, the French soldier; and with these were the Panyorangs Scherriff Ali, and Osman Bin Kassim Barkaba, the Demang Sapeedin, some smaller chieftains, Kiagoos Lanang, Bahdoo, and Moonchwa; and the Chief of the Chinamen at Palembang, the host of the wedding feast, Oey Soch Tchay and Lim Boo Seng; this was the array of judges, prosecutors and witnesses marshalled against me by the Government of Netherland India, on the morning of the fourteenth of February, 1852.

On the part of the defence; an American naval Commander, who had been begged to come, an American functionary whose presence had been solicited from the American Commissioner to China, and an American Consular agent at Batavia,—did not appear. Of the crew of the Flirt, four had gone to the hospital, and were no more heard of; stout Jim had been taken, out of charity, on board a homeward bound ship; the second mate, the lonely keeper of the vessel at Maceio, had gone to Singapore, to seek some diversion in my favor; and besides the mate, a prisoner with myself, there only remained poor, faithful, uncouth Pirez, as sole witness for the defence.

Some of you witnessed the management of that prosecution and defence. You know what influences were brought to bear; what leading questions, used to lead on a treacherous and hostile witness; what ready recording of an answer when favorable, and what delays and suggestions when doubtful; what gross injustice manifested by the one, and what skill or self possession, manifested by the other.

Yes, said the boatswain, interrupting, and explaining to the lady passengers. I saw it all; from the first day to the last; and they were a long time at it, ten whole days; from early in the morning, till late in the afternoon. There was the red-faced old president, whom I saw several times rather unsteady on his timbers, at the Rotterdamsche Hotel; and I was told that he got that way every day after dinner, like a good many of our judges at home. The bench is pretty strong on grog generally. There was one of the black gowns, as dark looking in the face, as that nice man Storm, related to the King of Dahomey; and the two mulattoes seemed to be pretty thick; in another black gown, was a man they called a Baron, and brother to the Adjutant of the Governor General; and in the fourth was an old fellow, past eighty, who could not hold his head up, and slept all the time. They did not look very imposing; a lot of hard Dutch faces, all but the mulatto; and the head government man was the hardest-looking one of the lot.

But those old chiefs from Sumatra, in speckled coats, blazing with diamonds, and holding their crooked daggers; they looked grand. It was a curious sight to see them stand up, sway their hands, sing a kind of song, and raise and lower the Koran three times on their heads, when they took an oath; and a funny sight to see a Chinaman lay hold of the head of a rooster, and another one cut it off, when a chin-chin was sworn; but from what I saw and heard all along, I think that Chinaman, Malay, and Arab, can swallow the rooster and the Koran, and swear black is white, about as easy as some of our folks can gulp down the gospel, and as many lies with it as you please.

By gracious king! I never heard of such swearing in all my life before. I knew nothing what the Dutchies or the chaps with the turbans said; but our ship-chandler at Batavia, was with me all the time; and gave me the run of their yarns as they spun 'em out. One Dutchman swore, that he had heard the Captain of the Flirt say, that he belonged to an association of young men in America, whose object was to set all uncivilized people a going on their own hook; this association had ten frigates armed with paixhan guns, unbeknown to the United States government; but where these frigates might be hid; whether moored to the North or the South pole, he did not say; and then the government man got up and showed to the Court a little piece of ribbon, that had on it in English; "member of the American institute;" and a paper, a travelling pass of some American order; and this was to confirm the story of the man, who swore about the frigates and the paixhans. I would not have believed such a stupid story could have been listened to, even by Dutchmen; but they spent half a day about it, in that Court; and it will be found in black and white, in their big pile of papers.

But the big gun of all, was a letter, which the government man took out of a strong copper box; it was a sheet of fancy white paper, all covered over with what looked like mice tracks, and this he handled as gingerly, as if it were the real original Declaration of Independence, written by Washington. He carried it with both hands, like a parson would the sacrament, and laid it before the chief judge. Then the Captain was called up to the desk; the paper was laid before him; the government man, watching, ready to spring; as though he expected a grab at the precious document. The Captain was told to look at it close; and to say, did he sign that paper or not. He plumped right out, no; he had never seen it before, never had such a piece of paper in his possession; never had authorized any such words, as were then translated; which said; that he would assist some Sultan there over in Sumatra with powder, balls, cannon and blunderbusses; that he would lend him the use of the United States Navy; that he would use up all the Dutchmen round about in those parts generally, and make the Sultan of Jambee a present of the territory of Palembang. The Captain said that he knew nothing of such stuff; he had ordered a letter to be sent, he had signed one; he had been asked if he had done so, when he came to Batavia; but never, till now, had he looked at the document. The one he had signed was on blue paper; this one was a miserable forgery.

Never did you see such a lot of Dutchmen, all struck of a heap. The tippling president pitched clean back in his seat; the old judge put on his spectacles wrongways up; and every body stared at the government man to see what he would have to say. He jawed and puckered up his mouth a while, and then he made a dive into the copper box again; and brought out a little yellow-covered book, knotched with the alphabet along the edges; and he turned over, and showed the Malay words for guns, cannon, ships; and a good many of the words found in the letter; this book was the vocabulary of the Captain, when at Palembang; and proved that he knew Malay words enough to make up the letter. The Captain said he had never put down such words in the blank book; he looked at it; and then pointed out to the Court, that all these ugly words were at the end of each list, and written in quite a different hand to those that had gone before them. The judges looked puzzled; and the government man seemed to be taken aback again, till he made another dive into the copper box; and brought out a cord of old papers belonging to the Captain; begging notes from school to a certain old governor for supplies; old love letters, tailors' bills; and something of that sort, I suppose, although I did not see; at any rate, they were brought out to show that there was writing, among them, that looked mightily like the signature of the mouse-track letter; and these papers were handed over to two schoolmasters, and they were to report, and they did so, the next day; saying that some pothooks and down strokes were like the signing of that Jambee declaration of Independence; but they could not swear that the same fist that signed it, had written all the schoolboy duns, love letters, and tailors' bills, they had been looking over.

The government man did not seem to make much out of the big gun; and then he tried some smaller ones, in overhauling the turbaned chaps. Every body that was looking on in Court;—and every American, English, German and French resident of Batavia was there, all the time;—every body I heard talk, said that the Government would get just such talk as they wanted out of the natives. But there never was such a lot of forgetful witnesses; they beat shy old salts at that game; except the two rascally servants, well known at Batavia as government policemen; all the rest did not say one word, that could be turned against the Captain; they all swore, they could not understand one word he said. But the government man had got some hook on to one, the grand old Arab Panyorang; he had let out somehow, to some Dutch officers, about some conversation with the Captain; and when he said that he did not understand the language of the Captain, the Dutch officers swore that he had said he did, and must be lying.

Then old turban stood up; the dark eyes of the Arab flashed; but there was not the move of a muscle in the face, nor a single quivering hair, in that splendid long white beard; he said that he had understood something of the thoughts of the American Tuan, but not by words; they had spoken with their hands, their eyes, and their brains. He was a splendid old man; and rose up and spoke, and sat down like the President of the United States of Arabia. The chief gown of the Court spoke to the venerable Chief; he said that he and his fellow-judges could not well believe such a story. The old man rose again, with a quiet look of contempt at the whole Court; he was sure that the American Tuan could prove his words true, on the spot;—he was skilful, let them try him.

Old toper whispered awhile to the mulatto, the Baron, and old sleepy head; then they called a translator to the desk; he wrote down something and handed it to the Captain, who was to repeat the contents with his hands to the Arab President; and he afterwards should repeat it to the Court. I have been to those French shows, where they do nothing but talk with hands; and never could make any thing out of their winking, and clawing and sawing of the air; but I never expected to see a show of pantomime in a Dutch court, by an American skipper.

The Captain faced the worthy old venerable, with the turban and the long beard; both looked hard at each other; but never moved a muscle; every body in the pit was crowding up to the foot-lights to see; and as I can make tracks in a crowd, I got a front seat. Our Captain pointed to the turban of the Panyorang; made little circles with his thumb and forefinger; counted fifty with his fingers; he pointed to the turban again, and then to his coat pocket, he waved his hands, and made all sorts of motions to make out that he went a sailing; he worked his feet like on a treadle, he swayed something with the left hand; and pitched something with the right, that looked mighty like weaving; and then he went a waving again, and looked like a man coming back from somewhere; and he seemed to pull something out of his pocket, he counted twenty with his fingers; and then looked at the Panyorang sort o' smiling, like one of our down-easters, asking a man to trade for a horse or a quintal of cod fish.

The old patriarch rose up and said; that the American Tuan proposed to give him fifty dollars for his turban; saying also, that he would take it home, and have others made like it, which he would sell him for twenty. The old man asked if he had spoken right; and wanted to know, if the judges had something besides propositions for buying and selling to try the skill of the American Tuan; but they were satisfied; and the show ended. All of this doing was written down by two quilldrivers in front of the chief bigwig's seat.

The next thing in the programme of this curious trial, was the hauling up of the Captain's nigger, who was not the handsomest Cuffee I ever saw; but the fellow looked as if he was made of some good stuff, far better than his cousin from Palembang, the relation of the King of Dahomey. A Portugue' man spoke to him, and he blubbered out some awful crotchety words, that set judges, and all of the crowd around me, in full grin. Cuffee jerked out something pretty hard, and looked marline spikes at the Van Breeks, and the bad do, or do bad man of the Captain. Old president wanted to know what he was driving at; Portugue' man could not tell; other chaps, sharp on lingo, translators of the Court, they tried and could do nothing; somebody said, let his master interpret; and then the Captain stood up, and looking solemn, said that the witness, Pirez, had seen upon the person of Bahdoo, who was present, a sash which had belonged to him; he had called him a thief; said that he had helped Dutch soldiers to plunder the cabin of the Flirt; and that such thieves, who wore combs in their hair like women, wouldn't eat pork, and didn't believe in Christ and San Antonio, ought not be let say one word against his master.

There was a break down after this, the grin went off into a galloping laugh; a man with a gilt stick pounded away awhile, old president looked sober, and asked Portugue' man to try Cuffee again; as he seemed to think that the Captain had been dressing a lttle, but nothing could be done with Cuffee by the Portugue' man; then all the blackgowns put noses together, whispered awhile; and after a time, old three sheets in the wind said, that the witness must be dismissed; as the Court was without a competent translator. The Captain protested against this; and said he was his only witness; it would not do; Cuffee was not wanted, and he stepped out.

And half the time was taken up by some more farces like this; all kinds of funny stories were told, that never would be believed in America. The Captain was chief lawyer all the time, overhauling every witness in his own lingo; and keeping up a running fight with the government man. They kept at it for nine days, and on the tenth, the government man made a pretty long yarn,—asking that the Captain have permission to stand in the pillory two hours, and then work twelve years for the Dutch Government to pay for his board in prison; which modest request was answered by two lawyers, who had not opened their mouths, but a chance time or two, all the days before. Then you know there was another grand sitting; every body in Batavia was crowding round the old Court House; the black gowns were in their places, the Captain standing up, whilst old president read off a long paper; saying, that the Captain did not come out East with the best of feelings to the Dutch, that if he hadn't taken Palembang, it was not for the want of the will to try; that they might thank their stars, that the old Flirt was not as in old times, when off in the Gulf with brave Nicholson, with seventy men and eight long twelve-pounders aboard; that it was clear that the Captain wanted to scrape up an acquaintance with them ragers and Sultans in Sumatra, that he had got some one to write a letter, and might have written it himself, if he had known how; and it was kind of insinuated that he did know how, and a good deal more than he had a right to, for the good of the Dutch; but after all, that this was not exactly high treason against Holland; he was not guilty of that crime; and it was decreed that he should have his vessel, and go on his way rejoicing. And then you know, we had a jubilee; and I whipped that big boxer at the Rotterdamsche hotel. But why the Captain did not get away; he can tell better himself.

Our friend, the Boatswain, said the Commander, resuming his narrative, has given you the chief features of the trial, with some of his own peculiar coloring. The test of the pantomime was an undignified proceeding for a Court of Justice, and was contemptuously proposed by the old Arab Chieftain, whose veracity had been so grossly doubted. The refusal to send for an interpreter who had understood Pirez on a former occasion, and thus depriving me of my only witness, was an act of wanton injustice. The alleged treasonable letter; and the words of hostile import, added to the vocabulary, were manifest forgeries, and so pronounced by my counsel, by many judges; and excepting the officers of the Government, by all who saw them there.

And fifteen months after that trial, the then arraigned prisoner was in the capital city of the country of his judges in Europe. He went there, though an alleged fugitive from justice; and the same spirit of blundering, that seized him in Sumatra, that did not know what to do with him during fifteen months in prison, that acquitted and condemned him four times, that could not keep him when he was ready to go; did there at the Hague, in the person of a Minister of Foreign Affairs, did in the eagerness of fear, at a time, when the government of the United States had assumed an attitude of decision to have wrongs redressed, did send to the late prisoner of Weltevreden, the convict of Dutch justice, walking abroad in the capital of Holland, did send to him deferentially, thinking it to be some other worthless matter,—the famous Jambee letter, all his own much deplored papers, his vocabulary; and voluminous evidences of the infamous policy of the Netherland India Government.

You will have been led to suppose, that I had none but friends in the local Court of Justice of Batavia; and such was the case, during the first proceedings instituted against me; the declaration of the absurdity of the charge alleged against me was then unqualified; it was repeated a second, and a third time; but prior to this public trial, the court had undergone some changes in its composition; it had been coerced so often, and driven into further action by a superior secret tribunal, acting under the direct influence of the Government, and holding a precarious judicial tenure under the absolute military government, which controls Java; it is perhaps not to be wondered at, that this Court in its last decision of acquittal, should this time have thought proper to make a concession to Government, by qualifying their decision, with many unfounded charges of evil intent alleged against me.

The mad lawyer uttered an unquestionable truth in his daily refrain: there is no law in Netherland India; not that there is no law administered; but no code that belongs to the country. A confusion of all law was jumbled up in my case; the jurisprudence of old Rome, the pandects, the Julian law of majesty, old English laws of attainder, the code of Napoleon, and German, and Italian codes; a medley of the laws of all nations, administered by a servile bench of judicial pensioners.

The Government had not obtained a condemnation, but some portion of their array of witnesses had given some color of excuse for my seizure, and thus one object of the trial was secured; but was the other, the influence on the native mind, realized? Who shall tell, what impressions were produced upon the stately Arab prince, and the Malay chieftains. Him whom they had seen fall into the hands of their hated oppressors, and then carried away in the ship, that was the decoy and prison of their great chieftain, whom they might have expected to see wasted in strength and broken in spirit, they now saw in the midst of his jailers, with the same front that they saw in Sumatra.

The native mind could not form any high conception of Dutch power, when they saw an unaided man magnified into a government foe; they could not have been much impressed with the dignity of Dutch justice, after witnessing the proceedings, which have been truthfully, though somewhat humorously described by our friend the Boatswain. The same power and the same justice, that was there, has been wielding a sway and exercising a jurisdiction in the Archipelago for upwards of two hundred years; and yet the native mind remains the same; unchanged as the native costume; the same ignorance of the religion that their masters profess to believe; the same indifference to the civilization they boast; for what has it done for them? And what single act can be pointed out in the whole history of Dutch rule in the East, that should cause the native mind to respect their religion, their laws, or their civilization?

But the people of the Archipelago are not so weak and base in character; so helplessly besotted in bigotry of superstition, as to prevent them from realizing an ameliorating change. No Asiatic races are so quick in perception as the Malay; none so truthful, industrious and docile as the Javanese; no Mahommedan or pagan nations, so entirely free from any cruel or degrading superstitions; and no people so willing to listen to differences of creed or opinion; yet they have learned nothing from one representation of European civilization, during upwards of two hundred years. And what might they learn from any other? Let us look a little farther into the native mind, as developed by my experience, and see.

On the last day of the trial, on the breaking up of the Court, there was a thronging around me of persons, and a good deal of inquiry and congratulation. Friend Brower, contrary to the strict injunction of the Fiskaal, allowed me a little liberty to range about, before returning to the prison. After talking awhile with some of you my friends, as you will remember, and other Americans, English, French and Dutch friends present, I then exchanged a few hurried greetings and cordial words of goodwill with my native friends from Palembang and Banca.

The venerable Scherriff Ali, was rejoiced to hear me speak like one of the sons of Pulo Percha; I had the tongue now, as well as the heart; all the people of Palembang were prepared to meet me with heart's wish and salutation. Abdallah should join me, when I came with my ship again; his mother would oppose no more. Captain Aboubakr was there, and grasped one hand, whilst the Panyorang his father grasped the other. A very old Malay chieftain stepped forward, the Demang Sapeedin, about seventy-six years of age; he had given me some old chronicles of Menangkabau, and a collection of pantuns. My son looks strong he said; he has been singing pantuns, he has not been weeping in the house of care. It is well; my children on the Ileer Keedookan will rejoice. Soch Tchay met me with his usual merry laugh, Company had spent much money to bring Chinaman, Arab and Malay from Palembang; but all got lock on their mouths. His friend Pood Djang had said, lock mouth fast, and leave key at home. When Tuan come to Palembang, Chinaman, Arab and Malay will open mouth again. Poor Lim Boo Seng looked rather dispirited; there was not the same cause to fear the Chinamen and natives at Banca as at Palembang; he had been very roughly treated by the Resident; and forced to come to Batavia, and leave his business without compensation; whilst those who came from Palembang had secured a good guaranty for their payment; and for their safe return before they left, which was the greatest, and most profitless expenditure that the Government had incurred in the case. I give no more kimlo to American Captain at Minto, said poor Lim Boo Seng.

The pleasant words of good will, so eagerly, though somewhat timidly, uttered by my native friends, were most grateful to my feelings, which I sought to return with full warmth and strongest expressions of regard for their welfare. Think of me in America, were the last words, that Panyorang Laksana had said; and such were the last I heard from the mouth of Panyorang Scherriff Ali.

Brower had come to hasten me; the prison carriage was waiting. In coming away, I saw in a recess in a passage way, part of a native dress; Brower passed by, and then it came forth; and Kiagoos Lanang came before me; he crouched down; he wanted to take my hand, I bade him stand up. He had felt heart sickness, ever since the night that he wrote the letter for the Sultan of Jambee. Moonchwa had told him the words he must put in that letter; he was afraid; Moonchwa was an oppas of the Company, and Kiagoos did as he said. Kiagoos was a dog; and his heart was sick; but he wanted to tell Tuan that his heart was not all bad. I was happy to hear him speak, I did not feel angry with him, or even with Bahdoo or Moonchwa; they were but weak children in the hands of a bad master. If I were free, he should eat rice with me, the same as before. Kiagoos grasped both my hands, Brower called; I hurried away from my late secretary; and this was my last and a gratifying experience with those whom I knew at Palembang

An old man stood at the main entrance of the Stadhuis; the sorrowful uncomplaining face of Wirojoyo was before me, that said in every line, no news of my poor child, no news of Sahyeepah; and I returned to prison with an oppressed mind, to await the decision of the great Star Chamber tribunal of Netherlands India.

FIFTY-SECOND DAY.

The thirteenth month of my stay in prison was gone; the fourteenth entered upon, and half passed away; and still no decision of the Star Chamber. Judges delaying, having a bad case; but Government pressing hard, fearful of rebukes and reclamations. Justice at Batavia, was waiting more than ever, for something to turn up; but there was nothing more than a very badly devised piece of Malay writing; some free words, the every day outspoken language of America, spoken to some Malay ears, there was nothing more for a government to urge; no other material, for the much needed conviction of high treason; and thus, many weary, anxious, hoping, doubting days were passed; waiting for the decision of the High Court of Netherland India; and in looking, also, even till I had ceased to look, for the return of Sahyeepah.

You will feel, that I am not going to say, that she never returned; but have sought to make you feel some of my own anxiety at that time; that you might the better appreciate my sense of relief, when I saw one day, at my cell door, all radiant with joy, beaming with good news, the simple, glad face of Wirojoyo.

Sahyeepah had come; had come alone; the old woman was gone, the boy was gone; and little horse, and cart, and all but Sahyeepah, all were gone, by the will of Allah. And she, poor child, was weary, was sick; her face was thin; she had come from a land of death, but was strong in heart; a brave child was Sahyeepah; would come to see Tuan his son, very soon. Such were the news of Wirojoyo.

And the day after this, I saw him again, more joyous in face than the day before. He felt that there was a pleasanter presence than his own, along with him. The faithful messenger was before me. Much altered indeed; two years of change had been produced by two months of fatigues and fears; the tracings of stronger feeling, of more enlarged intelligence, and of a deeper enthusiasm were to be seen in the wasted face. She had a strange, and a long story to tell; she did not tell it all on this first visit; but in the course of many more, after her return. I will put those separate tellings together, and some notes of hers, as she had learned from me to keep; and relate to you, in the words that I listened to, and read,

THE JOURNEY OF SAHYEEPAH.

When Diporo turned back at Bogor; Sahyeepah was alone, without father, without brother; the path was dark before her; but she did not look back on the lighter path behind. Her heart was little; but she would carry the message of great value on the dark road. Sahyeepah was a poor, weak slave to do this thing; but the voice of Panyorang Djaya Laksana, said in her heart; my little daughter, the wild rock deer can do the wish of Tuan, his son; and she would do it.

Ayum and the boy, had no voice whispering in their hearts; they wanted to follow the road that had light upon it, back to Batavia; but Djala, the little horse, has his head turned to the East, and they move on; they go along the great road of the Shetan Wolanda (the Dutch satan Daendels); Sahyeepah sees a great cloud from a hill top, she loses it in a valley; but from another hill top, she sees the same cloud; it is greater now; ayah! it is not a cloud; it is the great mountain Gedeh; higher than the clouds; and Suwanggee, the magician, who knows the will of Allah, lives at the foot of Gedeh; and she will speak with Suwanggee.

Sahyeepah speaks with a good woman, with a friendly face; she tells her of Suwanggee; he is like a man of the air; the eyes would see through him; he lives in a tchandy, one of the works of Raden Panji, a hero of the old times; of the days of Matarem. Sahyeepah enters the tchandy alone; she comes to a door, as the good woman had said; she calls out; Tuan Suwanggee, who is great, who has all knowledge in his heart, who knows the will of Allah, your slave, a poor woman, wants the fine ointment from the burning heart of Gedeh, to light her path on a great journey; and bring her back safe to her father and her brothers. She has spoken all her wish. A small voice, very little indeed; like the voice of a child, speaking through a reed; said, why did the woman speak with a crooked tongue; she was not poor, she had many rupees, and curious things of the rich city of Batavia; she must speak truth, all her thought, if she would get the help of Suwanggee, and the fine ointment from the burning heart of Gedeh.

Sahyeepah trembled, she had offended the man of air, who saw all her thought. She said, she had some little things of silver filigree, made by poor people of Pulo Percha; and she had some oil of fine herbs to sell. And she had only one hundred rupees to travel to Surakarta. The voice said it was well; she must place ten silver rupees in the buffalo's horn at the door; and she would find the fine ointment in the shell of a ketapan nut lying in her path, as she went out; with part of which she must anoint the palms of her hands and the soles of her feet; and the rest she must bury in the valley out of sight of Gedeh. Sahyeepah placed the money as commanded; and found a ketapan shell fitted very curious; and full of oil, that had the smell of fire, and of flowers; and she did as directed by Suwanggee.

Then Sahyeepah went forward with a stronger heart; she did not fear the night shade that came quick, hiding the top of Gedeh; as she went down into a deep valley, on the way to Tchanjore, there burying the ketapan nut. She had seen the roof poles of a dessa, from the hill top, near the tchandy of Suwanggee; she would soon pass the shade of the valley, and rest with some good people of the dessa. Djala puts down his feet very fast; Java pony knows where the dessa is, and the pahdee, and nice herb and water. Djala wants rest like Sahyeepah, Ayum, and Ambon. Adah! there is much grief, much woe, before Djala has rest.

Quick from the road border where thickest and darkest, sprang two men of Satan; their eyes burning in the night shade. Djala is stopped, Ambon falls from his seat; Ayum screams, Sahyeepah trembles. Where was the cunning work to sell, of the peddlers, and where were the rupees of the Company; quick, they cry; and Sahyeepah sees the klewang knife flash in the dark shade in the valley. Ayum gives the wallet of leather, that holds the money and the filigree; the robbers look, and cry; there are more rupees, only fifty in the wallet. Ayum has no more, her mistress has the rest fastened beneath her sarong. The foul men approach Sahyeepah; they will lay hands upon her; they will remove her sarong. Sahyeepah is the granddaughter of Panyorang Djaya Laksana; she carries the kriss of the daughters of Pulo Percha; the point is in the face of the djins; the point that never fails; Allah, the little hearts of evil draw back; there are the sound of steps in the valley; and the sons of Satan flee with the wallet.

Sahyeepah had thrown back her head proudly,—imitating the action of drawing the kriss, as she uttered the last words; her eyes lighted up with the pride of womanhood, and the pride of race; but I was thinking at the time, how that she, who had so boldly met two robbers, had trembled at the anger of the magician; who I doubted not was one of the twò, and was as I heard afterwards from other sources, one of those impostors, rather common in Java, as well as in more enlightened countries; who learn from the simple souls, who come to consult them, the weight of their purse and the way to it, and then rob them of it, by clairvoyance, astrology, spiritualism, or some ointment from the centre of Mount Gedeh. This I explained to Sahyeepah, who was quite ready to believe that she, and all the people of Java, were very silly to believe that Allah, who made the sun, moon, stars and the earth, should talk to his children in old ruins, in curious voices; and then ask ten rupees; what did Allah want with rupees when he made all rupees, and mount Gedeh too? Tuan, my brother speaks words that are good, said Sahyeepah; and resumed her story.

The sounds the robbers heard, were feet of buffaloes; a coolie was driving them, returning from the rice field, and going to the dessa of Tugu, near by. Poor women weeping, the coolie pitied them; he would have struck hard with the pachul, hoe, on his shoulder; but his feet were short; it was too late now. Kasih-an, poor women, come to the dessa; eat rice with his master, wash weary feet, and go and speak their grief to the Jaksa, the village justice; and he will send spearmen to follow the men of Satan, who have robbed poor travellers.

Djala was eating his pahdee, and Sahyeepah had eaten her rice; she goes to speak with the Jaksa. She speaks of the evil men in the valley; one was stout and old; the younger one was tall; and more Sahyeepah tells. Well told, my child, says the Jaksa, the spearmen shall find them, in all the road to Bogor; in all the great mountain Gedeh; but my child must give thirty rupees for the spearmen. Adah! the Suwanggee has ten, the robbers have taken fifty; and Sahyeepah has only forty to go to Surakarta. The spearmen must have the rupees; Sahyeepah cannot give, and leaves the Jaksa with a heavy heart.

I did not wish to tell her, that the cost and the delays of justice, was the same in my own enlightened country, as in simple, ignorant Java; that any one, half ruined by wrong, must complete that ruin, by giving up all he has to secure the aid of justice; and then too often he makes the sacrifice in vain.

Sahyeepah was on the road, early the next day with Djala, Ayum, and Ambon; her heart was full of trouble, how can it be well, when the sack has no rupees; but she did not look on the road behind; she looks before her; and there was Chipanas, the Hot mountain; like Gedeh; great towers of Allah, to guide her steps to Surakarta. She sees Chipanas in the clouds no more; the third, the fourth, and the fifth day of travel have passed; without loss, without grief; and lodging in peace, in the dessas on the way. The great tchandies of Tchanjore are passed; far on, the great hill of Tankuban Prahu is seen, where Panji sailed in the forest.

There is a petrifaction in this region of country, resembling a prahu; a huge stone ship in fact, in the forest, with which, as with the most of noted things in Java, the name of the hero Panji is associated.

Bukit Tunggil is another great tower of Allah; it guides the steps of Sahyeepah to Bandong. She draws near the town, and hears a mighty roar of feet and voices coming to meet her on the road. Ambon pulls back the head of Djala with fear. Adah! what terror is coming; clouds of dust, hiding the mountains, hiding the forest; shouts of men, eating the voice of Ambon, who cries to Djala; that hears not, that sees buffaloes foaming, rushing on; coolies striking, shouting; great wheels rolling behind; on they come, and Djala runs; his heart is in his eyes, and they see devils on the road; and Djala rushes to hide in the forest; rushes with Sahyeepah, Ayum, and Ambon. Allah, have mercy! they are all on the ground.

The clouds and the roar pass by; Djala is held by the hands of Ambon; but the cart is broken; one wheel in little pieces, Ambon cannot mend it; Ayum and Sahyeepah cannot. Weh! kasih-an! poor women must walk on foot to Bandong Sick feet and sick hearts they have in Bandong. It will take all their money to mend the cart; they must leave it; Sahyeepah sells it for a little sum; five times more was given for it in Batavia. This is great sorrow, great loss, and Sahyeepah learned at Bandong, that a Tuan, from the land of her brother, an American Tuan was in the carriage, with the buffaloes and coolies; he drank strong water, like the Dutchmen, he beat poor coolies; he beat them to give wings to buffaloes on the road.

This great loss of the poor travellers, was indeed caused by a fast driving American; who came to Batavia on some business for parties elsewhere in the East; obtained a privilege to visit the interior; and unfortunately for the good fame of America, was a representative only of some of her pot-house vices. Hard drinking, smoking, swearing, and mad driving, fit for the beer cellar and the race-course, were enacted by an old American debauchee at Bandong, and elsewhere in Java. This kicker of coolies, this beater of buffaloes, was a great admirer of the paternal rule of Holland in Netherland India.

What must Sahyeepah do? no cart, and so little money; she will not turn back, and it will be hard to go on. Ayum and Ambon are little of heart; how can they travel now? Sahyeepah thinks; Cheribon is not far off; her father has a foster brother there, a good old man, who will help her. They will reach there in a short time; the weak one shall ride Djala, not Sahyeepah alone; and so they travel; Ayum rides, and Ambon rides on Djala; a good little horse, not afraid of steep hills, stony paths, and dark waters rushing across them; he is only afraid of djins in the clouds of dust on the road; he takes them safe to Samedang; and safe, all the way to Cheribon.

Old Mas Prawiro has heart's joy to see the daughter of his foster brother, but where is Wirojoyo? where is Diporo Kasumo? where is Sareena? And what is Sahyeepah doing in Cheribon, without father, without friends? He must not ask all; he must help his niece to travel a long journey; he must not ask why; he must not ask where. Mas Prawiro wondered greatly, his wife, his children wondered; but Sahyeepah held close mouth; and Prawiro was good, all the same. He was not rich, he could not help much; he could not buy a new cart; but there is a saddle put on Djala, fit for nonna to ride; the sack of Sahyeepah has fifty more rupees in it; Ayum has many nice things in a new wallet; and they go with strong hearts again, on the way to Surakarta.

The road is now by the sea, the great sea of Java. Sahyeepah saw its waters, she knew its voice; she had slept, she had dreamed by the sound; Pulo Percha was beyond, on the other side; she heard the rambahya songs of the Moosie; she heard the sound of the waters of the Ogan; Panyorang Djaya Laksana was listening too, and thinking of his little daughter; thinking that she must never be little in heart; she must ride on the white elephant to Menangkabau. Now she must ride with a strong heart on the back of Djala; many days, foot sick and body sick, on she rides and walks, amid sunshine, amid darkness, in daylight and twilight; through stones and through waters in the path; on the way through Tegal, Pekalongan, stopping at Batang and Kandal, and for a time at the great city of Samarang.

Ayum was sick; she was old; she could chew sirih in the shade,—no more. Three days, Ayum has the cold in her bones; she takes much medicine, from a cunning dukun, a doctress of Java, who knows all the herbs of life and death; she gives Ayum of the herb of life; she makes her strong again. Allah, she makes Sahyeepah pay twenty rupees for taking the cold out of Ayum.

The practice of medicine; as well the chief part of the small trading, peddling, and money changing, is mainly confined to women in Java. They are famed, even among Europeans, to possess a skill for the preparation of the most subtle distillations and concoctions of herbs, ever known to the world. They have poisons more prompt than those so well known in Rome, that gave death in a pinch of snuff; they have others that only act six months after being taken; some that produce madness, some that produce strange effects, yet leaving the mind and body apparently well; such are the common beliefs among Europeans as well as natives at Batavia, of the skill of the women doctors of Java; who it seems, from the story of Sahyeepah, understand making large bills, as well as the profession elsewhere.

Djala is walking on the road, feet fast stepping; Ayum on his back; he pulls at the herb, he bites at Ambon; Djala is merry on Gunung Ungarang, the Mountain of Horses and Chariots. Proud necks are curving, hoofs pawing the air, manes flying in the wind; and chariots rolling; chariots of Chandra Kirana; the same in the days of Panji; the same on the day Sahyeepah is walking foot sore, on the road to the battle grounds of Dipo Negoro; where he fought with the Wolanda at Salatiga.

Sculptures in stone of beautiful horses and chariots; like Olympic triumphal cars, are to be seen in this neighborhood. Chandra Kirana was the wife of Panji; and a chief heroine of the wayang in Java.

Djala is stopped at Salatiga; and officers of the Company want to see the pass of Sahyeepah; they want to know why she goes to Surakarta;—to see a cousin who lived in Cheribon; the officers won't believe, they talk loud, they talk to Ayum; she trembles, her heart is little, a foolish old woman, and tells about Batavia, and a Tuan in the house of care. The officers say horrid words of Satan; Sahyeepah must go before the Jaksa.

Ayum speaks one way, Ambon speaks another; the Jaksa says Sahyeepah has a crooked tongue; she is shut up in a kandang, in a close room, like Tuan her brother, at Batavia. Two women come; they search all her dress; every little cloth; the sarong, the choolee, the scarf and koleeling; all but the pins in the hair; there is nothing that the officer wants, who stands outside the door. Sahyeepah goes free the next morning; but must pay the Jaksa for the trouble of the law, ten rupees; and she turns away from Salatiga, with a lighter purse and a heavier heart.

Sahyeepah stops at Karang Salan; she stops at Boyolalee; she is on sacred ground; lands of old Matarem, where Browijoyo ruled, and sent his Flowers of Victory, his mighty hosts to conquer lands on the Moosie, where Aria Damar reigned. Gunung Merapi; the mighty mountain of Red Fire; smoking top, between the clouds and the Eye of Day,—Gunung Merapi will light the way to the imperial city near by; but there is more woe, more loss for Sahyeepah, before she rests foot in Surakarta.

Allah is rolling the sun about above the clouds; there is thunder on the top of Merapi; and the sounds of rushing wings; and the hissings of Red Fire in the cloud tanks, eat up the voice of the king bird; and of Ambon speaking to Djala. The eye of day is shut; the face of Heaven is dark, and weeping; adoh! such torrents; the swelling Sunggee in the path. Tongues of Red Fire, show the rolling waters upon the bridge of the Sunggee.

Djala must bear Sahyeepah, Ayum and Ambon over; feet are too little for the deep water on the bridge. Two on the back of Djala,—Ayum and Ambon. He has crossed, he has come back; Djala is strong; but Ambon shakes with a little heart to cross again. Sahyeepah will hold the rein. Merapi bellows, tongues of Red Fire darting, and Sunggee swelling. Djala has stiff ears, eyes glaring; the rolling waters touch the feet of Sahyeepah. Djala beats against the water; the bridge groans; adah! it is going down the Sunggee. Djala plunges; the brave little horse and Sahyeepah are safe, but Ambon has gone down the Sunggee.

Poor Ambon is seen no more; and the wallet of Ayum with many rupees is gone. What sick, what poor, what desolate women to enter the city of the Susuhunan. They find rest for the night in a dessa. On the road early, the next morning, they see the waters of Solo; but Sahyeepah is heart sick, head sick; the cold is in her bones; and she has faint eyes to behold the tops of the walls of the Kraton;—pain of body kills her joy, on entering the city of Surakarta.

She will be brave, yet a little longer; the message in the hair knot has to be given; she searches, she asks; but the friend of Tuan her brother, is not in Surakarta; he has gone many days' journey in the lands of Preanger. No one can say, where he shall be found; Sahyeepah must wait; the pain of the body is now strong; head sick, heart sick, cold in the bones; the eyes see no more; and Sahyeepah lies many days, forgetting all things, in the house of a good woman of Surakarta.

Allah is good; the eyes of Sahyeepah open; she thinks of father and brothers; the cold is gone; her feet are strong; she is walking in the Kraton, and it is *pasar senen*, the gala day. She hears the gongs, and drums, and long trumpets; she sees the Flowers of Victory, the spearmen and the guards; the noble Radens, the golden sirih box, the mat of state, the great payung; and beneath it the son of wonder and brightness, Pakoo Boowono Senopati, Susuhunan of Surakarta.

This ruler over the relics of the ancient empire of Matarem, possesses but a nominal political power in Java; although still reverenced, or almost worshipped by the patriotic Javanese, so fondly clinging to all that belongs to the ancient state of their sovereigns, who once wielded an imperial sway in the Archipelago. The present emperor is the seventh of a dynasty, that has sold the best part of its power to the Dutch; yet the people of Java, think that the Europeans are mere farmers of the revenue for the advantage of the Susuhunan; as they understand the management of trade and rupees, better than he or his Radens. When the Susuhunan does not want the Dutchmen, said Wirojoyo to me, the people of Java, will drive them out of the island with bananas in their hands. And so they could, if they were roused to try;—eleven millions against two or three thousand Europeans; they might indeed smother them with fruit. The Dutch force is all on the coast; it does not come much in contact with the great mass of the natives in the interior:—half-breeds, and a few pensioned small chieftains, are the intermediaries of communication; and prevent the collisions that might take place between the rough, matter of fact of the European, and the sensitive etiquette of the Orientals; which rightly managed leads to a ready access to the native mind. In the East, everywhere, etiquette is power The emperor, who is absolute over about one million and a half of subjects, receives a large revenue from the Dutch Government, for allowing them the monopoly of all the coffee and sugar that can be produced in his lands. The neighboring independent State, the Sultanate of Yugya Karta, holds the same stipendiary relations with the Dutch; the princes selling the labor of their people, and their own political power, that they may enjoy, undisturbed with the cares of State, their oriental pomp and luxury; which is said to be most tastefully displayed at the imperial city of Surakarta.

Sahyeepah looks at the barungan, the great show of her land; and she sees the combat of the tiger and the buffalo.

The gamelan salindro, the kumpul, and the chelempung, musical instruments, call the people, men, women and little children, to see the chief show of Java. The buffalo that will let none but Javanese ride on his back, is the champion of the people; and the tiger, that will not kill the Europeans, is champion for them. The tiger is made hungry and weak; the buffalo bows his strong neck; the sharp claws are in the neck; Allah! that squall, that bellow; again the neck is bowed; weh! the horns are in the yellow skin, they drip with blood; Sahyeepah is sick; the people shout; the tiger is dead.

Malays and Javanese are inveterate show goers; the highest and the lowest; lone women boldly crowding their way; and taking places with the foremost. Besides combats with tigers, there are the topeng, or masked shows; the wayang, wherein are illustrated the wars and loves of the great heroes and heroines of Javanese history and fable; of Panji, Chandra Kirana, Rajamala, Dewa Kesuma, and Arjuna.

Sahyeepah walks in the Kraton; she looks at shows; but she is not happy. He who must receive the message does not return; and the rupees are all gone. What must Sahyeepah do? she cannot eat the rice of the good woman for nothing;—she can make wax printed cloths, and embroidery for the daughters of Radens; she makes the fine boddice, the scarf, the lace of the long bajoo; and the flowered sarong for the bride, and the lady of the court.

The Javanese or Malay woman, young or old, thus readily enters into business, and will support herself with a resolution, that may be equalled, but cannot be surpassed by the most self-reliant of the sex in any other part of the world. As I have said, they do all the small traffic of Java, except what is carried on by Chinamen. Wirojoyo said a Javan man, is a fool with money, he cannot take care of it; he gives it to his wife. The women are the chief bankers of Java.

The friend of Tuan her brother, comes to Surakarta; what wonder, when the coat of lacquer is torn from the head of the pin; what joy when the words are read. Other words are written, as Tuan, my brother, has received. His friend says; the way is bad to ride on Djala back to Samarang to Batavia,—must go in oar prahu down the Solo, to Gresik, on the sea; to Soorabayah; and in prahu with masts to Batavia. Djala is sold,—good, brave, strong, little Djala; she wept when he went away,—Sahyeepah will never ride on the back of brave little Djala again; but she is on the prahu, laden with rice; and Ayum is with her; and some women, who have merchandise for Soorabayah.

Tuan, her brother, has seen the Moosie, the Ogan, the Soonsang, and the Opang; let him look on them again, and he will see the Solo; but more houses, more people, more rice fields. Java is full of people, working hard for the Company; who keep a fort with cannon at Gresik, near the mouth of Solo; not far is Soorabayah, a great Dutch city, full of houses of merchandise,—many ships in the still water, and Sahyeepah saw the star flag of the country of Tuan, her brother.

There is a fire ship, of the Company going to Batavia. Sahyeepah has not many of the rupees, given by the friend of Tuan at Surakarta; she must give all for herself and Ayum in the fire ship. The sea of Java again; Sahyeepah loves the sea, like her grandfather, like Tuan her brother; she has heart joy, to hear the sound of the waters; and returning to father and brothers; but Ayum is sick, very sick; her sight is gone, the cold is in her bones; there is no dukun near; the chief of the fire ship gives medicine; the sight won't come back again, the cold will not go away, Sahyeepah rubs the poor old servant, and gives warm things; but the soul of Ayum goes to speak with Allah.

Adoh! Sahyeepah is alone; she weeps; the men of the fire ship drink strong water, and look at her with burning eyes; she shuts the door of her little room, she will not go out to eat;—for two days shut up with fear, and hunger, and then she hears the roll of the anchor chain; the great dayongs have stopped beating the water; there are the ships of the Company, and of all nations; there is Batavia; and Sahyeepah is in a boat; she walks with weak step; she can see no more; she feels only the arms of her father.

FIFTY-THIRD DAY.

My faithful messenger had but slight opinion of her own heroic exertions, as having contributed to the accomplishment of her mission. She had regarded her successful arrival at Surakarta, notwithstanding all her struggles and losses, as owing to the influence of the charmed ointment of the magician of Gedeh. This faith had led her to consult another man of charmed drugs at Surakarta; who for twenty rupees had given her an ointment to assist her return to Batavia; and also one to effect the enlargement of her brother from prison.

I had received the magic compound, enclosed in a nutshell, curiously carved and fastened, with which I must perform many minute, mystifying little ceremonials; and then the eyes of my jailers would become very heavy, and I should find no obstacle in going out. The pomatum emitted an odor, of many scents blended; and I thought I could distinguish some of the simples of the compound. I obtained them, and after many experiments produced an ointment of the color and aroma of the reputed charmed one. I thus sought to make a practical appeal to the common sense of Sahyeepah, to convince her of the folly of supposing that this preparation was some mystic extract from the centre of a mountain; but I found that I was running a risk of simply proving myself to be a magician, equal to suwanggee; and in this belief, I dare say that Wirojoyo remains fixed to this day.

The daughter listened, however, with more earnestness of thought, and with some exercise of reasoning powers; she was led to think of the influence of faith; and led to believe that Djala, and her sack of rupees, were the most effectual talismans, along with the resolution of her own heart, which enabled her to accomplish her journey. And talking of charms, and their reputed virtues, we were naturally led on to contemplate the source of the power that was ascribed to them.

It was not a hackneyed subject for Sahyeepah; it would not be for any simple, docile, inquiring heathen, to talk about the Author and Controller of life and death; it had never been a wearying class study upon her brain of childhood; it was a wonderful, and interesting thing to contemplate, the probabilities of a providence, a divine power, the same that controlled the universe, as watching over the life, and directing the foosteps of a weak, simple girl of Java.

The idea seemed to break upon the mind of Sahyeepah, with startling force, that the Ruler of Heaven would speak to her heart; and be her friend; true, she had some ideas at first, of gaining thereby the powers of a suwanggee;—but her mind soon cast away the contemplation of such a character;—a petty trader of the favor, which was pretended to be received from Allah. She began to feel, that the friend of the Maker of Heaven and earth, would feel but little interest in gathering rupees from poor people, seeking help and consolation.

There were some words in my mouth, about needy ones being called to come to the Source of abundance without money and without price; and I turned to the place in a large Malay Bible, which I had lately obtained; and as we followed down the page, the finger of my fellow inquirer stopped at the words, "Incline your ear, and come unto me; hear, and your soul shall live; and I will make an everlasting covenant with you." Who was speaking thus? And to whom? The Maker of all things, even unto Sahyeepah. Was it so indeed? That I affirmed with all positiveness, even more than I felt. The experience with Wongso had not developed more than an inquiring curiosity. I was to be startled again by the uncivilized mind, from uncheering speculations upon laws of necessity, of fitness of things, of progressions, developments, and harmonies. I was overwhelmed again with questions, that I was helpless fittingly to meet; but I must find some answer.

How was it that Javanese remained weak and poor so long, living and dying, the slaves of bad men? Had not the Maker of all things made the Javanese? We were turning over pages of the Bible; the Malay language is so well adapted to its simple, poetic style in some parts; more than all to the grand poetry of Job; and the Psalms and Isaiah speak in familiar figures to the Malay and Javanese mind. We were running over the pages of the latter prophet. I paused at words that struck me, that I had not seen before; messengers were spoken of, that were to be sent to "Javan and the isles afar off, that have not heard my fame, neither have seen my glory;"—a startling answer put into my mouth;—of moving power upon the mind of Sahyeepah;—the great Book of the Christians promised the mighty things of their religion unto her brethren and sisters in these isles afar off.

I was led to believe, from some after reading, that the Javan here referred to, was the land of a son of Japhet, situated in Asia; but I thought, at the time of first reading about it with Sahyeepah, that it referred to the sacred isle of the Hindoos, the modern Java of the Archipelago; and my earnest prison visitor thought so. The enthusiastic young mind, that had dreamed of some marvellous destiny for her race, the restoration of Menangkabau and Matarem; of some part that she might take;—the riding on the white elephant;—thought the time come, when the Satans of the Company should be driven out; and Flowers of Victory should perfume the banks of the Moosie and the Solo with Glory.

Earnest enthusiast of a child-like race; fitting instrument for the fanaticism of Brahma, the dark rites of Bohwanee, or the deadly imposture of Islam;—how it turned after a time with its enthusiasm, and woman's instinctive love of peace, to the contemplation of the life, character, and mission of the Son of Mary. What a wonderful story; so much power, so much poverty; so much love for hate, so much pain and suffering,—paying for the lack of poor aching hearts;—Sahyeepah one of these; and so much glory, to share even with her; the glory of one in white robes entering triumphant into a city, gorgeous with gems, and resplendent with the light of the beautiful face of the great Brother. Wonderful words of Revelations, speaking more to oriental imagination than to western intelligence, how they moved the heart and tears of this earnest soul of the Archipelago.

Where was the insignificant Malay city, with its bamboo and palm leaf, and paltry barbaric splendor? where was the pomp of riding upon an unwieldy beast after reading all this? What was the tawdry mat of state, the sirih box, the tinsel payung, the spearmen, and the guards; and all the pride of state of the vicious, indolent descendant of Browirjoyo, when reading of the throne of the King of Kings, and the Heavenly Host of *winged ones;* and *Sahyeepah* their names, even like the one on earth, who wished to be one of their number?

Gloomy walls of Weltevreden, heart-aching sounds of human woe and darkness; they chilled the spirit at times; but they were good; they had given seasons of reflection to thoughtlessness; they had quickened fellow feeling; they had widened the narrow scope of selfish aims; they had opened the way to new worlds of human souls,—to undiscovered regions of thought and sympathy. Walls of Weltevreden; Hotel of involuntary lodgers; College for the study of Humanity; unhonored Bureau of Governmental talent; and now, and since the jubilant words of the dying murderer, a Temple for the worship of the Most High.

How was I led into new paths by an inquiring pupil? My judges and jailers were forgotten, in following them; but the pupil outstripped the teacher,—not having the same encumbrance, of pride of knowledge, of self-sufficiency, of the speculation of a more presumptuous brain, of much contact with evil, and doubting at times of all things good and true; the pupil, the fellow inquirer rather, had none of these weights on the wings of enthusiasm, none of these blinds upon the eyes of simple, childlike faith, that read eagerly of the Word of Life; and said, Sahyeepah would wash the bleeding feet of her Great Brother, who was killed for the sake of poor weak children of the world, of Java, and Pulo Percha; Sahyeepah would be a Christian.

How much of that wish was owing to some sympathy with what was supposed to be, my belief and feeling? It matters not;—but only to show to you the workings of this guileless soul; brightening the prison; chasing away the demons of idle and hopeless moments; shaming the cold and skeptical spirit of civilization, and acting a part of earnest heroism, which only such prison influences could have developed; and perhaps might be met in few, but in enthusiastic, simple children of these isles.

And how the influence of the Redeeming Word had wrought upon the character and temper of Sahyeepah; even the Dutch were no longer children of Satan; but even of the same Good Maker who had made all. We talked of them, what they were in the past and the present; I had a copy of Tacitus,—the single book I was allowed and had asked for, on one occasion of tightening of prison discipline. Many a page of the Annals were translated into Malay; the brave stand of the Batavi, after whom this city was named; and their great struggles in their swamps, when led by Arminius against the mighty power of Rome, mightier than that of Iskander, of whom Sahyeepah had heard many a wonderful story.

We left the story of the Romans, and came down to later times, when the children of the Batavi fought against and conquered another great empire; that of the rajah, who sends ships to Manilla; and fought still a stronger one, the rajah of France; and when he pressed hard, they opened banks to let in the sea; and all resolved to leave their homes, to come and live in Java; and why? That they might have no master over them, and might worship God as they pleased; but they soon forgot their own struggles; and put forth all their skill and strength, to make slaves of Malay and Javanese; as Roman, Spaniard, and Frenchman wished to make of them.

But Sahyeepah must remember that the Susuhunan of Surakarta, the Sultan, and the Radens of Java; the Sultans of Sumatra,—all made slaves of their people; many were more cruel masters than the Dutch; though the people love their own tyrants best. The Susuhunans, Sultans, and Radens have no religion of peace and good will in their hearts; they have no Word of Life in their palaces; the men of Holland have; but they have hardened their hearts against its teachings; they shut out benevolence, brotherhood, and mercy; they worship a gloomy god,—no other but that one god. What! not the God of the Christians? No. They worship one whose name we looked for in the Testament; and we read of stories of those who had some thought of a treasure in Heaven; and others who had no thought but of treasures on earth; and these worshippers, and all Dutchmen were of the number, had no god but mammon.

Every effort of an industrious, skilful, and energetic government, has been put forth during more than two hundred years, to obtain by persuasion, force, cunning and fraud, whatever they could get of the fruits of the labor of a simple, industrious people, without making a single sacrifice for the moral welfare, or the intellectual advancement of these; nay, doing all in their power to prevent any such advantage being imparted by others. The people of Java seem of no more consequence in the estimation of the Government of Holland, than the soil of Java, and if the orang utan, and the baboons in the forest, could be trained to produce coffee and sugar, to greater profit than the human beings of these islands, there is no doubt but that the latter would be driven as ruthlessly into the sea, as once was done to many of the useless inhabitants of the Moluccas.

And if Susuhunan is bad; and Sultan, Rajah, and Raden, all bad as Company; what hope is there for poor people of Java; of Pulo Percha; and all the brethren and sisters of Sahyeepah? The eyes of the inquirer looked eager and sad. What hope for our brethren and sisters of these islands. What hope had Sahyeepah of the cold days of age, and sickness yet to come? were they of the pomp of fine robes, and music and applause? what was her joy in going the rugged way to Surakarta? the joy of pleasing some one, the joy of doing a good deed; and what was the hope, on the road she had been travelling in the Great Book; was there any honor, power, or glory in this world to be found in that? What has she found?

Sahyeepah spoke as a very little child; she forgot the wonderful words of the Great Book; she would hold them better in her heart. She had seen the prospect of better hopes, than in wealth and power; hopes of peace; hopes of constant songs, when the soul had wings; and they who would see all that, must not wish for the best that the world can give. The Great Brother, the Son of Mary, was very poor. Ayah! children of Susuhunans, who must be rocked in gold;—He lay in the trough of a beast's poor shelter. What poor people who believed! What great people who did not believe! The rajahs and panghulus of Juda mocked Him, whom fishermen and poor women followed, and Sahyeepah will follow; and her brethren and sisters must follow; and let the Wolanda, let the Dutchmen; kasih-an, pity on them; let them have all the power of Java and Pulo Percha, and hearts without love and without hope, if they will not follow. Such were the words of Sahyeepah.

Great change had come over the heart of the enthusiast; a change that startled my own; and carried me onward in paths I had never trodden before; but the dreams on the Moosie could not be all cast aside; some of the world's pomp and power must mingle with calmer hopes of the future. Sahyeepah with curious finger had paused on every island in the Indian and Pacific oceans, and questioned me about their people and their history; and above all, about the great island of the kangaroo, filled with the sons of England, who had often beaten the Dutchmen; one of whom was the great, good man Raffles, whom many children of Java and Pulo Percha hoped to see again;—would not the children of England in the island of the kangaroo, which was great, and they were many;—would not they come and be masters in Java; and one like Tuan Besar Raffles, rule over them?

It seems indeed likely, even as occurred to this simple mind, that the great Anglo-Saxon race of Australia,—founders of an Oceanican empire, will be the future arbiters of the destinies of these beautiful islands; and when it shall be so, perhaps it may not be happier for Malay and Javanese than now; yet better, in a thousand chances for their moral and Christian development, better in the hands of Anglo-Saxons, who love a little fair play, who have some regard for their fellow-beings as well as trade; and could such minds as Raffles preside, and a Xavier and Judson teach, then might the abundance of these isles be converted unto grateful tributes to the Redeemer of the world.

FIFTY-FOURTH DAY

The fifteenth month of my imprisonment was passing away; two months since the public trial; six weeks, since it had been declared in open court that I was not guilty of the crime for which I had been held in jail; and yet I had been waiting all this time, to learn the decision of the great secret tribunal, or rather the will of the Government. It seemed impossible, that after four deliberate decisions for my enlargement, by the court that had gone through the labor of searching out all the particulars of my history, cruise, associations, habits, thoughts, and conversations; impossible to suppose, that the Government could still try to sift out some plea, on this fourth occasion; and condemn me, even in spite of Netherland law and justice.

There was nothing else but a sense of justice to deter them from doing so; they felt that they had nothing to fear of retribution or reclamation. An American agent had said, it was better to hang troublesome men from America, of whom there were too many, than to run the risk of getting into trouble by dallying with any tedious formalities of justice. An American Commander had talked largely, got his eyes well dusted with Dutch suavity, and had done nothing. An American Commodore had passed out of the way of Batavia, saying that he had a treaty on hand that was to secure some Japanese trade; and he had no time to waste upon American citizens in jail in Java; and fifteen months had passed away, without receiving any notice from an American Secretary of State; so that there was nothing to fear from an American official interference; and though Dutch guards were knocked down, and their palace gates invaded by American Bassetts, and Smiths, and terrible American Boatswains; yet there was nothing to fear from the rulers at Washington, or their servants abroad; and they might do what they pleased with the American prisoners in Weltevreden.

At one time, there were some rumors that the American Japan squadron, was about to visit Batavia; I received visits and congratulations; it was coming no doubt to look after the Flirt and her people. There were rumors that I would be at liberty in a few days; one of my counsellors had learned from official sources that the High Court had come to a decision, after an incessant discussion of one month,—overhauling the mountain of documents; five judges being against, and four in favor, for some time; at last one had yielded in spite of the Government; the decision was in my favor, I would be afloat soon in my own Flirt, if her timbers still held together; I must say nothing about this matter to any body; as my counsellor would be suspected of disclosing judicial secrets. Of course, I would not tell; and yet I could not keep the secret out of my face; there were quick eyes to read it. Old Wirojoyo came to embrace me; every body said, the American Tuan was coming out of the house of care; and there would be jubilee in the campongs.

My Javanese friends came to offer me selamat,—the salutations of their simple customs, by which they notice every little event of joy. Wirojoyo, his son, and Sahyeepah, came; the other daughter having returned with her husband to Cheribon. Sahyeepah had come to surprise me; when she entered my room, she threw off the outer coarse dress, she usually wore; and disclosed

the rich, graceful costume, I had seen in Sumatra; the same fine, lace-bordered Japanese kabyah; the richly embroidered boddice; the curiously colored sarong, the golden girdle, the filigree clasp, the pearls, the studded slippers, the brilliants like buttons in the ear; and the same womanly tastes were all there; but how changed the face; the wild mischievous rock deer no longer laughed, but smiled so earnestly; the round merry face was lengthened with the lines of womanhood; not much of that dazzling prettiness, like many of her sisters of Java and Sumatra, of noble race; but European intelligence, and more than European enthusiasm beamed from her face;—she asked, would her grandfather think she had grown uglier? he never thought her beautiful like the Palm Tree, the Wave, and the Sweet Lip. I spoke of the comeliness of the heart; he must look into her new-born thoughts and feelings; and look as her brother looked; then he would see more beauty than possessed by the most dazzling daughters of Passumah.

Sahyeepah quickly replaced the coarse dress; saying, Sahyeepah is but a child still, when will she be a woman; when will the fine batek cloth, the flowered sarongs and the golden tali pendeng cease to please more than the white spotless robes that she must wear, to go and offer selamat to her Great Brother? She looked sad; did she feel reproached for having come in her bright garments, to remind her brother of his days of freedom, soon to come again? when he should sail on the waters of Java, when he should sail up the Moosie; to remind him of scenes that might woo him from sailing away to his own great land beneath the winds where the sun reposed. But Sahyeepah must not think thus; I would not sail away; I would eat rice again, by the will of the Almighty and the Loving One, with Panyorang Osman Djaya Laksana; we would tell him the stories we had talked over; and to many people on the Moosie; and in the lands of the Passumah. We would tell the story of the journey to Surakarta, to the Kraton of the Susuhunan; and that other journey of the soul, with hope and fear; in strength and weeping; through paths of meekness and humiliation; through a garden of agony, to a dire hill of execution; and beyond that to the everlasting city of gems, to the throne of the Great Brother. Sahyeepah would remember the robes to be worn, and would strive for no other.

The salutation of departure was given; the clasped hands; and the tchoom on the cheek; and I parted from my Javanese friends and they with me, with overflowing joy at the prospect of my speedy release

I packed up once more, my small wardrobe, my books, and papers, and all the little things that were to remind me of the strange days of my life within these walls; of my reveries and inventions; of my troubles and joys; of my studyings, teachings, and worryings at the hands of justice. I had seen new walls begin to rise, and a new hall of Instruction added to Weltevreden; but I should be wearied no more with questioning in that Hall; and those walls, the first creations of my machine, were not to add to the closer durance of the inventor. I thought all this, as I watched the finishing of the archway of the main entrance; awhile after my Javanese friends had left me: Tutup showed me in the afternoon the increased height and strength of the walls; the increase of the guard; and all the circumstances that now rendered hopeless any escape; as had lately been attempted by a wretched soldier about to be shot.

I saw the liveried oppas of the Attorney General enter the house of the jailer; no doubt with the ratification of my release,—the assurance to the jailer, that he might let me go free, as soon as he had received the order for my discharge, from the Greffier of the High Court. I finished my packing. I amused myself with some last charcoal scrawls,—some valedictory words, upon the walls of my cell; and then when weary, I went to look out on a magnificent sky of Java;—the clear deep blue, the thick studded glitter, and the soft shine of the great white face of the heavens, wrapping dull walls, and barred doors and gratings in a mantle of sphery beauty. I never saw such a lovely night;—but never one so quickly changed to darkness; not the darkness of storm clouds, but there was a shape of dread, that turned hope almost to despair. I saw in the shade of the ketapan tree, right before my door, a form moving, and something glistening in the moonbeams;—a sentinel on especial guard before my door.

What was the meaning of this? some order from the Attorney General; he had demanded that I should be put to death; the High Court had so decided; the decision would be declared in a few days; the Attorney General apprehended some designs of my friends to effect my escape, and had ordered an extra guard:—when the decree of condemnation should arrive, I would then be placed in a condemned cell. All this I partly learned from the turnkey, who came to speak to me at my door, and was confirmed the next day, by my counsellor from the city.

For the first time I felt the grip of ruthless power. I had not felt much of the fury and denunciation that accompanied my first imprisonment; and I had felt that my after sufferings from close confinement, bad food, and other hurtful circumstances of life in prison, were merely a test of my mental and physical constitution; which I would have to bear awhile; but sooner or later must be let out, or taken out. I had kept mind and body too busy to realize very forcibly my prison condition; but now, there was a change, a determination to end all this blundering, and tedious workings of law. I must never be allowed to go free among the people of the Archipelago;—it would be too much risk to hold me imprisoned. I must be put to death;—no government will interfere to stay their hands; American officials in the East Indies are too much occupied with other matters. Hang him, said the American agent; it is your safest course; and the Government has resolved to follow his advice.

I thought of the many cruel and bloody scenes, I had witnessed within these walls—the hangings, the bastinado, the chainings of a man's wrist down to his ankle for many days, till he roared with the agony of an excruciating back; the torture that preceded execution; and then the pitiless jailer, the brutal turnkey, the stolid guards, and the hard ruthless character of the men of Holland was all before me; there was no hope; the Government feared no intervention from America, and furthermore, had received from thence some cowardly denunciations of a pitiful enemy:—I would surely die, if I did not escape.

I had thought of leaving prison before, at a time when it would have been easy to get away, to get beyond the walls at least; but then, all Java is a jail for an European, unless there is some friendly ship ready to take him away; and there were few captains willing to run the risk of imprisonment and a fine of ten thousand rupees, for taking any one away from Batavia without a passport. I could not hope to find a ship ready to sail, when I was prepared to leave, and so had planned to have a certain means in readiness, to aid me in my flight, when it became necessary to go.

I had become intimate with one of the translators of the Court of Justice, a man of much talent, and pleasant conversation, who became a frequent visitor in prison. I began to place confidence in him, placed in his hands a large portion of the proceeds of my machine making; and he was to purchase a small swift-sailing prahu to be left in charge of a native in my confidence; this prahu was to cruise along the coast, apparently engaged in fishing, and to be ready at any point I should name; when I should be ready to leave.. But I had trusted to a traitor, who had a hand with Storm in making spurious documents and many false things. My funds were applied to other purposes; I lost them and other trusts confided to the hands of that translator of the court of Justice of Batavia.

There was another visitor, a singular character, a reputed exiled count of Russia; his father, a wealthy boyard; a sister, companion of the princess Dolgorouky; and he had been obliged to flee in consequence of some wrong to a lady of the court of St. Petersburg. A relative at the Hague had furnished him the means to go to the East Indies; the usual field selected for the expenditure of the exuberant vice and energy of the youth of Europe. He came to see me, became interested in my fate; and as he showed many bold and generous qualities, won my confidence, and another investment of my funds.

He was, for a time, a protegé of the Resident of Batavia; he had the run of the city, without fear of being called up at the Stadhuis: he used government servants, and government horses at his will; and after a time took a fancy to make use of a small government cruiser, one of the gun prahus for the revenue service;—this was done in my interest; to take a survey of all the creeks and bays in the neighborhood of the roads; to find a sure place for a rendezvous; and to prepare the way for the rescue of another, when I myself should get out. He cruised thus freely with a government boat, till a note was intercepted; he was to be arrested; he ran the cruiser upon Onrust Island, drowned seven of his crew, and escaped to Singapore with the connivance of a high functionary at Batavia.

At Singapore he joined my second mate; communicated with me; and I was led to forward money; nearly all of my prison earnings, to purchase a small cutter. A craft of forty tons, with a crew of twelve men, mostly Spaniards, was soon under his command. He went to Lingen, to the mouth of the Soonsang, to Banca; and then to points on the coast of Java, according to my direction; he ran into a creek near Cramat, and communicated with a friend in Batavia; he was discovered by a Dutch cruiser, was chased, got away; and when last I heard of him, the day after the sentinel had been placed at my door, he had been seen from the telegraph station, standing off and on, near the point of Ontong Java, and a cruiser had been sent in pursuit of the bold Russian count.

There was no hope of help at this hour of need from that quarter: fearful rumors came to my ears, from turnkey and sentinel; the fate of Wongso rose up before me; and I felt that no philosophy or spirit of resignation of mine could ever consent to that; any desperate measures, even a frenzied, hopeless run in daylight, a run-a-muck indeed, rather than that; but whatever was to be done, must be done quickly; any moment might bring the decree of death, and then I would at once be fastened in the condemned cell. Where were my friends, my faithful Javanese friends, and the faithful Pirez? the gates were shut upon them, although I knew it not: the prospect looked dark and desperate; when a ray of hope burst in,—the presence of my friends here,—the Captain and the Boatswain.

Breakers ahead there, said the Boatswain, interrupting;—heard it was a bad case with the Captain; and thought I would ask leave to go and see a dying countryman. By gracious king, I never meant to look at a dying codfish, much less a countryman in the hands of a Dutchman: I went to see how to scatter those bricks that your machine had been piling up about the jail; never went to preach any sermon, or any talk of give-up of any kind. Our friend looked a bit worried; observed the Boatswain, turning to the ladies; and it was time to be getting up some sort of anxiety: I had heard every where about Batavia, that the Government never meant to let him out alive; he had made himself too agreeable to the yellow skins; and old Dutchy thought he might wake up some morning, and see the skipper of the Flirt riding through the streets of Batavia on top of an elephant, with a hundred thousand or so, of Malay run-a-mucks in his wake; so he thought it best to put those dreams out of his head, by giving the neck of the Captain a twist. But he said he did not mean to wait for that experience of Dutch justice in the East Indies; he thought he had seen enough, and had waited long enough; and was bound to get out; and if his heels couldn't save him to die a kicking with his neck clear at least. That was the talk I wanted to hear: The "old man," who was along, told him, there was a berth on board the Palmer for him; she was all repaired, ready for sea; would lay in the outer Roads, waiting for him; but he must get out of the walls himself; and I, and the mate, and whole crew of the Palmer, were to be ready with the long-boat to take him on board. I hated to leave him then in prison, but could do nothing; he had to get help on shore to get out; but we kept a sharp look out,—myself and mate, and the crew; forty two of 'em, I had every night in that long-boat; all armed from the boots up to the coat collar; and as crooked a lot to handle of tough, good fellows, as ever sailed out of the port of New York;—every man full charged with fight, and ready to make a rush on the jail; which, by gracious king, I meant to do, if they got you into the close jug. Now let's have the full yarn how you got out, which I have been getting along in bits.

I had studied well the topography of the prison; and all the chances of a night evasion,—of getting over its walls; and all seemed hopeless: a round of sentinels, and a broad ditch, guarded every outer wall; sentinels were in each court, and especially on the alert at night; and then there was risk of being challenged at all points by the numerous police, that swarm in the streets of Batavia after dark. I needed a horse to take me swiftly to the boat-landing;—my counsellor agreed to come with one, his heart failed him, and the arrangements failed for that night; another one agreed to come; and he also failed; the prospect was darker than ever, notwithstanding the assurance that my friends of the Palmer were waiting for me every night with a boat and stout crew; all the sure means and friends I had counted upon, failed; and the chances of escape grew more desperate than before.

It was rumored that the decree of death was issued, and probably was in the hands of Brower; the next day, there would no longer be any hope. After the sun had set, I made preparation to leave. There were two bars in my rear window, which I had weakened by many well-concealed drillings and cuttings,—made during the unobserved leisure of less perilous times, when making preparation for some possible future need; which I could easily remove now. When out, I would have to pass the door of the room of the crazy lady, and run the risk of raising a cry from her; and then the door of the turnkey; with the risk of rousing his ever watchful dog;—if safely passing these without disturbance, I had to cross an outer wall, on the side of the great canal; and then I could not hope to clear that without drawing upon me the attention of the sentinel; but there was the deep-shaded park, behind the palace for a refuge; and after running the risk of a shot, I then had a clear run before me of four miles, to reach the boat.

I had taken a look at the sentinel in front, under the ketapan tree: he was indulging in a forbidden pipe, and a gaze at the moon. I was at work upon the rear bars: I heard a sliding sound upon the outer wall, and a slight thump on the ground; there was a dark object, moving under the shadow of the wall inside; it crossed the court stealthily, and came near my window; and then I could distinguish the rude outline of brave, faithful Pirez.

My joy to see him was hardly so great as my surprise. He soon had his feet in the crevices of the wall, and holding on to the bars of my window, told me as follows, in that wild jargon, so incomprehensible to the Court of Justice of Batavia, which if understood, would have told rather too strongly in my favor. He had been locked up at a police station; no doubt, immediately after the resolve upon severe measures towards me; he could not come to me, he could not send; and had been in despair about his master. People came into the yard of the police station to speak with friends fastened up for a day or two;—he could speak with them; but there was no one could tell him any thing. This morning he saw a young peddler woman, with filigree of silver work from Palembang to sell; the good face that his captain knew; who was no longer afraid of Pirez because he was ugly; but was kind like a good Christian lady, San Antonio bless her: she put her finger to her lips; Pirez looked only at the things to sell: he handled the silver filigree, whilst the good peddler said; Pirez, help master; papa Wirojoyo sampan sunggee Anchol, prahu Pulo Edam.

Faithful Javanese hearts needed no message, no advices.

The prahu of the old demang was then lying off that little island on the border of the outer roadstead, which contains some curious haunted ruins; relics of the old Dutch company; and his little boat was waiting for me that night, at a rendezvous on Anchol Creek. I was prepared for any act of generous devotion from the brave daughter; but had not expected such risk of person and property from the timid old Javanese father. Pirez was then told, where he could easily leap a back wall of the police station, to get out that night; and trust to the Great Helper, and his own stout heart and limbs, to join me, in Weltevreden, and help me out. My Javanese friends had some strange ideas about this poor fellow, that he was a kind of djin, which I had confined to earth, and mortal labor; and could make him help me in moments of extreme necessity: they firmly believed that Pirez could jump out of one prison and get into another, whenever it was absolutely necessary that he should do so in my behalf; and that faith has no doubt been fully confirmed, in the mind of Wirojoyo at least, by the exploits of my follower.

Pirez was not locked up in his room; and he who could outrun a monkey up the straight stem of a palm-tree, was quickly over the police station walls; he passed the house of my noble young friend; he startled him in his bed, without having roused any one else in the house. Few words were needed to explain what he was about: much was said, which Pirez could not understand, who continued to reiterate my name and that of the prison; but after some parley he received a note, some money, and certain things from my friend; which he began to remove from his person, after letting himself down from my window. Under his clothes was another suit; a loose hunting coat, and other garments, such as worn by gentlemen on excursions in the neighborhood of the palace of the Governor General at Buitenzorg; an officer's uniform cap, some false hair, a wig and moustaches, a dye for the face, a dirk, and some money. The note explained, that the writer had not dared to come near me, on account of so much suspicion resting upon him; the court had not decided, but would the following day: his relative, the judge of the court, had told him that Brower would hold the decree four and twenty hours, before serving it at the prison; the good-hearted sheriff believing that my friends were taking measures for my escape: the boat of the Palmer had come regularly every night; and would come twice more;—after that, she must sail; my chance was this night; (the writer supposed that this note would be delivered the following morning;)—a little after sunset, when the guard was about to be relieved, and just before placing a sentinel at my door; a friend would enter the court; and then I must trust to my own ingenuity and good fortune to find a chance to walk out with him.

From some other remarks it was evident, that the writer had not supposed that Pirez was going that night with the intention of breaking into prison, and of getting me out; but had supposed that he would come to see me in a regular way the next morning: it was indeed a difficult matter to understand the faithful fellow's dialect of uncouth sounds; and perhaps because I had succeeded so well in understanding, that he was there ready to carry me out forthwith upon his back, to scale walls, to fight the guard; and swim to the Palmer if necessary.

He was grieved to hear me say, that I would stay in prison that night; but a few words soon persuaded him that it was best. I had a while ago resolved to try; because it seemed too great risk to defer; but the next day the chances would be better. At this hour the boat of the Palmer would be gone,—no longer expecting my coming. He must return as he came; take some messages to my friends this night, and then get off with some boat before morning, on board the Palmer.

Pirez retreated with tiger stealth across the yard. I could dimly see his shadowy form approach a piece of new wall, near a building then designed for the insane. This portion was not quite finished, and easy to be scaled by such as Pirez, at least.

The dark form is ascending the wall; but no movement to be observed; mounting with invisible rise like the moon. It is on the wall: the head cranes over; it is disappearing; there is a rumble of something falling from the wall; a loud challenge; a rush of feet; bang! a musket fire; a heavy thump; a cry and groan; a clatter of a bayonet upon stones; and the last sounds heard were fast-running feet, soon lost in the park behind the palace, long ere the alarmed guard of the prison had turned out.

I learned the next morning from the turnkey, that a sentinel had been found at his post, lying bleeding and senseless; struck on the head with a brick. When recovered a little, he swore that a great black fiend, like an enormous bat with wings, had leaped down upon him from the top of the new mad-house. He could give no better account; stuck to it that it was no mortal; had just swept by him and he fell after firing, without knowing what hurt him. He had, in fact, pulled trigger in his fear without taking aim. Pirez has not joined me as I hoped; and I am often grieved to think what accident could have befallen the faithful steward of the Flirt.

I have not spoken of my other follower, and fellow-prisoner; my late navigator on board the Flirt. He had some British friends in the city; although British authorities had made no interference; expecting that the government of the flag under which he had been serving, was the proper party to take cognizance of his case. He had found employment like myself; being very skilful with pencil, in mapping and drafting; though not in my more profitable, inventive way; and he did not partake of any of my sympathies in regard to the people of the Archipelago; looking upon the entire race, as being generally, despite certain good appearances, all after the fashion of Babdoo and Moonchwa; natural born traitors, thieves and cut-throats. These sentiments caused my officer to be regarded in a much more favorable light by Dutch officials; also "in consideration of his youth, and the pernicious influences that had been exercised over him," as a Dutch minister afterwards said; although there was only the difference of a year and a half in our ages. There was no doubt that if I, the principal, was out of the way, the Government would let him go; he and his friends felt assured of this; and I was well assured, from his own mouth, that it was not necessary to have any anxiety about his safety, when it should become necessary for me to escape.

(And such has been the case; he having been pardoned, shortly after condemnation; and that condemnation was unquestionably changed after the escape of the commander from sentence of death, to the one demanded by the Fiskaal at the trial; to stand in the pillory; and afterwards undergo twelve years of hard labor in the mines of Banca, or at the penal fortress of Soorabayah; which sentence now hangs over the head of the unpardoned commander of the Flirt, to be put into execution, whenever he can be captured upon Dutch territory.)

A bright, still cloudless Sabbath morning dawned; the 24th day of April, 1853. It wore away with moments of deep emotion with me; some emotion to think I was looking for the last time upon walls that were traced deep upon memory, even as I had traced on them; they would soon be lost to my sight, flying away with the wings of a ship; or lost to sight within the walls of my last cell. There was some emotion in thinking of leaving for ever, my prison pupils,—Conan, Gedeh and others; the visits of Umbah, the fruits and the teachings; and those more earnest and interesting associations with another pupil, might never be repeated with such interest, as in this prison;—but then there was home, liberty, country; and then thoughts rose up of possibly following the footsteps of Wongso, to that horrible field of death; oh! rather death in warm blood, in a thousand other cruel shapes than that.

And one came to propose an evasion out of the hands of the hangman, if other chances failed; my good-hearted friend, the Baron, had got leave to see me: he believed my case to be desperate, knowing nothing of my plans:—safe enough he was to be trusted; but the fewer in the secret of such matters, the better; he had some propositions to make, but not feasible; and I might have told him not necessary to try;—he had a last resort for me in his pocket; one of the subtle poisons of Java, quick and certain, and leaving no evidence of the cause. It was not strange for the rough soldier to propose such a thing; it was an act of friendship, the same as to aid in a duel; but I declined to retain the poison, however desperate might be the future.

He had a little written message from Umbah; some words of sorrow and affection from the true-hearted child, most grateful to my heart, in those troubled moments. In thinking of her, I recalled Bassett to mind: he was then with me: his presence at my heels would betray me; he must go with the Baron, whom he often followed; but now he crouched close in a corner; he would not stir, and snarled at my friend, who approached him with caressing voice and action: he could not be carried out; I must trust to other chances during the day, to prevent the faithful animal from following my steps; but much I regretted that I could not put on board the Palmer the courageous, faithful namesake of the brave and generous friend, I hoped to meet at home.

With words of warmest friendship I parted with my honest-hearted late fellow-prisoner; words warmer than his; though would not have been, had he known my resolve for that evening;—and that evening was near at hand; the last rays of a glorious Java sun were streaming through the tops of the almond, the tamarind, and the waringin trees before the great gate. The disguise was on, beneath an outer thin dress, ready to be thrown off at a moment; my long beard, well softened from time to time, to be ready for the razor at the last minute; the last thing to be done, when ready to step forth. Minutes are counted; not many before the guard would go the rounds; and a sentinel be placed at my door for the night. I had stained beneath my eyes, to alter the expression of my face; the dark, well-fitting wig covered my lighter-colored hair;—Tutup opens my door;—I am in bed, concealed by a small curtain, affecting illness and surliness;—do not wish to talk; and Tutup, who had sometimes found me in silent moods, passed on; but would return in five minutes to close my door, after going the round of other rooms. Conan deposits the evening meal; the guard has assembled in the archway; twilight, the quick coming twilight of the tropics has set in; but no friend is in the court; still I must go now; the beard is off in one minute, and false hair fastened on the upper lip; the outer garments are thrown off; my supper put on the floor, for poor little Bassett,—fastening him under the bed, as he devours the food. And now all was ready; I saw some visitors, coming from other blocks, leaving on account of closing gates; and I stepped forth and marched straight for the archway leading outside.

What moments were those. The air was full of dancing shapes;—and buzzing sounds were in my ears for a while; only a little while;—the rush of fresh air, the sight of free ground beyond that gateway. The guard was drawn up in file, with the sergeant at their head; just about to start on the rounds. This sergeant had seen me a hundred times; but I, trusting to my altered face, and garb, and a well practised change of gait, looked him straight in the face; and carelessly acknowledged a salute as I passed. I had made one step, and heard him wheel around. I dare say he had some doubts about the person he saw by that dim twilight; he might bid me stop, and then all was lost, but the chances of a desperate rush for the park; or to strive for a death in hot blood, at the hands of the guard;—there was a large cigar in my mouth; I did not smoke; but put there as additional means of concealment; I paused before a soldier not on duty, seated under the archway, smoking his pipe; I stooped for a light; puffed a moment with my cigar; it seemed to draw badly; bit an end, muttered, and growled some Dutch words; it was time for the guard to move; the sergeant wheeled around and faced the court again; the man with the cigar must be all right. With what emotion I then stepped from beneath that archway; I passed the outer walls and moat; and was in the free highway; but where was the horse?—there is a low sound in the park; the friend is there; and the horse, a little way off; and then how shall I tell how fast I went; or how I passed the by-lanes and suburbs of Batavia on the way to the rendezvous for the boat of the Palmer.

It had not come: it was indeed a little before the time. There were moments of intense anxiety and of deep interest in the little wood near the rendezvous;—friends were waiting to see me;—there was Diporo Kasumo, three stout Javanese prahu men, and his sister. I had a few words alone with Sahyeepah; she was readily convinced, that it was best that I should go on board the ship of my country; but would I not get on board some other one in the Straits of Sunda, and proceed to Singapore as I intended to do? her father would go there with his prahu, when they heard from me; and we would all meet again; and if not here, surely in the bright city of the Great Brother.

The sound of oars was heard, the dipping blades of the well-manned boat of the Palmer. Some last warm words and tokens of affection of simple, Javanese hearts; and then I heard the voice of our gallant Boatswain; what a sound was that; and what a sight, the well-armed, brave crew, and the home faces. I feared no longer all the garrison of Weltevreden at my heels.

But it was a close rub; said the Boatswain, interrupting, not a moment had we to lose. All hands ready for fight,—the boys were really primed for a brush,—our mate especially: I being in command, and having strict orders from the Captain, thought it best to wait for the Dutchies on board the Palmer, if they were going to come on. We were off, and dashing across that still bay; and not a word till we passed close by the Flirt; then our friend broke out; taking on about his gallant little craft. I believe he wanted to go on board of her, and persuade our men to cut her out from under the guns of the Boreas. I had thought of that often afore. But there was not the shadow of a chance, and it made my heart real sore too, as we passed her, lying hard and fast in the roadstead of Batavia.

Yes, said the Commander, I felt a keen pain of regret on passing my stout little ship, that had been such a pleasant home, on many a delightful day's sail; but my last thoughts were certainly not with the Flirt; nor busied with schemes for cutting her out;—but thinking at that moment of the people I was leaving behind me, who had so won upon my sympathies; and one more than all, who could still be dimly seen on the farthest reaching point of the shore of Java; and with upraised waving hands seemed to say, Forget not me, and all the words and resolves made about my people in the prison of Weltevreden.

The Palmer had her anchor apeak; her sails all loosened; and soon after the fugitive had received the warm greetings of her commander and the passengers on board,—the noble ship began to move through the waters of the bay. The sturdy boatswain, mate and crew were in a high state of excitement; they seemed wishful to wait for pursuit; the two long twelve-pounders, the ship's armament, were run out, all the small arms were on deck;

signal lights went up from the shore; the commander could not risk his vessel in any wild adventure of fight; orders are given to hoist every sail; the breeze freshens, and onward she surges. There is a flash, and the Boreas has fired a gun; the men of the Palmer are frantic, and her twelve-pounders hurl back defiance to the Dutchmen. But there is success and glory enough; better now to catch every breath of that freshening breeze. The smoke of a pursuing steamer is seen;—the Palmer must keep on her way; and the next morning beholds the clipper, as we have seen; threading her rapid way through the lovely isles of the Straits of Sunda; whilst the fugitive,—grateful to God for glorious freedom, yet with sadness in his joy, turns a last look towards the Island of Java.

www.ingramcontent.com/pod-product-compliance
Lightning Source LLC
LaVergne TN
LVHW021305110826
845150LV00003B/490

* 9 7 8 1 4 2 5 5 5 9 5 1 9 *